God
Heaven
and
Har Magedon

God, Heaven and Har Magedon

A Covenantal Tale of Cosmos and Telos

MEREDITH G. KLINE

Wipf & Stock
PUBLISHERS
Eugene, Oregon

GOD, HEAVEN AND HAR MAGEDON
A Covenantal Tale of Cosmos and Telos

Wipf & Stock Publishers
199 W. 8th Ave., Suite 3
Eugene, OR 97401

ISBN: 978-1-49824-804-4

Cataloging-in-Publication data:

Kline, Meredith G.
God, heaven and Har Magedon / Meredith G. Kline.

p. cm.

ISBN 1-59752-478-6

1. Covenant theology. 2. Covenant theology—Biblical teaching. 3. Eschatology—Biblical teaching. I. Title.

BS680 K55 2006

to our three sons

—

MEREDITH M.
littérateur-theologian

STERLING
architect

CALVIN
musician-maestro

Contents

APPENDICES

Key to Abbreviations

BOOKS

BOC — *By Oath Consigned: A Re-interpretation of the Covenant Signs of Circumcision and Baptism.* Grand Rapids: Eerdmans, 1968.

GOM — *Glory in Our Midst: A Biblical-Theological Reading of Zechariah's Night Visions.* Overland Park: Two Age Press, 2001.

IOS — *Images of the Spirit.* Grand Rapids: Baker Book House, 1980.

KP — *Kingdom Prologue: Genesis Foundations for a Covenantal Worldview.* Overland Park: Two Age Press, 2000.

SBA — *The Structure of Biblical Authority.* 2nd ed., rev. Grand Rapids: Eerdmans, 1975.

TGK — *Treaty of the Great King: The Covenant Structure of Deuteronomy, Studies and Commentary.* Grand Rapids: Eerdmans, 1963.

FESTSCHRIFT CONTRIBUTIONS

CSW — "The Covenant of the Seventieth Week" in *The Law and the Prophets: Old Testament Studies in Honor of Oswald T. Allis,* ed. by J. H. Skilton. Nutley: Presbyterian and Reformed, 1974, pp. 452-469.

DLM — "Death, Leviathan, and the Martyrs: Isaiah 24:1–27:1" in *A Tribute to Gleason Archer*, ed. by Walter C. Kaiser, Jr. and Ronald R. Youngblood. Chicago: Moody Press, 1986, pp. 229-249.

OOS — "The Oracular Origin of the State" in *Biblical and Near Eastern Studies: Essays in Honor of William Sanford LaSor,* ed. by G. A. Tuttle. Grand Rapids: Eerdmans, 1978, pp. 132-141.

TBO — "Trial by Ordeal" in *Through Christ's Word: A Festschrift for Dr. Philip E. Hughes,* ed. by W. Robert Godfrey, Jesse L. Boyd III. Phillipsburg: Presbyterian and Reformed, 1985, pp. 81-93.

ARTICLES

BNR	"Because It Had Not Rained" *Westminster Theological Journal* 20 (1957/58): 146-157.
CONE	"Comments on an Old-New Error" *Westminster Theological Journal* 41 (1978/79): 172-189.
DK	"Divine Kingship and Gen 6:1-4" *Wesminster Theological Journal* 24 (1961/62): 187-204.
DT	"Double Trouble" *Journal of the Evangelical Theological Society* 32 (1989): 171-179.
FCO	"The Feast of Cover-over" *Journal of the Evangelical Theological Society* 37 (1994): 497-510.
FR	"The First Resurrection" *Westminster Theological Journal* 37 (1974/75): 366-375.
FRR	"The First Resurrection: a Reaffirmation" *Westminster Theological Journal* 39 (1976/77): 110-119.
GUL	"Gospel Until the Law: Rom 5:13-14 and the Old Covenant" *Journal of the Evangelical Theological Society* 34 (1991): 433-446.
HMEM	"Har Magedon: The End of the Millennium" *Journal of the Evangelical Theological Society* 39 (1996): 207-222.
STGC	"Space and Time in the Genesis Cosmogony" *Perspectives on Science and the Christian Faith* 48:1 (1996): 2-15.

Preface

It could be this octogenarian's last book and there were several things I wanted to do. One was to provide a primer in covenant theology. Another was to make more accessible the gist of some of my previous biblico-theological studies and to do so in a form serviceable to a wider readership than most of my publications, which have been oriented to the professional community of biblical research and to my students in the academic setting of theological schools.

The major move in this democratic direction was to enliven the analysis of the covenants by introducing the series of covenant administrations within the intriguing story line of Har Magedon, the mountain of God. Extending as it does from creation to consummation, the tale of Har Magedon readily accommodates the total history of the covenants and invites excursions into areas that have been of special interest to me, like pneumatology, cosmology, eschatology, and common grace and culture (cf. the "cosmos and telos" specifications of "a covenantal tale" in the subtitle). Moreover, quite apart from such considerations the current spate of secularized and dispensational versions of "Armageddon" (fantastic fiction all) makes a review of the biblical Har Magedon motif timely.

Though the covenants remain the theological foundation and heart of the matter, by its adoption as our narrative framework Har Magedon becomes the dominant surface theme. As we track this theme through the Scriptures we discover a recurring pattern, an eschatological megastructure that appears in each of the typological world ages culminating respectively at mounts Ararat and Sinai/Zion and then once again, climactically, in the antitypical New Covenant age. This Har Magedon paradigm, which shapes our telling of the covenantal tale (cf. Part Three), consists in the following complex of elements: establishment of a kingdom covenant by the Lord of Har Magedon; a meritorious accomplishment by the covenant grantee, triumphant in the Har Magedon conflict; a common grace interim before the coming of the covenanted kingdom; an antichrist crisis; consummation of the Glory-kingdom through a last judgment victory of the covenant Lord in a final battle of Har Magedon.

If only in condensed, digest fashion the present work is thus a comprehensive biblico-theological survey of the kingdom of God from Eden to the New Jersusalem. As such it complements my *Kingdom Prologue* (which focuses on kingdom developments through the history recorded in the Book of Genesis) and might then have been appropriately entitled *Kingdom Come* or *Kingdom Consummation.* With so vast a terrain to be surveyed, the treatment has had to be highly selective in the inclusion and coverage of topics and in the adducing of the relevant Scriptural data and other evidence in support of conclusions advocated on controversial subjects. It is hoped, however, that these explorations will at least serve to bring more clearly into view the grand biblical vision of God's heavenly kingdom in its eschatological movement from Alpha to Omega.

As a step towards a less academic form of presentation footnotes are limited to an occasional reference to a pertinent, more ample discussion elsewhere in my writings. To facilitate this referencing process several earlier articles are reproduced in full here in the section of appendices.

For his amanuensis assistance in the production of the computer document and indeed for his coordinating of the whole editorial-publishing process of bringing this book to see the light of day I am indebted beyond words to Jonathan B. Kline.

In biblical quotations non-AV translations are my own unless otherwise noted.

The cover picture is a reproduction of an oil painting (53½ x 33) by Muriel G. Kline.

Meredith G. Kline
January 2005

Part One

God and Heaven

Chapter One

Naming the Metaworld

Heaven and Cosmos

The Bible tells us of the existence of a realm our mortal eyes cannot see. In the biblical vocabulary (as in our own) this invisible celestial realm is called by the same name as the visible region of the star-studded sky (viz. "heaven"). We shall be reflecting later on the significance of this name sharing.

Living in an age when intensive astronomical probing has been rewarded with astonishing discoveries concerning the cosmos, we are bound to wonder how the biblical heaven is to be correlated with all this. How are we to fit into our scientific cosmology this mysterious realm beyond human perception? Until we can comprehend the heavenly reality presently inaccessible to scientific investigation and incorporate it into our analysis, the quest for a unified field explication of the totality of creation must prove elusive. But meanwhile in biblical revelation we may catch a glimpse of something of the nature of heaven and how heaven relates to our visible world, something that brightens our religious contemplations, whatever its limitations for our scientific constructions.

In theological reflections heaven is sometimes considered to be a place outside the cosmos, out beyond our universe. Or if it is regarded as within our space-time-matter-energy continuum, it is thought of as a separate part of the cosmos, at some distance from the environs of planet earth. There are biblical indications, however, that suggest otherwise. For instance, in Isaiah 6 the heaven-temple (vv. 1,4) is identified with the whole earth (v. 3). And there are those episodes reported in Scripture when the eyes of earthlings have been supernaturally opened to perceive heavenly phenomena and they discover that the very spot where they are is the gate of heaven (Gen 28:16,17) or that it is filled with heavenly beings (2 Kgs 6:17). Heaven, it would seem, is not remote from us but present right here, even though unseen. Also, there does not appear to be anything in Scripture that would contradict the assumption that the invisible heaven is coextensive with the visible cosmos in its entirety.

As an analogy to this inter-permeation of the invisible and the visible worlds we may point to the proposal of current cosmologists that so-called dark matter is present throughout the universe, in quantities apparently far surpassing visible matter, yet unseen. And analogous to a heaven that is perceptible to angels and others but is impervious to ordinary human vision is the familiar fact that sectors of the electro-magnetic spectrum, though detectable by the sensory organs of some earthly creatures, are beyond the perception of others. But such analogous phenomena do not really explain what it is about heaven that distinguishes it from the visible cosmos and renders it invisible to us. That mysterious aspect of heaven is beyond our knowledge. In order to discuss it, all we can do is adopt some conventional term for it, preferably one that keeps in sight the intermeshing of the visible and invisible realms. We shall use the term "dimension." To signify that this heavenly reality is something beyond our present experiencing we shall prefix meta-, thus metadimension. To give this distinguishing meta quality of heaven a more specific name we may call it a Glory-dimension or, resorting to the Greek, a Doxa-dimension.

The appropriateness of this name will become clear as we proceed to take a look at what the Bible discloses concerning the substance and structure of heaven. Approaching the subject from the spatial or cosmological point of view, our particular interest will be in the topography and architecture of heaven. But since God's Glory-Presence is the preeminent reality of heaven, the cosmological and theological perspectives are inseparable here. Heaven is a holy location and it contains, indeed it consists in, sacred architecture. It is a Glory-temple-city.

Here in Part One we shall also examine the beginning of heaven and its consummation. This will contribute to our probing of the interconnection of heaven and the visible cosmos. It will also emerge that our distinction between the visible and invisible realms is not something absolute and permanent, but relative to human experience and limited to the first stage, the pre-consummation stage, of man's historical existence. As a result of man's glorification-metamorphosis heaven will no longer be beyond his perception. For man too, as already for God and his angels, heaven will then be cosmos and cosmos will be heaven.

Heaven: Glory-Temple

To help us envisage the better country he has prepared for those who love him (1 Cor 2:9; Heb 11:10), God has provided some visual aids. For one thing, before the coming of Christ, the people of God were given earthly buildings, a tabernacle and a temple, as miniaturized models of his holy heaven, and an earthly land flowing with milk and honey as a suggestive image of the paradise character of their heavenly inheritance. When we focus on the subject of heaven on earth in Part Two we shall be dealing further with this theme of the replication of the heavenly archetypes in earthly symbolic copies, visible shadows here below of the invisible world above, and foreshadowings of the world to come.

Secondly, from time to time the Lord favored his prophets with visionary experiences of heaven. Accounts of these visions have been included in the Scriptures so that we might all be able to see heaven as it was descried through the prophets' supernaturally opened eyes. Of course, even when unveiled in such revelations of the Spirit, heaven remains cloaked in symbolism. Typology is the idiom of apocalyptic vision. What is seen in these visions still bears the shape of the earthly models. Heaven appears to the prophets as a glorified version of the temple on Mount Zion. Because of our inability to apprehend the heavenly reality itself, it was necessary that these prophetic disclosures be cast in such symbolic forms. Yet this imagery does convey to us a true conception of heaven, enough for now to serve as an anchor of the soul, even if, with our natural curiosity about the spatial-topographical nature of our everlasting habitat, we long for something more, eagerly awaiting the unveiling of heaven at its ultimate apocalypse.

Totally dominating the scene in biblical revelations of heaven is the presence of God, the God of Glory. No creature can see God, who is Spirit, in his transcendence above and apart from all creation, visible and invisible, but the eternal unseen One does manifest his personal presence within his creation. As beheld by the prophetic seers in their visions of heaven and described in their literary accounts of those experiences, the Glory theophany, like the topographical and architectural features in such visions, is a likeness of something belonging to the earthly scene. It is portrayed as a Shekinah-like luminous cloud of smoke and fire that fills a royal sanctuary, a resplendent theophanic cloud that occupies the throne in the holy of holies between cherubim guardians. Needless to say, the relationship is actually the other way around. The Shekinah cloud is the likeness or copy, a projection of the archetypal Glory into this world in a form accommodated to mortals. The Glory-Presence is the original, and it is this Glory epiphany that is the paramount, definitive, quintessential feature of heaven.

As we examine the nature of this divine Presence in heaven we are led back to our special point of interest, the architectural identity of heaven. It turns out, in fact, that there is a soft edge (as the watercolorists say) between the divine Resident and the heavenly residence. As we look, the edge indeed becomes lost; the line of distinction disappears.

The glory of the heavenly Presence is a royal glory, the glory of a king with myriads of servants in attendance about his throne. So it was in Isaiah's vision of heaven. The prophet saw "the Lord sitting on a throne, high and lifted up" in the midst of the seraphim (Isa 6:1,2) and he exclaimed, "my eyes have seen the King, Yahweh of hosts" (v. 5). When heaven was opened to Ezekiel and he saw "visions of God" (Ezek 1:1), a wondrous cherubim-chariot appeared to him, a chariot-throne with a bright radiance suffusing it (vv. 4ff.) and investing the enthroned Deity (vv. 26f.). Such "was the appearance of the likeness of the Glory of Yahweh" (v. 28). And when a door was opened in heaven for the apostle John (Rev 4:1) and he was "in the Spirit" (v. 2a), "behold, there was a throne set in heaven and one sitting on the throne" arched with emerald glory (v. 2b), one acclaimed by the heavenly retinue as the Creator-Lord, worthy to receive the glory, honor, and power (v. 11). There are also the familiar great white throne judgment scenes in the visions of heaven in Dan 7:9,10 and Rev 20:11, with the radiant divine Judge again seen as seated on a fiery chariot throne. Consistently, the center of the unveiled heaven is occupied by the Majesty on high, the enthroned King of creation. Hence, architecturally, heaven is a palace, a royal court.

Because heaven's King is the Lord God, the thrice-holy One (Isa 6:3; Rev 4:8) whose Presence sanctifies a place, the royal house of heaven is at the same time a holy house, a temple. Qōdeš, "holiness," is an Old Testament designation of heaven (cf., e.g., Deut 26:15; Jer 25:30) and its earthly replica is called miqdāš, "sanctuary" (1 Chr 22:19; Ps 74:7; Isa 63:18).

The equivalence of the palace and temple images of heaven is exhibited in passages where heaven is both depicted as a royal court and denoted as a hêkāl, "temple," a term which means "great house" according to its ultimate derivation and is itself also used for the house of a king, a palace (cf. Ps 45:16; Dan 1:4). Isaiah refers to the heavenly place where he saw the King on his throne as the "temple" (Isa 6:1). In Psalm 11, David's affirmation that "Yahweh's throne is in heaven" (v. 4b) is paralleled by the statement that "Yahweh's holy seat [cf. Ps 47:9] is in the temple" (v. 4a). Here "temple" is a synonym for heaven and this heaven-temple is said to be God's throne site, the royal court of the righteous Judge of all the earth (vv. 4c-7). Other Old Testament instances of the identification of the heaven from which God emerges for judgment as hêkāl, "temple," are Ps 18:6,9,13 [7,10,14] and Mic 1:2,3. Likewise, the New Testament Apocalypse repeatedly designates the heavenly site of God's judgment throne as a "temple" or the holy "tabernacle" of the covenant (cf. Rev 11:19; 14:15,17; 15:5-8; 21:11,23).

The spatial-architectural nature of heaven is thus defined by its central, all-dominant feature, the God-King resident there. By virtue of his holy Glory-Presence, heaven is a royal, sacred space, a palace-temple. But the relation of the divine Glory to heaven viewed as an architectural structure goes beyond imparting to it the formal, functional significance of palace-temple. There is in addition a remarkable identity between the Glory-Presence and the heaven-temple, a kind of substantial oneness. God, that is, the epiphanic heavenly manifestation of God, *is* the temple.

This identification of God with the heaven-temple is stated quite simply in Rev 21:22. Referring to New Jerusalem, the cosmic city of the consummation, heaven unveiled, John declares, "I saw no temple therein, for the Lord God Almighty and the Lamb are the temple thereof." The apostle is not making a pantheistic identification of God with the cosmos-temple. Rather, the Glory manifestation of God is here called God. What John declares is that the radiant theophany formation constitutes the temple structure; the heaven-temple consists of, is made up of, the Glory.

A similar coalescence of God's Glory and temple is found in Isa 4:5,6 in a vision of the heavenly Zion, representing the consummated messianic kingdom. The Glory epiphany, as usual the dominant feature of the heavenly scene, is depicted as a canopy covering the temple mount, a pavilion sheltering Zion's holy assemblies. [Cf. *IOS* 36.] The underlying concept here is that of God's house serving as a tabernacle-shelter for his people (cf. Rev 7:15 and 21:3). And the Shekinah-Glory is identified as the primary sheltering component of the holy house, the protective roof overhead. Echoed here is the imagery of the paschal-event at the exodus, where the Glory-cloud hovered over (cf. Isa 31:4,5) the blood-smeared dwellings of the Israelites, shielding them from the destroyer-angel when he passed over the land of Egypt. [Cf. *FCO*.]

A variation on the conception of the Glory as constituting the temple structure appears in Isaiah 6. This vision of heaven contains two symbolic images of the theophanic Glory, each of which is declared to fill the heaven-temple. The first Glory image is that of the royal robes of the enthroned King (v. 1; cf. Luke 12:27). So extended, so global, is their sweep that they fill the cosmic sanctuary. The second thing that is said to fill the temple is smoke (v. 4). Elsewhere, smoke is found as a feature of theophany, as in God's appearances to ratify covenant with Abraham (Gen 15:7) and with Israel (Exod 19:18). In the nearby Isaiah 4 prophecy, the Glory-theophany is described as "cloud and smoke by day" (v. 5), that is, as antitypical to the Shekinah pillar of the exodus. And the apostle John, speaking of the heavenly temple as filled with smoke, identifies the smoke as "from the glory of God and from his power" (Rev 15:8; cf. Exod 40:34,35; 1 Kgs 8:10,11; 2 Chr 5:13,14; 7:1,2). It is then the smoke of the epiphanic Glory that fills the holy house of the God-King in Isa 6:4.

This Isaiah 6 imagery of the diffusion of the epiphanic smoke throughout the temple identifies the divine Glory not with the outer structure that encased and shaped the temple space, as did the canopy-roof symbolism in Isa 4:5,6, but with the inner volume or space of the temple, with its atmosphere. Yet the distinction is not so sharp in the case of this wondrous heavenly architecture. The divine radiance that is ethereal and serves as atmosphere is at the same time a plastic, shaping, sculpturing substance that eliminates the need of separate bounding walls and roof. Out of this Glory-dimensioned epiphanic stuff, now invisible to earthlings, is heaven constructed.

As we shall see below, the Glory epiphany complex, though a fully trinitarian manifestation (see, e.g., Rev 4:2,5; 5:6; cf. 1:4,5), is peculiarly identified with the Spirit. Accordingly, heaven is the Spirit realm and to enter heaven is to be in the Spirit (Rev 4:1,2). This throws an interesting light on the atmosphere of the heaven-temple constituted by the Glory-Spirit. For the Spirit is the breath of life (Gen 2:7; John 20:22) and hence the picture that emerges is that of heaven dwellers, those in the Spirit-atmosphere, breathing continually afresh the breath of life. That is the secret of immortality.

Conclusion. What we can glean from the biblical revelation concerning the metaphysics of heaven thus lends support to the suggestion that Glory-dimension serve as our designation for that meta(beyond)dimension which characterizes the invisible realm, distinguishing it from the visible creation. We might add that in view of the identification of the Glory with the Spirit, Spirit-dimension would also be an apt name.

Chapter Two

Alpha Radiation: The Creation of Heaven

The Big Blaze

The heaven the Bible tells us about is a part of creation. This Glory-dimensioned realm does not belong to the eternity of God before and apart from the created cosmos. Wherever we find it in the Scriptures, heaven is a place where God is present within creation, a place where he is seen in relation to his creatures, revealed to them in epiphanic Glory, enthroned among them as their Shepherd-Sovereign. And belonging to the creation as it does, heaven, though it will have no end, did have a beginning.

That beginning is announced in the opening verse of the Bible. The phrase "heaven and earth" in Gen 1:1 denotes the upper (invisible) and lower (visible) spatial spheres respectively, which together comprise all of creation. The interpretation of "heaven" here as the invisible realm of the divine Glory and angelic beings is supported by the apostle Paul's exposition of the role of God the Son in the creating process. Reflecting the language of Gen 1:1, he declares that the Son created "all things that are in heaven and that are in earth, visible and invisible, whether they be thrones, or dominions, or principalities, or powers" (Col 1:16; cf. John 1:1-3). The equation of heaven and the invisible realm is clear. Similarly, Nehemiah, referring to the heaven of Gen 1:1, identifies it with the realm of angels (Neh 9:6).

That the "heaven" of Gen 1:1 is not the visible heavens of lower register space is also indicated by the Genesis 1 context itself. The origin of the heaven of v. 1 is assigned to "the beginning," which, in the reflections on the Genesis 1 creation account in Prov 8:22,23, is identified as the era before the developments traced in Gen 1:2ff., in particular, before the production of the visible heavens or "firmament" (v. 8). Also, while the visible sky-heavens are, according to Gen 1:6,7, derived from what is called "earth" in Gen 1:1,2, the "heaven" of v. 1 does not take its origin from that "earth" but appears as a separate product created alongside the "earth." It must then be the invisible heaven. And to this invisible heaven Gen 1:1 attributes an origin, a coming into existence "in the beginning." [On the above cf. *STGC* 4B, 5A, and 9B.]

Though the visible world, the "earth" of Gen 1:1,2, was not completed until the end of the creation "week," completion of the invisible heaven (with its angelic hosts) had evidently been accomplished "in the beginning." Job 38:7 indicates that the celestial sons of God existed at the point in earth's development described in Gen 1:2ff. and were joyous observers of the progress of the Creator's cosmic architectural achievements. As we shall be noting further below, the presence of the angels at the climactic event of the creating of man is intimated in Gen 1:26,27 (cf. Prov 8:30,31).

Since the origination of the invisible heaven is fused with that of the visible cosmos in the beginning of creation, and the starting point to which cosmologists trace the visible universe is popularly called the Big Bang, the simultaneous bursting into being of the Glory-heaven might be called the Big Blaze.

Introduced into the Genesis 1 narrative in the opening verse, the invisible heaven remains in view as that narrative continues the panoramic two-register (heaven and earth) format throughout its treatment of the creation "week." In fact, the primary perspective of the account is that of the upper register; the story of creation is told from the point of view of the Creator in the heights of heaven.

In Gen 1:2 the Spirit, with whom (as we have noted) the Glory theophany is especially identified, represents the upper register, invisible space, and the deep and darkness over which the Spirit hovers is the lower register, visible space.

In Gen 1:3-31 the heavenly register perspective is carried forward in the several creative fiats by which visible space was fashioned into a habitable world in the course of the "six days." The scene evoked by these fiats is the throne of the King of Glory, the King invisible, the only God, dwelling in light unapproachable (1 Tim 1:17; 6:16). A particularly important indicator of the heavenly source of these fiats is the "let us" form of the fiat in the record of the creation of man (Gen 1:26). This consultative form reveals the setting to be the angelic council, a standard feature in the portraiture of heaven. Also pointing to God on his throne above is the motif of divine surveillance and judgment found in the refrain "and God saw that it was good," which signifies God's approbation of what had been made as in accord with the masterplan (cf. Prov 8:30,31). For such judicial scrutiny is repeatedly mentioned as a function performed by God on his heavenly throne: "The Lord looks down from heaven; he beholds all the sons of men" (Ps 33:13) . . . "His eyes behold, his pupils try the sons of men" (Ps 11:4c). Hence, the "let there be" refrain that resounds throughout the account of the "six days" is an utterance of God from the upper, invisible realm. The carrying out of his commands in the visible, lower register world is recorded in the accompanying formula, "and it was so." The Spirit executed in the earth below the fiat of the Logos-Word from heaven above.

Heaven is very much the focus of the seventh day also (Gen 2:1-3). For it is concerned with God's sabbath, his royal rest as the One who has finished the work of creation, his enthronement in the supernal realm. Indeed, what is signified by the divine sabbath, the everlasting royal session of the King of Glory, is the essential reality of heaven. That was the nature of heaven from its original creation, but the seventh day marked a distinctive stage in the history of heaven, the Creator-Author henceforth assuming the additional title of Finisher of heaven and earth and all their host. [On the heavenly focus of the creation account see *STGC* 5B and 6A.] Such was the origin of heaven and the nature of its relation to the visible creation from the "beginning" to the seventh day. According to the Master Architect's design for creation there is yet another phase to be reached in the on-going seventh day of God, another stage in the history of heaven and earth. The King of heaven will at the hour appointed consummate his cosmic temple.

The Endoxation of the Spirit

The invisible heaven came into being in God's opening act of creation. What we have just been saying about this has been in terms that related the creation of heaven to the origin of the cosmos. But now we want to consider that creational act in relation to the doctrine of God.

Above we suggested "the Big Blaze" as a designation complementary to "the Big Bang," the term the cosmologists use for the beginning singularity. The additional name was intended to draw attention to the supernal aspect of the event, the heavenly counterpoint melody in the song of creation. That suggestion must now be refined; terminology is needed that will reflect what we have discovered about the Glory phenomenon being the manifested Presence of God. The creation of heaven was an epiphany. It was a beaming forth of the One who gives himself as Creator the name of Alpha (Rev 1:8; 21:6). More precisely then, the Big Blaze was an Epiphanic Effulgence. It was an Alpha Radiation.

As an epiphany, the Glory that constitutes heaven is identifiable with God. At the same time, this Glory epiphany is a created phenomenon. The account of the creation of heaven in Gen 1:1 is the record of the origin of the Glory epiphany, the creational investiture of Deity with majestic splendor (Ps 104:1,2). The heavenly Glory is then a created embodiment of Deity. It is, moreover, a permanent embodiment. It is not a temporary theophanic manifestation but an eternally enduring epiphany, for the Glory-heaven has no ending, only a consummation.

We have previously observed that it is with the Spirit of God that the Glory is particularly identified. Much of the evidence for this is found in the biblical accounts of the Shekinah-cloud, the earthly projection of the heavenly Glory. In a further discussion of this below we shall be noting how this theophanic cloud is referred to as the Spirit. Hence, the heavenly Glory reality itself, the permanent manifestation of God which we have spoken of as a divine epiphanation is more specifically an epiphanation of the Spirit.

This Glory-manifestation of the Spirit and the Incarnation of the Son are alike in that each is a permanent embodiment of a person of the Godhead in a created entity, the epiphanic glory and human nature respectively. To signalize this correspondence we shall coin a term for the Spirit epiphany that parallels the term Incarnation conceptually and phonetically. We shall call it the Endoxation of the Spirit.

Both the endoxate Spirit and the incarnate Son (particularly but not solely in his exalted state) are creational revelations of the Glory of God. Before and apart from creation, expression of the divine Glory is also central in the forms of subsistence of the second and third persons within the triune Godhead. The eternal procession of the third person is a manifesting of the Glory of the Father in the Spirit. The eternal filiation of the second person is a sonship relationship, a relationship that signifies likeness to the Father and is thus an effulging of his Glory. Now the Endoxation of the Spirit and the Incarnation of the Son represent a creational continuation of these eternal intratrinitarian, interpersonal dynamics. The Spirit's Endoxation is a creational projection of the eternal procession of the Spirit; the Son's Incarnation, of the eternal filiation of the Son. Within the realm of creation each affords a resplendent revelation of God's Glory. Each is a glorious image of the divine Being.

In the endoxate Spirit-heaven the revelation of God's Glory was present in substantive form from the beginning. And the prospect of a consummated Epiphanation of the Glory-Spirit, an eternal temple, a heaven peopled with glorified humanity, was proffered from the outset in the promise sanctions of the creation covenant. A primal eschatological paradigm was thereby established in that covenant and basic to it was the goal of a sabbatical consummation of Glory.

This original sabbatical pattern of eschatology was resumed in the subsequent program of redemption administered through the Covenant of Grace. The purpose of redemption is to bring to pass, in spite of the Fall, the realization of the eschatological goal of a consummate revelation of God's Glory, as originally set for creation. Redemption is thus subordinate to revelation, in particular, the revelation of the divine Glory. Also, if we confine our analysis within the sphere of redemption, which itself affords a revelation of God's glorious nature, we are once again bound to affirm the primacy of this revelation of God over redemption viewed as a soteriological program, simply because of the fact that teleologically the Glory of God outranks the salvation of man – and everything else.

As part of the redemptive program the Incarnation of the Son also subserves the purpose of achieving the cosmic telos set in the primal eschatological paradigm. And this means that the Incarnation is ancillary to the consummating of the Endoxation of the Spirit, which is that telos. In this sense, the Endoxation of the Spirit has the primacy.

Alike as creational manifestations of the eternal Glory of God, the Endoxation of the Spirit and the Incarnation of the Son are also alike as manifestations of something else at the heart of God's purposes in creating the world. Both embody the Immanuel principle. This principle of personal divine immanence, of God's accompanying Presence, came to expression in the Endoxation of the Spirit from the beginning, altogether apart from the process of redemption. The Incarnation is a redemptive version of the Immanuel principle. It enhances the revelation of that principle afforded by the Endoxation of the Spirit for it entails a messianic mission of divine grace that requires of the Son that he undergo humiliation and suffering as an atonement for sins and so bring the reconciled world back into union with God, a union in the Spirit sent by the Father and the Son. The Endoxation of the Spirit in the original creation of heaven did not involve those elements found in the Incarnation of the Son; it was not a matter of grace. It did, however, exhibit the Immanuel principle. It manifested the fatherly heart and goodness of God. Creation of the Spirit-heaven as the temple-dwelling for ʾĕlōhîm-creatures displayed from the outset God's desire to vouchsafe his blessed Presence to his creation. The Endoxation of the Spirit was an intimate drawing near of God to his worshipping creatures in divine love to welcome them into the beatific embrace of his heavenly Glory.

The Spirit and Filiation

In formulating the doctrine of the Trinity the church has seen in the economic relations of the three persons analogues of their eternal immanent forms of personal subsistence. In particular the Son's sending of the Spirit at Pentecost – symbolically anticipated in Jesus' breathing the Spirit on his disciples (John 20:22) – has been regarded as warrant for including the Son (cf. "*filioque*") along with the Father as a subject in the eternal spiration of the Spirit. It is through the Son that the Father spirates the Spirit. In terms of this procession of the Spirit, the Son is the second person of the Trinity and the Spirit the third.

A reverse ordering of these two persons of the Trinity obtains when they are viewed in terms of the eternal generating of the Son – proper account being taken of what we have been observing about the Endoxation of the Spirit and its relation to the Incarnation of the Son. It is not simply that in this economic relationship there is a temporal priority of the Endoxation of the Spirit to the Incarnation of the Son, but that the endoxate Spirit performs a fathering function with respect to the incarnate Son. It is by the Holy Spirit that Jesus was conceived, the Glory-Spirit, the Power of the Most High, coming upon Mary and overshadowing her (Luke 1:35). The Father begets the Son through the Spirit. In this process the Spirit is the second person and the Son the third. And as in the spiration of the Spirit so in the begetting of the Son the economic relations of the divine persons are to be seen as analogues of their eternal immanent relations. The fathering of the incarnate Son by the endoxate Spirit warrants inclusion of the Spirit along with the Father as a subject in the eternal divine begetting, the generating process of which the Son is the object. It is a desideratum, therefore, that a reference to the Holy Spirit corresponding to the *filioque* phrase in the creedal account of the spiration of the Spirit find a place in our confessional formulation of the eternal filiation of the Son.

Supporting this proposal, there is another economic analogue for the immanent order of Spirit and Son, with the Spirit as subject and the Son as object. This analogue is found in the messianic sonship of Jesus (cf. Ps 2:7; Matt 3:17; Mark 1:11; Luke 3:22; Rom 1:3,4). The Spirit performs the anointing of Jesus whereby he is constituted the Christ-Son of God (cf. Isa 61:1-3; Luke 4:18,19), a process manifested in the avian descent of the Spirit on Jesus at his baptism (Matt 3:16; Mark 1:10; Luke 3:22; John 1:32-34) and the transfiguring overshadowing of Jesus by the Glory-Spirit on the holy mountain (Matt 17:1-5; Mark 9:2-7; Luke 9:28-35; 2 Pet 1:16-18).

Mystery within the mystery of the triunity of the Lord our God: the Son and the Spirit are each before and after the other and each both subject and object in relation to the other in the simultaneous eternal communicating of the numerical divine essence from the Father through filiation and spiration.

We are confronted with paradox again in connection with the Father's place in these intratrinitarian processes. He is the subject in both filiation and spiration and object in neither. Yet if they are viewed under the aspect of the revelation of the divine Glory, the Father is the telos of both. As we have noted, the begetting of the Son is the producing of an image-likeness of the Father's Glory and the spirating of the Spirit is an effulging of that Glory. As revelatory expressions of the Father, the Son and the Spirit radiate back to him his Glory and so are also subjects in the eternal immanent self-glorification of God. And the Father is thus simultaneously fontal and final in this perpetual divine self-glorifying through the two modes of communicating the divine essence.

Chapter Three

Omega Apocalypse: The Consummation of Heaven

Consummation and Glorification

Since man's Fall it is through a redemptive process, in fulfillment of the terms of a covenant of grace, that God brings his creation-kingdom to its consummation. But this consummation, with the glorification of humanity as its principal operative mechanism, was God's announced goal from the beginning. The Lord presented this eschatological prospect through the symbols of the Sabbath and the tree of life in the garden-sanctuary of Eden. This consummated kingdom was the promised blessing sanction of God's original covenant with man in Adam, the inheritance to be secured as the reward for obedient service.

Under the terms of that covenant of works, glorification-consummation would not have been, as it is now, a gift of redemptive grace and it would not have involved a Christological presence and mission. Its achievement would however have required a supernatural intervention of the Creator-Spirit.

A parenthetical observation may be allowed here to indicate the relevance of the point just made for on-going discussion of world origins.

It has been argued that we impugn the wisdom and power of the Creator unless we hold that he produced man by a process in which the potentiality of the ultimate human form was present in the primal product from the absolute beginning, capable of evolving without being subjected to special, supplementary divine intervention. But quite apart from the evidence in Gen 2:7,21,22 for the special creation of Adam and Eve, that contention is contradicted by the biblical disclosures concerning the eschatological structure of creation history, in particular, the predestined consummation of the created order. As revealed in Scripture, the consummating of heaven and earth is as much a direct, miraculous act of God as the original act of creation. The sheer supernaturalism of the glorification of man is all the more evident once that event becomes part of the redemptive process. For divine redemption is antithetical in principle to a merely natural development of any potential or inclination supposedly present in fallen mankind. In fact, the whole Christological-soteriological program introduced after the Fall belies the charge that there would be a defect in God's creating if direct divine intervention is required after the original act of creation in order to achieve the ultimate goal of the divine plan and bring creation to its omega-point. That goal was not attainable apart from a fresh, climactic interposition of divine might.

The consummating touch of the finger of God effects a change; it results in something new, as is reflected in the case of the redemptive consummation in the denoting of the post-consummation cosmos as a "new heaven and new earth" (Isa 65:17; 66:22; 2 Pet 3:13; Rev 21:1).

For heaven, the dwelling place of God, this newness would consist not so much in a change of heaven itself as in a difference in man's experiencing of heaven. By virtue of the glorification-metamorphosis (which perfects the divine image in him) man would have his eyes opened to what was hitherto invisible. He would be able to apprehend the wondrous realities of the Glory-dimension, previously beyond human ken. As a result of this ultimate unveiling, heaven would no longer be invisible space; the distinction between an invisible upper register of the cosmos and a lower visible register would cease. In that sense, that is, relative to man's experience of it, heaven as a spatial-cosmological reality would be changed; it would enter a new, consummate stage, a stage of unveiled glory.

There are of course other ways in which the post-consummation heaven would have been different. For example, it would no longer be a field of conflict. Satan and all evil powers would have been totally banished in the consummating event of final judgment. And something new would have been introduced into heaven. It would be peopled by an innumerable company of glorified human beings, a heavenly nation born in a day, in a moment, in the twinkling of an eye. That would be a day of such spectacular newness in the history of heaven as to match the day of the epiphanic flash in the beginning, when heaven was filled in a moment with the countless myriads of angels.

And what of the visible world? Here too the consummation would bring change and newness. When the distinction between visible and invisible space disappeared and man's perception of the world included its Glory-dimension, the cosmos as an integral, unified whole would take on a new face for him. For glorified man, earth would become "heavenized." All would be aglow with glory.

More broadly stated, man's glorification would mean the perfecting of his dominion over all the works of God's hand (cf. Heb 2:5-10). He would enjoy the capabilities that we see displayed in the resurrection appearances of Christ, the second Adam, whereby, without recourse to external technology, the Lord transcended space-matter (passing through closed doors and ascending into the sky). Hence, even if the post-consummation earth were much the same in its material composition as it was originally, man, because of his new endowment with mastery over it, would find that it had become for him a different place. And the time dimension would also assume a quite new character in the experience of one invested with immortality, with aeons of joyous heavenly life extending before him into infinity.

Consummation and Cosmology

From the perspective of the human participant in the Omega-apocalypse event, the space-time world would be transformed. But would the newness of the new earth include something besides this difference relative to the human spectator? Would there be a radical change in the physics, in the structural dynamics and configuration of the universe, and in the morphology of life below the elohim-level? Or would there be substantial continuity in these respects between the pre-consummation and post-consummation earth?

In our discussion so far the consummation event we have been referring to has been the eschatological prospect presented in the creational covenant, though what we have said would apply equally to the consummation of redemptive history. As we now focus on the question of the structural continuity/discontinuity of the pre-consummation and post-consummation cosmos, we shall assume a postlapsarian stance. The consummation immediately in view will be the one actually reached via redemptive covenant. Much, however, of what we will be saying about that consummation would, *mutatis mutandis*, have been true of a consummation reached apart from the Fall and redemption.

Prophecies of a Cataclysmic Finis

One thing obviously relevant to the difficult question of the impact of the consummation on the structural dynamics of the cosmos is biblical prophecy to the effect that God's eschatological intervention in final judgment involves in some sense a catastrophic ending of this present world. We read that as a prelude to the appearance of a new heaven and earth the present visible heavens and earth will dissipate like smoke and vanish (Isa 51:6); that they will flee from God's presence; that they will pass away and their place will be found no more (Rev 20:11; 21:1b; cf. Mark 13:31). Isa 34:4 and Rev 6:14 picture cosmic convulsions, with mountains and islands uprooted and the heavens removed like the rolling up of a scroll. In the language of Ps 102:26 quoted in Heb 1:11,12, the earth and heaven, in contrast to the Lord who continues unchanging forever, will perish, put off and replaced like garments. Other passages speak of a shaking and removing of heaven and earth in contrast to unshaken things that remain (Isa 13:13; Hag 2:22; Heb 12:26,27). And 2 Pet 3:10-13 foretells a passing away of the heavens and a consuming of the earth in a final conflagration. These disclosures are anticipated in God's ancient common order covenant revealed to Noah. The guarantee given there of the permanence of earth's ecological order is qualified by the phrase, "while the earth endures" (Gen 8:22), an ominous intimation of an eschatological terminating event in earth history (cf. 2 Cor 4:18).

How are these biblical declarations to be understood? It would contradict the redemptive nature of God's response to the debacle brought on the world by Satan and man's Fall to suggest that the present physical universe is to be obliterated and another universe created *ex nihilo*. Redemption is a recovering and restoring of the original. The person who experiences redemption in Christ remains the same person, even though the transformation from the sinner dead-in-sins to the saint alive-forevermore-in-Christ is so radical as to be called a new creation. Likewise it is the heavens and earth that undergo the convulsive shaking and consuming conflagration of the final judgment that re-emerge as the "new" heavens and "new" earth, however great the alteration that has taken place in that eschatological crisis. This understanding of the matter finds support in the passage where Peter foretells the passing away of the world that now is in the coming day of the Lord. For in that same context he also says that the prediluvian heavens and earth "perished" in the flood waters, making way for the present heavens and earth, and yet there is solid continuity between our postdiluvian world and the prediluvian world that "perished" (2 Pet 3:5-12).

The continuity implicit in the restorative or preservative nature of the redemptive principle becomes sharply focused in the biblical doctrine of the resurrection of the body. It is the present mortal body that undergoes resurrection. In the case of those who live to the return of Christ the identification of their suddenly "changed" bodies with their previous bodies of flesh and blood is especially clear (1 Cor 15:51,52). The glorified bodies of the saints thus constitute an incorporation of the present world into the new heavens and earth, a continuation of at least the physical stuff of the original creation into the consummated creation – and more than that.

The conclusion is then warranted that the cosmic eschatological crisis does not entail the annihilation of the original creation. The primal energy-mass which has become the multi-galactic universe familiar to us will be continued – in some form. It is the original creation that emerges transformed into the new, consummated cosmos.

While the catastrophic termination of the present world order will not constitute a complete break between this world and the world to come, it obviously will result in discontinuity of some kind. Elements of this world will be destroyed, never again to appear in the post-consummation world. As to this dross that will be eliminated when the Lord comes as a refiner's fire, there is good biblical reason to identify it with the products of fallen man's history. It will be the outward technology, material paraphernalia, and all external expressions of man's present cultural life that will be done away with (cf. 2 Pet 3:10).

Even apart from the Fall and redemption, human culture would have functioned only as a temporary substitute until the coming of the permanent consummation-culture, the supernatural God-produced culture that consists in the community of glorified humanity. At the advent of that consummation city of Metapolis, what mankind had produced by way of carrying out the cultural mission mandated in the creation covenant (cf. Gen 1:28; 2:15) would become obsolete and pass away. Since the Fall, the evil that infects human culture is an additional and compelling reason for the elimination of the pre-consummation world order.

Man's culture finds its historical embodiment in political structures and characteristically God's destroying wrath against man's works is depicted as a judgment directed against these nations of the earth. For example, when Haggai predicts the eschatological shaking of the heavens and earth, he expounds this in terms of an overthrowing of the evil kingdoms of the nations (Hag 2:2). The ultimate disappearance of the very institution of the secular state, it may be noted, is inherent in the temporary character of the common order arrangements within which the state was instituted. As we observed above, those arrangements are limited by covenant stipulation to the duration of the present earth (Gen 8:20–9:17, esp. 8:22). The day is coming when the common order ceases and that will spell the end of the present network of nations. If we are familiar with the typological idiom of biblical prophecy, which portrays God's kingdom in the world to come under the symbolism of the Old Covenant kingdom of Israel in the midst of the nations, we will not be misled when we find the nations of the earth mentioned in the prophetic portraiture of the consummated heaven (cf., e.g., Rev 21:24-26). The current national embodiments of fallen man's culture must be banished from the scene in the final judgment. For the new heavens and earth will have room for the holy kingdom of God alone.

Hypothesis of Basic Cosmic Continuity

It would not be inconsistent with the conservation principle of the redemptive process if the consummating event effected some outward changes in the earth beyond the removal of the surface incrustation of human culture. It will be in order then to attempt a tentative probe of the question whether such changes should be expected and if so what might be their extent and character. Suppose we start by testing the hypothesis that this expanding universe of ours with its current thermodynamics will be perpetuated into the eternal state in substantially its present form. This possibility might be combined with at least a minimal version of the scenario of an earth-convulsing final judgment.

If we adopt this view we must be prepared to deal with questions arising from the calculations of scientific cosmology about the future of this universe. According to theorizing in recent times the universe is destined for either expansion to a state of complete entropy or recollapse into the singularity of the "Big Crunch," the former option being the current favorite. To be sure such a fate is reckoned to be in the extremely remote future, but it would still have relevance for immortal beings living in such an evolving universe. Given that challenging eventuality, faith might find a solution to the dilemma in the omnipotence of the faithful Creator. His power offset the aging, disintegrating effects on Israel's clothing the forty years in the wilderness (Deut 8:4; 29:5; Neh 9:27) and preserved Daniel's three friends through the contraction of their world into the fiery confines of the fiercely heated furnace (Dan 3:19-27). He raised Jesus from the dead. Therefore, even if the Glory-dimensioned bodies with which God endows the overcomers in the consummating act of glorification did not already render them transcendently invulnerable against all such lower-dimensioned phenomena, he could be counted on to do whatever was necessary to counteract any cosmic extremity for their benefit. And presumably this cosmic crisis would prove to be a transitional moment in a recycling of the new heavens and earth.

It must be admitted, however, that such a (possibly recurring) process of gradual dissolution and refashioning of the cosmos does not seem appropriate to the consummate stage of creation designed from eternity for eternity by the divine Architect and Masterbuilder.

Hypothesis of Radical Cosmic Restructuring

A more likely option then is the hypothesis that a radical cosmic convulsion will occur at the end of this world-age, followed at once by a restructuring (2 Pet 3:13) that yields a cosmos which is a stabilized, optimal spatial environment for glorified humanity. Such a consummated world might differ markedly from the pre-consummation world. It might not have a planetary focus for the citizens of heaven within a stellar system with a galactic distribution pattern akin to that of the present universe. Its "earth" might be a kind of Glory-suffused cosmic orb beyond our imagining. On the other hand, the stabilized new earth produced by the re-creation might more or less resemble the old earth. By way of assessing whether the continuity or discontinuity possibility deserves the preference all we shall attempt to do here is to reflect briefly on certain biblical data that have been seen as relevant to this question.

On a more literal interpretation of the prophecies of the coming kingdom in Isa 11:6-9 and 65:25, they would indicate that the future world will contain fauna and flora recognizably like varieties found on the present earth, even if with some remarkable changes like carnivores turned herbivorous. And if the morphology of sub-human life would be similar to that of this world, a corresponding continuity would presumably obtain in the meteorological sphere, the general physics, and cosmic framework of the new earth.

An incidental problem for this or any other view that posits a continuation of present plants and animals in the future world is how they manage to survive the cataclysmic ending of this age. One possibility would be to postulate some antitypical functional equivalent of Noah's ark in which the animals and vegetation were preserved through the diluvian prototypical ending of the world (2 Pet 3:5-7). Another possible solution would be to assume restoration by re-creation. An interesting related question would concern the particular species that would be perpetuated: just those that remained on the scene at the end of the world, or all that ever existed (including the non-human hominids), or some selection according to the Creator's wisdom?

The more literal interpretation of Isa 11:6-9 and 65:25 does not, however, commend itself. The animal imagery is no more to be taken literally than the contextual references to the nations of the ancient Near East (Isa 11:11-16) or the old Jerusalem (Isa 65:18) – or the lamb with seven horns and seven eyes in the heavenly scene in Rev 5:6. But it might be acceptable to see the figurative imagery as pointing to some new kinds of representatives of the animal and vegetable kingdoms, just as the typological politico-cultural features in these passages point to the new glorified society of the New Jerusalem. As a matter of fact, that is what these prophecies would really point to even on the more literal approach, rather than to the thoroughgoing continuity suggested above. For the functional changes in the animals would entail a morphological restructuring tantamount to the creation of new species. And with the predatory element gone, the present food-chain would be radically altered. We would have to assume that a fundamentally different ecological order was to be substituted for the present system.

Whatever the meaning of Isaiah's prophecies, there are considerations that favor the prospect of a new earth with fauna and flora of some sort. Although an earth with an ecology like the present earth's would not be a biological necessity for those inspired by the heavenly Spirit of life, it would not be an incongruous life-setting for glorified man. Human procreation would no longer figure in this biological-ecological order (cf. Luke 20:35,36), but Glory-dimensioned beings could function within it in other ways, if we may judge from the analogous situations of earthly visitations of angels (cf., e.g., Gen 18:8; 19:3) and the activities of Jesus in his resurrection appearances (Luke 24:43; cf. Luke 24:30; John 21:13). And positively favoring the expectation of some kind of fauna and flora (more likely new forms) is the consideration that there would not then be any diminution of the riches of the original creation. There is some warrant then for entertaining the speculation that the new creation will contain a biosphere of non-elohim creatures, an arena in which man finds royal enjoyment in the works of God's hand (Gen 1:28; Ps 8:5-8; Heb 2:6-9) as he engages with songs of praise in the cosmic dance of the redeemed before the Lord their Maker (cf. 2 Sam 6:21; 1 Chr 13:8; Prov 8:30,31).

In connection with that speculation a question arises with respect to the nature of God's sabbath. If the Creator's entrance upon the seventh "day" marked the closing of the "six days" era devoted to the making of all the significant "kinds" of creatures, would the production of different fauna for the new earth contradict his sabbath relation to his creation? Or might these new creatures be regarded not as new "kinds" but as divinely mutated forms of present varieties, just as the human creature is not regarded as a new kind of being in spite of the radical transformation of the body that occurs in the glorification event?

Rom 8:19-22 has also been seen as biblical evidence relevant to the question of the continuity between the pre-consummation and post-consummation earth. Speaking of the earth in panoramic, age-spanning terms, this passage points back to a lamentable development, no doubt associated with the Fall, and it looks forward to an eschatological deliverance from that unhappy situation. Traditional exegesis finds here a reference to a curse that blighted nature, introducing into it features inimical to fallen humanity (changes even at the level of thermodynamics, according to promoters of the young earth dogma). The longed for deliverance is then understood as the removal of this curse and a restoration of the original order of nature, usually thought to be one without animal death (a notion without biblical warrant and contrary to the evidence of natural science). Rom 8:19-22 as traditionally interpreted would then suggest a substantial continuity between the present and future earth, though even on this view the passage would not necessarily imply that the new earth is a simple restoration of the pristine creation without significant alteration.

However, the traditional exegesis of this passage must be challenged. The apostle Paul (reflecting the treatment of death and resurrection in Isa 24:4ff.) is referring here to the fact that when man broke God's covenant and brought down on himself the curse of death, the earth was obliged to take on the function of graveyard. The personified earth is pictured as groaning because of its new role as depository for the corpses of men, and particularly because it must cover over the blood of the martyrs. Agreeably, the anticipated deliverance is identified with the redemption of the bodies of the saints at the resurrection (Rom 8:21,23). On this interpretation, Rom 8:19-22 does not speak precisely to our particular concern with respect to the continuity between the realm of nature now and hereafter. [Cf. *DLM* 229-249.]

Conclusion. Our vision of the future cosmos is dim. Certainty eludes us in our inquiry into the new earth's spatial-cosmological likeness to or difference from the present earth. But greater assurance is possible when it comes to the new earth's religious character, its nature as a holy place. Under the prophetic image of a descent of the heavenly city of God to earth, biblical prophecy portrays a coalescence of heaven and earth. The new Jerusalem – festal gathering place of God, the Judge of all, and of Jesus, the mediator of the new covenant, and of the innumerable angels, and of the assembly of the firstborn enrolled in heaven (Heb 12:22-24) – this new Jerusalem comes down to the earthly mountain, great and high (Rev 21:10–22:5). By virtue of this union of the new heaven and new earth, the earth is "heavenized." The new earth is the focal site of the enthroned triune Presence, the center of a cosmic holy of holies (cf. Rev 11:19; 21:16).

The consummated cosmos is the tabernacle of God where he dwells with men (Rev 21:2,3; 22:3,4). Jesus told his disciples he was going to prepare a place for his own in this house of his Father and would come again to receive them unto himself that where he was they might also be (John 14:2,3). This is Immanuel's land. This is the realm of the endoxate Glory-Spirit. This is the heaven, the everlasting home our spirits long for in the midst of our present mortal existence (2 Cor 5:1-5).

The heavenly city of God on the high mountain, focal center of the eternal cosmic kingdom, recalls the mountain of God in Eden, focal cultic site for the projected global theocracy. Therein lies a tale – the tale of Har Magedon.

Part Two

Heavenand Har Magedon

Chapter Four

Earthly Replicas of Heaven

Glory Replication

Earth, the visible cosmos, was made to mirror the invisible world of heaven. The lower, terrestrial register was so designed that it contained replicas of realities in the upper register Glory-realm, including likenesses of the God of heaven. Nor was the visible world alone the scene of such ectypes. Heaven too was filled with images of the God of Glory in the form of the angel "sons of God," like Elohim their Creator-Father and accordingly also called ʾĕlōhîm, "gods" (Ps 82:1).

As we have attempted to probe deeper into the mystery of the replication of the divine Glory it has appeared that the creating of heaven itself was a replicating of the eternal, uncreated Glory of God. This is most clearly seen when the heavenly Glory-Temple is perceived as an epiphanation of the Spirit. Further it has appeared that the replicating of eternal divine Glory in the creation of the cosmos points back to a radiating of divine Glory involved in the dynamic forms of subsistence within the Trinity apart from creation. Within the divine ontology the filiation of the Son is an imaging of the Father's Glory, and the procession of the Spirit is an efflorescence of that glory, itself eternally unseen and beyond our comprehension, evoking our unending wonder and worship.

The replication principle is then a dominant aspect of the exhibiting of the Glory of God, which is teleologically the ultimate tenet of theology.

Our focus here will be on the earth with its lower register reproduction of the supernal realm, for it is to this sphere of terrestrial images of heaven that Har Magedon belongs. Har Magedon is indeed a standard feature in these symbolic earthly representations of the upper register reality of heaven, the holy cosmic temple and royal residence of the King of Glory.

The paradise-sanctuary of Eden was the original such symbolic replica of heaven, produced by God in the process of the original creation. And as we have observed, later, in the premessianic stage of the redemptive era, there were other such earthly copies of heaven in the form of architectural structures fashioned by God's people at his direction and according to his design specifications – ectypes of the archetypal heavenly sanctuary. At the climax of the history of the prediluvian world, "the world that then was," the Lord had Noah construct the ark as a miniaturized version of the three-storied cosmic temple of God, the royal house in which heaven serves as his throne and earth as his footstool. The most familiar of the symbolic renderings of God's heavenly house are found in the postdiluvian world, in the typological history of Israel: the Mosaic tent of meeting and the Solomonic temple. Each of these was patterned after the heavenly exemplar revealed by the divine architect (Exod 25:9; 1 Kg 6:38; 1 Chr 28:12,19; Heb 8:5; 9:23). The erecting of these divine dwellings was thus a redemptive re-enactment of the original creation, as well as a foreshadowing of the eschatological temple of God in the new heaven and earth at the consummation of history. And in each of these replication episodes we find that a Har Magedon mountain is part of the symbolic complex.

Replication in the Genesis Prologue

Since the Har Magedon image emerges at the outset of human history as part of the original earthly mirroring of heaven, we turn now to the biblical narrative of creation to see how the replication principle figures in that account. It becomes apparent at once that replication is of fundamental importance in the cosmography of the Genesis prologue.

The basic structure of that passage, as we have previously indicated, is one of alternating heavenly and earthly scenes. This alternating of upper and lower level perspectives begins with the opening statement in Gen 1:1 about the origin of "the (invisible) heaven and earth." And what we find as we follow the development of these alternating perspectives through the narrative is a striking, extended pattern of reproduction of the archetypal upper level in lower level ectypes. Because of its theological importance, the case of man, created on earth as image of his Maker, the God of heaven, attracts most attention, but it is only one component in a pattern of replication which is pervasive in the Genesis prologue.

We propose then to trace this imaging motif in Gen 1:1–2:3. This will involve a reiterating of the series of indicators of the upper register perspective examined above, but this time the overview of the archetype will serve to introduce a survey of elements found in the lower register sections that are ectypal of the heavenly realities.

The first indicator of the upper register is the designation "heaven" in Gen 1:1. (Exegetical evidence for this interpretation was given in a discussion of Gen 1:1 in Part One above.) Since "heaven" is also used to denote the visible heaven (Gen 1:8), the sky that is produced in the process of developing the lower register world called "earth" in Gen 1:1, the appearance of "heaven" as a name for the supernal realm in the opening verse signalizes at once the replication relationship between the upper and lower registers, a relationship in virtue of which the latter is a rich resource of metaphors for the former. We shall return to the specific instance of the sky as an analogue of the invisible heaven when dealing with the productions of the second day.

The next indicator of the upper register is the reference in Gen 1:2 to "the Spirit of God" situated above the deep and darkness of the lower, visible world. Key to the interpretation of this verse is the use of "Spirit" elsewhere as a designation for both the Glory Presence that is the center and fullness of the invisible heavenly realm and for its visible earthly projection, the theophanic Shekinah cloud. Evidence for the Spirit identification of either one, the invisible or its visible projection, will constitute evidence for that same identification of the other.

The Scriptures at times attribute to the Spirit acts narrated in the Pentateuch as having been performed by the theophanic cloud in guarding and guiding Israel in the days of Moses (cf. Neh 9:19,20; Isa 63:11-14;

Hag 2:5). Also, "Spirit" appears as a synonym for other designations of the Glory cloud (e.g., Isa 59:19; Luke 1:35).

Further, there is the evidence of significant parallelism between what is done by the Shekinah and by the Holy Spirit in comparable historic situations. Notable is the extensive correspondence that obtains between the Glory cloud at the establishing of the Old Covenant at Sinai and the Holy Spirit at the inauguration of the New Covenant at Pentecost. The parallels are in the areas of sight and sound phenomena and of function. The latter includes the shared role of Shekinah and Spirit in providing the confirmatory witness of covenant documents, namely, the two covenant tablets and the New Testament canon. Patently, the Shekinah was a theophanic manifestation of the Spirit.

Another similar case of corresponding acts is found in Deut 32:10,11. This is of special interest because it involves an allusion to Gen 1:2. To convey the idea that the exodus-redemption of Israel was a kind of re-creation event, Moses depicts the operation of the Shekinah cloud in behalf of Israel in the wilderness in terms that recall the creational situation described in Gen 1:2. The allusion is unmistakable for he employs two terms he uses elsewhere only in Gen 1:2, one to picture God as hovering over (mĕraḥephet) his people Israel and the other for the uninhabitable (tōhû) character of the wilderness. What the Spirit did in the original cosmic creation was repeated by the Shekinah in a redemptive typological version. Clearly then the Spirit who hovered over the inchoate earth in Gen 1:2 is to be understood as the Glory-Presence manifestation of God.

The avian, overshadowing imagery they share in Gen 1:2 and Deut 32:11 establishes a link between the Spirit and the Glory-Presence, heavenly and earthly, and that link is reenforced by the association of both of them with that same imagery elsewhere in the Scriptures. Overshadowing is a familiar function of the Shekinah cloud in the Old Testament. The Shekinah hovered over the Israelites' dwellings when the death angel was passing over the land of Egypt (Exod 12:13,23, with the verb pāsaḥ properly translated as "hover over"); and as a cloud-pillar it overshaded the Israelites journeying through the wilderness (Exod 13:21,22; Num 14:14; Ps 105:39; cf. the image of the eagles' wings in Exod 19:4); and as a cloud of glory it overshadowed the tabernacle of Moses at its completion (Exod 40:35 [LXX]; Num 9:15; cf. 2 Chr 7:1,2). Similarly the cherubim of the Glory overshadowed the mercy seat in the holy of holies (Heb 9:5). In the prophetic idiom of Isa 4:5,6 the image of the Glory-cloud as a sheltering canopy over Mount Zion is used to typify the archetypal Glory in the consummated cosmos. Also, this protective, shielding function is entailed in the passages noted above where the Shekinah is denoted "Spirit" (Neh 9:19,20; Isa 63:11-14).

In the New Testament the avian overshadowing metaphor reappears at critical junctures in the life of Jesus, again with the Spirit and the visible theophanic cloud alternating as subjects of the action. In the angel Gabriel's announcement to Mary, her conception of Jesus is attributed to her being overshadowed by One called the Power of the Highest and the Holy Spirit (Luke 1:35). At the baptism of Jesus, the heavens being opened, the Spirit was seen descending on him like a dove (Matt 3:16; Mark 1:10; Luke 3:22; John 1:32,33). At the transfiguration it was the theophanic cloud that overshadowed the holy mountain (Matt 17:5; Mark 9:7; Luke 9:34).

Our conclusion is then that "Spirit" in Gen 1:2 is indeed an indicator of the upper register. The first indicator, the term "heaven" in Gen 1:1, refers to the upper register as a cosmic realm, a glory-dimensioned world. The "Spirit" in verse 2 confronts us with a personal Glory, the King of Glory, the Lord of the heavenly temple, the endoxated Glory-Spirit who himself *is* the Glory-temple of heaven.

In the further unveiling of the upper register it is the Glory-Spirit's identity as Sovereign over the creation that continues to be most conspicuous. His royal authority is manifested, as has been noted, in the fiat-decrees that omnipotently structure the earth and bring the multitudes of its occupants into being, and in the series of the Creator's judicial pronouncements declaring his own works, one after another, to be "good," each such verdict of approbation an anticipation of the final comprehensive judgment that all that he made was very good (Gen 1:31). We shall find that it is this dominion aspect of the upper register revelation of the Creator that figures prominently in the Genesis 1 instances of the archetype/ectype principle.

The record of the Creator's royal sabbath rest (Gen 2:2,3) directs us once again to the throne of heaven, the central and dominant object in the heavenly scene. And along with the palatial-spatial perspective of the picture of the reign of the King of Glory, the divine sabbath introduces a temporal dimension. For together with the preceding six days the seventh day constitutes a sabbatical week schema representing heaven time as an eschatological movement from kingdom construction to kingdom consummation.

In the course of our review of the upper register certain earthly replicas of the heavenly archetypes have already come into view. But now, as we seek to demonstrate the prevalence of the replication principle in the Genesis prologue, we want to examine more directly and fully the theme of the ectypes that appear in the creation account.

Most explicitly the replication principle comes to expression in the creation of man as the image of God. [For further treatment of this subject beyond the present brief digest of the more salient data, see *IOS*.] The Glory-Spirit-Presence referred to in Gen 1:2 as the "Spirit of God" is associated with the creation of the human bearers of the divine image in both Gen 1:26,27 and Gen 2:7. As previously noted, the "let us" fiat of Gen 1:26 identifies the scene as the heavenly council of angels, the site of the Glory-Spirit of Gen 1:2. Such is consistently the significance of this consultative plural (see Gen 3:22; 11:7; 18:2,21; Isa 6:8; cf. Isa 41:21ff.). And the divine creative breathing on man in Gen 2:7 is identified as an act of the Spirit by the interpretive words of Jesus, "receive the Holy Spirit," on the occasion of his counterpart redemptive act of breathing on his disciples (John 20:22). The creative breathing of Gen 2:7 was an act of fathering by the Spirit comparable to his overshadowing of Mary in the conception of Jesus (Luke 1:35). The child then born of Mary was accordingly called "the Son of God," and similarly by virtue of the Spirit's fathering of Adam, Adam was a "son of God" (cf. Luke 3:37). The conceptual connection between such sonship and bearing the divine likeness is underscored in Gen 5:1-3 by the juxtaposition of God's creating man in his image and Adam's fathering a son in his likeness. The *imago Dei* is thus primarily a matter of replication and representational likeness rather than representative status.

Since the paradigm replicated in man is the Glory-Spirit, man's likeness to God consists at a creaturely level in outstanding glory elements found in the divine Archetype, the holy enthroned God of Glory. These glory components are royal-judicial dominion, ethical purity and integrity, and visual luminosity. The connection between man's being made in the likeness of God and his rulership over all the earth and its creatures is clearly established in the fiat-decree to create man in God's image (Gen 1:26).

Subsequent references to man's likeness to God repeatedly identify this likeness with man's dominion and his performing of judicial functions (cf. Gen 3:22; 9:6; Ps 8:5-8). By virtue of that royal office man is an elohim being (Ps 82:6), as are the angel members of the celestial council (Ps 82:1). Ethical excellence is most explicitly identified as a second component of the image of God in references to the redemptive renewal of the image. Thus Eph 4:24 and Col 3:10 describe the re-creation in the likeness of the Creator as a renewing in righteousness, holiness, and knowledge of the truth, the moral qualities that are the foundation of the heavenly throne of the Judge of all the earth (Ps 89:14). The third component of man's likeness to the divine Glory, a visual splendor that mirrors the invisible Glory of the divine Original, comes as an eschatological reward. Since the first Adam failed to achieve this and it is now attained through Christ, the Redeemer of the elect, it is in passages presenting the prospect of the parousia and ultimate glorification of the redeemed that their likeness to God or Christ is identified with this visual brilliance (cf., e.g., 1 Cor 15:40-53; Phil 3:20,21; 1 John 3:2). When that transpires, the replication of the Glory-Spirit in man is perfected and the eternal predestined purpose of God fulfilled that all whom God foreknew should be conformed to the likeness of his Son, that he might be the firstborn among many brothers (Rom 8:29,30).

Another notable instance of replication appears at the climactic seventh day of the Genesis Prologue. This closing day of the creation week, like the "beginning" at the head of that week, is an upper register reality. The Creator's sabbath rest (Gen 2:1,2) is his royal session as the Majesty on high, the divine enthronement that is the nucleus of the archetypal heaven, now in its new phase as an enthronement in the completed cosmic temple. And Gen 2:3 tells us that God made a lower register ectypal sabbath after the pattern of his heavenly sabbath by appointing for his human image bearers the ordinance of the earthly sabbatical schema. (For the interpretation of Gen 2:3 as the origin of the ordinance of the Sabbath, see Exod 20:11.) Calling for six days of work crowned by a sabbath day, the Sabbath ordinance shapes man's succession of days so as to exhibit week by week the temporal pattern in which God was pleased to reveal the origination of the world – the Genesis prologue being the canonical version of that revelation.

Comparing the main ectypes contained in days six and seven, man and the Sabbath, Jesus tells us that the Sabbath was made for man, not vice versa. The Sabbath was a blessing to man in that it instructed him concerning his heavenly Father's way, holding forth the promise that as he imitated that way he would at last arrive at God's own archetypal sabbath rest. Accordingly, the Creator's archetypal sabbatical history, which was replicated symbolically in the recurring seven day cycle prescribed by the Sabbath ordinance, would also be replicated on the grand scale of the overall structure of human history. That sabbatical history like its heavenly archetype was to be an eschatological movement to consummation, from a time of earthly kingdom labor to the time of glory-kingdom inheritance.

Made in the likeness of heavenly archetypes, the earthly replicas become in turn images for our picturing the invisible originals of the upper register; they are put to use as literary figures to depict analogically the heavenly reality beyond man's ken. Thus, for our contemplation of God, analogies are drawn from his ectypal likeness, man; God is described in all manner of anthropomorphisms. In the Genesis prologue the Creator appears as a workman who performs his task and then takes his rest – or, more specifically, he is portrayed as a king who builds himself a palace and then occupies the throne.

The temporal aspect of this analogy further illustrates how an earthly ectype may serve as a figure for something in the upper register. Since the chronological schema of the Creator's sabbatical week begins and ends with upper register phenomena (viz., "in the beginning" and God's eternal seventh day of sabbath enthronement), certainly the six work days (each divided into evening and morning) that form the central part of the schema connecting the beginning and the seventh day must also refer to heavenly time. This description of upper register time is then another instance of the use of a lower register replica as a metaphor for its heavenly archetype. The temporal image of an earthly sabbatical week is one of the features of the broadly anthropomorphic portrait of the Creator as a royal builder. The chronological framework of the creation account is not intended to be understood literally. God in his wisdom revealed the temporal dimension of his upper level creational history under the figure of his human replica's lower register week as formulated in the Sabbath ordinance, the divinely appointed replica of the archetypal sabbatical reality.

A final observation apropos the recurrence of the replication principle in the Genesis prologue: featured in virtually every "day" in the narrative is at least one natural phenomenon or object that functions in this account in a manner metaphorical of the King of heaven or that readily lends itself for literary use as a metaphor of heaven.

The theme of the first triad of days is creation kingdoms, and the products of these days provide images for conceptualizing the heavenly realm. The light of day one affords a figurative analogue for the luminous glory of heaven. The clouds (the waters above) of day two are a constant accompaniment, insignia, and vehicle of the divine Glory, and the overarching firmament of that second day is a likeness of the overshadowing canopy of heavenly Glory (cf. Isa 4:5,6) – indeed, as we have noted, the earthly "heaven" provides the name for the upper register realm. Similarly, the trees of day three with their overspreading branches and association with the birds of the heaven are an arboreal kind of heaven, a semblance of the sheltering celestial Glory (cf. Dan 4:10-12). Also, entailed in the production of the land on day three was the formation of the mountains with their heads in the clouds of heaven (cf. Pss 90:2; 104:5-9; Prov 8:25), a natural image of heaven of special relevance for the topic of Har Magedon.

The theme of the second triad of days is creature kings and a figurative analogue for the heavenly Ruler, the Creator King (theme of the seventh day), is provided by each of these terrestrial kings: the astral bodies of day four that rule the night and day; the birds and fish of day five that exercise their sway over sky and sea; and the royal creatures of day six, the animals with their dominion over the vegetation, and especially man, the earthling appointed lord over all the creation.

In sum, the entire lower register strand in the creation narrative is a continuous series of instances of replication of the upper register Glory, ectypes that provide us with God-language and conceptual imagery for our reflections on the Glory-heaven until the day when our eyes will be opened.

Chapter Five

Mountain of God

Eden As Replica of Heaven

In Gen 2:4ff. there is a shift from the cosmic perspective of the prologue to a concentration on the local scene of Eden, man's original homeland. Prominent still, however, is the principle of replication. For the garden sanctuary that the Lord planted in Eden (Gen 2:8) was a terrestrial image of the upper register, an image not just of one or another feature of the invisible world but of the Glory-realm as a whole. And within this complex replica of heaven, Har Magedon comes into view.

The Glory-Spirit, whose dominant presence in the heavenly temple is evidenced by Gen 1:2 and 26, was present in his visible theophanic form in Eden. This is attested by Gen 2:7 and 3:8, the former relating his immediate involvement in the creation of Adam and the latter his fearful judicial intervention in the garden after the Fall "as the Spirit of the (judgment) day," attended by the cherubim (cf. Gen 3:24). Sanctified by this Glory theophany, Eden was a holy site, a temple, "the garden of *God*" (Ezek 28:13,14; 31:8,9), "the garden of the *Lord*" (Gen 13:10; Isa 51:3), an earthly copy of the heavenly temple. The celestial sanctuary was replicated in Eden – but there was something more here than simply symbolic representation. In the personal presence of the Glory-Spirit there was in Eden an actual projection of the heavenly reality into the visible world below.

The paradise nature of the holy site of Eden, evident from the designation of its defining center as a garden, is also intimated by the name Eden itself according to one view of its etymology (cf. Gen 3:23 LXX). Agreeably, it was celebrated in subsequent times as a fertile land of abundance, an arboreal delight (cf. Gen 13:10; Isa 51:3; Ezek 31:9; 36:35; Joel 2:3). Its vivifying role is accented in the Genesis 2 description. In it were the tree of life and the river of life, which refreshed the garden and watered the world around Eden. The heavenly reality, the archetypal land of abundant life and delight, is portrayed in Scripture as Eden-like, another instance of an earthly replica serving as a metaphor for its supernal original (Isa 35:6; 41:18,19; Ezek 47:12; Joel 3:18; Rev 22:1,2).

Eden was also a representation of heaven in that it was a sabbath land, a trait closely related to the fact that Eden was a holy land. We may approach this matter by examining what the Scriptures say about the land of Canaan, a redemptive restoration of Eden. Like Eden a paradise land and holy land, Canaan was also a sabbath land; it was a replica of the heavenly realm of God's seventh day rest. God's enthronement in heaven is his sabbath rest (Isa 66:1; cf. 11:10) and correspondingly, as Isaiah's comparison of God's cosmic and Canaanite houses shows, his enthronement above the ark in his earthly tabernacle or temple is a sabbath rest (cf. Ps 132:8). As the location of God's temple enthronement, the earthly projection of his celestial seventh day enthronement, the promised land of Canaan was a sabbath land. And accordingly the failure of many Israelites of the exodus generation to enter Canaan is said to have been a failure to enter into God's own sabbath rest (Heb 3:18–4:5; Ps 95:11).

Canaan was a sabbath land from another point of view: it was a prototype of the sabbatical inheritance that awaits God's people, their eternal heavenly rest (cf. Heb 4:9). Canaan was the place of coming to rest at the end of their journey (cf. Num 10:33-36; Deut 12:9). It was the place where God gave them rest from their enemies (Josh 21:44; 23:1; 2 Sam 7:1), a foreshadowing of the peace of heaven, the resting of the saints from the labors of their warfare as they enter into God's own rest (cf. Rev 14:13).

Further, Canaan was a sabbath land in the sense that the Sabbath ordinance (with its extensions in sabbatical and Jubilee years) shaped the cultural life for which the land was the infrastructure. That ordinance even arranged for the land's own enjoyment of sabbatical rest (Lev 25:1-12).

Though a sabbath land, Canaan was not the real sabbath land. Not Joshua but Jesus leads God's people into the true sabbath land of God's heavenly seventh day (Heb 4:8). Jesus, our great high priest, has already passed into heaven and entered his royal sabbath rest above (Heb 4:14). His session on the right hand of the throne of the Majesty on high is a participation in the seventh day royal rest of God, the King of creation.

However rich the sabbatical typology of Canaan, the primary factor in its identification as a sabbath land was its privileged position as the site of the sabbath enthronement of the Glory-Spirit. That is also the basic consideration in our identifying of Eden as a sabbath land. Eden had sabbatical significance as a prototypal stage of the royal rest covenanted to man beyond his probationary mission and the carrying out of the kingdom commission to fill and subdue the earth. But it is primarily from the viewpoint of God's own sabbatical resting in Eden that Eden was a sabbath land.

The main thing we must do then to establish the character of Eden as a sabbath land is to show that Eden was the locus of a replication of the celestial throne scene, with a heaven-to-earth projection of the Glory-Presence, divine occupant of the sabbath throne above. To do that will involve an exploration of the biblical revelation concerning the mountain of God in Eden. That is our next topic, but first a brief excursus pursuant of our discussion of the connection between sabbath and theocratic land.

By reason of their interconnection within the history of the replication of heaven on earth, sabbath and kingdom land are mutually conditioning concepts. As the site of God's sabbath enthronement, the holy land (whether Eden or Canaan) is a sabbath land. Conversely, the sabbath partakes of the nature of Eden and Canaan as a place, a land. It takes on a spatial dimension along with its more obvious temporal dimension. As we have seen, in the Hebrews 3 and 4 analysis of redemptive history the sabbath is identified at the typological level with the land of Canaan and at the archetypal level with the realm of heaven.

The sabbath is a place and conspicuous in Hebrews 3 and 4 is the idea of entrance into this sabbath place of rest. Later in the Book of Hebrews this entrance theme emerges again. When it does, the Hebrews 4 prospect of our entering into God's sabbath rest is translated into the hope of our eschatological entering into the true holy of holies beyond the veil, into the throne room of the heavenly temple (Heb 6:18,19; 10:19). The substitution of temple for sabbath rest in the development of the entrance theme in Hebrews is natural for God's holy house is his resting place (Isa 66:1; Acts 7:49).

Concretely, then, the spatial aspect of the sabbath takes the form of holy land and holy house or temple. Ultimately these two images – along with holy city – coalesce in the eternal sabbath. In the case of the promise of eschatological entrance into the holy of holies, once again the fulfillment is through the sacrificial ministry of Jesus, our high priest. He has opened the way and has gone before us, not into a typological holy place but into the heavenly sanctuary itself, now to appear in the presence of God for us (Heb 6:20; 9:12,24,25; 10:19,20), a high priest whose permanent sanctuary service in our behalf is performed as the One invested with all authority in heaven and earth, enthroned at God's right hand (Heb 8:1,2).

The Mountain of God in Eden

Eden was a sanctuary, a paradise, a sabbath land. A further contribution to the symbolism of Eden as an ectype of heaven was made by a prominent feature of its topography. Dominating the landscape of Eden was the mountain of the Lord. This motif of God's mountain is a pervasive element in biblical symbolism from creation, through redemption, to consummation. It is most familiar in the form of Mount Zion, which brings out clearly the nature of this mountain as the site of the temple residence of the Lord, the sanctuary of his theophanic Glory-Presence, the place of his royal sabbatical rest as he sits enthroned amid the cherubim.

Mount Zaphon and Mount Zion

Isaiah 14 contains a graphic picture of the sacred mountain. In a taunt against the king of Babylon (cf. vv. 4ff.) the defiance of this king against God is depicted as a boastful lusting for an ascent to heaven. He would elevate himself above the hosts of heaven, challenging the supremacy of the Most High, enthroned amid the epiphanic clouds (vv. 13,14). This celestial seat of sovereignty is identified as a mountain. The evil king would sit enthroned in a place called "the mount of assembly" (har môᶜēd), the mount where the angelic council gathers for judicial session at the throne of God (v. 13). Har môᶜēd is the Hebrew term that gets transliterated in Greek as har magedōn and we shall be returning to this designation again below.

Parallel to har môᶜēd in v. 13 is the Hebrew expression yarkĕtê ṣāpôn, "the heights of Zaphon." Yarkĕtê can refer to the utmost point, whether high or low. In God's counter-challenge, the king is threatened for his antichrist aspirations with a judgment that will bring him down to the pit of destruction, the yarkĕtê bôr (v. 15). But in v. 13, as a synonym of har, yarkĕtê clearly signifies not extreme depth but extreme height, the mountain heights of heaven. Agreeably, the conjoined term ṣāpôn at times refers by itself to the celestial realm (cf. Ps 89:12 [13]; Job 26:7; 37:22; Ezek 1:4). In a mythologized version of the concept of a mountain of deity, Baal's residence is on Mount Zaphon, a terrestrial representation of the cosmic abode of the gods. Besides Isa 14:13, yarkĕtê ṣāpôn appears in Ezek 38:6,15 and 39:2 (which will be discussed below) and in Ps 48:2 [3]. In Psalm 48 it stands in apposition to Mount Zion. The mountain of God and his city, Jerusalem, blend together here as the psalmist extols the Lord:

> Great is Yahweh and greatly to be praised, in the city of our God;
> the mountain of his sanctuary, paragon of peaks, joy of all the earth;
> Mount Zion, the heights of Zaphon, city of the Great King
> (vv. 1,2 [2,3]).

Mount Zaphon is thus identified with Mount Zion. They are two names for the mountain of the Lord. Hence what we learn about the heights of Zaphon in Isaiah 14 (and Ezekiel 38 and 39) contributes to our total picture of God's holy mount.

The Original Zion in Eden

We have stated that the topography of Eden featured an instance, the original instance, of the Zion/Zaphon phenomenon. We must now indicate the grounds for that conclusion. One line of evidence involves a recognition that Israel in Canaan recapitulates in basic ways the situation of man in Eden. In each case there is a theocratic order, with a sanctuary of the Glory-Spirit to be guarded; with a holy paradise land flowing with milk and honey to be cultivated and enjoyed; with a covenant of works and its dual sanctions of blessing and curse. The Israelite sanctuary provides graphic pictorial evidence of this reproduction of Eden in the reflections of paradise in its decorative motifs. There is then a presumption that Zion, the mountain site of the temple and Glory theophany, was also part of this pattern of recapitulation, that Zion was a restoration of an original holy mountain in Eden.

Similarly, the New Jerusalem of the new heaven and earth is portrayed as a final, consummating restoration of Eden, as a garden with its tree and river of life and as a holy site of the throne of God (cf. Rev 22:1ff.). And again the presumption is then that the great high mountain that is the site of the New Jerusalem at its appearing out of heaven (Rev 21:10; cf. Isa 2:2,3; 4:1-5; 25:6–26:2; Mic 4:1,2; Ezek 40:2) is another feature of this eschatological realm that harks back to Eden, pointing to the presence of such a holy mountain in the primal garden of God.

Ezekiel 28 takes us beyond presumptive indicators. Like Isaiah 14 this oracle is directed against a king with arrogant, antichrist pretensions, in this case the king of Tyre. Once again the true Judge of heaven and earth casts down the tyrant from his imagined heights as enthroned deity (v. 2) to the depths of the pit of death (v. 8). In a concluding lament (vv. 11ff.) this fall from heaven to Sheol is likened to an event that transpired in Eden, an event variously understood as an experience of Adam or of Satan.

The scene is clearly set in v. 13: "You were in Eden, the garden of God." The regalia of the one thus addressed, an adornment of precious stones and gold, suggests the opulence of Eden, where those gem-stones were available in abundance (cf. Gen 2:11,12) to be used in symbolic replication of the Glory of God – as they were in the breastplate of the high priest in the redemptive recapitulation of Eden in Israel. Indeed, the resemblance of the list of precious stones in Ezek 28:13 to the list of stones in that breastplate as described in Exod 28:17-20 and 39:10-13 has misled some to identify the figure in view here as the Israelite high priest, rather than Adam or Satan. This matter will call for further consideration below, but at the moment what we want to call attention to is the statement in Ezek

28:14 about the location of the king. Sharpening the focus of verse 12, which stated: "You were in Eden, the garden of God," verse 14 declares: "You were on the holy mount of God." Together, verses 12 and 14 plainly reveal that the mountain of God stood in the midst of Eden.

The "stones of fire" (ʾabnê ʾēš) associated with the holy mount in Ezek 28:14 are comparable to fiery phenomena connected with God's mountain elsewhere, including coals of fire (gaḥălê ʾēš) flashing among the cherubim (Ezek 1:13; 10:2) or aflame on the altar (Lev 16:12; cf. the live coal [reṣep] in Isa 6:6) or issuing from a theophanic display of wrath (2 Sam 22:9-13; Ps 18:13,14). Here on this awesome sacred peak in Eden the mysterious figure behind the king of Tyre in Ezekiel 28 was originally stationed (v. 14) and from this holy height he was subsequently thrown down (vv. 16,17).

When Genesis 2 is read in the light of Ezekiel 28 hints of the presence of the mountain of God in Eden can be discerned there. The flowing of the river of Eden into the surrounding terrain, which in any case suggests that Eden was higher ground, is probably to be seen as the origin of the biblical motif of the river of life that flows from the mountain sanctuary of the Lord (cf., e.g., Ezek 47:1ff.). There would be an explicit reference to such a mountain in Gen 2:6 on the (not widely accepted) view that the problematic ʾēd refers to a mountain that rises up from the earth. Also, the nearby availability of gold and precious stones mentioned in Gen 2:11,12 suggests that the mountain of God is the assumed setting since elsewhere in the biblical trajectory of the theme of a profusion of gem stones they are associated with the glorious city of God on his holy mountain (cf. Isa 54:11,12; Rev 21:18-21). And most significant is the presence of the Glory-Spirit in Eden. This evokes the image of the mountain of God for in the restoration of Eden at Sinai, in the typological holy land of Canaan, and in the antitypical holy land of the new heaven and earth the Glory-Spirit appears on the summit of the mountain of God. A particular point in this regard is the correspondence between the thunderous judicial manifestation of the Glory-Spirit in Eden recorded in Gen 3:8 and that narrated in Exodus 19–24, where Mount Sinai is the mountain of God on which the theophanic Spirit appears.

Sacramental Icon of Heaven

The mountain of God in Eden shared with the land of Eden as a whole in its basic symbolic significance as a representation of God's celestial realm. Indeed, the mountain was the heart of the terrestrial replication of God's heaven. As the site of the focal revelation of the enthroned Glory on earth the mountain afforded to man a sacramental access to participation in the invisible heaven while he was in his preglorified state. It was the cultic focus for the earthly people of God in the garden. In the event of a successful probation the mountain would have continued to be the cohesive epicenter as humanity expanded from Eden to the appointed global fullness. Like its redemptive counterpart, Mount Zion, the mountain in Eden was to be the spiritual capital, the place to which from afar prayer would be directed, to whose summit the holy throng would ascend with their tribute of worship and praise (cf., e.g., Ps 43:3,4; Isa 27:13; 30:29; 56:7).

By virtue of God's residence on the mountain it was the holy temple mount, the mount of the palace of the Great King of heaven and his angelic entourage, the administrative center for cosmic government, the seat of the sovereign Judge of the whole world. Since it is a function of the theophanic Glory-Spirit enthroned on the mountain to execute the dual sanctions of the covenant, the blessing and the curse, the mountain was the source of life and death. From it emanated a river of life, a stream of blessing, which, however, in the fallen world can become a torrent of fire inflicting the curse of destruction. At the beginning, before the Fall, the mountain was the site of an overhovering, sheltering Presence of God. As mentioned above, this shielding function of the Glory-cloud is strikingly exhibited in redemptive history in the Shekinah's hovering over (pāsaḥ) the doors of the Israelites' houses, warding off the angel of death who was passing through the land of Egypt. Similarly Isa 31:5 compares the Lord's defensive covering of Jerusalem (gānan, root of the noun gan, "garden," as in the garden of Eden) to the protective hovering of birds (pāsaḥ – cf. the avian imagery for the Creator Spirit in Gen 1:2). Hence the mountain in Eden signified that this theocratic realm was a protectorate of the Suzerain, a fortress, a refuge under the overshadowing wings of the Almighty (cf. Isa 4:5,6).

Viewed as a whole from top to bottom the mount of God in Eden was a representation of the cosmos – the foot of the mount, the earth; its summit, heaven. In terms of cosmographic symbolism the mountain was thus the heaven-earth axis, located at the center of the earth, just as Zion, its redemptive restoration, was regarded as the navel or center of the earth (Ezek 5:5; 38:12). The mountain slopes leading from the bottom to the peak and the crowning glory of the divine Presence were then a passageway to heaven. Psalm 24 envisages the approach of God-seekers to stand before him in his Zion sanctuary as an ascending of the mountain of the Lord (v. 3). As an ascending passageway the slopes of the mountain were a staircase. Architecturally this image was embodied in the ziggurat, the symbolic cosmic mountain of the ancient pagan world, a mythologized version of the pristine Edenic reality. It is found again in the vision of Jacob in Gen 28:12ff., where the stairway is the intersection of the invisible and visible worlds, the interconnection by which ministering heavenly beings (cf. Heb 1:14), sent on earthly mission, move back and forth between the upper and lower registers. The staircase represents the mediation of God's blessings. In the redemptive context this is a mediation of salvation and of the right of access to heaven, and Jesus is the staircase (John 1:47-51).

The mountain staircase leads to the entrance gate of the temple-city at the summit. The access way points to the welcome at the opened gates of heaven. In Psalm 24 the thought of the ascent of the hill of the Lord leads to the thought of the opening of the gates for the entrance of the King of Glory (vv. 7-10). Likewise Jacob recognized that the site of the staircase of his dream was the site of the gate of heaven, the house of God (Gen 28:17). And Jesus, the true staircase-mediator, is also the true temple gate, the true entryway to the temple-city of Glory on the heavenly summit of the cosmic mountain (John 2:19-21; 10:7,9; Rev 21:22).

Chapter Six

Har Magedon: The Mount of Assembly

The Meaning of Har Magedon

One biblical name for the celestial mountain of God is Har Magedon. According to the more traditional view of this term it does not refer to the holy mount but signifies Mount Megiddo. However, the biblical evidence against the Megiddo view and in favor of understanding har magedōn as a designation of the mountain of the Lord is quite conclusive. [The present account of this matter is a recasting of material in *HMEM* 207-22 and *GOM* 212, 213.]

The Hebraisti Clue in Rev 16:16

The term har (mount) magedōn appears only once in the Scriptures, in Rev 16:16, but a decisive clue to its meaning is found in that passage. Referring to the mustering of Satan's forces for the final battle, Rev 16:16 states: "he gathered them to the place that in Hebrew (Hebraisti) is called Har Magedon." Har magedōn is thus identified as a Hebrew term that has been transliterated into the Greek text. Identifying transliterated Hebrew and Aramaic words as Hebraisti is a peculiarly Johannine trait within the New

Testament. Besides two cases in Revelation there are four in John's gospel. Now what proves to be decisive for the interpretation of har magedōn is the fact that these transliterated Hebraisti terms are consistently accompanied by an explanation of some sort, even by a translation sometimes.

In three of the cases in the gospel the word in question is the name of a place. In each case the context furnishes at least an identification of the place thus denoted, even if not a translation. In John 5:2 Bethesda (with variants Bethsaida, Bethzatha, Belzetha) is identified as a particular pool in Jerusalem having five porches or colonnades. Similarly, in John 19:13 the Aramaic Gabbatha (of uncertain meaning) is identified by the Greek term Lithostrōton ("stone pavement or mosaic"), the designation of Pilate's judgment seat to which Gabbatha is appended. In the case of the reference to the site of the crucifixion in John 19:17 the Greek name Kraniou ("of the skull") affords a translation of the Aramaic name Golgatha, which is added to it. In John's resurrection narrative the Aramaic rabbouni is at once explained by the Greek didaskale, "teacher" (John 20:16).

Again in Rev 9:11, the one other appearance of Hebraisti in Revelation besides 16:16, an explanation of the Hebraisti term is provided: "They had a king over them, the angel of the Abyss, whose name in Hebrew is Abaddōn, and who has in Greek the name Apollyōn (Destroyer)." This instance is especially significant because Abaddon and Har Magedon form a pair in the Book of Revelation, linked not only by the term Hebraisti but by their parallel placement in the literary structure, each at the climax of one of the corresponding sections (the trumpets and the bowls of wrath) in the over-all chiastic arrangement of the book. Moreover they form a (contrastive) conceptual pair, for (as we shall be observing further) they denote antipodal positions in the cosmos, Heaven and the Abyss.

Surely, in light of this consistent stylistic pattern, the Hebraisti term in Rev 16:16 will also prove to have its explanation in its immediate context. It is then necessary to show that this is the case on whatever interpretation of har magedōn one proposes. What we shall find is that the Megiddo view fails this crucial test and the mountain of God interpretation is validated by it.

Associated with har magedōn in Rev 16:16 is the concept of gathering, expressed by the verb synagō ("he gathered [synēgagen] them to the place called in Hebrew har magedōn"). According to the pattern of Hebraisti terms, har magedōn will then signify Mount of Gathering. We came upon precisely that name in our discussion in Isaiah 14 in the preceding chapter. As observed there, the term har môᶜēd, "Mount of Assembly," appears in Isa 14:13 as a designation of the mountain of God. The noun môᶜēd is derived from the verb yāᶜad ("appoint"; niphal, "assemble by appointment"), which is rendered in the LXX by synagō, the verb used in Rev 16:16 in the interpretive word play: "he gathered them to the Mount of Gathering."

Har Môᶜēd, Mount of Assembly

We are thus pointed to the har môᶜēd of Isa 14:13 as the Hebrew term transliterated har magedōn in Rev 16:16, and we hope to show that there is considerable evidence confirming the connection between the two and thereby establishing the interpretation of har magedōn as the Mount of Assembly/Gathering, the mountain of God.

The basic phonetic equivalence of har magedōn and har môᶜēd is at once apparent. The first three consonants of magedōn correspond to the three consonants in môᶜēd – the Greek gamma (g) being used at times to render the Hebrew ᶜayin (cf., e.g., the LXX rendering of names like Gaza and Uthai). The -ōn is an afformative in Hebrew nouns, including place names. The vocalic differences reflect adjustments that occurred in the adaptive process of transliteration.

Supporting the identification of the har magedōn of Rev 16:16 with the har môᶜēd of Isa 14:13 is the fact that each of these expressions in its single biblical appearance is paired with Hades as its polar opposite on the cosmic axis. In the Isa 14:13 context the contrast is drawn between the heights to which the king of Babylon aspires as the site of his throne and the depths to which he is actually to descend. He will not ascend to the har môᶜēd, to the yarkĕtê ṣāpôn, "heights of Zaphon," as he boasts (vv. 13-14), but will be brought down to the yarkĕtê bôr, "depths of the Pit" (v. 15). Correspondingly, in the Book of Revelation har magedōn (16:16) is contrastingly paired with Abaddōn (9:11), another Hebrew term, here the name of the angel of the Abyss, and in its Old Testament appearances a synonym of Sheol. The Abaddon of Rev 9:11 is then the equivalent of the Sheol and Pit of Isa 14:15. And the har (mountain) element in har magedōn (Rev 16:16) of course contrasts with the Pit of Abaddon, as does the har in har môᶜēd (Isa 14:13). The correspondence of the har môᶜēd of Isa 14:13 and the har magedōn of Rev 16:16 within the framework of these parallel contrastive pairs is indicative of the identity of these two terms.

We shall presently return to our argument for the equivalence of har môᶜēd and har magedōn, particularly the evidence for their shared association with the theme of gathering. But first we shall develop further the case for the identification of har môᶜēd as the mountain of the Lord, Zion/Jerusalem. For if har môᶜēd is Zion, then to demonstrate that har magedōn is the equivalent of har môᶜēd will be to establish the Zion/Jerusalem identity of har magedōn.

Har Môᶜēd – Mount Zaphon/Zion – Har Magedon

In Isaiah 14 there are several other terms besides the already mentioned yarkĕtê ṣāpôn that are appositional to har môᶜēd and serve to identify har môᶜēd as the celestial mountain of God. One is šāmayīm, "heaven" (vv. 12,13), which is paired with Sheol (vv. 9,11,15; cf. ʾereṣ, "netherworld," v. 12) to denote the opposing cosmic poles. This pair, synonymous with the yarkĕtê ṣāpôn/yarkĕtê bôr pair, like the latter corresponds to the har magedōn/Abaddōn combination in the Book of Revelation and thereby reenforces the identification of har magedōn with har môᶜēd. Other such appositional terms in the Isaiah 14 context that bring out the heavenly nature of har môᶜēd are "above the stars of God" (v. 13) and "above the heights of the clouds" (v. 14). But of the alternate terms for har môᶜēd, yarkĕtê ṣāpôn is the most important.

Zaphon (ṣāpôn) was the name of a mountain to the north of Israel that was regarded as the residence of Baal, an earthly localization of the cosmic Zaphon, the abode of the gods. A secondary meaning which ṣāpôn acquired was "north," but in the Old Testament, as we have seen in Isaiah 14, yarkĕtê ṣāpôn may denote the heavenly mount of God, polar opposite of Sheol. Ps 48:2 [3] and Ezek 38:6,15; 39:2 offer additional instances of yarkĕtê ṣāpôn used for the celestial mountain of deity or for Mount Zion as the earthly projection of God's heaven.

Psalm 48 celebrates the supremacy of Yahweh the Suzerain and his mountain-city. A cluster of phrases in vv. 1,2 [2,3] denoting the divine fortress concludes with: "Mount Zion, the heights of Zaphon, city of the

Great King." By placing yarkĕtê ṣāpôn and Mount Zion in apposition this passage identifies the two as we noted above and this establishes that har môᶜēd, the equivalent of yarkĕtê ṣāpôn in Isa 14:13, is Mount Zion.

As in Isaiah 14, yarkĕtê ṣāpôn in Ezekiel 38–39 denotes the mountain of deity from the perspective of antichrist ambitions. These ideological claims to the divine throne are reified in Ezekiel 38–39 in the form of a pseudo-Zaphon over against Zion. Yarkĕtê ṣāpôn here is a designation for that false mountain of deity, antichrist-Gog's place from which he launches his assault against the mountain of God, the true yarkĕtê ṣāpôn. The final eschatological crisis is depicted in terms of the historical situation in the old typological era when there were rival pagan mountains of deity, like Baal's at the Mount Zaphon north of Israel, over against Zion-Jerusalem in Israel.

The identification of har môᶜēd with Zion is also attested by references to Zion (in passages like Ps 74:4 and Lam 2:6) as the place of God's môᶜēd and of the assembled congregation (ᶜēdâ) of his people, and most graphically by the actual locating of the ʾōhel môᶜēd, "tent of meeting," its replacement (2 Sam 6:17), and its successor, the temple, on Mount Zion (1 Kgs 8:4).

The Gathering Against Zion

Having demonstrated, especially through the yarkĕtê ṣāpôn linkage, that har môᶜēd is Zion/Jerusalem, the mountain-city of God, we may now support our case for equating the har magedōn of Rev 16:16 with the har môᶜēd of Isaiah 14 by pointing to the equation of the Rev 16:16 Har Magedon episode with the eschatological event elsewhere in Scripture located at Zion, the mountain of God.

The central, totally dominant theme in the har magedōn passage (Rev 16:16) is that of the great gathering, the gathering of antichrist hordes against the Lord and his people at Har Magedon. As we have seen, it is this gathering that is signified by the very name har magedōn. And what we find is that this theme of a universal hostile, antichrist gathering appears repeatedly in the har môᶜēd, mountain of God, passages and that it is, indeed, this mountain-city of God against which the gathering is directed. Mount Zion/Jerusalem, har môᶜēd, occupies in these passages the position of Har Magedon in Rev 16:16, a clear proof that this har môᶜēd stands behind and explains har magedōn. Among such passages are the following:

Psalm 48, having identified yarkĕtê ṣāpôn (and thus har môᶜēd) as Zion/Jerusalem (v. 2 [3]), goes on to relate how the rebellious kings gather (yāᶜad) there against Yahweh (v. 4 [5]), who shatters their advancing armies and secures the eschatological peace of the city (vv. 5ff. [6ff.]). All the key elements of the Har Magedon gathering event of Rev 16:12ff. are combined in this picture of the gathering against the har môᶜēd/Zaphon site of God's mountain-city, Zion/Jerusalem.

The most elaborate portrayal of the final Har Magedon gathering is found in Ezekiel 38–39, the account that is the chief source drawn upon in the series of prophecies of that satanic deception and gathering of the nations in the Book of Revelation (Rev 12:9; 13:14; 16:13-16; 17:12-14; 19:17-21; 20:7-10). As related in Ezekiel 38–39, Gog's antichrist challenge takes place according to God's pre-announced purpose and his sovereign orchestration of the event. Lured by the Lord to this final confrontation, Gog advances against "the mountains of Israel" (39:2,17). It is God's chosen Mount Zion in the heart of those mountains that is his main point of attack. The indications for this are clear, even though Zion is not mentioned by name. God does speak of the mountains of Israel as "my mountains" (38:21) and of the land of Israel as "my land" (38:16). Implicit in that is the royal mountain-city where Yahweh dwells and rules over the mountainous domain he claims as his own. Also, such a capital city on the cosmic mountain was regarded as the center of the earth, and in 38:12 Gog is described as scheming to assault the people of God dwelling at "the center [lit. navel] of the earth" (cf. 5:5). Confirmation of this understanding of the destination of Gog's campaign is found in the interpretation of this event provided in the Gog-Magog prophecy of Rev 20:7-10 (on which, see below).

Prominent in Zechariah's prophecies of the end of the age is the feature of a final crisis, marked by a gathering of the nations for final judgment (Zech 12:3; 14:2). As in Ezekiel 38–39, the Lord is seen as the one who arranges this crisis; it is he who gathers the hostile forces to their place of doom. And once again here the gathering place of the eschatological battle is the city of Jerusalem.

Similarly, Zeph 3:8 relates the Lord's determination to assemble the kingdoms of the world for judgment and the context indicates that the place of this gathering is, as always, Jerusalem, God's holy hill (cf. 3:11,14,16). The prophecy concludes with the promise of another kind of gathering to Zion. As a correlate of God's gathering the enemy nations for destruction he will gather the remnant delivered from their foes to Jerusalem as a place of honor and joy forever, to Zion the object of God's delight and love.

Likewise Joel 3:2,9ff. [4:2,9ff.] reveals God's intention to gather all nations in order to enter into judgment against them. Reflecting this, the gathering place is called the Valley of Jehoshaphat ("Yahweh judges"). The place where God sits and engages in judgment (v. 12) is his royal throne, which is located on his "holy mountain" (cf. v. 17). This becomes explicit in the further exposition of this day of the Lord event in vv. 14ff. The gathered nations are now referred to as "multitudes, multitudes." The location is now called "the Valley of Decision," that is, the valley where the divine Judge pronounces his verdict, and this judicial act is depicted as a roaring from Zion, a thundering from Jerusalem (v. 16). The sentence of doom is issued from the heights of Mount Zion and is executed in the Valley of Jehoshaphat/Decision below, the valley becoming the winepress of the wrath of God (v. 13; cf. Rev 14:17-20, where the event is pictured as a final harvest-gathering and trampling of the grapes of wrath in "the winepress outside the city" (v. 20), which can only be the city of Jerusalem).

Other relevant mountain of the Lord passages include Isa 2:2,3; 4:5-6; 24:21-23; Mic 4:11-13; Dan 2:35; 11:45; Zech 6:1; 14:4.

Of direct and decisive bearing on the interpretation of the gathering against Har Magedon in Rev 16:16 are the parallel accounts in the Apocalypse of the satanic deception of the nations and the gathering of them for the battle on the great day of God Almighty: Rev 12:9; 13:14; 19:17-20; and 20:7-9. The last of these is particularly relevant for our present purposes. Resuming the Ezekiel 38–39 imagery of Gog and Magog, the Rev 20:7-9 account of antichrist's gathering of the nations from the four corners of the earth at the end of the millennium relates how the satanic forces march against God's people and surround "the camp of the saints and the beloved city." That city of God's people, the city beloved of God, is of course Jerusalem (cf. Ps 87:1,2 [2,3]; Zeph 3:17; Rev 21:2).

Jerusalem/Zion/the Mount of Assembly is the counterpart in Revelation 20 to the Har Magedon of Rev 16:16.

Conclusion. The biblical evidence is conclusive for the identification of har magedōn with har môᶜēd, the Lord's Mount of Assembly, Mount Zion with its city of Jerusalem, the city of our God.

The customary interpretation of magedōn as the city of Megiddo fails the decisive exegetical tests. It cannot meet the demand of the Johannine Hebraisti pattern that the context contain an explanation of the meaning of har magedōn. Also (and surely this is a fatal flaw) whereas the site mentioned in the biblical passages dealing with the gathering is the target under attack by the gathered armies, on the Megiddo view har magedōn in Rev 16:16 is not the place attacked but a battle-field (the valley of Jezreel) where opposing forces clash. The place that is the target in the hostile gathering of nations is regularly identified as Zion; this mountain-city of the Lord is an integral and essential element in biblical descriptions of the final gathering and judgment. When, therefore, we come to a climactic vision of the final antichrist gathering in Rev 16:12-16 and find there a reference to a mountain (har) it can be no other mountain than the mountain of the Lord. But on the interpretation of magedōn as Megiddo there is no reference to the mountain of the Lord. The attack on God's mountain challenging his dominion – the distinctively antichrist aspect of the gathering that is definitive of the episode – is completely missing. And in place of the mountain of God, that standard feature in accounts of the eschatological crisis event, a mountain of Megiddo is intruded – a mountain mentioned nowhere else in Scripture, a mountain that does not even exist in the topography of Palestine. The notion of Har Magedon as the Esdraelon plain (strangely called a mountain) does not fit in the biblical portrayal of the antichrist gathering of nations to seize the throne of God. The Megiddo interpretation ought not be entertained as a serious option.

Har Magedon – well named, this heavenly mount, the mountain of God. For it is the mount of gathering in multiple senses. Primarily and forever it is the temple-mount, the assembly place of the worshipping, celebrating entourage of the King of glory, a myriad congregation of angels and men (cf. Heb 12:18-29; Pss 47:9; 48; 102:21,22 [22,23]). Here is the council chamber where God assembles the heavenly elders for deliberation (cf. Ps 82:1). This celestial mount is the paradise to which

God's exiled people of every nation are regathered (cf. Deut 30:3-5; Isa 27:12,13; 43:5; Jer 32:37-41; Ezek 11:17-20; 36:24). Har Magedon is the palace-fortress against which Satan's antichrist, aspiring to the throne on this mountain, gathers his hordes in the final battle of Har Magedon (cf. Ezekiel 38–39; Rev 16:14-16; 19:19; 20:8), an event which, from the perspective of God's sovereignty, is a divine gathering of the nations to Zion for their final judgment (cf. Joel 3 [4]; Zech 12:3; 14:2; Matt 25:31,32). This Mount of Assembly is the heavenly hearth to which the Lord gathers his elect, one by one in their passing from the earthly scene (cf. Isa 26:20; Luke 16:22; Rev 6:9-11) and as a resplendent multitude raised from the dust in resurrection glory at his final harvesting of the earth at his parousia (Dan 12:2; Matt 13:30; 24:31; Mark 13:26,27; 2 Thess 2:1; Rev 14:14-16).

Part Three

Har Magedon Warfare: An Eschatological Megastructure

Chapter Seven

Eruption of the Har Magedon Conflict

Sabbath, Eschatology, and Covenant

The shape of things to come for man was set in the pattern God adopted in creating heaven and earth in the beginning. As revealed in the Genesis prologue (1:1–2:3) the history of creation had a sabbatical form. An era of divine work (the six days) issued in the divine sabbath (the seventh day).

That seventh day continues forever (cf. Heb 4:1-11). It is the consummation stage of the cosmic reign of God, the reign of the divine Glory-Presence that was initiated at the absolute beginning of creation. Viewed in its entirety, God's sabbatically structured reign is one of movement to cosmic consummation. And since man's activity is patterned after his Creator's, human history has, like its divine archetype, a sabbatical structure; from the outset mankind has been on the way towards a predestined eternal sabbath. Informed by this consummation-directed dynamic, man's history has had from the beginning an eschatological character.

The reproduction of the archetypal divine sabbath pattern in man's earthly existence is explicitly expressed in the Sabbath ordinance (cf. Exod 20:11). This ordinance, made when God made man (Gen 2:3), was made for man, not man for it (Mark 2:27,28). Man was indeed to honor the Sabbath; observance of it was a duty. But the Sabbath was a blessing and privilege for man. It was given to be a source of refreshment and joyful hope (Isa 58:13). By imprinting the sabbatical pattern on man's days God was promising nothing less than that he would bring his human image-bearer to participate in the royal rest of his own seventh day. The Sabbath ordinance conveyed a divine commitment to consummate man's beatitude.

To be sabbatically structured meant that human existence was from the beginning covenantal as well as eschatological. For such divine commitment as was given in the instituting of the Sabbath ordinance is precisely what is definitive of the divine-human arrangements which the Bible designates by the terms we translate "covenant." Covenantal transactions are those that involve divinely sanctioned commitments. In some biblical covenants the divine sanctioning is the divine witnessing and enforcing of a human commitment; in others, it consists in God's making the commitment himself – as in God's original sabbath covenant. It thus appears that the very fact that the creation of man and his world is revealed in the form of a sabbatical week serves to identify this creational order as a covenantal order. The Sabbath ordinance was itself a sign and seal of the original covenant in Eden.

Covenant Proposal of Sabbath Grant

What we want to consider in this chapter is how Har Magedon figures within this primal covenant informed by the eschatological-sabbath principle. First we will need to have a more circumstantial account of the nature of this covenant. Of particular importance is the aspect of it that accounts for its being traditionally called a covenant of works. We may get at this by returning to the pattern of God's activity in the process of creation as presented in the Genesis record, the pattern of a series of creative accomplishments leading to the sabbath goal. One further feature calls for attention within this simple scheme of works and rest. It is repeatedly stated that God saw that the work was "good" – climactically, "very good." The divine architect-builder of the cosmic house engages in an assessment of his work and registers his satisfaction: what has been produced corresponds perfectly with his architectonic plan. As expressed in the Prov 8:22-31 version of the creation week, the divine Wisdom takes delight day by day in the progress of the cosmic structure (vv. 30,31). In this scrutiny of his works of creation and the pronouncing of his approbation we see the God of the heavenly throne sitting in judgment on his own work. The archetypal sabbatical pattern is then one of works-judgment-rest.

Since the sabbatical pattern that structures human existence is a replica of God's archetypal sabbatical pattern, man too comes to the promised consummation only by way of work and (favorable) judgment. According to the terms of the covenant in which the sabbath principle was encapsulated at the beginning man must accomplish a specific divinely stipulated work and receive God's judicial approbation in order to gain entitlement to ultimate entrance into the heavenly kingdom of glory.

Though the earthly replica of God's sabbath pattern, like the original itself, contained the feature of judgment, there are of course certain differences as to the kind of judgment found in the two cases. For one thing, in God's judgment of his own creative works no question of moral right or wrong was entailed. It was simply a matter of assessing the architectural progress. Also, while God's creational productions were the necessary prelude to his sabbath rest, they were so simply in the way that the first stages in any construction project are necessary to the final completion of the building. It was not as though by the "good" works he accomplished God was earning in a legal sense a right to honor and dominion that he did not already have. In the case of the sabbatically shaped covenant with man in Eden, however, God's judgment was the rendering of a verdict as to whether man's work was morally-religiously righteous or sinful, obedient or rebellious. And the nature of Adam's performance, whether good or evil, was the legal ground of the outcome, whether good or evil, life or death.

According to the terms of this probation arrangement, the promised sabbath rest must be merited by obedience, while, on the other hand the hope of that blessing would be forfeited by disobedience. A fundamental principle of divine governance emerges here, namely that consummation blessing, in contrast to pre-consummation benefits, must be earned through successful probation (cf. Rom 2:6-8). Eternal life in glory is a reward for meritorious service rendered to the Creator. This principle applies to angelic beings as well as to man. Their eternal tenure as residents of God's heaven had to be achieved through a probation crisis, the crisis which was the occasion of Satan's defection.

It is then with good reason that the customary designation for God's covenant with Adam as federal representative of mankind has been Covenant of Works, "works" signifying that the inheritance of the kingdom of glory was a reward to be earned by man's probationary obedience. "Works" here is the opposite of "grace," the gospel principle whereby fallen sinners, elect in Christ, are given the heavenly inheritance as a free gift in spite of the forfeiture of any and all blessings through the disobedience of the first Adam. Under the gospel the legal ground of the elect's reception of the inheritance is the meritorious accomplishment of Christ, the second Adam. The merit of his one act of righteousness is imputed to elect sinners, who receive it by faith alone – by faith that it might be by grace.

Unfortunately there are currently not a few revisionists who deviate from these tenets of traditional covenant theology. It is their opinion that the reward of eternal heavenly life that God promised to Adam was more than any creature could merit. The operative principle in the covenant was then not simple justice but justice qualified by some kind of "grace." This blurring of the works concept and contradiction of the law-gospel contrast inevitably leads to a Judaizing subversion of the gospel.

Also involved in this radical revision of covenant theology is an assault on the justice of God, for entailed in the discounting of the merit of the act of probationary obedience is the setting up of a standard of justice above God and his judgments. To refuse to acknowledge the pure and perfect justice of God's covenantal stipulation of a heavenly reward for the performance of the mandated probation task is to fail to recognize that God's covenant Word is definitive of justice. It is to deny that the name of the Judge of all the earth is Just.

The fallacy of the revisionists' position becomes even more evident when we examine their assault on God's justice with respect to the negative sanction of the covenant, the penalty threatened for disobedience. Indeed, the inescapable implication of their view is that God would be guilty of appalling injustice in his judicial response to man's sin. For if, as they argue, Adam's ontological stature was not such that any good he might do would be worthy of eternal life, then by the same token neither would any evil he might do be deserving of Hell's eternal death. Yet precisely that was God's judgment on man's transgression – the judgment which in the case of the elect was visited on the Son of God. The denial of the simple justice of the appointed blessing sanction of the Creator's Covenant of Works with Adam thus has as its consequence the turning of the Cross of Christ into the ultimate act of judicial malfeasance. However unintended, such is the evil fruit of the rejection of the traditional doctrine of the covenant of works.

Covenant and Har Magedon Conflict

Only by way of meritorious work might man arrive at the eternal sabbath. It was by performing the specific probation assignment stipulated in the Creator's covenant of works with him that Adam must earn for himself and the human race the reward of entitlement to the consummated kingdom. This critical probationary task had to do with Har Magedon, the mount of assembly, celestial site of God's royal court.

Diabolical evil had broken out in heaven. Satan had challenged the God of Har Magedon. And Adam was assigned the role of standing in the name of his Creator Lord and withstanding the assault of Satan at the mountain of God in Eden, the earthly projection of the heavenly mount of assembly (as we have seen above). That was *the* probation task. It was by victory over the enemy of heaven in this battle of Har Magedon that Adam was to win the promised reward of everlasting glory.

There is an apparent allusion in Ezekiel 28 to the calamitous event of Satan's rebellion in heaven. In our appeal to the lament in Ezek 28:11ff. as evidence that Eden was the site of the mountain of God, we noted that the sin of the king of Tyre and the judgment threatened against him are depicted as a kind of reprise of something that happened in Eden. Someone back there had been guilty of high treason and had been expelled from the mountain of God. According to one view the allusion is to the fall of Adam but preferable is the view that the figure alluded to is Satan.

If we follow the Masoretic text at the key points, reading ʾatt ("you") in v. 14 and wāʾabbedĕkā in v. 16, there is only one figure, the cherub, whom God drives out. The view that the allusion is to Adam, with the cherub as a second figure, one who is first associated with Adam (v. 14) and then drives him out (v. 16), requires revocalizing the text, reading ʾet ("with") in v. 14 and wěᵓibbaděkā ("and he drove you out") in v. 16. The reading ᵓatt (a form of the second masculine singular pronoun also found in Num 11:15 and Deut 5:24) is favored in v. 14 as a resumption of the ᵓattâ, "you," in v. 12, something to be expected since vv. 14,15a continue addressing the person confronted in vv. 12,13 (the ᵓattâ of v. 12). And in favor of the first person (i.e., God) vocalization, wāᵓabbeděkā, in v. 16b are both the first person wāᵓăḥalleěkā in the preceding parallel clause (each clause declaring the divine judgment of expulsion from the holy mount) and the first person hišlaktîkā in the following statement, v. 17, which repeats the thought of v. 16b, namely, God's casting the offender from heaven down to earth.

Also problematic for the Adam view is the prominence given on that view to an association of Adam with a cherub figure in his original unfallen state. There is no basis for this in the Genesis narrative. Further, the heavenly sphere of the figure in question and his adornment with heavenly glory from his very creation are not compatible with Adam, for whom such honor was not a creational endowment but had to be won through a process of probation. Another difficulty for the Adam view is the finality of the judgment immediately inflicted on the offender. For fallen Adam a door of redemptive hope is opened and all those elect in the promised messianic seed of the woman are ultimately delivered from the final perdition of expulsion from the heavenly mountain. On the other hand the punitive sequel to the offense described in Ezek 28:16 is altogether agreeable with the fate of Satan.

Moreover, where the Ezekiel 28 imagery appears elsewhere in the Scriptures it depicts Christ's redemptive triumphing over the devil. In the subduing of the demons by the seventy-two sent out in his name, Jesus saw Satan falling like lightning from heaven (Luke 10:18). At the imminent approach of his exaltation through the Cross and resurrection, Jesus declared the time was come for the prince of this world to be driven out (John 12:31). And when that exaltation had transpired, heaven rejoiced that the great dragon, the ancient serpent called the devil and Satan, the accuser of the brethren, had lost his place in heaven and had been hurled down (Rev 12:8-10; cf. Zech 3:2).

According to Ezekiel 28, Satan's treasonous disobedience originated in pride over his exalted status as cherub-attendant of the throne on the mountain of God (cf. especially vv. 14,17). Such self-pride in the creature contradicts the prime objective of creation – the praise and glory of the Creator. It is tantamount to putting the creature in the place of the Creator and invites quick destruction (cf., e.g., Acts 12:22-23). A similar view of the nature of Satan's primeval evil can also be discerned in Isaiah 14. The king of Babylon denounced there is, like the king of Tyre in Ezekiel 28, a prototype antichrist figure and thus a bestial reproduction of the satanic dragon (cf. Revelation 13). Accordingly, the pride of Satan, like that of his antichrist replica, will have involved a lusting for an even higher dignity than the Creator had favored him with, a seditious grasping for the occupancy of the throne of the Creator himself on Har Magedon (cf. Isa 14:13,14), the very throne whose holy glory he, as anointed cherub, was supposed to guard.

Recorded in Gen 1:26 is the particular development in the history of heaven and earth that was, it would appear, the catalyst for the emergence of the lust for deity in the heart of the anointed cherub, blameless in his ways from the day he was created until then (Ezek 28:15). The satanic hubris will then have been a jealous reaction to God's plan to create man, an image-son of the Most High, an elohim being like the angels (Ps 8:5; cf. Heb 2:7; Ps 82:1,6), and to grant him dominion over all the works of God's hand. Gen 1:26 indicates that a disclosure of this divine purpose was made to the heavenly assembly. That is the significance of the plural "us" in the divine decree, "let us make man." As noted above, this divine consultative plural consistently involves the presence of God's celestial retinue (cf. Gen 3:22; 11:7 and 18:2,21ff.; Isa 6:2,8; 41:22,23). God's intention to create the majestic man-creature was announced to the angelic council on Har Magedon and it was evidently this disclosure that precipitated the anointed cherub's devolution into the devil.

Satan's blasphemous challenge to the authority of the God of Har Magedon was an intolerable idolatry. The defilers of the heavenly temple must be banished from the holy place of God's Glory-Presence. However, though driven from that sanctuary, now guarded by the faithful cherub-remnant, Satan and the angels who fell with him were not yet driven into the fiery Abyss, the place of perdition prepared for them (Matt 8:29; 25:41). An interim form of existence was permitted to the devil and demons in which they would function within the history of man – serving the ultimate purposes of God in spite of themselves. The Har Magedon conflict that had erupted in heaven would be continued on earth as well as among the armies in the invisible world.

Bent on foiling God's announced purposes concerning man and the perfecting of a kingdom of the son of man, Satan contrived to maneuver his way into Eden, there to encounter man at the mountain of God and to subvert his allegiance to the Lord of Har Magedon. It was in anticipation of this satanic act of trespass in defiance of the decree of banishment that God charged Adam with the guardianship of his Eden sanctuary. Gen 2:15 summarizes man's role in relation to the garden of Eden: he must cultivate it and guard it. The Hebrew šāmar, "guard, keep," used here is frequently employed for the priests' function of protecting the sacred precincts against defilement. Adam was invested with responsibility and authority beforehand to repulse Satan's profane encroachment into God's sanctuary.

This would involve Adam's performing the judicial function of discerning between good and evil, the function referred to in the name given to the probation tree: "the tree of the knowing of good and evil" (Gen 2:17). In Gen 3:22 man's knowing of good and evil is identified as an aspect of his likeness to the members of God's judicial council. In 2 Sam 14:17,20 and 1 Kgs 3:9,28 such judicial discernment between good and evil is attributed to kings engaged in rendering verdicts and is said to be a mark of their likeness to God or the Angel of God. The probation tree had a negative aspect – its fruit was forbidden; but it also pointed to the positive, God-like task Adam was to perform. When confronted by the evil intruder, subtly exploiting the negative aspect of the tree to malign the name of God, Adam must carry out that positive judicial assignment. Taking his stand as God's warrior-priest, guardian of the holy ground of Har Magedon, he must declare the evil one evil, condemn his trespass, and repulse him. This task, signalized by the name of the tree of the knowing of good and evil, was indeed the critical task.

Man's covenant obligations were not limited to this one duty of guarding the sacred garden. There were other, long-range requirements, assignments pertaining to his offices as king and priest. In the event of a successful probation man must carry out the kingdom commission by culturally forming his world – populating it, taking possession of it, appropriating its resources, ruling it (Gen 1:28). He was also to be engaged in the fundamental function of priestly ministry, that is, the worship of God. But man's immediate challenge was to answer the call to holy war, to guard the gates of heaven as God's vicegerent and to vanquish the archenemy of Har Magedon. To take a stand against Satan was to make a decision for God against evil; it was an act of righteousness. While not the sum total of the covenant's requirements, the summons to perform this one act of righteousness was the central hinge on which the whole covenant order would turn whether for weal or woe. By failure here all would be lost but by obedience here heaven would be won.

As manipulated by Satan the testing at this key point took on the aspect of a temptation that could have a disastrous outcome. As arranged by God the probation testing afforded an opportunity for man's eschatological advancement to the sabbath land. Faithful performance of the critical probationary mission of guardianship at Har Magedon would result in the divine judgment of approbation placing man beyond probation, a status involving his confirmation in righteousness and eternal life, and ultimately his glorification. Entry into the realm of eternal sabbath rest, translation to the consummate glory and shalom of the heavenly heights of Har Magedon was offered as the reward for victory in this battle of Har Magedon.

Satan's approach was camouflaged and subtle, the sinuous serpent his fitting agent. But his blasphemy was none the less blatant. He called in question God's goodness, veracity, and supreme authority – his Godness. Plainly, serpentine Satan was a hostile presence in that holy place whose guardianship had been entrusted to the residents of Eden. And at this critical juncture they were found wanting. They defaulted in their duty as guardians of the sacred garden, their duty to discern between good and evil. They fell in with the counsel of the evil one and despised the covenant of the good One. They forsook their God and sealed a covenant with the devil, partaking of the satanic sacrament of the forbidden fruit. Their performance in the crucial probationary test was a failure, an appalling, tragic failure. Instead of opening the door to the shalom of the sabbath, they brought sin and death into the world (Rom 5:12-19).

Such was the outcome of this opening battle of Har Magedon in the earthly arena, a total triumph for the tempter. Or so Satan might have thought for a moment. But this day's combat was not over. The God of heavenly Har Magedon was still to appear on the field of battle and take action at the earthly Har Magedon. This day would yet prove to be a primal day of the Lord.

Chapter Eight

Messiah: The Coming Victor of Har Magedon

Decretive Inauguration of Redemptive Holy War

The qôl yahweh, the thunderous sound of the Lord's parousia, frightened the guilty pair in Eden into hiding. It was a stormy theophany, not a stroll through the garden "in the cool of the day" (as Gen 3:8 is traditionally rendered) but an advent "as the (Glory-)Spirit of the (judgment) day."

Had Adam carried out his duty as guardian-judge of the Eden sanctuary, his encounter with Satan would have turned into a final judgment, a banishment of Satan and his demonic company to everlasting perdition. That did not happen, but Satan's success against Adam did not mean that he had toppled God from his Har Magedon throne and delivered himself from perdition. It meant only that the final judgment – for Satan, the day of doom – was postponed until the appointed time.

Confronted by the challenge to his throne, the Lord of Har Magedon responded with a manifestation of his absolute sovereignty. The would-be supplanter was not to be allowed to leave the battle scene uncondemned. Coming in wrath, the Judge of heaven and earth pronounced against Satan the sentence of inescapable, shattering defeat (Gen 3:14,15). The Har Magedon conflict would continue. The holy war would enter a new phase and move on to the final day of the Lord. Intimated in the judgment decree was God's determination not to abandon his original design for an eschatological temple, a temple of glorified Adamic earthlings, incorporated into the heavenly assembly. Prophetically outlining the age-spanning warfare, the Lord's judicial declaration pointed not only to the ultimate destruction of Satan but to the messianic dawning of sabbath glory on Har Magedon.

"Cursed are you" (Gen 3:14). The divine malediction addressed to the devil declared his ultimate everlasting doom, a fate described under the figurative imagery of the serpent that Satan had made his agent: "Upon your belly you shall go and dust you shall eat all the days of your life." Satan's subjugation and destruction would be effected through God's human representatives in the on-going war of Har Magedon. For in spite of the discomfiture of Adam and Eve in the encounter in Eden, God would raise up from their descendants an army bearing the banner of their Maker-Savior, steadfastly opposed to the archfoe of Har Magedon. The allegiance of mother Eve to the Lord would be restored and she would assume the status of mother-in-the-faith of those being mustered into the army of the Lord: "Enmity will I put between you [Satan] and the woman, and between your seed and her seed" (Gen 3:15). This new, redemptive phase of the war, commencing with the woman and continuing in the growing company spiritually like her, would come to its decisive climax in the emergence of the descendant of the woman whom subsequent divine revelation identifies as Jesus, the Christ of God. In fulfillment of his role as second Adam, true guardian of Har Magedon and champion of the holy army of God, this coming one would conquer the dragon and cast him down from the heights to Hell: "He will crush your head."

Eternal Covenant of the Father and the Son

The future course and outcome of the Har Magedon conflict disclosed in the judicial pronouncement of Gen 3:14,15, particularly the triumphant mission of the messianic warrior-king, would take place in fulfillment of the terms of a divine covenant made before the world began. Involved in the eternal divine decrees were commitments of the persons of the Trinity to one another with respect to their relationships in the creation and in the redemption of the world, and such divine commitments constitute a divine covenanting. All three persons of the Trinity participate in this covenanting but we shall focus here on God the Father and God the Son.

On the Son's part there was a commitment to undertake a messianic mission on earth, to enter the fallen world as a second Adam, as the representative and savior of an elect multitude from among mankind fallen in the first Adam (Rom 5:12-20; 1 Cor 15:45-49). And the Father promised to reward the Son's faithful carrying out of this commission with highest exaltation. This eternal divine covenanting is revealed to us in various ways in Scripture. [On this see further *KP* 138-141 and *GOM* 222, 227, 235-237.]

Jesus sets forth his earthly mission as the performing of a previous heavenly commissioning: "For I came down from heaven, not to do my own will, but the will of him that sent me" (John 6:38; cf. 10:18; 17:4). He claimed to be the Messiah, the one sent and anointed by the Father, consecrated and empowered to fulfill the Father's redemptive commission. Presupposed in this messianic identity of Jesus is the prior covenantal arrangement, the mutual Father and Son commitments sealed in heaven before the Incarnation.

The Father's prior commitment to grant the merited reward to the obedient Son is revealed in Old Testament messianic passages. For example, God's decree to establish his Son as his king on Zion with universal dominion is disclosed in Ps 2:6-9 and God's oath appointing the Son to an eternal royal priesthood is made known in Psalm 110. Jesus echoes this revelation of the Father's covenantal promise of royal inheritance: "As my Father appointed unto me a kingdom, so I appoint unto you that you may eat and drink at my table in my kingdom and sit on thrones judging the twelve tribes of Israel" (Luke 22:29,30). This statement is embedded in the context of our Lord's instituting of the New Covenant (cf. Luke 22:20) and therefore the parallel he draws between his covenantal appointment to his disciples and the Father's prior appointment of the kingdom to him amounts to an identification of the latter as also a covenantal transaction. In fact, since the verb translated "appoint" (diatithēmi) is the verb to which diathēkē, "covenant," relates, Luke 22:29 may be rendered: "As my Father covenanted unto me a kingdom." Here then is a plain explicit corroboration of the theological construct of a pre-Incarnation intratrinitarian covenanting.

The obedience the Son must render under his commissioning as a second Adam had both active and passive dimensions. His active obedience consisted in his victorious prosecuting of the Har Magedon warfare. That was the probationary task whose accomplishment was prerequisite to gaining the eschatological blessing of consummated glory, the assignment which the first Adam failed to fulfill. It was by performing that "one act of righteousness" (Rom 5:18) as the second Adam that the Son would merit for the people he represented the sabbath inheritance originally offered in the creation covenant. Meeting the evil foe of the holy One of Har Magedon and overcoming him would at the same time be a redemptive act of deliverance by which the Son set his people free from their bondage to Satan, sin, and death.

To this mission of redemptive judgment God the Son committed himself even though it meant he must undertake the burden of passive obedience, the ordeal of suffering unto the death of the Cross. As the prophetic declaration of Gen 3:15 puts it, he would suffer the bruising of his heel in the process of trampling on the serpent's head. He must undergo the curse that was incurred by the first Adam's breaking of the Creator's covenant with man in Eden. He must become a victim of death in order to become the Victor over him who had the power of death. As Isaiah foretold, the Servant of the Lord must be brought low as the way to being lifted on high (Isa 52:13–53:12; cf. Phil 2:6-11). The active and passive obedience are interwoven. The dragon is overcome by the blood of the Lamb.

Like the covenant with the first Adam, the Father's covenant with the Son, commissioning him as a second Adam, plainly exhibits the works principle of inheritance. In each case there is the proposal of an eschatological grant to be bestowed on the meritorious ground of the fulfillment of a probationary assignment. The nature of the grant as something that is earned is especially clear when the promised grant takes the form of the Son's securing the church as his inheritance possession. For the Scriptures identify this prize as something he has purchased. He "gave himself for us that he might redeem us" as "a people for his own possession" (Titus 2:14). It was "with his own blood" that he acquired the church (Acts 20:28; 1 Pet 1:18,19). In their new song the worshippers about the heavenly throne acclaim the Lamb as all worthy: "for you were slain and have purchased to God by your blood (a throng) from every tribe and tongue and people and nation" (Rev 5:9). The church, Christ's bride, belongs to him by virtue of his paying the purchase price stipulated in the Father's covenantal grant. [Cf. *GOM* 238.]

Jesus appealed to the works-merit principle in the Father's promissory covenant with him when his mission as the suffering Servant was about to be completed. Declaring that he had glorified the Father on earth, finishing the work he was given to do (John 17:4), Jesus presented his claim on the grant of glory he had earned: "And now, O Father, glorify thou me with thine own self with the glory which I had with thee before the world was" (John 17:5).

The Father's Covenant of Works with the Son is then an appropriate designation for the eternal intratrinitarian covenant, and has the advantage of calling attention to the two-Adams linkage between it and the creational covenant of works.

The Lord's Covenant of Grace with His People

Subsumed under the traditional designation, "Covenant of Grace," is the whole series of redemptive administrations of the kingdom from the Fall to the consummation, culminating in the New Covenant. Manifestly, this Covenant of Grace and the eternal intratrinitarian covenant are interrelated. It is through his fulfilling of his probation assignment as Servant in his eternal covenant of works with the Father that the Son is entitled to be the Mediator-Lord of the Covenant of Grace. And it is in and through the succession of administrations of the Covenant of Grace that the Son secures the reward promised to him in the eternal covenant, the reward of the countless company redeemed from all generations and nations to be his holy bride.

But though these two covenants interlock in this way, they differ in basic respects and therefore must be distinguished from each other. We have already noted the contrasting roles of the Son: Servant in the intratrinitarian covenant but Lord in the Covenant of Grace. Secondly, there is the contrast in the principle of kingdom inheritance in the two cases: works in the eternal covenant but grace in the Covenant of Grace. In the former the Son earns the kingdom reward by the meritorious accomplishment of his messianic mission, but in the latter it is as a gift of gospel grace that ill-deserving people are granted the transcendent blessing of the heavenly Har Magedon inheritance. In the Covenant of Grace the Son by grace makes his people co-heirs with him of what he has earned by works in the eternal covenant. It is by the obedience of the One in the intratrinitarian covenant of works that the many are made righteous and obtain the glory inheritance in the Lord's covenant of grace with the church (Rom 5:19).

Also distinguishing the two covenants from each other is the difference in their principal parties. The eternal covenant is between the persons of the Godhead – with the elect of mankind also in view in so far as the Son is contemplated as the second Adam, the representative of the elect. But the parties to the Covenant of Grace are the Lord and a company of earthlings, the community of those who profess faith and pledge troth to Christ the Lord together with those under their household authority. Whereas only the elect of mankind are (representatively) in view in the eternal covenant, in the administration of the Covenant of Grace the covenant community includes some who are not elect – "they are not all Israel who are of Israel" (Rom 9:6; cf. 11:21).

The overarching Covenant of Grace, which was to unfold in several premessianic administrations (including the Noahic, Abrahamic, and Mosaic covenants) and have its full, culminating expression in the New Covenant, was inaugurated by the divine declaration of Gen 3:15 and the divine act of symbolic sealing recorded in Gen 3:21. In anticipation of his assured redemptive triumph over Satan in the fullness of time, the Son, as Lord of the Covenant of Grace, was administering this covenant and its salvation blessings from the Fall onwards.

Viewed from the perspective of the Har Magedon conflict, the inaugurating of the Covenant of Grace instituted a new phase in the Lord's holy war against the rival claimant to Har Magedon's glory and dominion. The Son's administering of the Covenant of Grace was a warring against the Devil. As we have seen, in this new phase the Lord's prevailing is by way of redemptive judgment, a judging of Satan and his demonic hosts that entails the freeing of God's elect from their bondage as captives in Satan's kingdom of darkness and the transforming of them into victorious warriors of Christ, the true Lord of Har Magedon.

The Har Magedon Pattern in Premessianic Typology

According to the prophetic decree of Gen 3:15 the advent of Messiah, God's champion, would mark a decisive turning point in the Har Magedon conflict. He would repulse the would-be usurper of God's throne and bring God's holy war against Satan to a triumphant conclusion.

Once the decree was issued proclaiming the messianic Son the guardian of God's mountain and indeed the destined sharer of God's throne, Satan's anti-Har Magedon campaign assumed an antichrist character, with antichrist figures carrying out his machinations (cf., e.g., Isa 14:4ff.; Ezek 28:2ff.; Dan 7:8ff.,20ff.; 8:9ff.,23ff.; 11:28ff.,36ff.). They are bestial likenesses of the dragon (cf. Rev 13:1ff.) and they culminate in the man of lawlessness (2 Thess 2:3-10) in the final satanic assault on Har Magedon. That final antichrist crisis marks the closing hour of the Har Magedon confrontation of Christ and Satan. It merges into the last judgment and the eternal establishment of God's victorious Messiah and his people on the consummated Har Magedon, the heavenly Mount of Assembly of the new creation.

This outcome of the Har Magedon warfare, first announced in Eden (Gen 3:15), reflects the arrangements determined upon in the intratrinitarian covenant, the Father's covenant of works with the Son. In terms of that proposal-of-grant covenant, Christ receives the Har Magedon throne as the reward for his faithful service as the incarnate Son and second Adam, fighting the good fight against the evil foe of Har Magedon.

Filling out the pattern of the Har Magedon conflict in the era between Christ's decisive victory over Satan at his first advent and the age-closing antichrist crisis and last judgment is the transitional period of the present church age. Though Satan operates under divinely imposed restraints in the interim age, his agents continue their devilish opposition to Christ and his people.

We have then this over-all pattern of the eschatological warfare as waged by the Son of man in these last days: covenant of royal grant – meritorious service of the messianic warrior – interim era of continuing hostilities – antichrist crisis – Christ's redemptive judgment – kingdom consummation on heavenly Har Magedon. We shall later elaborate on the unfolding of this pattern in the course of the messianic age. But first we want to demonstrate the presence of this same eschatological megastructure in the typological premessianic history of the Har Magedon conflict.

We are alerted to this parallelism in the shape of the earlier and later history by the observation of Jesus likening the days of the parousia of the Son of Man to the days of Noah (Matt 24:37-41; Luke 17:26,27). Examination confirms that the history of the prediluvian world, the world that then was (2 Pet 3:6), contains all the components of the Har Magedon pattern found in the messianic era. In fact, this pattern repeats in the premessianic stage of the history of the postdiluvian world that now is. And true to the pattern, in each of these world aeons the Har Magedon conflict moves to a climactic representation of the consummate Har Magedon, the new Jerusalem on the mountain of God, great and high (Rev 21:10). In the old world the Ararat mountain is that prototypal Har Magedon and in the new world beyond the Deluge it is Sinai/Zion.

Chapter Nine

Ararat: Old World Type of Har Magedon

The Ark Covenant

The story of Ararat, the Har Magedon of the world that then was, has its beginnings in God's covenant with Noah (Gen 6:13ff., esp. v. 18). An administration of the overarching Covenant of Grace, this Noahic covenant is to be clearly distinguished from the subsequent covenant of common grace that God made with all mankind, providing not for the inheritance of heaven but simply for a measure of earthly benefits (Gen 8:21–9:17). The ark covenant with Noah arranged for the deliverance of his family from the Deluge, the age-ending judgment of the old world. More than that, it provided for them a place in the consummate kingdom of God in the symbolic form of the ark on Ararat.

As in all other administrations in the Covenant of Grace series, the blessings of the covenant with Noah were a gift of grace to ill-deserving sinners, fallen in the first Adam. Yet there was a principle of works in this covenant in connection with the messianic aspect of the typology of the ark-salvation event. The covenant was a covenant of grant, bestowing kingdom benefits as a reward for faithful service rendered to the Lord of the covenant. Noah was a type of Christ, the faithful Servant of the Lord, and as such he was the grantee of the ark covenant.

Righteous Noah, Covenant Grantee

The Lord said to Noah: "Come, you and all your house, into the ark, because I have found you righteous in this generation" (Gen 7:1). Noah's exemplary conduct as a covenant servant receives God's approbation and this righteousness of Noah is declared to be the ground for granting to him salvation from judgment and inheritance of the kingdom in the ark. Divine approbation of Noah is also found in Gen 6:8, which states that in contrast to corrupt mankind, whom God intended to destroy, "Noah found grace in the eyes of the Lord." The regular meaning of this expression is to be applauded for good service deserving of favorable recompense. This same assessment of Noah as "righteous" and "perfect" is repeated in Gen 6:9. Particularly in view in God's commendation of Noah and the covenantal grant based thereon would be his steadfast stand as a prophetic spokesman for God (Gen 6:9; 2 Pet 2:5) amid spreading apostasy and in the face of the satanic opposition of the world rulers of this age.

Special covenantal grants bestowed in return for notable services are attested in the case of others beside Noah. We will take up the case of Abraham at the appropriate point. There were also David (Ps 89:3; 1 Sam 13:14; cf. 1 Sam 16:7; 2 Samuel 5–7) and Phinehas (Num 25:10-13; Ps 106:30). The eternal salvation of these individuals was, of course, a matter of divine mercy and grace through Christ. But it pleased the Lord to invest their exemplary righteousness and outstanding acts of covenantal devotion with special significance so that with reference to a typological manifestation of God's kingdom they prefigured Christ as one who received the kingdom of glory for the faithful performance of the messianic mission stipulated in his eternal covenant with the Father. And in the case of some of these grantees, including Noah, their righteous acts were the grounds for bestowing kingdom benefits on others closely related to them (cf. Noah's household – Gen 7:1), just as in the case of Christ the many are made righteous by the obedience of the One (Rom 5:19) and become joint-heirs with him of his kingdom inheritance.

Covenant Community in the Interval

Between the original revelation of the covenant of grant to Noah and the actual salvation experience in the ark there was an interval of some hundred and twenty years. We are assuming that God's disclosure to Noah of his purpose to save him from the deluge judgment that was coming on the world (Gen 6:13ff.) dated to about the time of the Lord's declaration that sinful mankind's days were numbered – only a 120 more years to doom's day (Gen 6:3). That warning was probably made known to Noah and through his prophetic witness to his doomed contemporaries. And if so, it is not likely that God would have made that disclosure of his intention to destroy mankind without at the same time letting Noah know that he would be saved from this catastrophe – the promise contained in the covenant revelation recorded in Gen 6:13ff. (Subsequently, as Noah's sons were born and married [cf. Gen 5:32; 7:6; 11:10] the covenant promise will have been up-dated to include Noah's family [cf. Gen 6:18; 7:1].)

As just noted, the interval period was marked by the birth of Noah's sons (cf. Gen 5:32). This was in continuation of the previous perpetuating of the covenant people that is chronicled in the genealogy of Gen 5:1-31, which traced Adam's line through Seth to Noah. This genealogical continuity of the covenant line was attributable to the Lord's providential blessing on the successive generations. But there is a strong indication that a special kind of divine intervention was involved in the procreation of Noah's three sons during the 120 years interval. It was after Noah was 500 years old that he became the father of Shem, Ham, and Japheth (cf. Gen 7:6; 11:10). This is a far more advanced age than in any other case in the genealogies in Genesis 5 or 11:10ff. and this period before the begetting of children is in proportion to Noah's total life span much greater than is attested in all the other cases. We are then probably to understand that Noah's experience was similar to that of Abraham who did not beget Isaac, the son of covenant promise, until he was a hundred years old (which in the briefer life span of Abraham's day was comparable to Noah's age of 500 [cf. Gen 11:30; 15:2ff.; 17:17ff.; 18:11ff.; 21:1,2]). It would then appear that in Noah's case as in Abraham's the procreational perpetuating of the covenant line was due to supernatural intervention.

This process of generating the family of Noah was a temple building process, for God's people are his dwelling place in the Spirit. It was one of two temple buildings taking place in the days of Noah; the other, as we shall see, was the construction of the ark-temple.

A window on the nature of the interim period before the Flood is provided by Jesus' reference to the days of Noah as comparable to the days of his own parousia. Although what Jesus emphasizes is the unthinking, unprepared character of the world when suddenly overtaken by the flood, his observation also reveals those days to have been a time of eating and drinking, of marrying and working in the field and in the house (Matt 24:38,40,41). That is, more or less the usual common grace conditions obtained. There was that measure of stability in the natural world and human society that the Lord has promised to mankind in spite of their perverseness, the common grace benefits that he had bestowed from the Fall on and will continue to provide as long as the world continues, according to his covenant formally promulgated after the Flood (cf. Gen 8:21–9:17).

Structuring the common world order were the divinely appointed institutions of the family and the city of man, or the state. And in the midst of this common world with its common institutions there was also the holy institution of the covenant community. Gen 4:15–6:4 traces the development of this common order in the old world through the concluding 120 year period of the days of Noah. In Gen 4:25–5:32 the account focuses on the people of God. They were part of that common world. They were citizens in the city of man. They made their contributions to the advancing culture. But what was distinctive of them was their additional identity as the holy community of faith. They called on the name of the Lord (Gen 4:26b); that is, they identified themselves as belonging to the Lord, as Yahweh-people, as his covenant community. Their calling on the Lord's name was a confession of him as covenant Suzerain and Father. It was also a prayer for his protective care over them as his servant-sons.

In the center of the covenant community stood the altar (Gen 4:4; cf. Heb 11:4; Gen 8:20), visible symbol of their identity as a cultic congregation, a holy priestly assembly. It was to the altar they resorted to call on God's name in praise and petition. And as a public monument set up within the city of man the altar was a witness of the covenant people to the world, a legal testimony to the denizens of the earth that Yahweh was the Lord and Owner of creation, who summoned them to turn from their idol-lords and render allegiance to him as their sovereign. This altar-claim of Yahweh's world ownership is enhanced if the altar is seen as a symbolic replication of the heavenly mountain of God, site of the Lord's cosmic throne. [Cf. *KP* 372-376.] Along with the covenant community's priestly witness involved in their erecting altars in the name of the Lord God, a prophetic witness issued from their midst in the form of individuals raised up by God as bearers of his word, agents of his lawsuit against the ungodly world (Gen 5:22; cf. Jude 14,15; Gen 6:9; cf. Heb 11:7; 1 Pet 3:20; 2 Pet 2:5). And within the 120 year period the prophetic witness to the incredulous world, warning of imminent judgment, was dramatically reinforced by the ark taking shape before their eyes under the direction of prophet Noah, a visual portent of the threatened deluge-doom (cf. Heb 11:7; 1 Pet 3:20).

As for polity, the altar congregation was strictly a cultic community. It was not a geo-political organization in competition with the ordinary political entities. It was not a holy nation or theocracy but rather a family community. Indicative of this is the casting of the history of the covenant community in the form of the genealogy of Seth (Genesis 5). The authority structure of this holy company was one with that of the patriarchal family of Seth and his successors. To be sure, that family also existed as a component of the common world order, but as an altar community it was not of that world. While its stance in relation to those outside included a welcoming evangelistic call to come under the protective sovereignty of the living God of salvation, its altar and prophetic witness – along with the ark under construction – challenged and threatened the devotees of pseudo-gods and their antichrist lords.

Inevitably then, the interval period was a time of tension, testing, and tribulation for the witnessing people of God. Although God's faithful generating and preserving of the covenant line was a major feature of these days of Noah, that covenant community was a minority remnant and indeed a decreasing remnant in the earth. During this phase of the Har Magedon warfare Satan's dark sway was such that he becomes known as the deceiver of all the earth. Only the advent of Christ in the last days would turn the tide of battle, with the gospel penetrating Satan's iron curtain and proving to be the power of God unto salvation among all the nations.

Antichrist Crisis

Through the period from the covenant with Noah to the Flood the Har Magedon strife intensified, moving on to its antichrist climax. We may best trace this continuing conflict by surveying developments in the city of man in this era, first taking notice, however, of the earlier instituting of the city.

The origin of the city of man, or state, is recorded in Gen 4:15. Cain complained that the world into which he was being driven would be anarchical, a society without a system of law and order to deter the family of slain Abel from wreaking vengeance on him (Gen 4:13,14). Correcting Cain's false assumption, the Lord assured him there would be a divinely authorized administration of justice. There would be a deterrent against any would-be killer of Cain: he would be avenged sevenfold (Gen 4:15a). Properly translated, Gen 4:15b repeats the thought of v. 15a. Referring to the Lord's assertion in v. 15a as an "oath" (Hebrew ᵓôt, usually rendered "mark"), v. 15b says that the Lord thus made an oath commitment that it would not be the case that any who wished would be free to kill Cain with impunity. There would be the appointed minister of God's wrath to reckon with. By this oath pronouncement God instituted the state with its sword of justice. Following naturally upon this record of the granting of the charter of the city is the account of the building of the first city by Cain – or, on another reading, by his son, Enoch (Gen 4:17).

The extremely compact history of the city of man in Gen 4:17-24 sets the stage for the world crisis in the days of Noah. Cain's evil dynasty perverted the common grace provision of the state, turning it into an instrument of tyrannical oppression. Climactic in this development was the reign of Lamech. He showed contempt for the institution of the family as well as the state. He violated the family ordinance by practicing bigamy (Gen 4:19). And he perverted the state's administration of justice by using it as a means of personal vengeance. Moreover, in doing so, he ignored the lex talionis principle, the just standard of a life for a life. As he boasted to his wives, he took a life in revenge for a bruise (Gen 4:23,24). But worse than all this, Lamech manifested the antichrist spirit, exalting himself above the Lord of Har Magedon. Referring to the Lord's sevenfold vengeance by which he would repay the killing of Cain, Lamech blasphemously claimed superiority to God: "If Cain is avenged sevenfold, Lamech will be avenged seventy-sevenfold" (Gen 4:24).

The theme of the city of man is resumed in Gen 6:1-4 after the intervening account of the covenant community from Adam to Noah (Gen 4:25–5:32). The grievous situation exemplified by Lamech's reign is now described as an antichrist crisis that provoked the Lord's determination to limit this stage of the city of man to a 120 more years and then to wipe man from the earth (Gen 6:3,7). The tyrannical rulers are characterized by the same offenses attributed to king Lamech. Their abuse of the ordinance of monogamous marriage took the form of the royal harem. From the large pool of attractive women available in the expanding population (Gen 6:1) they seized as wives "all that they chose" (Gen 6:2). Their administration of justice was turned into a reign of terror conducted through the mighty princes born in the royal household (Gen 6:4), powerful warriors who filled the earth with violence (Gen 6:5,11-13). But, as in the case of Lamech, the final intolerable affront of human kingship against the God of Har Magedon in the days of Noah was the antichrist claim to deity. Adopting the ideology of divine kingship prevalent in the ancient world and traceable to prediluvian times, the evil monarchs entitled themselves sons of the gods, the term the biblical author took over from their blasphemous mouths to designate them in the summary indictment of Gen 6:1ff. The antichrist character of this development in human kingship is heightened if we conclude that 1 Pet 3:19,20 and Jude 6 refer to the involvement of demons in this Genesis 6 episode. These titans of old will then have been demoniacally impelled. A diabolical impulse is in any case clearly present in this crisis stage in the prediluvian unfolding of the pattern of the Har Magedon warfare.

The city of man had become an idolatrous theocracy in which man had assumed the position of deity. All culture and cult, every sphere of life, had been brought under the dominion of the absolutized rule of the divine king. To allow the co-existence of any other cult would not be consistent with the antichrist ideology of the state-cult. In particular, the altar of the Yahweh people, staking out a claim of world sovereignty for him and for themselves as his children was intolerable to the Cainite god-kings. Suppression and elimination of these rival claimants to ultimate possession of the world was inevitably the policy of the antichrist regime. With the tempo of mankind's rebellion against heaven ever increasing, the hatred of Satan's brood for God's children will have reached a crescendo under the final generation of the demon-driven, self-deified dynasts. For the community of faith it was a time of suffering for the sake of God's name. The severity of the persecution is evidenced in the reduction of the covenant community to a remnant of eight at the time of the Flood (cf. 1 Pet 3:20). And the devil had infiltrated even that remnant family of Noah, producing his ugly likeness in Ham, the accursed.

Satan could taste triumph in the war of Har Magedon. The fierce oppression under the bestial world power resulting in martyr death and apostate defection had all but cut off the seed of the woman from the earth – and therewith the messianic hope itself. The covenant Protector of the faith community could no longer delay; he must respond to their appeal (cf. Psalm 94). For their sake and for the sake of his own name which was identified with them he must remember his covenant with Noah (Gen 8:1). It was time for the Judge of all the earth to come quickly, time for the Har Magedon conflict pattern to move on from antichrist crisis to the divine redemptive judgment and the consummation of the holy assembly on the mountain of God.

Parousia-Judgment and Gathering

Virtually synonymous with the eschatological day of the Lord, the day of final judgment, is the parousia of the Lord. So in the case of the final judgment of the old world, the Lord's advent was central. Psalm 29 suggests that the storm clouds bearing the flood waters were an instance of the theophanic manifestation of the Lord as the One who mounts the cloud-chariot and rides to battle. Comparing the royal Presence of God in the Deluge judgment to his Spirit-Presence at creation (Gen 1:2) and his thunderous advent at the judgment in Eden (Gen 3:8), the psalmist declares: "The voice of Yahweh is over the waters; the Glory-God thunders; Yahweh is over the mighty waters . . . Yahweh has sat enthroned from the flood; he has sat as king from of old" (vv. 3,10). The Flood narrative itself invites a comparison of God's action by means of the wind (rûaḥ, Gen 8:1) upon the flood waters (which recalled the primal creation conditions) to the hovering of the Spirit (rûaḥ) over the deep at the beginning (Gen 1:2). Also indicative of a visible personal presence of the Lord is the narrative detail that after Noah had entered the ark with his family, "Yahweh shut him in" (Gen 7:16b).

The judicial procedure employed by the Lord was the divine ordeal. The rival claimants – God's people and their antichrist foes – were subjected to the ordeal of passage through the waters of death. We may incidentally note that Peter identifies the flood waters as a baptismal event (1 Pet 3:20f.), so advising us that the rite of baptism is a symbolic undergoing of a death ordeal. Peter also calls attention to the ordeal nature of the last judgment, with fire instead of water as the ordeal element (2 Pet 3:5ff.). In such trials by ordeal the Lord renders a verdict in favor of those in the right by bringing them safely through the ordeal, while the condemnation of the false claimants is registered in their being overcome by the deadly ordeal medium. In the Deluge ordeal God provided Noah with the plans for the ark as the means of deliverance, secured his family in the ark, controlled the mounting waters, and brought the ark to rest on the far side of the flood. By their resurrection-emergence from the death waters (cf. 1 Pet 3:21) the remnant people were declared justified in the sight of God and heirs of the heavenly kingdom. Heb 11:7 brings out the nature of the Deluge as an ordeal judgment with two-sided outcome of vindication and condemnation: "By faith Noah, being warned of God of things not seen as yet, moved with fear, prepared an ark to the saving of his house; by the which he condemned the world, and became heir of the righteousness which is by faith."

For Noah's family the Deluge was a redemptive judgment, a salvation event. As Peter says, they were "saved by means of the water" (1 Pet 3:20). It was for them a redemptive experience in several ways. We have already seen that the ordeal procedure of the flood waters rendered a judicial verdict of vindication for those in the ark, validating their claim to world inheritance. Also, in so far as the waters were the waters of death, a manifestation of the wrath of God, the safe passage of the ark occupants through these waters typified the saving of all who are in Christ from the divine wrath to come. The Flood was also redemptive in that it rescued the godly remnant from the wrath of ungodly men. It delivered them from the antichrist persecution that threatened their very existence by cutting off (circumcising) their persecutors from the face of the earth and leaving the faithful as a now victorious remnant in the new world beyond the flood. Discriminating as they did strictly in terms of the religious status of the opponents, blessing God's people and cursing Satan's followers, such redemptive judgments were intrusions of the principle of final judgment into the era of common grace, prototypes of the eschatological judgment.

A distinctive feature of the redemptive judgment segment of the Har Magedon conflict pattern is an act that is reflected in the name Har Magedon. This is the act of gathering associated with the parousia of the Lord. The divine gathering is a redemptive gathering of the saints out of the doomed world, a harvesting of them into the heavenly garner. In the days of Noah the ark was the refuge into which the remnant people were gathered. This theme of the gathering into the ark is given great prominence in the composition of the Flood narrative. It is the theme of the second of the seven concentrically arranged sections of the account (Gen 7:1-5) and it is recapitulated at the beginning of both the third section on the flood proper (Gen 7:6-12) and the fourth section on the prevailing of the judgment waters (Gen 7:13-24). This triple mention of the gathering is indicative of its importance in the Flood judgment seen as a redemptive act. That the Lord himself is the Gatherer-Harvester is manifested by the fact that the entry of the remnant people into the ark was sealed by his act of securing them within the sanctuary place of refuge (Gen 7:16). His hand can also be discerned even in the coming of the animals to Noah to be herded into the ark (Gen 6:20; 7:9,15).

The place of gathering, a sanctuary in the sense of refuge from the stormy deep, was also a sanctuary in the sense of holy house of God. That is another feature common to the occurrences of the Har Magedon pattern we are examining: each involves the building of a temple as the site of assembly for the meeting of the Creator-King with his worshippers, men and angels.

The ark was designed to be a replica of the cosmos conceptualized as a three-storied house, the temple residence of God (Isa 66:1). Besides the three-storied structure, the door and window are mentioned as architectural features of the ark, and these too have counterparts in the cosmic creation house with its window of heaven (cf., e.g., Gen 7:11; 8:2) and door of the deep (cf., e.g., Job 38:8-11) – the two access points for the flood waters. As in the case of other replicas of the heavenly sanctuary, like the tabernacle and temple as well as the visible cosmos, so in the case of his ark-house it was God who provided the architectural plans (Gen 6:14-16).

That the ark was a sanctuary, a holy theocratic formation, and its occupants a holy nation, a kingdom of priests, is also evidenced by the introduction of the clean-unclean distinction in the regulations governing the gathering of animals and birds into it (Gen 7:2,3). Elsewhere this distinction appears again in the Israelite theocracy in connection with dietary rules. During their residence in the ark-theocracy Noah's family was restricted in their eating of meat to clean creatures – one of the reasons for including seven pairs of such animals. After they left the ark and returned to the common grace order, they were given permission to eat all kinds of meat again (Gen 9:3). Similarly, with the termination of the Israelite theocracy, the temporary clean-unclean distinction was discontinued (cf. Acts 10:10ff.).

Kingdom Consummation on Ararat

As we follow the ark-temple to its resting place on the mountains of Ararat we come to the final component in the Har Magedon pattern. Here the ark becomes a prophetic sign of the consummated cosmic house of God, the temple of the new creation. Peter directs us to see the Flood history as typological not only of the last judgment but of the creation of the new heavens and earth (2 Pet 3:5-7,13). The way the literary form of the Flood narrative in Genesis 6–8 reflects the style and structure of the creation account in the Genesis prologue is calculated to identify the Flood episode as a (re-)creation event. To similar effect is the way the physical phenomena of the flood recapitulate the course of the original creation from the stage of the unbounded deep to the (re)appearance of dry land and vegetation and the (re)emergence of animals and man. [See further *KP* 221-225.]

The human occupants of the ark add striking details to the typological picture of the consummation of history. By virtue of their glorification the redeemed will attain to that mastery over the world to which man was commissioned in the creational covenant, the goal that was set before him in promissory fashion in the Sabbath ordinance. That ultimate destiny was typologically portrayed by the circumstances within the ark. All the orders of creation were there placed under man's dominion and by means of the ark man surmounted the extreme onslaught of the elements of nature. Glorification of the redeemed will involve their resurrection and this too was prophetically portrayed in the experience of those in the ark in that they survived the passage through the death-waters and came forth alive to inherit the new earth beyond the sea of death.

To depict the fulfillment of man's historical task as projected from the beginning, the expansion of the holy community to world-wide dimensions, Scripture employs the model of the city of God as well as the house of God. Man's carrying out of the cultural mandate would produce Megapolis, the global theocratic city, the holy city whose king was the Lord God, enthroned on Har Magedon, the cultic center of the city. And by the glorification of the citizens of the city, the people-temple, God would transform Megapolis into Metapolis, the Beyond-city, the heavenly city. The equivalence of the two models – temple and city – is seen in the cuboid holy-of-holies form of the eschatological city, New Jerusalem (Rev 21:16). Accordingly, the ark, replica of the cosmos, with prototypically glorified occupants, was in typological symbol the consummate cosmic holy city as well as the cosmic heavenly temple.

The acts of resurrection and glorification that bring the temple-city to its consummate state are manifestly acts of God. So too is the accompanying event of the last judgment, the coming of Christ the Lord taking vengeance on his foes, destroying antichrist by the breath of his mouth. Likewise in the Noahic flood event, the prophetic type of the last judgment, the primary actor was God. In the last analysis, he was the builder of the ark, the temple-city. And clearly he was the one who, by unleashing from his arsenal the mountain-surmounting waters, prevailed over the ungodly world, obliterating the antichrist powers who challenged his throne on Har Magedon. The Flood was a parousia event, a prototypal final battle of Har Magedon in which the Lord was the Victor and Consummator.

While the building of the ark-temple, the overcoming of the satanic world, and the salvation of the remnant community are in an ultimate sense to be attributed to the power of God and his name is to be exalted in the praises of his creatures, the Scriptures at the same time attribute these accomplishments to Noah. Thus, Heb 11:7 states that Noah "prepared an ark to the saving of his house" (cf. Gen 6:17,18,22; 7:5-7). The explanation for this is that the eschatological acts of God are performed through the Christ of God and in the typological portrayal of these acts Noah represented Christ. In Noah we see a prefiguration of Christ in various capacities: as the grantee of the covenant, whose faithful service secures the kingdom blessings for the covenant people; as the prophet-mediator of the covenant revelation; as the builder of the sanctuary house of God; as the savior-king, who delivers his people from the divine wrath and rescues them from the satanic powers; as the champion descendant of the woman who slays the dragon.

The Flood event culminated in the ark's settling on the Ararat mountain (Gen 8:4) and the building of an altar there (Gen 8:20). The Hebrew term hārê ʾărārāṭ, "mountains of Ararat," might be rendered "one of the mountains of Ararat" but that still does not amount to Ararat being the name of the mountain. It would therefore be more accurate to refer to the particular landfall of the ark within the range of mountains in the Ararat region as the Ararat mountain rather than as Mount Ararat, but in deference to popular usage we may refer to it as Ararat or Mount Ararat.

Ararat was constituted the holy mountain of the Lord by the positioning of the ark-temple there, by the erection of the altar on it, and, most emphatically, by the sanctifying Presence of the Lord himself – a presence manifested in his revelation of his acceptance of the offerings presented on the altar (Gen 8:20,21). With the temple-city of the ark situated on it, Ararat was the equivalent in Noah's days of Zion, the site of the temple-city of Jerusalem. And along with Zion, Mount Ararat was a type of "the great and high mountain," landfall of the temple-city of New Jerusalem on its descent from heaven at the eschatological finale (Rev 21:10). The final chapter in the pattern of the Har Magedon conflict as it unfolded in prediluvian history thus brings us in typological figure to the consummate Har Magedon, Mount of Gathering.

For the Noahic community of faith to be gathered to Ararat/Har Magedon was to be brought to the sabbath realm. The sabbath theme emerges in Gen 8:4, which tells of the ark coming to rest on Ararat in the seventh month. The Hebrew term for this resting (nwḥ) is the word used in Exod 20:11 for God's sabbatical resting on the seventh day of creation. The sabbath theme has its main exposition in the seventh section of the seven-part chiastic arrangement of the Flood history (Gen 8:20-22), the counterpart to the seventh day-stanza of the creation account (Gen 2:1-3). Recounted in this closing section is the altar consecration of the ark-kingdom to the Lord, which is precisely the symbolic import of the sabbath. The climactic last scene of this Har Magedon pattern is then a prophetic sign of the consummation not only in its spatial dimension as the heavenly temple-city of New Jerusalem on Har Magedon but in its temporal-eschatological dimension as the eternal sabbath of the new heaven and earth.

Noah's agency in God's establishing of his kingdom community in its sabbath stage on the mountain of the Lord was adumbrated in Lamech's oracular explanation for naming him "Noah": "He will bring us relief from the toil of our hands, from our work made painful as a result of the Lord's curse upon the ground" (Gen 5:29; cf. Gen 3:17). The explanation involves a play on the similar sounds and meanings of the name Noah, which comes from the verb nwḥ, "rest," and the verb nḥm, "comfort, give relief." In the subsequent narrative the verb nwḥ is echoed in connection with the consequences of acts of Noah. As we have seen, the ark Noah built came to rest (nwḥ) on Ararat (Gen 8:4). Then in Gen 8:21a Noah's offerings on the altar he set up on Ararat are said to produce a restful, soothing (hannîḥōaḥ, a form of nwḥ) fragrance for the pleasure of the Lord. The resultant promise of the Lord (Gen 8:21b) alludes to Lamech's prophetic naming of Noah (Gen 5:29), declaring that within pre-consummation history the divine curse on the ground will not be intensified into another Deluge-scale destructive assault of nature on earth's living creatures. Positively put, the status of the Noahic ark-community on Ararat was (typologically) that of a remnant who had been rescued from the catastrophic escalation of the curse into an overwhelming outpouring of divine wrath and had been brought into a place of eternal rest. As interpreted by these echoes of Gen 5:29, Noah's name designated him a prototype of Christ, the second Adam, who, following the eschatological pattern set by God in the process of creation, performed the works necessary to earn the heavenly reward and then entered into Noah-land, the realm of God's sabbath enthronement.

One further aspect of Noah's prefiguration of Christ was entailed in the priestly role we noted in the closing episode of the Flood event. As a king, the Lord's royal servant, Noah had built the ark-temple, the kingdom of God in symbolic replica, and had overcome the opposing powers of man and nature. That was penultimate. Ultimate was his priestly service. As a priest Noah took this world subjugated, this kingdom of God completed, and consecrated it to God in the token form of the offerings burnt on the altar. Answering to this is the eschatological act of consecration by the messianic priest-king. Of Christ it is foretold that standing in the heavenly heights, having completed the building of the temple-kingdom of God and the subjugating of all his enemies, he will then as priest deliver over the kingdom to the Father – a final act of sabbatical consecration – that God may be all in all (1 Cor 15:24-28).

Chapter Ten

Zion: New World Type of Har Magedon

The Abrahamic Covenant

Introduction. The road to Sinai/Zion, the dual typological Har Magedon, begins with the covenantal call of Abraham. Unlike the ark-covenant with Noah, which concerned only the Flood episode, the Abrahamic Covenant involved all the subsequent unfolding of the Covenant of Grace through the Old and New Covenants. And the Abrahamic Covenant was, of course, not without rootage in the past. For the kingdom promises given to Abraham renewed the kingdom prospects of the redemptive prophecies of Gen 3:15 and 9:25-27, in which the kingdom hope originally given to Adam was resumed, now adjusted to reflect the new redemptive realities. The lines of kingdom continuity thus reach back from the Abrahamic Covenant to the creational covenant and its promise of sabbatical Har Magedon, as well as forward to the New Covenant's attainment of that eschatological goal.

Indicative of the continuity of the Old and New Covenants with the Abrahamic Covenant is the identification of the redemptive accomplishments associated with those two covenants as in each case a divine remembering of the covenant with Abraham, Isaac, and Jacob. For the Old Covenant, see Exod 2:24; 6:5; cf. 32:13; Lev 26:42,45; Ps

105:8ff.,42. For the New Covenant see Luke 1:54,55,72,73; cf. Acts 3:25. The Old and New Covenants are thus correlated with two stages in the fulfillment of God's kingdom promises to Abraham. The establishing of the Old Covenant coincided with the Mosaic-typological stage of the coming of the kingdom; the promulgation of the New Covenant, with the inaugurating of the messianic-antitypical stage. Each of these covenantal transactions was attested by documentary witness, the Old Testament and New Testament respectively, each the canonical constitution for its phase of the kingdom.

The two-stage structure of the history of the promised kingdom can best be displayed by tracing the fulfillment of each of the individual components of the kingdom: the king, the people, and the land. Before setting forth this two-stage unfolding of the kingdom we shall look at the prelude to the Abrahamic Covenant provided in Genesis 9–11 and consider briefly the theologically critical question of the principle that governs kingdom-inheritance in the Abrahamic Covenant and in the two covenants that are correlated with the two stages in God's remembering of that covenant.

From Ararat to Abraham

Genesis 9–11 sketches the historical setting of the Abrahamic Covenant, picking up the story at the climactic completion of the prediluvian Har Magedon pattern on Mount Ararat. This passage first relates how the common grace order with its institutions of family and state was renewed by means of a rainbow-sealed covenant (Gen 8:20–9:17). [For an analysis of the covenant of common grace see *KP* 244-262; cf. 153-180.] Then it concentrates on the close connection of the on-going Covenant of Grace with the line of Shem. Under the Abrahamic Covenant, this ethno-centralizing of the covenant community, which had also occurred in the prediluvian history, would take the form of the national election of Israel as the people of God, heirs of the typological Har Magedon, Mount Zion.

The distinctive covenantal identity of the Shem-Eber-Peleg-Abraham line is brought out by the separate genealogical treatment of this branch of Shem in Gen 11:10-26 (cf. Gen 10:25) after the general genealogical account of the three sons of Noah in Gen 10:1-32. In the general table of nations and the following Babel episode (Gen 11:1-9) the non-covenantal lines are identified with the city of man and especially with its evil propensities. But within Genesis 9–11 the most remarkable expression of the antithesis between the covenantal and non-covenantal lines is found in the prophetic oracle of Noah (Gen 9:24-27).

This oracle presents a panoramic forecast of redemptive history in the new world comparable to the prophetic decree of Gen 3:14,15 at the outset of the redemptive program in the old world. A formula of election and reprobation (i.e., the declaration of one brother's subservience to another) marks the rejection of the Ham-Canaan line and the acceptance of the lines of Shem and Japheth. This antithesis is underscored by the pronouncing of the curse of subjugation on Ham-Canaan and the promises of blessings on Shem and Japheth, the blessing of bearing God's covenant name for Shem and the blessing of ultimate entrance into the covenantal tents of Shem for Japheth. And more than antithesis, there is antagonism. There is a flaring up of the ancient enmity between the woman's seed and the seed of the serpent, a major eruption of the Har Magedon conflict. Shem's descendants, Israel, will wage holy war against the descendants of Ham-Canaan. Canaan will be conquered and dispossessed; Israel will conquer and take possession.

Noah's oracle prepared for the Abrahamic Covenant by its emphasis on the coming national election of Israel but it also did so by its two-stage perspective on the eschatological course of redemptive covenant. While the center of gravity for the Shem-Canaan encounter is the typological, Old Covenant situation, the oracle looks beyond that. The blessing on Shem, his covenantal identification with the Lord God, comes to expression in the covenant made with Abraham, which contemplates not only the old, typological order but the messianic age of the New Covenant. And the oracular blessing on Japheth promising entry into the covenant anticipates the gospel promise given in the Abrahamic Covenant, the promise of the ultimate inclusion of the Japhethites and indeed all the nations through the promised messianic Son (Gal 3:8).

Covenant of Promise

Clearly, the Abrahamic Covenant is a grace arrangement, a subdivision of the comprehensive Covenant of Grace. The apostle Paul identifies it as a covenant informed by the principle of promise, the opposite of the principle of works that was operative in the Law (Gal 3:12,17,18; Rom 10:4-10). According to Paul the salvation blessings offered in the Abrahamic Covenant are obtained through faith in Jesus Christ (Gal 3:22). In particular, the principle of justification by faith alone plainly operated in the case of Abraham himself (Rom 4:3) and that assures all who walk in the footsteps of the faith of father Abraham that they likewise obtain the promise by grace (Rom 4:16). Righteousness will be imputed to all who believe in him who raised from the dead the Lord Jesus, who was delivered up to death for our sins and was raised again for our justification (Rom 4:23-25). Again, the apostle pronounces God's promise that all nations would be blessed through Abraham to be an announcing of the gospel beforehand (Gal 3:8,9).

The manner of the ratification of the Abrahamic Covenant manifests its grace character. It is the Lord God who makes the solemn oath commitment that ratifies the covenant, guaranteeing the fulfillment of the promises. In the ritual of the passage of the symbolic theophany through the midst of the slain and divided animals, the Lord swore that he would undergo the cutting-off curse of the Cross in order to fulfill his kingdom promise (Gen 15:9-21; cf. Gen 22:16; Heb 6:13-18). As an administration of the overarching Covenant of Grace, the Abrahamic Covenant with all its kingdom blessings, whether temporal-temporary-typological or heavenly-eternal, is the fruit of the Son's meritorious performance of passive and active obedience according to the terms of the Father's covenant of works with him.

Carrying forward the Abrahamic Covenant as they do, both the Old and New Covenants are, like it, administrations of the Covenant of Grace. Foundational to both these covenantal orders is the purpose and program of individual election in Christ unto salvation and the heavenly inheritance. At the same time the Scriptures indicate that in the Mosaic economy there was superimposed as a separate second tier on this foundation stratum of gospel grace a works arrangement, the Torah covenant with its "do this and live" principle (cf. Lev 18:5), the opposite of the grace-faith principle

(Galatians 3 and 4; Rom 10:5,6). The introduction of this Law arrangement centuries after the covenant of promise to Abraham did not abrogate the earlier promise of grace because its works principle did not appertain to individual, eternal salvation (cf. Gal 3:17). The works principle of the Law was rather the governing principle in the typological sphere of the national election and the possession of the first level kingdom in Canaan. It is this works principle that explains the otherwise inexplicable termination of the typological kingdom of Israel through judgment curse.

With the abolishing of the Mosaic order, the second level kingdom of the messianic age was initiated under the Lord's New Covenant with the church. Jeremiah, speaking of the new covenant to be made in the coming days (Jer 31:31-34), drew a sharp contrast between it and the covenant made at Sinai (i.e., the stratum of it concerned with the typological kingdom). He described the Old Covenant as breakable and in fact as having been broken by Israel, which means that it was informed by the works principle of inheritance. And he asserted that the new covenant would be unlike the Torah covenant. It would be unbreakable; it would be an administration of gospel grace and forgiveness. While then we will want to affirm the New Covenant's continuity with the foundational gospel stratum of the Mosaic economy and with the Abrahamic Covenant of promise, we must also acknowledge the works-grace discontinuity between the new and the old (at its typological level), the difference that Jeremiah so emphatically asserted.

Two-Stage Fulfillment

We have already remarked on the law-gospel contrast between the Old and New Covenants. Another aspect of the discontinuity between them emerges when they are viewed as two stages in the fulfilling of the kingdom promise of the Abrahamic Covenant. The Old Covenant kingdom is only a temporary type, a provisional symbol, while the New Covenant kingdom is the permanent antitypical reality. Emphasizing this difference, the Book of Hebrews declares the discontinuity to be such that with the initiating of the New Covenant, the Old Covenant becomes obsolete and vanishes away (Heb 8:13). To be sure, a certain continuity is involved in the typological relationship itself, the continuity of the earlier prototype to the later antitype, the continuity of promise to fulfillment. Nevertheless, the New Covenant fulfillment entails the discontinuance of the Old Covenant. The Old Covenant is abrogated and replaced by the New Covenant (cf. Heb 7:18; John 1:17; Rom 10:4). At the same time, we recognize that there is solid continuity between the Old and New Covenants when the Old Covenant is viewed not at the overlay stratum to which the typological kingdom and the works principle appertain but at the foundational gospel-grace layer. Indeed, from this perspective the New Covenant continues the Old Covenant.

Let us now see how the two-stage fulfillment structure, with its continuity and discontinuity aspects, comes to expression in the history of the separate kingdom promises of king, people, and land. Each of these will be found to involve two levels of meaning, which correspond in general to the two stages of the coming of the kingdom.

The King. Both Abraham and Sarah receieved the promise of royal descendants (Gen 17:6,16). In Jacob's testamentary blessing on Judah (Gen 49:8-12) the kingship promise came into sharper focus: the royal dynasty was to be established in the tribe of Judah (level one) and was to culminate in the messianic Shiloh, whose reign would be universal and eternal (level two). In anticipation of the establishment of the monarchy the Lord prescribed the manner of the king who should serve as his representative (Deut 17:14-20). With the appointing of David as king – the level one fulfillment – the king promise was elaborated in a special covenant guaranteeing the perpetuity of the Davidic dynasty (2 Sam 7:11-16; cf. Ps 89:3ff.). At the typological level the Davidic line was interrupted at the exile, the kingship at that time being part of the Old Covenant order, a works arrangement Israel failed to keep. But in remembrance of the Lord's covenant with Abraham, Isaac, and Jacob, the promise of the king found fulfillment beyond the exile at the second, antitypical level (cf. Lev 26:42-45). The advent of Jesus was heralded as the realization of the royal seed promised to Abraham; Jesus was the ultimate dynastic scion covenanted to David (Matt 1:1; 2:6; Luke 1:32,33,69-73). In Jesus Christ the Davidic dynasty attained everlasting status and through him the construction of God's house, typified by Solomon's temple project, is being carried out at the antitypical level in the building of the church-temple of these last days. Between the first level kingship, the Davidic dynasty under the Old Covenant, and Jesus Christ, the second level king in the New Covenant order, there is the obvious continuity of a dynastic, genealogical succession. Equally obvious is the discontinuity marked by the difference between king David, the typological figure, and king Jesus, the antitypical successor of David and David's Lord, who has no successor, whose throne is cosmic and forever.

The People. Besides the individual royal seed, Abraham was promised a numerous corporate seed, a nation of people. Indeed, Abraham and Sarah would become father and mother of a multitude of nations (Gen 12:2; 13:16; 15:5; 17:4,16). The development of the twelve sons of Jacob into the twelve-tribe nation of Israel was the level one fulfillment. By Solomon's day the people of Judah and Israel were as numerous as the sand on the seashore (1 Kgs 4:20). At the second level the promised seed consists of those who are the spiritual children of Abraham, like him believers justified by faith, and that irrespective of whether or not they are his physical descendants (Rom 4:11,12,16,17; Gal 3:16,29). In the face of the fall of Israel, the apostle Paul's defence of God's faithfulness in honoring the seed promise rests squarely on the identification of the promised seed with this second level, spiritual seed, the elect remnant within Israel (Romans 9–11). The apostle treats the spiritual meaning as *the* meaning of the promise, declaring that they are not all Israel who are of Israel (Rom 9:6). Also, as previously mentioned, he points to the promise that all nations would be blessed through the messianic seed of Abraham – of which the promise that Abraham would be the father of many nations is the equivalent – as an announcing of the gospel beforehand. Thereby the many nations of Abrahamic descendants are identified as the universal company of believers, elect in Christ (Gal 3:29).

Elements of both continuity and discontinuity appear when we analyze the two stage fulfillment of the seed-promise. There is continuity in that the fullness of the elect Jews and the fullness of the elect Gentiles together constitute one spiritual family of father Abraham. This continuity – indeed unity – comes to plain expression in Paul's identification of Christ as *the* seed (Gal 3:16) and his assurance to believers that Jews or Gentiles they "are all one in Christ Jesus" and that in Christ they "are Abraham's seed" (Gal 3:26-29). To the same effect Paul declares in Eph 2:11-19 that the Gentile Christians, formerly foreigners and aliens, were now fellow citizens as Christ creates out of believing Jews and Gentiles one new man, one body.

By means of its olive tree imagery Romans 11 instructs us concerning two kinds of continuity between the two stages. One is the continuity of the elect, spiritual seed (as we shall see) but along with that is the continuity of the covenant community as an institution, which is a broader circle than the election. That the olive tree as a whole represents the covenant institution, not the election, is evident from the facts that some (alas many) Jewish branches have been broken off and that Gentile branches who do not continue in God's kindness are threatened with the same excision. Moreoever, the engrafting of Gentile branches into the upper part of the tree shows that this part of the symbolic image represents the New Covenant, the second stage. The two stages, old and new, are thus joined together in the organic unity of the one tree. The church as holy covenantal institution is the continuation of Israel as a holy covenant institution (though quite different in organizational polity). Also discernible in the image of the olive tree – beneath the surface – is the other kind of continuity, that of the spiritual seed. For implicit in this arboreal figure is the inner living core of the tree, extending from its roots to its crown, which represents the spiritual children of Abraham, continuous through the two stages of kingdom fulfillment. The realization of the promise of the seed at its second level of meaning already in the premessianic era (a distinctive feature of the people promise) is a further continuity factor in the relation of the two stages of fulfillment.

Further, a typological relation, involving continuity-with-a-difference, obtains between the Old Covenant, Abrahamite people and Christ. Isaiah's treatment of the Servant of the Lord theme establishes this typology. The prophet presents the Messiah as God's servant, his chosen, the royal descendant of Abraham, the Davidic Branch, a witness and light to the Gentiles. Similarly, Isaiah describes the Israelite remnant, the holy seed (Isa 6:13), as God's chosen servant (45:4), the seed of Abraham who loved God (Isa 41:8; 45:4), God's witness to the nations (Isa 42:19; 43:9,10). With respect then to the seed of Abraham as servant of the Lord there is a prototype-antitype continuity between Israel and Christ, a continuity which also involves the discontinuity of the difference between Old Covenant symbol, Israel, and New Covenant substance, Christ the true Israel.

The Land. As the promise of the kingdom-land was gradually disclosed, its boundaries were clarified; the Abrahamites would possess the land of Canaan from the Euphrates on the northeast to the river of Egypt on the southwest (Gen 12:1,7; 13:14-17; 15:18-21). At the first level the promised land was occupied by Israel to the specified bounds in the days of the monarchy (Josh 21:43-45; 1 Kgs 4:21; 8:65). Canaan was a symbolic restoration of the creational kingdom in Eden, a paradise flowing with milk and honey, a holy land with Zion/Har Magedon, the mountain of the God of Glory, in the midst. More precisely, since Canaan was for Israel a land of rest (Deut 3:20; 12:9; 1 Kgs 8:56), it was typological of God's kingdom when it shall have attained its promised sabbath-consummation. Hebrews 4 reminds us that Canaan was not the actual heavenly sabbath land but only a prototype of heaven. The first level fulfillment of the land promise thus pointed beyond itself to the second level, sabbatical realm.

There was an indication of this sabbatical, eternal, antitype level of the promise in the characterization of the promised inheritance as "everlasting" (Gen 13:15; 17:8; 48:4). The second level of meaning of the land promise is also attested in the description of the kingdom of the second level king: Messiah's domain would be global (Pss 2:8; 72:8; Zech 9:10). Again, Rom 4:13 states that Abraham was heir not merely of Canaan but of the cosmos and agreeably he and other recipients of the land promise set their hope not on an earthly country but on the better, heavenly country (Heb 11:10,16), the glory-dimensioned new heaven and earth, the eternal Har Magedon. As in the case of the people promise, we do not merely find that a second level meaning is attested for the land promise but that this second level meaning is regarded in the New Testament interpretation of it as *the* meaning and that the first level meaning is virtually discounted. Thus, with reference to all the people of God of premessianic ages, including those who under the Old Covenant had participated in the first-level fulfillment in the land of Canaan, Heb 11:39 declares: "These all . . . received not the promise" (cf. v. 13).

The typological continuity-with-a-difference relation of the two levels of meaning of the land promise and the coordinated two stages of fulfillment is brought out by the portrayal of the eschatological kingdom as a new Jerusalem/Zion (Rev 21:2,10). Particularly striking is the New Jerusalem's combining of the twelve gates bearing the names of the twelve tribes of Israel and the twelve foundations of the walls which have on them the names of the twelve apostles of the Lamb (Rev 21:12-14). Here, translated into urban architectural imagery is the Pauline teaching of the identity of the inheritance hope of New Covenant believers with that of the Old Covenant people of God. The Gentile believers are not only fellow citizens but fellow heirs with their Jewish brothers (Eph 3:6). Heavenly Mount Zion is the shared ultimate destination common to all who are in Christ (Heb 12:22-24; cf. 11:40).

Obedient Abraham, Covenant Grantee

Like Noah, Abraham became the recipient of a covenantal grant of the kingdom because of faithful service he rendered. Once again the kingdom in view is a prototype version, not the eschatological reality. Unlike the kingdom grant to Noah, which was fulfilled in his lifetime, the typological kingdom in Canaan of which Abraham was the grantee was not bestowed until generations later.

Gen 15:1 depicts the Lord as a suzerain who bestows a royal grant on an officer for notable military service. Abraham had led a campaign against invaders of the land on which the Lord's claim had been laid and he had given the tributary tithe of the battle spoils to his divine sovereign (Gen 14:14-24). In response the Lord declared: "Your reward will be very great" (Gen 15:1) – also read: "Who [i.e., the Lord] will reward you greatly." The term sākār, "reward," is used for compensation for conducting a military expedition (cf. Ezek 29:19,20).

Genesis 22 records another episode in which an outstanding act of obedience on Abraham's part is said to be the basis for the Lord's bestowing on him the blessings of the covenant: "By myself have I sworn, declares the Lord, because you have done this thing and have not withheld your son, your only son, that I will surely bless you . . . because you have obeyed my voice" (vv. 16-18). From the perspective of Abraham's personal experience of justification by faith, this act of obedience validated his faith (Jas 2:21ff.; cf. Gen 15:6). But from the redemptive-historical/eschatological perspective, Abraham's obedience had typological import. The Lord constituted it a prophetic sign of the obedience of Christ, which merits the heavenly kingdom for his people.

That Abraham's obedience functioned not only as the authentication of his faith for his personal justification but as a meritorious performance that earned a reward for others (and thus as a type of Christ's obedience) is confirmed in the Lord's later revelation of the covenant promises to Isaac (Gen 26:2ff.). The Lord declared that he would bestow these blessings on Isaac and his descendants "because Abraham obeyed my voice and kept my charge, my commandments, my statutes, and my laws" (v. 5; cf. v. 24). Abraham's obedience was not, of course, the ground for anyone's inheritance of heaven, but it was the ground for Israel's inheritance of Canaan, the prototypal heaven, under the terms of the Mosaic covenant of works. Eternal salvation would come because of Christ's obedience, but because of Abraham's obedience Christ would come as to the flesh from Israel (Rom 9:5) and thus salvation would come from the Abrahamites, the Jews (John 4:22).

Covenant Community in the Interim

The 430 Years

On the occasion of the ratification of the Abrahamic Covenant by divine oath, the Lord foretold an interval of four hundred years (also described as four generations) that was to elapse before the promise of the kingdom (at the typological level) was fulfilled (Gen 15:13-16; cf. Acts 7:6). As indicated at the time of fulfillment this period was more precisely four hundred thirty years (Exod 12:40,41). The Exodus passage is also more specific as to the location of Abraham's descendants during this time. In Genesis 15 the Lord describes the four hundred years as a time of oppression in some country not their own (v. 13). Exod 12:40 (Masoretic text) identifies the four hundred thirty years as the time the Israelites lived in Egypt. When Paul referred to the Law as having been introduced four hundred thirty years after the covenant of promise (Gal 3:17) he did not include in that period the two centuries of the patriarchs' sojourning in the land of Canaan (as is done in the Septuagint and Samaritan Pentateuch texts of Exod 12:40, which add "and Canaan" to "Egypt"). The apostle rather viewed the whole time of Abraham, Isaac, and Jacob in Canaan before Israel's descent into Egypt as the time of the giving of the covenant of promise. In doing so he was adopting the perspective of Psalm 105: "He remembers his covenant forever, for a thousand generations the pact he prescribed, the covenant he made with Abraham, the oath he swore to Isaac and which he confirmed to Jacob as a decree, to Israel as an everlasting covenant" (vv. 8-10).

Pilgrims and Good Neighbors

For the Abrahamites the four centuries interval was a postponement of the occupation of their promised inheritance. For the Amorites this period was a delay in judgment while their iniquity was ripening. On both accounts the interim was a time of common grace. While the kingdom was in abeyance the covenant people were to be cultivating common grace relationships. It was a time for toleration and cooperation with the current occupants of their promised land. Those who had the promises must recognize that for the present they were strangers and pilgrims on the earth (Heb 11:9,13; Gen 23:4; 47:9). Until the day of march and conquest came they must practice pilgrim politics. They must follow customary common grace procedures in their social and economic dealings with their Canaanite neighbors. When the hour arrived for Shem to inflict the Noahic curse on Ham, the Canaanites were to be utterly destroyed; no covenants might then be made with them (Exod 23:32; 34:12,15; Deut 7:2). But during the interim era, before the time came to establish the theocratic kingdom, the patriarchs could properly enter into covenantal arrangements with them, such as economic contracts and military confederations (Gen 14:13,24; 21:22ff.; 23:3-18; 26:26ff.).

Beyond merely respecting the property rights and honoring the political authority of the peoples among whom they lived as resident aliens, the patriarchal family proved to be agents of temporal, common grace benefits for their neighbors. Outstanding in this regard was the career of Joseph in Egypt (Gen 40:14ff.; cf. 47:7,10). The appropriate attitude towards the world realm in which they found themselves was to be one of prayerful solicitude for its peace and prosperity, such as Jeremiah recommended to the Israelites in Babylonian exile (Jer 29:7) and Paul to the Christians in the Roman world of his day (1 Tim 2:2). Agreeably, Abraham prayed for king Abimelech (Gen 20:7,17) and Jacob blessed the pharaoh (Gen 47:7,10).

Continuing Remnant

A fundamental feature of the interim period in each instance of the Har Magedon pattern is the divinely assisted generating of those who make up the continuing remnant community. We observed this in the days of Noah, and again in our own interadvental interval the Spirit's bringing forth the expanding family of Jesus through the witness of the church is a central motive. In the case of the patriarchal interim the supernatural aspect of this procreation process is emphasized. Daunting natural impediments were overcome by divine intervention in order for Abraham's covenant line to be continued in Isaac and then in Jacob (Heb 11:11). And during the sojourn of the sons of Israel in Egypt it was in the face of the most adverse circumstances that they "were fruitful and multiplied greatly and became exceedingly numerous, so that the land was filled with them" (Exod 1:7, NIV). The explanation for this remarkable multiplying of Israel was that "Yahweh made his people very fruitful" (Ps 105:24).

At the same time (again as in the days of Noah) there was an overwhelming quantitative superiority of the non-covenant peoples to the house of Israel. While the continuing existence of the remnant community reassured those with eyes of faith that Satan would not succeed in cutting off the people of God from the earth and thwarting God's redemptive purposes, their faith was tried by the fact that they were only an island of light in the world-sea dominated by the darkness of the devil's deception.

This situation is adumbrated in the Genesis 10 survey of nations that sets the stage for the unfolding of the Har Magedon conflict in the postdiluvian world. The homeland promised to the Abrahamites, suggestively referred to by the listing of the Canaanites who occupied the land before the Israelite conquest (Gen 10:15-19), is positioned at the center of the world-map, completely overshadowed by nations that proved to be enemies of Israel and defiant of Israel's God. Virulent among these surrounding powers was the antichrist spirit. It was manifested in the heaven-scaling builders of Babel and in Nimrod, a gibbōr (hero figure) like the prediluvian "sons of the gods" (Gen 10:8). And there were the rulers of Mizraim, Egypt (Gen 10:6), claimants of divinity. Of special interest, at the head of the list in Gen 10:2 are nations (especially Magog) that reappear in biblical prophecy of the final battle of Har Magedon, associated there with the antichrist figure of Gog (Ezekiel 38 and 39). And in that passage the point is that in the final crisis when Satan is loosed to be, as of old, a deceiver of the nations (cf. Rev 20:7,8), there is a return to the state of affairs that obtained before Christ's coming, indeed far back in the world portrayed in Genesis 10, a world in which the covenant remnant was a small enclave of faith, with all the other encircling peoples of earth deceived by Satan's deadly lie.

Even more distressing for God's people than the success of Satan's cause in the world outside the chosen family was his subtle penetration of the covenant community itself. The seed of the serpent were to be found among those bearing the covenant sign of circumcision. Ishmael persecuted the son born by the power of the Spirit (Gal 4:29) and godless Esau spurned his covenantal inheritance (Heb 12:16,17). Apostasy from the holy fellowship of the servants of God is a recurring theme throughout the history of Har Magedon warfare. Virtually an entire generation of rebellious Israelites was sentenced to perish in the wilderness. Later, the nation, repudiated as Lo-Ammi, "Not-My-People," was exiled to Babylon. Subsequently, identified as the seed of the serpent, though boasting of being the children of Abraham, and indicted as slayers of the prophets and of the Son, the Israelites suffered a national fall. Again in New Covenant history, there emerges a harlot-church, the great city Babylon, the apostate church, prostituted to the satanic beast and false prophet, shedding the blood of the martyrs. Persecuted by satanic powers from without and undermined by satanic deceivers within, the faithful in every interim era, though never forsaken, find that their fellowship in the hope of the kingdom is one of suffering and patient endurance (Rev 1:9) as they fight against the demonic powers of this dark world and the spiritual forces of evil in the heavenly realms (Eph 6:12).

Covenant Family Polity

The examples of Job and Melchizedek remind us that in the patriarchal age the Covenant of Grace was represented by other family units besides Abraham's. But in the covenant the Lord made with Abraham it became clear that henceforth his family would be the main channel for the flow of the covenantal river. Theirs was the national election to the inheritance of the typological kingdom in the promised land and of them would come the Messiah, he who by the Spirit fathers the New Covenant family of God, heirs of the true, heavenly kingdom.

Until the Abrahamites developed into a nation and took on the form of a kingdom, their simple family structure served as the polity of the covenant community. Membership in the Abrahamic family meant membership in the covenant community. Of particular interest is the way the parental-household principle informs the regulations governing the administration of circumcision, the sign of membership in the covenant: along with Abraham, those under his household authority, including infant sons, were to receive this sign. While the family relationship initially conveys holy status, that is, membership in the holy covenant institution, it does not guarantee continuance in the covenant. The children of the covenant might fail to own it. We have mentioned the defection of Ishmael and Esau as conspicuous instances of this in the patriarchal period. It is to be noted that the parental authority principle for determining covenant membership continued to be valid when the form of the covenant community changed from simple family to theocratic kingdom of the twelve tribes of Israel and eventually to church of the New Covenant.

Within the familial covenant structure Abraham had the status of father of all the covenant people. As the paternal source and patriarch of the covenant family (cf. Isa 51:1,2) Abraham was a prototype of Christ, the second Adam, the patriarchal father of the new mankind, the family of the redeemed (cf. Gen 5:1; Matt 1:1).

The polity principle of patriarchal authority prevailed throughout the interim era. This can be observed in the area of the community's cultic life. There was no separate order of cultic officers, no special priesthood apart from the patriarchs, who officiated at the altar as *primus inter pares* and disciplined their covenant households. Illustrative is the role of Jacob on his return with his family from Paddan-aram (Gen 35:1-4). The patriarchal authority over the cultic family had a prophetic dimension (Gen 20:7; Ps 105:15). The patriarchs were the recipients of special revelation. Their priestly pronouncements of blessings on their family were inspired prophetic forecasts of the future outworking of the covenant blessings and curses (cf. Gen 27:27-29; 49:1-27). Also attributed to the patriarchs is the priestly-prophetic function of intercession (Gen 20:7; cf. 18:22-32).

Altars and Divine Presence

Like the covenant community in the Noahic era, the Abrahamic community was altar-centered. They played their part in the affairs of the profane world of common grace, but what was distinctive of them was their identity as a holy company, a priestly congregation. The altars they set up within the boundaries of the promised kingdom staked out Yahweh's claim to this land – and ultimately to the whole world, since Canaan was a prototype of the consummated cosmos. Besides signifying that divine claim of ownership, the altars Abraham erected at Shechem and Bethel on his first passage through the land (Gen 12:1-10) were an expression of his faith here at the outset that despite all present circumstances to the contrary God would at last fulfill the promise to give him this set-apart territory. Witnessing to the name of the Lord as sovereign over all, the patriarchal altars issued a warning that the coming of his kingdom and the judicial dispossessing of the nations that currently occupied the land would not be indefinitely postponed. The appointed time was set; the four hundred years of common grace delay would run their course and the pilgrim people of the Yahweh-altars would turn into the invincible army of the Lord, seizing and cleansing the land by holy war. Then there would be raised up a central kingdom altar on the Mount of Assembly, a victory monument of Yahweh on Har Magedon, the place of his enthronement. But not yet in the interim period. The patriarchs possessed the kingdom, both typological and eschatological, only in the promises, only by faith (Heb 11:13).

Although the people of God did not arrive at the promised Har Magedon during their patriarchal era journeying, along the way there were certain anticipatory pointers to their Zion-Jerusalem destination. It was at Salem (Jerusalem) that Abraham found Melchizedek, priestly representative of God Most High and type of Christ, king of Zion, whose priesthood is forever, after the order of Melchizedek (Gen 14:18; Hebrews 7). And one patriarchal altar was erected on what would become the mountain of the Lord. For Mount Moriah, to which God directed Abraham for the sacrifice of Isaac (Gen 22:2), is identified in 2 Chr 3:1 as the site of Solomon's temple. Abraham's revelatory experience there was a foretaste of Zion, the temple mount, preeminently the place of the vision of God.

While it was at Bethel, not at the site of the future temple, that Jacob too had a vision of God and built an altar to him, the mountain of God was symbolically portrayed in his dream (Gen 28:12ff.). The stair-structure rising from the earth to heaven and traversed by angels recalled the Glory-crowned Har Magedon in Eden, of which Zion would be a replica. The site of this vision was therefore, as Jacob declared, the house of God and gate of heaven (v. 17). The staircase formation of this true mountain of God had a pseudo-counterpart in the Babel ziggurat (a cosmic mountain – see further below). Within redemptive typology the symbolism of Jacob's visionary mountain-stairway, serving as a link between heaven and earth, found its true fulfillment in Jesus, the mediator between God and man (John 1:51). Christ is the Har Magedon way to heaven.

Altars are associated with manifestations of deity (cf. Exod 20:24). The mode of the divine presence in the patriarchal period was indicative of the pre-kingdom status of the Abrahamic community. With the coming of the (typological) kingdom in power in the Mosaic age the Lord appeared in theophanic glory, in the radiant majesty of the Shekinah-cloud. To the patriarchs he appeared in the more veiled form of the Angel of the Lord. Jacob, reviewing his own experience and that of Isaac and Abraham before him, identified God with the Angel: "God before whom my fathers Abraham and Isaac did walk, the God who shepherded me all my life long to this day, the Angel who delivered me from all evil" (Gen 48:15b,16a). Whatever foretastes of parousia theophany were afforded, they were partial, private, occasional, not yet the continuing, public manifestation of the Glory-Spirit that marked the kingdom age. Nevertheless, as Jacob's testimony affirms, God's superintending presence was with his people, promoting the growth of the community and preserving it as a remnant in the earth unto the advent of the kingdom. "When they were but few in number, few indeed, and strangers in it [i.e., the land of Canaan], they wandered from nation to nation, from one kingdom to another. He allowed no one to oppress them; for their sake he rebuked kings: 'Do not touch my anointed ones; do my prophets no harm'" (Ps 105:12-15, NIV). Moreover, though the Spirit was not present in the outward glory of the Shekinah, he was mightily at work as a divine presence within. The Genesis narrative is replete with the evidences of this in the transformation of individuals, producing in them justifying faith and hope, and in the remolding of the flawed, tension-torn covenant family into a healed community united in brotherly love. The patriarchal interval era was not yet kingdom time but it was not without its realized eschatology. It will be recognized that not just in the various common grace aspects of the community's life but in this internal presence of the re-creating Spirit the patriarchal interim finds its echo in the final interim time, the present already/not yet church age.

Antichrist Crisis

Pseudo-Har Magedon at Babel

In the postdiluvian world the city of man was soon exhibiting again the religious animus that had brought down the Deluge judgment. As we have observed, Genesis 9–11 sketches this setting of the patriarchal interim history and it is especially in the Babel episode narrated in Gen 11:1-9 that we can see the evil proclivity of the city of man. The program of erecting a temple-tower complex that would reach to the heavens (Gen 11:4; cf. Gen 28:12) gave expression to an incipient antichrist spirit (cf. Isa 14:13).

The explusion of man from Paradise and his dispersion over the earth had meant the loss of the access to the celestial glory-life and of the focus for an expanding humanity that had been provided for by the original Mount of Assembly in Eden. Babel was an attempt to reverse the divine judgment of dispersion by achieving an ecumenicity of humanity in defiance of deity. But Babel was a pseudo-focus city. It was an experiment in salvation by human works; its trademark was Made-by-man; its number was six hundred sixty-six. It was an idolization of man, a refashioning of the city of man into the cult of man, an affront to the Lord God, architect-artisan of the heavenly city. And the ziggurat-staircase-mountain structure at Babel was a pseudo-Har Magedon, a challenge to the true Har Magedon that God raised up in the original creation and that was destined according to covenant promise to be consummated by the Christ of God through redemptive re-creation.

God's descent on Babel in judgment disrupted this antichrist enterprise lest the mystery of iniquity reach its climax prematurely. But the exposure of the latent evil of the city of man at Babel was ominous. That evil would try the patience of the patriarchs throughout the appointed interim centuries. And in the days of Moses it would culminate in a crisis of animosity that threatened the existence of the covenant community and thereby seemed to preclude the prospect of the Lord's ever attaining triumphant glory on the Mountain of God, whether the typological Sinai/Zion or the eschatological Har Magedon.

Pharaonic Antichrist

As we have seen, it was disclosed to Abraham early on that the four centuries before the full measure of iniquity was reached in the city of man were to be for the covenant people a time of mistreatment and eventually oppression and enslavement at the hands of the pagan powers (Gen 15:13-16). More specifically the oppressor nations would be two of "the sons of Ham," Mizraim (Egypt) and Canaan (cf. Gen 10:6). The latter was already singled out in Noah's oracle as the branch of Ham against which the curse of reprobation and subjugation would be executed (Gen 9:25). But the extreme of enmity against the patriarchal people of God would take place in "Egypt . . . the land of Ham" (Ps 105:23; cf. v. 27; 78:51; 106:22). It was these Egyptian Hamites who came to hate Jacob, conspiring against the Israelites and bringing them into cruel bondage (Ps 105:25). It was in Egypt that the evil in the city of man escalated into an antichrist crisis.

The antichrist ideology of divine kingship that had precipitated the judgment of the Noahic world (Gen 6:1ff.) appears again in Egypt in the dominant doctrine of the pharaoh's divinity. The claim of the pharaohs to be gods is in view when the Lord's blows on Egypt, especially the tenth plague, are described as a bringing of judgment on the gods of Egypt (Exod 12:12; Num 33:4). Whatever allusion there may be to deified natural phenomena or creatures associated with various gods that were objects of the plague judgments, the primary reference is to the self-proclaimed gods of the royal house. In the one other biblical appearance of the motif of the gods of Egypt pharaoh is again conspicuous (cf. Jer 46:25).

The dominance of the concept of the pharaonic god-king in the culture of Egypt finds most remarkable expression in the royal pyramid tombs. These monumental architectural enterprises commanded and exhausted the material and manpower resources of the whole land in the interest of providing for the divine pharaoh's immortal existence. Like the ziggurats, artificial mountains, the pyramids too represent a perverted, mythological development of the pristine, genuine Har Magedon. They were identified as a stylization of the primeval hill of Egyptian creation myth. At his first emergence, shining forth in royal glory, the creator god makes a mound of dry land in the midst of the primordial chaos in order to have a place on which he might stand and rule. Since this mound was the place from which all life originated, the conceptualizing of the pyramids as the primeval hill was apt, designed as they were to be the channel of the re-creation of life beyond death. The nature of the primeval hill as the site of radiant sunrise-like manifestation of royal divine glory is conveyed in its hieroglyph, which pictures a mound with the rays of the rising sun emanating above it. This hieroglyph also serves for the verb which means "appear in glory." Unmistakably there is here a distorted echo of the mountain of God that was the center of creation in Eden, Har Magedon, the site of the Creator's enthronement in radiant glory.

The pharaohs with whom the Israelites had to deal exhibited various other antichrist traits. When the Lord through Moses demanded that his people be liberated so that they might gather at the mountain of God to serve him, pharaoh challenged the messenger-representative of the God of Har Magedon with a scornful "Who is Yahweh that I should obey him?" (Exod 5:2). And he defiantly countered the witness of the true wonders performed through the hand of Moses and Aaron (Ps 105:26,27) with lying signs performed by his court magicians (Exod 7:11,12,23; 8:7; cf. 2 Thess 2:9,10). The deceptive subtlety that characterized the pharaonic tactics (Exod 8:29 [25]; Ps 105:25; cf. Gen 3:1) betrayed the satanic aegis and inspiration of the Egyptian antichrist.

A life of bitter bondage was the lot of the people of God in the antichrist crisis in Egypt. The imposition of ruthlessly enforced grinding labor was one pharaonic measure calculated to reduce the Hebrew male population and thus diminish the viability of the Israelite community (Exod 1:8ff.). Another appalling scheme for reducing the remnant to an ineffective, negligible element swallowed up in the Egyptian populace was the pharaonic decree requiring Israelite infant boys to be killed (Exod 1:22). As it turned out this became in effect an attack on God's destined deliverer of his people, the type of the coming Messiah (Exod 2:1ff.), a distinctively antichrist act.

According to biblical prophecy, at the final battle of Har Magedon there is a massive gathering of antichrist's global forces to besiege the community of faith, the company of witnesses to the name of Jesus Christ, the Lord. Similarly at the climactic exodus episode at the sea there was a mobilizing of all pharaoh's military might and a hemming in of the covenant people, bearers of Yahweh's name, caught between the sea and pharaoh's horses and chariots (Exod 14:6ff.). Since the Glory-Spirit cloud, the theophanic Presence that crowns Har Magedon, was present with the Israelites as their divine guide and shield (Exod 13:21,22; 14:19,20), this gathering of pharaoh's forces against them was a peculiarly antichrist challenge to the name, authority, and power of the God of Har Magedon.

Divine Judgment

Parousia

The founding of the typal kingdom was heralded by the advent of the divine King, come to judge the antichrist world and redeem his people. The form of the divine advent was consonant with the arrival of the day of the Lord and the establishing of the kingdom in power and glory. In the earlier, patriarchal era God had manifested himself as the Angel of the Lord, a glory-muted mode of theophany. There is a continuing presence of this divine Angel during the Mosaic mission, but associated with the Angel now is a parousia of the Glory-Spirit, an appearing of God in majestic splendor. The intervention of God in earth history for the salvation of Israel by means of this Glory Presence is indeed a primary motif of the exodus narrative. The literary development of this theme unfolds in a comprehensive concentric pattern. The opening and closing sections of the account (Exodus 1–4 and 19–40 respectively) portray the divine Glory as present in the midst of the covenant people and the middle section (Exodus 5–18) recounts the mighty acts of redemptive judgment performed by the King of Glory.

The revelation of God in the flames of the burning bush at the call of Moses, the fiery kind of manifestation distinctive of Glory-Spirit theophany, is identified as the Angel of the Lord (Exod 3:2). We see here the bonding in redemptive mission of the second and third persons of the Trinity that culminates in the New Covenant age in the synchronized operations of the incarnate Son and the Pentecostally bestowed Holy Spirit. This appearance of the Lord to Moses as a consuming fire betokened his holy wrath about to be directed against the despisers of his rule. At the same time, the presence of this theophanic fire in the bush (symbol of the covenant community) without consuming it was a disclosure that this judicial visitation would be, for God's people, redemptive. In the hour of judgment they would be spared from the destructive impact of his burning anger. The presence of God in the burning-but-unconsumed bush portrayed the miracle of gospel grace: a sinful people saved from wrath – more than that, transformed into a temple residence of their holy Lord.

The firebrand form of the revelation of God's Presence on this occasion recalled the flaming torch theophany at the ratification of the Abrahamic Covenant by divine oath (Gen 15:9ff.). The Lord's identification of himself as the God of Abraham, Isaac, and Jacob (Exod 3:6) and his announcement of his intention to deliver his people from oppression and give them the land of the Canaanite nations (Exod 3:7-10) also mark the revelation at the bush and the ensuing Mosaic mission as a fulfillment of the promises of that covenant given to the patriarch (Gen 15:13-21). Indeed, the inauguration of the promised kingdom by the making of the Torah covenant is foreshadowed here in the burning bush theophany, the Glory-manifestation of the divine Presence in both episodes being at a holy mountain of God (Exod 3:11) – as it was originally in Eden. In fact, the mountain of the burning bush is the very mountain of the kingdom covenanting, Horeb-Sinai, which like the bush (sěneh, a play on Sinai) is described as "burning with fire" (Exod 3:2; Deut 4:11; 5:23) by virtue of God's advent on it. There is the further resemblance that again on this later occasion Sinai was the scene of a burning that did not consume. This time however what was involved was not just a symbol but the reality of the covenant people, assembled at the mountain of fiery theophany.

Such was the setting of Moses' call, the mount of theophany. It was as Lord of that holy Mount of Assembly (cf. Deut 33:16) that God appeared and confronted Moses. It was as the divine warrior, the Sovereign of Har Magedon, that he appointed Moses as his lieutenant in command of the holy war army, commissioning him to conduct a new phase in the unremitting battle of Har Magedon.

Public theophany in the form of large scale meteorological phenomena witnessed by the covenant people as a whole, Glory-cloud-parousia theophany, was (re-)introduced in the postdiluvian history in connection with the exodus event. Explicit reference is made to this cloud theophany as the director and protector of the Israelites in their departure from Egypt and their passage through the sea and the wilderness (Exod 13:21,22; 14:19,20,24; cf. Num 14:14; Deut 1:33; 9:3; Ps 78:13,14; Neh 9:11,12,19,20). It was indeed in the Glory mode of the Angel-attended Shekinah-Spirit that the Lord was present throughout the entire process of inflicting final judgment on the pharaonic kingdom and bringing his redeemed people to their promised mountain of inheritance.

Redemptive Judgment

Visitation of wrath though it was, the exodus judgment was for the Israelites a rescue operation delivering them from the rage of their enemies. It was an intervention of the Lord their God whereby he became the salvation of his people (Exod 15:1-3).

In this event we see the principle of redemptive judgment intruded into common grace history. Redemptive judgments, whether typological anticipations of the ultimate judgment or the antitypical eschatological judgment itself, discriminate strictly along covenantal lines in the execution of the curse and blessing. The exodus narrative repeatedly mentions the Lord's distinguishing of his people from the Egyptians. He is said to put a difference between the Israelites, their land and cattle on the one side and the Egyptians and their property on the other (Exod 8:22,23 [18:19]; 9:4,6,26; 10:23; 11:7). Climactic in this display of Yahweh's sovereignty were the tenth plague and the crisis at the sea. In the last plague, while striking the firstborn of every household throughout Egypt, the angel of death (cf. Ps 78:49; 2 Sam 24:15-17; 2 Kgs 19:34,35) spared the Israelite dwellings. They were shielded by the divine Presence, which hovered over their blood-smeared entryways (Exod 11:7; 12:12,13,29,30), even as the Spirit hovered over the deep and darkness in the beginning and would overshadow the Israelites in the wilderness. [On the paschal episode, see *FCO*.] And in the confrontation at the sea, the waters became a dry-ground pathway through which the whole Israelite nation passed safely, whereas those waters swept over the entire army of the pharaoh, not one of them surviving (Exod 14:19-30; 15:1-12,19; Ps 78:53).

This separating, discriminating judicial process was a trial by ordeal, a subjecting of the rival legal parties to divinely wielded ordeal elements, so rendering verdicts, whether of vindication and deliverance or of condemnation and destruction. In judicial ordeals the vindicated party might take over the estate of his adversary and agreeably the favorable verdict of the Israelites included their plundering the treasures of the Egyptians (Exod 3:22; 12:36).

Water was the ordeal element in the exodus event as it had been in the Noahic Deluge judgment, and just as Peter interpreted the Flood as a baptism (1 Pet 3:20,21) so Paul identified the ordeal at the Egyptian sea as a baptism: "They were all baptized into Moses in the cloud and in the sea" (1 Cor 10:2). [See further, *BOC* 55-61.] It appears then that the basic or generic signification of the covenantal rite of baptism is that of a passage through the ordeal waters of death. This baptismal judgment can take either of two forms. The death waters can be safely negotiated by means of a divinely provided vehicle or agent of salvation – whether Noah's ark or Moses or Jesus. In these cases passage through the baptismal death issues in resurrection. However, undergone apart from the Lord's provision for deliverance the baptismal ordeal of divine judgment, the judgment that looms over all (Heb 9:27), issues in condemnation, destruction, perdition. So it was for the world in Noah's day and for the pharaoh's pursuing armies – and so it will be in the final judgment for those who have not sought refuge in Christ, the true ark, the new and greater Moses-mediator (Heb 10:26-31; 2 Pet 3:5-7).

In Paul's exposition of the Red Sea crossing as a baptism, "the cloud" is mentioned along with the sea as a second ordeal element (1 Cor 10:2). The reference is to the theophanic pillar of cloud and fire that executed the dual sanctions of the covenant, functioning as a light to lead the Israelites to safety (Exod 13:21; 14:19,20) but flashing fiercely to destroy the Egyptians (Exod 14:20,24). It was then the King of Glory, the One beheld by Israel as a consuming fire on Mount Sinai (Exod 19:18; 24:15-17), who was himself the ordeal power at the Egyptian Sea. The Shekinah parousia there was an advent of the Lord of Har Magedon in glory with his judgment angels (cf. Isa 63:11-14). [See further *BOC* 68-70.]

This same combination of water and Spirit as instruments of divine judgment appears in the messianic judgment-baptism. John the Forerunner, comparing his own baptismal rite with the baptismal ordeal to be executed by Jesus, declared: "I baptize you with water . . . He will baptize you with the Holy Spirit and with fire" (Matt 3:11). The collocation of water and Spirit-fire (here distributed between John's sign and Jesus' actual baptismal judgment) links the messianic baptismal ordeal to the Mosaic baptismal event. And involved here again in the messianic judgment are both the ordeal outcomes of blessing and curse. For believers, Christ's baptism with the Spirit and fire was a Pentecostal anointing unto justification and life in the heavenly kingdom, but for the apostate Old Covenant community the messianic baptismal ordeal was unto condemnation and the desolation of Jerusalem.

From the fact that it was the Glory-Spirit, the Lord himself, who performed the role of the fiery ordeal power in the Mosaic baptismal judgment it is evident that the deliverance wrought for God's people was not just a matter of rescuing them from the hostility of their antichrist enemies (though it was that too); it was also a deliverance from the wrath of God. Repeated in the exodus salvation is the gospel of the burning but not consumed bush. And in the repetition it becomes clear that the salvation from divine wrath is based on the accomplishing of an atonement for sin. The sacrifice of the paschal lambs (Exodus 12) and the whole Mosaic sacrificial system echoes the Gen 3:15 prophecy of the bruising of Messiah's heel, preaching beforehand the gospel of the Cross.

Gathering of the Kingdom People to Mount Sinai

As it develops the theme of the establishing of the typal kingdom of God, the Book of Exodus deals first with the way the Great King secured his kingdom people for himself (Exodus 1–18). Since they were in a state of bondage an act of redemption was required, delivering them from pharaoh's dominion. And since the Israelites were enslaved in a foreign land, their redemption also involved a regathering to the homeland promised to their fathers. The full story of this homecoming takes us beyond the Book of Exodus to the history of the occupation of the kingdom land of Canaan, culminating in the assembly of the twelve-tribe nation at Mount Zion (cf.

Exod 15:13,17; Ps 78:54, reading "holy mountain"). Within the Exodus account the gathering of Israel by the hand of Moses and Aaron (Ps 77:20 [21]) leads to a national assembly at Mount Sinai (Exod 19:1,2).

God's gathering of his people is portrayed as a shepherding of his flock (Ps 78:52-54; Isa 63:11-14). At the same time the gathering to Sinai is depicted as a military mustering. The flock of Israel departing Egypt was organized in divisions (Exod 12:17,41,51), an army of the Lord marching to the holy war in battle array (Exod 13:18). They are already engaged in battle with the Amalekites along the way to Sinai (Exod 17:8-15). But the martial character of this operation is more pronounced in the subsequent advance of the twelve tribes from Sinai to Canaan. Military terminology is used in the prescriptions for the encampment of the tribes under their standards (cf. Numbers 2). The particular interest of the census the Lord orders is in the number of the warriors in each of the tribes (cf. Numbers 1). The stages of the journeying are described in the style of military annals (Numbers 33) and the signaling of the advance of the several tribes by trumpets fits the imagery of an army on the march (Numbers 10). And the march of course culminates in actual warfare. The gathering of God's people was a deployment of troops for a major battle in the war of Har Magedon.

Sinai/Horeb was the immediate, intermediate destination of the warrior companies of Israel. Its identification as "the mountain of God" (Exod 3:1; 1 Kgs 19:8) arose from God's choice of this mountain as the site of his appearance to Moses at his commissioning call and his revelation to Israel through Moses at the ratification of his covenant with them (Exod 19:2).

Since the Shekinah theophany was an earthly expression of the divine Glory of the archetypal, heavenly Har Magedon, whatever earthly mountain it settled upon became a symbolic-typological Har Magedon. The duration of the tenure of a particular mountain as a prototypal Mount of Assembly might be longer or shorter but none of the prototypes retains its symbolic identity as God's holy mountain under the present New Covenant dispensation. The hour has come when only the heavenly reality remains (John 4:21-24). Those with understanding of the times patiently await the eschatological advent of the Glory of the heavenly Har Magedon. Others, not understanding the new era inaugurated by Jesus Christ, entangle themselves in "holy" wars for the control of obsolete sacred heights, seemingly indifferent to the terrible toll of human suffering and the threat posed to the stability of the whole world order.

Along with the presence of the Glory theophany, another identifying feature of the prototypal mountain of God was a replica of the cosmic heavenly temple. The ark on Ararat and the temple on Zion were such structures. They constituted the mountain on which they were situated a dwelling place. This residential aspect is especially clear in the case of Mount Zion where the house of God is firmly founded on the mountain, continuing thus over a lengthy period of time (cf. 1 Kgs 6:13; Ps 74:2). The tabernacle, the royal dwelling at Mount Sinai, was designed for repeated dismantling and re-assembling; it was not firmly fixed there at the mountain. Sinai was then only a temporary encampment of the Lord as he accompanied his people along the way to the promised land. Nevertheless, by virtue of the appearing of the theophanic Presence on Mount Sinai it was stamped a holy mount of God, a Har Magedon, and it retained that status during the old typological era, even when the tabernacle was replaced by the temple on Mount Zion (1 Kgs 19:8). Similarly, even after the Sinai encampment was left behind, the Lord continued to the be known as "the One of Sinai" (Judg 5:5; Ps 68:8 [9]).

Israel's gathering to Sinai was a wilderness experience. The wilderness character of Sinai is brought out by the alternative term, Horeb (desolation, waste land), as well as by the designation of the Sinai site as the wilderness or desert of Sinai (e.g., Exod 19:1). Intensifying the image, Deut 32:10 calls the area a barren, howling waste, employing the term tōhû used in Gen 1:2 for the inchoate stage of the primeval earth. This passage suggests the theological significance of the wilderness setting when it refers to it as the place where the Lord "found" the Israelites. Sinai's wilderness character connotes the desperate plight of the Israelites. It speaks of their helplessness, of their dependence on the mercy and might of the Lord to rescue them out of this bleak, lifeless realm and lead them on into the promised paradisiacal inheritance (cf. Deut 32:13,14).

But Sinai was to be something more than a reminder to Israel of the perilous wilderness from which they were delivered. It was to stand in Israel's memory as the place where their national election as God's kingdom people was confirmed by covenant. The gathering of Israel to Sinai was a gathering to the covenant assembly. Above all else, Sinai was the mount of the covenant.

Prophesying of the Messiah's covenantal union with the church, Hosea pictures that New Covenant event in terms of the typological Sinai event, which he portrays as a marital covenanting with an exchange of vows (Hos 2:14-16 [16-18]). On his part, the Lord pledges to transform wasteland desolation into wedding delight. Similarly the Lord declares through Jeremiah that he remembers the Sinai era as a time when Israel was devoted to him by marriage commitment and followed him as a bride through the wilderness, the land not sown (Jer 2:2). Likewise in the allegory of Ezekiel 16 the covenant solemnizing at Sinai is imaged as a wedding. Vivid once again here is the forlorn, destitute state of Israel until the compassionate, transforming intervention of the divine Groom. In its Mount Sinai version Har Magedon is a nuptial gathering in celebration of the redemptive (re-) union of God and his people.

Kingdom Consummation: Inauguration of the Typal Kingdom at Sinai

Introduction. The coming of the typal kingdom begins with the redemption of the chosen kingdom people by their Great King (Exodus 1–18). Our analysis of the redemptive judgments against the antichrist power brought us to the national assembly at Sinai. There the official constituting of the kingdom by covenant took place (Exodus 19–34), concluding with the enthronement of the King in the royal tabernacle, constructed for him as stipulated in the treaty (Exodus 35–40). This formalizing of the relation between Yahweh and Israel may be construed after the analogy of a wedding, as we previously observed, with Israel as wife. It may also be seen as an act of adoption, with Israel as God's son (cf. Exod 4:22,23; Rom 9:5). Here, however, we are viewing the Sinaitic transaction as the formal instituting of the typal kingdom and in that model Israel is the servant or vassal of Yahweh, their Suzerain, the Sovereign indeed over every dominion in heaven and earth. [Cf. *KP* 46, 47.]

Surveyed from the perspective of the covenant as its primary theme, the Book of Exodus falls into two major sections. Exodus 1–18 is concerned with the figure of the one who is to be the mediator of the covenant (cf. Heb 3:4) and especially with the validating of his appointment to that position by the role he plays as the agent of Israel's almighty Lord in accomplishing their salvation. The second section (Exodus 19–40) narrates the solemn ratification of the covenant.

In this over-all pattern the Book of Exodus anticipates the form of the New Testament Gospels. The latter also have two main divisions. The first part, like Exodus 1–18, presents the covenant mediator, Jesus, the new and greater Moses, the Messiah-Son sent by the Father and certified for his mediatorial role by his unparalleled words and deeds. The second division of the Gospels is the passion narrative section, which, like Exodus 19–40, is the record of covenant ratification, the blood of the Cross being the blood of the New Covenant. We may, therefore, speak of the Book of Exodus in its over-all structure as the Gospel of Moses, a covenant witness document, which is what a gospel is. [For a full exposition of this identification of the Book of Exodus cf. *SBA* 172-203.]

The covenant making process recounted in Exodus 19–40 consists first of all in ratification ceremonies (narrated in Exod 19:1–24:11). Prominent here are the covenant documents, the two stone tables and the book of the covenant. Exod 24:12–34:35 then traces further the history of these documents, in particular the two tables. This is interwoven with an account of the breaking and renewal of the covenant, which has its symbolic-judicial counterpart in the breaking and renewing of the tables. Also in this section of Exodus are the prescriptions for the tabernacle, while the concluding section (Exodus 35–40) relates the confirming of the covenant relationship through the actual construction of the tabernacle and God's taking up residence there in the midst of his people.

If we change our perspective on the Book of Exodus, subordinating covenant to kingdom and taking the inauguration of the kingdom as the primary theme, the ratification of the covenant described in Exod 19:1–24:11 becomes the covenantal constituting of the kingdom. And Exodus 25–40 becomes the record of the consummating of the Sinai stage of the typal kingdom by the erecting of the royal tent of assembly and the enthronement of the Lord God of Har Magedon there in that earthly replica of his royal house above.

Covenantal Constituting

By the days of Moses the Abrahamic family had become the twelve tribe nation. The national aspect of the covenant making at Sinai is displayed in the united participation of all the people throughout these proceedings. Particularly significant is the group of elders and the role they played as representatives of the whole nation, especially at key points like the initial voicing of Israel's commitment to the terms of the covenant (Exod 19:7,8) and at the communion meal that sealed the covenant (Exod 24:1,9-11; see also Exod 3:16,18; 4:29; 12:21; 17:5,6; 18:12). Also manifesting the involvement of the nation as a whole were the twelve witness pillars set up to represent the twelve tribes (Exod 24:4).

Through the Sinai covenanting this national community was constituted a kingdom, the theocratic kingdom of Yahweh, the divine Suzerain. The Lord's declaration that the Israelites were to be to him "a kingdom of priests and a holy nation" (Exod 19:6) made clear from the outset the objective of establishing the kingdom. In due time the kingdom structure would be completed in the instituting of the monarchy with its earthly representative of Yahweh, as had been prophesied in Jacob's blessing on Judah (Gen 49:8-12) and legislatively provided for in the Deuteronomic renewal of the Sinaitic covenant (Deut 17:14-20).

Indicative of the kingdomization of Israel, the documentation of the Sinaitic covenant was in the form of treaties employed in the diplomacy of kingdoms in the Mosaic age. The two stone "tables of the covenant" (Deut 9:9,11,15; cf. Exod 34:28; Deut 4:13) reflect the customary arrangement of preparing duplicate copies of the treaty, one each for the great king and the vassal king. And the contents of the two tables follow closely the outline of the extrabiblical treaties: preamble, identifying the Great King (cf. Exod 20:2a); historical prologue, rehearsing the Great King's previous favorable treatment of the vassal (cf. Exod 20:2b); stipulations, imposing obligations on the vassal in his service of the Great King (cf. Exod 20:3-17); sanctions, pronouncing the blessings that would attend obedience on the vassal's part and the curses that would be visited on disobedience (cf. Exod 20:5,6,7,12). Two other standard features of the international treaty pattern, namely the document clause dealing with the enshrinement of the treaties under the feet of the deities and the section containing the invocation of the gods to be witnesses and enforcers of the covenant, have parallels in the context of the Exodus 20 account of God's covenant words (cf. Exod 25:6; Deut 4:26; 30:19; 31:28). [On the kingdom-treaty form, see *SBA* 115-130.]

Equivalents of the basic elements of the treaty form are found again in the book of the covenant (cf. Exod 20:22–23:33), which was read to the people when they were about to swear their covenant ratifying oath (Exod 24:7). Obedience to the divine Angel was mandated by the preamble-like identification of him as bearer of God's name and by the reminder of the guidance and protection he provided for Israel, an historical prologue equivalent. Also there were commandments, noteworthy among them the corporate commission to wage holy war against the occupants of Canaan, and the associated sanctions, especially the promise that the Lord would overcome the enemy and establish the covenant people as a theocratic kingdom in the promised land (cf. Exod 23:22-31).

This prospect of fully kingdomized Israel was prophetically symbolized in the process of ratifying the covenant at Sinai. For one thing, there was the arrangement of the altar with the twelve stone pillars, most likely positioned in the form of a square around the altar. The altar was the locus of the Lord's Presence and the pillars represented the twelve tribes stationed around the holy residence of their King. This was the arrangement prescribed for the Israelites' encampment in the wilderness. It may be that the witness pillars also represented kudurru stones (i.e., boundary markers). The scene at the foot of Sinai was then a symbolic model of the promised kingdom, anticipating the typal fulfillment in the kingdom land of Canaan with Zion, the Har Magedon mount of the altar, situated in the midst of the surrounding tribes. And all this typological symbolism finds its antitypical realization in the holy city-kingdom situated on the high Mount of Assembly in the new heaven and earth. There the altar-throne-temple-city of the Glory Presence has about it a square-shaped, twelve-sectioned boundary wall with twelve gates, three on each side, having the names of God's typal-stage people, and with twelve foundations, having the names of the apostles of the Lamb, representing the people of the New Covenant.

The communion meal on the mountain (Exod 24:1,9-11) was another feature of the Sinai covenanting symbolic of an aspect of the emergent kingdom, in this case, the personal relationship of the God-King and his people. Israel, represented by the seventy elders and their special mediatorial officers, participated in a sacrificial meal (cf. the peace/fellowship offerings, v. 5) in the presence of God. The parallel between this theophany and the Glory vision in Ezek 1:22, with a crystal clear firmament-like pavement beneath God's feet in each instance, indicates that in the Exodus 24 episode too God appeared as the enthroned Glory, viewed by the elders of Israel from a perspective at his feet (cf., e.g., Matt 28:9; Luke 7:38; John 13:5ff.). This communion meal anticipated the situation when the Glory-Spirit would reside in the midst of Israel and the people would partake of peace-offering feasts as guests at the Lord's house, as prescribed in the cultic provisions of the Mosaic covenants. And these communion meals were in turn prophetic of the eschatological banquet of the redeemed in the consummated kingdom on the heavenly Har Magedon, the banquet of which the Lord's Supper is a sacramental foretaste in the worship of the church of the New Covenant.

Enthronement of the Covenant Lord

The original pattern for eschatology was set in the creation history. The Creator's achievements of the six days led to his sabbath rest, a royal session, an enthronement. In keeping with this image the creating process is viewed as the construction of a cosmic royal house. This pattern repeats in redemptive history, only now the palace construction follows upon divine victory over the enemy. The slaying of the dragon precedes the building of the place of God's enthronement. Final judgment is the prelude to the emergence of God's palace-temple and his occupying of the throne therein. It is of vital theological import to maintain the distinction between the creational and redemptive forms of the basic eschatological pattern. The loss of that distinction marks fallen man's mythological perversions of the pristine primal tradition of mankind's beginnings, the creation process being then misconstrued as one of conflict with and victory over some prior evil power. [On this see further *KP* 26-30, 147, 148.]

The redemptive form of the paradigm (conquest-construction-coronation) informs the history recorded in the Book of Exodus. God vanquishes the Rahab monster of Egypt (cf. Ps 74:12ff.; Isa 51:9f.; Ezek 29:3ff.; 32:2ff.), then mandates the construction of the tent of gathering with its cherubim-guarded ark, footstool of the Glory-throne.

The builders are required to adhere strictly to the architectural model revealed to Moses on the Mount of Assembly (Exod 25:9), subsequently articulated in Moses' instructions to the people (Exodus 25–31). The actual construction follows, the tabernacle being fashioned as prescribed, detail after detail (Exod 35:4–40:33). When Moses finishes the work, the divine enthonement takes place. The Glory-Spirit descends over the tent of gathering, the earthly replication of God's celestial courts, enveloping, entering, filling it (Exod 40:34,35). So the Lord of the covenant assumed his throne there in the midst of his people. Though it bore the image of the eternal Glory-temple on the heavenly Har Magedon, the style of the royal residence of the King of Glory was accommodated to that of his people's dwellings, temporary structures suited to a journeying existence, not yet arrived in the kingdom-land of rest (cf. 2 Sam 7:6,7). For the King of Glory is the condescending Immanuel.

Re-creation

Entailed in the construction of the tabernacle and God's enthronement therein is the re-creation dimension of the kingdom consummation at Sinai. Suggestive of this re-creation aspect is the allusion to the beginning (rēšîṯ) of time (Gen 1:1) in the Lord's declaration that the month of the paschal event was to be the beginning (rōš) in Israel's reckoning of the annual round of time (Exod 12:2). And the appearance of the Glory-cloud hovering creatively over the tōhû sitatution of Israel (Deut 32:10) was evocative of the hovering of the Creator Spirit over the dark depths at the beginning (Gen 1:2).

Already within the course of the ten plagues (themselves a process of de-creation) the major creational feature of separation and bounding appears as the Lord distinguishes between his people and the Egyptians. The bounding of the darkness by the introduction of day-light on day one of creation (Gen 1:3) is recalled by the presence of light in the area occupied by the Israelites, setting limits on the dense darkness of the ninth plague that covered Egypt for three days (Exod 10:21-23). And the bounding of the deep by the dividing of the waters vertically on day two and horizontally (by the appearance of the dry land) on day three found its counterpart in the climactic dividing of the Egyptian sea and the consequent emergence of a dry-ground passage for the Israelites through the waters of death (Exod 14:21,22; 15:8; cf. Josh 2:10; 3:13; Ps 78:13; 66:6; 106:9; Neh 9:11; Isa 51:10).

Since the tabernacle represented the cosmos in symbolic miniature [cf. *IOS* 35-42] the account of its construction is equivalent to the record of the creation of the heavens and the earth in the Genesis prologue. The nature of the building of the tabernacle as a re-enactment of creation is brought out by the literary form of the narrative of that event. Echoing the fiat-fulfillment structure of the Genesis creation account, Exodus 25–31 presents the divine fiat-commands and Exodus 35–40 the fulfillment. Again, within the Exodus 40 narrative of the actual setting up of the tabernacle, the divine directives are given first (vv. 1-15), then their execution (vv. 16-33). And the concluding statement: "And so Moses finished the work" (v. 33) clearly recalls the declaration of Gen 2:2 that the Creator "finished his work."

The redemptive re-creation under Moses also included the replication of the divine Glory-likeness in man, a climactic feature of the original creation (Gen 1:26,27). One way in which this fashioning of man in the image of the Glory-Spirit came to expression was the transfiguring of Moses so that his countenance reflected the divine Glory (Exod 34:29-35). Another symbolic representation of the creation of man in God's image is seen in the priestly investiture of Aaron (Exodus 28). His holy garments were designed "for glory and for beauty" (Exod 28:2). The flame-colored linen material and the gleam of golden threads and gems set in gold contributed to the impression of radiant glory, with the holy mitre as the crowning expression of the Glory-likeness. [Cf. *IOS* 42-47.]

Calling for separate notice as a re-creation feature in connection with the typal consummation of the kingdom at Sinai is the sabbath motif. Before the Sinai covenanting there was the providing of the manna as a sabbatically structured process (Exod 16:23-30). But principally there is the formal republication of the creational ordinance of the Sabbath (Gen 2:2,3) in the fourth of the ten stipulations of the Sinai treaty (Exod 20:8-11) and in the elaboration of these stipulations in the book of the covenant (Exod 23:12). The promulgation of the Sabbath is prominent in the account of the tabernacle project. It marks the close of the fiat-command section (Exod 31:12-17) and the beginning of the fulfillment section (Exod 35:2,3). And as we have noted, the statement that Moses finished the work, found at the conclusion of the account of the construction, erection, and consecration of the tabernacle (Exod 40:33), reflects Gen 2:2, which relates the Creator's finishing the heaven and earth and entering into his royal sabbath rest of the seventh day. Indeed, the Exodus 40 account goes on to report the sabbatical enthronement of the Glory-Spirit in the tent of assembly, earthly reproduction of the sabbath throne room on the celestial Har Magedon, Mount of Assembly (Exod 40:34,35).

Kingdom Consummation: Culmination of the Typal Kingdom on Zion

Introduction: Sinaitic Covenant and Abrahamic Promise. Sinai sealed the national election of Israel. They had now been brought into being, gathered together to the mountain of God and constituted by covenant the kingdom people of Yahweh. The kingdom promised in the Abrahamic Covenant was thus in process of realization at the typological level. Indeed, with God's tabernacle-enthronement in the midst of his kingdom people at Sinai, the theocracy had, in principle, been founded. But still to be fulfilled were the other two kingdom promises given to Abraham besides that of the people – the promises of the kingdom land and of the king, earthly vicegerent of the King of kings. To trace the history of Israel beyond Sinai is to witness the completing of the typological theocracy by the fulfillment of the land promise through the conquest and occupation of Canaan and the fulfillment of the king promise in the establishment of the Davidic dynasty.

This history unfolds within the framework of the national covenant ratified at Sinai and (as we have noted) under that covenant continuance in possession of the typal kingdom was governed by the principle of works. Israel's situation was like Adam's in the creational covenant of works, Israel's probation, however, being corporate and continuing through their generations. As it turned out, the typological picture with all the elements of people, king and land was eventually completed in the Davidic kingdom centered on Zion. As for the legal basis of such fulfillment of the kingdom promise as there was, the explanation is found in what we earlier observed concerning Abraham, the grantee of the covenant of promise. His exemplary obedience was invested by the Lord with typological significance as the meritorious ground for his descendants' inheritance of the promised land and their continuance as the kingdom-people until the arrival of Abraham's messianic seed. It was within these assured parameters secured by Abraham's obedience that Israel's probation unfolded and as a result there was a time of over-all fulfillment of the promised kingdom at the typal level.

However, the course of fulfillment was not a simple matter of steady development. Not only were there interruptions and delays along the way to the Zion kingdom, but after the heights of Zion had been attained the kingdom was disrupted and at last terminated. These vicissitudes in Israel's kingdom fortunes reflected the fluctuations in their allegiance to Yahweh, under probation as they were in the Sinaitic covenant of works with its dual sanctions of blessing for faithfulness but curse for infidelity. Israel being incorrigibly prone to apostasy, it was inevitable that their history under the Law would be one of the rise and fall of the typological kingdom. The Law was good but it was rendered impotent by the weakness of the Israelites' flesh.

In the rejection of John and Jesus, Israel filled up the measure of the sin of their fathers who had slain the prophets. On that generation was visited the blood of all the righteous shed on the earth. The Old Covenant dispensation came to an end with the pouring out of the decreed desolation on Jerusalem (Matt 23:29-39; Dan 9:26,27). Nevertheless, as the apostle Paul declares, there had been much advantage for the people of Israel in the Sinaitic arrangement. Theirs was the adoption as sons, the divine Glory, the covenants, the receiving of the law, the temple worship and the promises. They had been entrusted with the very words of God and of them Christ had come (Rom 3:1,2; 9:4,5). The Old Covenant order, theirs by national election, was one of highest historical privilege. And while a works principle was operative both in the grant of the kingdom to Abraham and in the meting out of typological kingdom blessings to the nation of Israel, the arrangement as a whole was a gracious favor to fallen sons of Adam, children of wrath deserving no blessings, temporal or eternal. The Law covenant was a sub-administration of the Covenant of Grace, designed to further the purpose and program of the gospel. By exhibiting dramatically the situation of all mankind, fallen in and with Adam in the original probation in Eden, the tragic history of Israel under its covenant-of-works probation served to convict all of their sinful, hopeless estate. The Law thus drove men to Christ that they might be justified by faith. All were shut up in disobedience that God might have mercy on all (Rom 11:28-36; Gal 3:19-25). Indeed, in the unsearchable wisdom of God, Israel's ultimate act of satanic rebellion against the Lord of Har Magedon – their repudiation of the Messiah, delivering him up to death on the Cross – became the occasion for the accomplishing of salvation and the gospel's going out to the Gentiles (Rom 11:11,12).

Occupation of the Kingdom Land

Prophetic Victory Hymn. The song of Moses (Exod 15:1-18) belongs to the victory hymn genre. [On this cf. *SBA* 76-88.] It celebrates Yahweh's triumph in judgment over the Egyptian empire and, prophetically, the anticipated establishment of his royal sanctuary. Later, in connection with the Lord's victories through his servant David, victory hymn re-appears in the oracle of the Davidic Covenant (2 Samuel 7) with its combination of the themes of conquest and construction of a house for the divine Victor on Zion. And in this same tradition is the hymn sung by the victors over the beast as they stand by the sea of glass, "the song of Moses the servant of God and the song of the Lamb" (Rev 15:3).

While each of these songs is primarily doxological, as victory hymns sung in the face of vanquished foes they are also taunt songs. The taunt element is especially pronounced in the Hallelujahs of the saints over the fall of Babylon (Rev 18:1ff.), cast like a stone into the deep (Rev 18:21), a judgment reminiscent of the fate of pharaoh's armies (Exod 15:1,4,5,10). The victory-taunt song complements the imprecatory psalm. It celebrates the divine vengeance that overtakes the cruel enemy in response to the imprecatory plea of God's people. The saints' use of these prayer genres of imprecation and taunt belongs to the final judgment crisis, but also to the intermediate state (cf. Rev 6:10) and to episodes involving typological intrusions of the principle of final judgment. The victory hymn of Exodus 15 thus signals the transition from the kingdom prologue era of the patriarchs to the Mosaic age of the coming of the kingdom, the shift from common grace relationships and pilgrim politics to the waging of holy war against the foes of the covenant people in a foreshadowing of the eschatological judgment on the wicked. [On the concept of intrusion ethics cf. *KP* 155-159; *SBA* 154-171.]

There is a sustained emphasis in the Song of Moses on the fact that the Lord God is the chief actor in all that transpires. The history of Israel's deliverance and eventual occupation of Canaan is first and last the story of God's triumph and God's sovereign appropriation of his rightful domain for the glory of his name. It is the divine warrior, Yahweh, who fights and wins the battle of Har Magedon, maintaining his claim to lordship over the holy mountain.

In the Exodus 15 hymn the destination beyond Sinai to which the Lord would lead his people, the land where he would plant them (Exod 15:17; cf. Ps 44:2; Isa 5:1ff.), is designated "the mountain of your [God's] inheritance." This terminology is used for the royal shrine of deities and agreeably the destination is further described in Exod 15:17 as the sanctuary the Lord's hands had made for his royal session, the place where he would reign forever (v. 18). "The mountain" could refer to the whole mountainous region beyond the Jordan (cf. Deut 3:25), the entire holy land (cf. Ps 78:54), or more specifically to Mount Zion. Exod 15:13 calls the goal of Israel's procession "your [the Lord's] holy domain (nāweh)," a term with pastoral coloring, referring to the shepherd's tent encampment. Although there might be a preliminary reference here to Sinai, the term is elsewhere used primarily for Mount Zion (2 Sam 15:25; Isa 33:20; Jer 25:30; 31:23).

The procession to Canaan was preeminently Yahweh's march of conquest to establish his kingdom rule on the Mount of Assembly (cf. Deut 33:2-5; Judg 5:4,5; Pss 68:7,8 [8,9]; 114:2; Hab 3:3-7). It was Yahweh's doing that his people were brought to the holy mountain his right hand had won. It was he who drove out the nations before them and settled them in their lands (cf. Ps 78:52-55).

Moses-Joshua: Conquest Phase. Moses and Joshua constituted a founding dynasty at the establishing of the typal kingdom. The close relationship between the two leaders and the interlocking of their missions is reflected in the way the prophetic hymn of Exodus 15 fuses the judicial water ordeals that launched the two stages of the warfare conducted by them in turn, the ordeals at the Red Sea and the Jordan River (cf. Psalm 114; Habakkuk 3). The Mosaic stage was one of deliverance from the Egyptian representative of Ham and the Joshuan stage was one of dispossession of the Canaanite branch of that accursed line. Together they made up the conquest phase of the Old Covenant's typological Har Magedon judgment.

Moses of course stands by himself as the one set over all God's house (Heb 3:2,5), the mediator of the Sinai Covenant. Along with his mediatorial function in the covenant ratification process and his supervision of the construction of the tabernacle he composed the covenant documents that constituted a national constitution, a priority task at Sinai in view of the imminent organization of Israel as a kingdom in the promised land.

Foundational covenant documentation was provided in the tables of the covenant and the book of the covenant, enough for the purpose of ratifying the covenant. But the maintaining of Israel's on-going relationship with their holy God would involve an elaborate priestly ministry of purification, sanctification, consecration and tribute, and the details of this liturgical service to be rendered to the Lord in his sanctuary-residence were given by revelation to Moses within the period – upwards of a year – that Israel was encamped at Sinai. Such was the origin and purpose of the Book of Leviticus.

Whereas Leviticus prescribes the cultic order, the Book of Numbers deals with Israel's corporate cultural task of filling and ruling her appointed domain. Israel's historic mission was to wage a holy war of conquest. In stark constrast to the church's great commission to evangelize the nations of the world, Israel's mandate was to extirpate the nations of Canaan. The Book of Numbers covers the history of this program of conquest in the first stage under the command of Moses, with Joshua as his adjutant. It records the prescriptions and preparations for the military advance and it narrates the actual setting out in battle array from Sinai, the rebellion at Kadesh resulting in a defeat at Hormah and a generation-long postponement of the advance against Canaan, the resumption of the advance, and the victories and beginning of tribal settlement in the Transjordan area.

The office of the priest entailed in the cultic program and the appointment of Aaron's line to that dignity had been dealt with in the Exodus document. This theme is carried forward in Leviticus with an account of the investiture and consecration of Aaron and his sons and the commencement of their altar ministry. In the Book of Numbers the role of the priests as guardians of the sacred tent is graphically conveyed in the arrangement prescribed for the encampment of the twelve tribes

(Numbers 2). Reflecting ancient Egyptian military camps, the over-all formation was a square with God's royal tabernacle in the center. We have previously called attention to a similar arrangement in the form of the altar surrounded by the twelve pillars at the Sinai covenant ceremonies. We noted that this formation was a reduced scale version of the later Zion-centered theocratic kingdom in Canaan, which was in turn a type of the heavenly kingdom symbolized in the Book of Revelation as the temple-city, New Jerusalem. According to the instructions in Numbers 2 for the disposition of the Israelite tribes in the wilderness, three of them were located on each side of the square at a distance from the tabernacle. And between them and the tabernacle on each side the priests and Levites were positioned, the priests being on the entrance side, which was a clear index of the priests' function of serving as the immediate protectors of the sanctity of God's sanctuary. Redemptively reproduced here – and again in the subsequent tribal allocations in the promised land – was the original situation in Eden where man was assigned the priestly task of negative consecration, the guardianship of the earthly Har Magedon. Archetype and antitype of all these terrestrial scenarios is the holy mount of God's heavenly enthronement, with the encircling twenty-four thrones of the elders and, in the center, the four living creatures (cf. Rev 4:4ff.).

Israel's campaign of conquest was identified as a holy, priestly undertaking by the leading position of the priests in the line of march. Carrying the ark of God's Presence they went before, with the Glory-cloud above them directing the advance (cf. Num 9:15-23; 10:11-13,33-36; Josh 3:3,4; 6:6; 8:33). Similarly in the final battle of Har Magedon the armies of heaven that follow the priestly-garbed Christ are a company of priests, robed in fine linen, white and clean (Rev 19:11-14; cf. 1:13).

For God's people in every age the Har Magedon warfare is at its core a wrestling against the spirit powers of darkness, a resisting of the challenge of the evil one against our Lord, the lord of the holy mount (Eph 6:10-18). It was Israel's failure in this invisible sphere of conflict (cf. Numbers 11–14) that accounts for their defeat at the outward military level at Hormah (Num 14:41-45). The alarming measure of Satan's success is seen in the postponement of the program of conquest and the dying off of the exodus generation in the wilderness.

This period of roughly forty years was comparable to the later time of the nation's removal to Babylon. It was a virtual exile from the promised land even before they entered it, an executing of the curse sanction of the Sinaitic covenant of works. Here we must recall our earlier, introductory analysis of the relation of the Sinaitic covenant to the Abrahamic kingdom promise. The Law did not abrogate God's promise covenant to Abraham. The Lord's sovereign grace relationship to the promised seed of Abraham, the true Israel, remained intact during the forty year hiatus in the typological kingdom program. Moreover, since (as we observed above) God's typological kingdom grant to Abraham assured the continuance of the Israelite covenant nation until the advent of the messianic seed of Abraham, the renewal of the broken Law covenant and the typological order after the forty years disruption was assured.

Meanwhile the simultaneous operating of the Abrahamic grace covenant and the superimposed Sinaitic covenant of works resulted in the peculiar ordering of Israel's encampment described in Exod 33:7-11 (a dischronologized passage within the Sinai narrative, which actually refers to the later, wilderness situation). Because the Israelites were still God's covenant people by the terms of the Abrahamic administration of the Covenant of Grace, there was still a theophanic Presence of God with Israel at the tabernacle. But because there was a rupture in the relationship defined by the Sinaitic covenant pertaining to the national election, the tabernacle was not located in the center of the tribal encampment but outside the camp, some distance away.

In various other ways the covenantally disrupted nature of the forty year period becomes evident. There was not a regular performance of the prescribed liturgical service during this time (cf. the implications of Num 15:2ff.; Amos 5:25,26; Acts 7:42,43). We are told that the practice of circumcision lapsed (Josh 5:4-7) along with the observance of the paschal feast (Josh 5:10). At the same time, it appears that the Aaronic priesthood still retained its authoritative cultic status and performed its distinctive functions on occasion during the interval era (cf., e.g., Numbers 16 and 17).

In the fortieth year, with a new generation on the scene, the advance on Canaan was resumed. The old complaining, rebellious spirit was in evidence again, but sin was confessed and the mediatorship of Moses was sought (cf., e.g., Num 21:7). A victory over the Canaanites at Hormah (Num 21:3), where Israel had experienced defeat at the outset of their wilderness exile (Num 14:45), highlighted the beginning of a new (the final) phase of Moses' leadership, with Israel moving forward from Kadesh to Moab. The persisting inner, satanic dimension of the conflict confronts us in the Balaam episode and the seducing of certain Israelites into the idolatry and immorality of the worship of Baal (Numbers 22–25). This, however, proved to be an opportunity for a display of zeal for God's honor by Phinehas, son of Eleazar, son of Aaron, for which God bestowed on him and his descendants a covenantal grant of perpetual priesthood (Num 25:10-13; cf. 1 Chr 6:4ff.).

Although the entrance into and conquest of Canaan was to take place after Moses' departure, there was a series of preliminary military successes in his final year. Most notable of these were the victories over the Amorite kings Sihon and Og in the Transjordan area on the eastern border of Canaan. Moses' assignment of this territory to the two and a half tribes as their inheritance marked the beginning of the process of Israel's entering into the possession of their covenanted domain.

There, east of the Jordan in the plains of Moab, the mission of Moses came to a close with his mediating a renewal of the Sinaitic covenant. The documentation of this covenant is found in the Book of Deuteronomy, whose over-all structure, like the Sinaitic treaty tablets, conformed to that of the international suzerain-vassal treaties of the second millennium BC [On this see *SBA* 131-153.] This summons to Israel to swear anew their covenantal commitment to Yahweh was more specifically a call to affirm their acceptance of his new representative, Joshua, the appointed successor of Moses (Num 27:15-23; Deut 3:28; 31:3,7; 34:9). The Deuteronomic Covenant was a dynastic covenant. Such covenants became of force at the death of the current king – in the case of Deuteronomy, the death of the heavenly Sovereign's earthly representative. Accordingly, the Book of Deuteronomy closes with a notice of the death of Moses, attesting that the Deuteronomic Covenant was now in effect.

Joshua's position as Moses' successor was sealed by the duplication of Israel's passage through the sea under Moses in their crossing the Jordan under Joshua. In the Joshuan phase of the prosecution of the divine holy war Canaan proper was invaded (Joshua 1–11) and the Israelites received their tribal allotments (Joshua 12–21).

Several ceremonial events confirmed the restoration of the new generation's covenantal relationship to their God. The first two occurred at Gilgal after the Jordan crossing. One was the circumcision of the whole nation, those born in the wilderness not having received the sign of covenant membership during the years of wandering (Josh 5:1-9). Also signalizing the return to normalcy was the national celebration of the paschal feast on the evening of the fourteenth day of the first month, the fortieth anniversary of the original observance (Josh 5:10; cf. Exod 12:3). The passing of the wilderness era was underscored by the cessation of the provision of manna at that time (Josh 5:11,12). A third covenantal ritual confirming Israel's restored relationship to the Lord occurred at mounts Ebal and Gerizim after key military victories at Jericho and Ai (Josh 8:30-35). What took place on this occasion was the second act of the covenant renewal begun under Moses. The Deuteronomic treaty itself had stipulated there should be this concluding ceremony after Israel had entered the land (Deuteronomy 27). [See further *KP* 377.] This two-stage covenant ratification interlocking the Mosaic and Joshuan administrations is an index of the dynastic unity of these two leaders. The point is strengthened by similarities in ceremonial procedure between the Sinai and Shechem episodes, like the inscribing of the contents of the covenant on stones and the reading of these to the Israelites in preparation for the covenant oath-taking.

The Lord's parousia is paramount on the day of judgment. His presence as the divine warrior in the conquest of Canaan is highlighted by the manifestation of the divine Angel with sword in hand, identifying himself to Joshua as "commander of the army of the Lord," providing the strategy for the attack on Jericho, and assuring Joshua that he has delivered Jericho into Israel's hands (Josh 5:13–6:5). That the battle was the Lord's and the victory his was the message of the altar Joshua built to him on Mount Ebal (Josh 8:30; cf. 23:3). It was a victory stele celebrating Yahweh's triumph over the gods of Canaan by the supernaturally abetted crossing of the Jordan and the victories over the cities recorded in Joshua 6–8. The altar was a symbolic mountain of God set up in the mountainous holy land, claiming the land and proclaiming Yahweh as the Lord of this Har Magedon terrain.

During its Joshuan phase the role of the priests continued to identify the campaign against Canaan as a holy war. The high priest Eleazar was associated with Joshua as the medium of oracular directions from the Lord (Num 27:15-23; Josh 14:1; 19:51). And the priests with the ark of the covenant were positioned in front of the Israelite army at the crossing of the Jordan and again, with the sacred silver trumpets, at the demolition of Jericho. Another indication that the Joshuan campaign did not fall under the category of just war but rather of holy war is the intrusion of the principle of final judgment. Israel's taking the territory of Canaan away from the long-time occupants of the land, overriding the common grace conventions and anticipating the eschatological day of the Lord, is indeed the paramount example of intrusion ethics. Instances of the intrusion principle are also found in various episodes within the program of conquest as a whole. For example, there was Rahab's divinely approved deception of the Jericho authorities to whom she would normally owe her allegiance (Joshua 2). And underlying the case of the Gibeonites' deception (Joshua 9) was the prohibition against the Israelites' making covenants with the occupants of the land – contrary to normal common grace policy attested in the practice of the patriarchs (cf., e.g., Gen 14:13). The Joshuan holy war against Canaan, with its intrusion of the ethics of final judgment, was a prototype of the final battle of Har Magedon on the last great day of the Lord. [On the concept of intrusion ethics cf. *SBA* 154-171; *KP* 157-159, 357-359.]

The day of the Lord culminates in the sabbath rest of God and his people. So the intrusion of the final judgment in the Joshuan conquest of Canaan issued in a sabbath experience for Israel: God gave Israel rest on every side from all their enemies (Josh 23:1). In Josh 21:43,44 this rest is equated with the land Israel was given to settle in. Reflecting this sabbatical view of the land Joshua allotted to Israel, Heb 4:8,9 affirms that the true, eschatological sabbath rest (of which Canaan was only a temporary type) still awaits God's people. For the present, we look unto Jesus, who has gone before us, entering that sabbath realm to appear before God's Presence for us, already occupying the sabbath throne of God's seventh day rest (Heb 6:20; 9:26; cf. 1:3,13).

Mention of the sabbath rest (Josh 23:1; cf. 21:44) is followed by the record of an assembly (or two assemblies if Joshua 23 and 24 describe separate occasions) called by Joshua to set the kingdom in order. Like his master Moses, Joshua at the close of his life summoned the nation to renew their covenantal vows to the Lord. The elements of the treaty pattern that informed the Sinaitic and Deuteronomic Covenant documentation are found again in Joshua 24. Thus, preamble (v. 20); historical prologue (vv. 2b-13; cf. vv. 17,18); stipulations (vv. 14,23,25); document clause

– incorporation of this treaty in the Torah documentation (v. 26); sanctions (vv. 19,20). Note also the common ceremonial features of ratificatory oath (vv. 15-24) and witnesses (vv. 22,26,27). Unlike the concluding covenant mediated by Moses, this was not a dynastic covenant. It did not appoint a successor to Joshua but rather marked the end of the Moses-Joshua phase of the establishing of the typological kingdom in Canaan.

Judges: Consolidation Phase. Though the Israelite tribes had gained firm control of the land through the decisive victories under Joshua, local centers of resistance remained. The task of eliminating the Canaanites carried over into the transitional period from Joshua to David. Consolidation of Israel's position was hampered, however, by their failing to prosecute the holy war and by their falling into idolatry. For these violations of the covenant they were given into the hands of their enemies (Judg 2:10-15), so that deliverance from oppression became a prominent facet of the struggle to complete their acquisition of the promised inheritance.

During this period prior to the Davidic monarchy and Solomonic temple on Zion, the royal tabernacle continued to bear witness to the reality of God's Presence. The mountain site of Zion on which God's house was ultimately to be located was among the pockets of resistance not yet overcome in the Joshuan phase of the conquest. This site (ruled back in Abraham's day by Melchizedek) was occupied by the Jebusites (Judg 1:8,21; cf. Num 13:29; Josh 11:3; 15:8; 18:16) and did not come entirely under Israel's control until David's day. Meanwhile the tent of meeting was located at Shiloh and other places (Josh 18:1; 1 Sam 21:1; cf. Mark 2:25,26; 2 Sam 6:12; 1 Chr 16:39).

The presence of the Lord God as Israel's actual, active Monarch was also manifested in the giving of oracular revelation through priestly mediation at the royal sanctuary and in the provision of Spirit-inspired Scriptures supplementing the foundational five books of Moses in an expanding covenantal canon. [On canon and covenant see *SBA* 21-110.] Further, the reality of God's kingly rule, directing and protecting his people, was evinced in his raising up specially endowed theocratic agents, prophets and judges. God's hand in this was the more apparent in that these offices were not transmitted through family descent but by direct, individual, charismatic appointment. Especially significant was the calling of the prophets by a visionary rapture into the Glory council on the heavenly Har Magedon, from which they were then dispatched to earth as the spokesmen of Yahweh to his covenant people (cf., e.g., Isa 6:1ff.; Ezekiel 1–3). Most public of the evidence of the intervention of Israel's divine King in her history were the remarkable exploits of those on whom the Spirit came mightily to be judges (Judg 3:10; 6:34; 11:29; 13:25; 14:6,19; 15:14; Heb 11:32ff.) and prophets, like unto Moses even if not his equal in the performance of awesome deeds (Deut 34:10-12).

In the Joshuan phase of the conquest we noted the theophanic appearing of the Lord in the form of the Angel of the Lord (Josh 5:13-15), warrior captain of the army of the Lord. The divine Angel appears again in the period of the judges, now in the new role of God's prophet conducting the covenant lawsuit, a major function of the Israelite prophets from Samuel to the close of the typological kingdom order (Judg 2:1-3; 5:23; 6:8-10; 10:11-14; 13:3ff.). [See further, *IOS* 75-79.]

The Theocratic Monarchy

The Promised King. Completion of the typological picture of the kingdom in the land of Canaan required the fulfillment of the king promise given to Abraham. The Deuteronomic Covenant had anticipated that after taking possession of the land and settling down there Israel would desire a king to be appointed over them and it had prescribed the kind of king they should have, one chosen by God and observant of the words of the Torah-covenant of the Lord his God (Deut 17:14-20). After the delay of the period of the judges and the disappointment of Saul's term as king, the covenantally promised and prescribed kingship was realized in the divine choice and Spirit-anointing of David for this office of vicegerent of Yahweh in the theocratic kingdom.

Conquest and Victor's Palace. We meet again here the pattern of conquest followed by the building of a royal residence for the victor. [For an extended treatment of the interrelated themes of temple construction, kingship, conquest and covenant, see *SBA* 76-88 and *GOM* 146-162.] This pattern appears whether the history is viewed from the perspective of David or of the Lord as the royal warrior. In the case of David the record of the building of his palace (2 Sam 5:11) is embedded in accounts of his military victories over the Jebusites at the fortress of Zion (2 Sam 5:6-10) and over the Philistines (2 Sam 5:17ff.). The connection with the capture of Zion is particularly significant since that was to be the site of David's palace – and of the Lord's royal house. 2 Sam 7:1 brings into parallelism as complementary sabbath components David's victorious emergence from the strife of battle and his palace residence: "When the king took up residence in his palace and the Lord had given him rest from all the enemies around him." The rest from enemies is the sabbath as completion of kingdom work and the palace residence is the sabbath as the rest of session on the throne of the kingdom.

As 2 Sam 7:1 indicates, David's victories were the Lord's victories (cf. 2 Sam 7:11). To the same effect is the oracular word to David during his battle against the Philistines, instructing him to move out promptly at the sound of marching in the tops of the balsam trees, "for then Yahweh has gone out before you to smite the army of the Philistines" (2 Sam 5:24). Similarly Psalm 89 extols Yahweh as the warrior-savior of his people, who declares concerning David, "I will crush his enemies before him and strike down those who hate him" (v. 23 [24]; cf. Ps 132:17,18). Recognizing that it was the Lord who had defeated the enemies and that this triumphant prosecution of the holy war called for enthronement in a palace-sanctuary, David proposed the building of such a royal house for God (2 Sam 7:1f.; Ps 132:2-5). The Lord's endorsement of this project came in the form of a covenant (2 Sam 7:5-16; 1 Chr 17:4-14; 2 Sam 23:5; Pss 132:11,12; 89:3,4,19-37).

The Davidic Covenant. Conjoined with the commission to build the temple in the Davidic Covenant was the Lord's commitment to perpetuate the dynasty of David unto the coming of the son of David who was David's Lord. Royal dynasty and temple building are closely related matters, since temple building was a task of kings and divine appointment to construct the temple was a validation of an individual's right to the crown. In the covenant with David the perpetuation of dynasty and the construction of the temple are contemplated in relation to both the typological order of the Old Covenant and the messianic order of the New Covenant.

The dynastic guarantees were a grant to David as the faithful servant (1 Kgs 3:6), who had waged the Lord's battle, secured the mountain city for his enthronement, and brought the ark-throne to Zion, the city of David, so identifying his kingdom as God's kingdom (1 Chr 13:1-13; 15:23-28). Significantly, the record of the Davidic Covenant comes immediately (2 Samuel 7) after the account of David's service (2 Samuel 5 and 6). In this respect David was a type of Christ, who earns the eternal kingship by fulfilling the intratrinitarian covenant of works, triumphing in the Har Magedon conflict over Satan. In so far as the dynastic grant to David referred to the typological level of the kingdom it was an administration of the Sinaitic covenant of works, and accordingly it included a warning that for failure to obey the law of the theocratic king, occupants of David's throne would incur the curse of the covenant (2 Sam 7:14; Ps 89:30-32). At the same time, in so far as there was a reference to the New Covenant level of the kingdom, the Davidic Covenant was an administration of the Abrahamic Covenant as a covenant of sovereign grace and the promised dynasty of David culminated in the Messiah, the king in whom the dynasty was confirmed for ever (2 Sam 7:15,16; Ps 89:3,4,28f.,33ff.).

Similarly, the building of God's house was realized at both the typological level in the Solomonic temple (cf. 2 Sam 7:12,13; 1 Kgs 5:3-5; 8:17-21; 1 Chr 28:2,3) and the antitypical level in the church-temple built by Christ through the Spirit – the former within the program and under the terms of the Mosaic administration of the Law and the latter in accordance with the gospel principle of the Covenant of Grace.

Temple Construction, a Re-creation. The literary form of the biblical narrative of the construction of the Solomonic temple follows a pattern found in extra-biblical accounts of temple building at that time. "Standard elements included: the decision and commission to build (1 Kgs 5:15-19); the acquisition of building materials (1 Kgs 5:15-26) and drafting of craftsmen (1 Kgs 5:13ff.; 7:13); description of the temple and its furnishings (1 Kings 6 and 7) with statement of completion as specified (1 Kgs 6:9,14,38); dedication and deity's entry of his residence (1 Kgs 8:1-11,62-66); dedicatory prayer (1 Kgs 8:12-61); blessings and curses (1 Kgs 9:19)" [*GOM* 148].

The identity of Israel's tabernacle-temple as an earthly replica of the heavenly temple was evidenced by its architecture, furnishings, and theophanic resident (cf. Heb 9:11,23f.). The Glory-cloud that filled the structure was the visible manifestation of the Glory-Spirit who occupied – who *was* – the invisible, archetypal temple. Moreover this cloud theophany was represented architecturally by the two bronze pillars at the sanctuary entrance. These corresponded to the theophanic pillars of cloud and fire, themselves anthropomorphic symbols of the legs of God. The cherubim-guarded ark in the holy of holies was clearly a replica of the cherubim-attended heavenly throne. The bronze altar, understood as a stylized mountain, was an icon of the mountain of God and thus of the heavenly kingdom. The cosmic nature of the archetypal temple in its Glory and sub-Glory dimensions, the cosmos being conceived of as a three-storied house, was mirrored in the ectypal sanctuary's horizontal floor plan with holy of holies, holy place, and outer court. Or if a two-level model of the cosmos is assumed, Israel's sanctuary copied this in the vertical sectioning of each of the three divisions of its over-all floor plan into the two spheres of heaven and earth. Temple building was then a process of cosmic re-creation, a redemptive (re-)making of heaven and earth. [See *IOS* 39-42.]

Besides reflecting the primal creation house as a cosmic whole the Solomonic temple recalled the microcosmic projection of the celestial Glory-temple in Eden. Edenic floral motifs appeared in the decorative detailing of the temple and it was located in a paradise-like land flowing with milk and honey. Moreover it was situated in a holy land, on a mountain of God.

This mountain site of the temple heightened its cosmic, heavenly temple symbolism. For Mount Zion, as we have noted earlier, is identified in Ps 48:2 as the heights of Zaphon, a synonym of har mô^{c}ēd, Har Magedon, preeminent figure for God's holy heaven. Also, like the temple, Zion recalled the original paradise sanctuary; associated with Zion-Jerusalem in its eschatological stage are the Edenic features of river and tree of life (Pss 46:4; 48:2). And, most obviously, Mount Zion was a restoration of the mountain of God in Eden. Like that Har Magedon, Zion was the cultic center, the focal point of the kingdom, the place to which God's people were gathered, the mountain of assembly for exalting the name of Yahweh, the Great King, in worship, the mountain of the judicial council for the execution of divine judgment. "From Zion, the perfection of beauty, God shines forth . . . he summons the heavens above and the earth for the judging of his people: 'Gather unto me those committed to me, who made a covenant with me by sacrifice'" (Ps 50:2,4f.).

Like the Ararat-ark the Zion-temple was a prophetic type of the consummate cosmic house of God, the new heavens and earth, the New Jerusalem, urban holy of holies on the great high mountain, the ultimate Har Magedon.

Enthronement of the King of Glory on Zion. Once the temple was completed and the ark of the covenant installed in the holy of holies (1 Kgs 7:51–8:9), the climactic event took place – the advent of the King of Glory in the theophanic cloud and his entrance into the temple to assume his throne between the cherubim (1 Kgs 8:10,11; 2 Chr 5:13,14; 7:1-3). As was the case at the completing of the tabernacle (Exod 40:34,35), the Glory-Spirit filled the temple on Zion, so identifying with it and proclaiming it to be the earthly manifestation of the Glory-temple of the heavenly Har Magedon.

Since the Solomonic temple was a representation of the cosmic creational kingdom with its Eden hub, the enthronement of Yahweh in this royal house on Zion signified that while he was covenantally identified with Israel as their theocratic King he was the Sovereign over all nations, Ruler of heaven and earth. Solomon recognized that the temple he built was only a miniature symbol of the heavenly Glory-Temple, itself only a creational revelation of the Creator God, pointing to the Eternal, the uncontainable, incomprehensible One before and apart from creation (1 Kgs 8:27; 2 Chr 6:18; cf. Isa 66:1,2; Acts 7:48-50).

It is as Creator of all that the Lord is Owner-King of all, all nature, all nations (Pss 24:1,2; 89:9-13; 95:3-5; 96; 97:1-9). His universal kingship thus obtains from the founding of the world (Ps 93:1,2). Indeed, the divine Presence over the deep and darkness in the beginning as a Glory-Spirit-Temple was already a manifestation of God as King enthroned in the midst of the celestial council. If we speak of the Glory Spirit's occupying the holy of holies in Solomon's temple as an enthronement we are not suggesting that God's kingship was only then initiated. It was not as though God's triumphs over the enemies in David's age had attained a kingship not possessed before. These triumphs were rather a maintaining and enforcing of the everlasting sovereignty of the Glory-King of Har Magedon in the face of Satan's continuing challenge. Yahweh's enthronement in the royal house on Zion was simply a timely, typological statement of his perpetual status as King of kings.

Yahweh's residence in his holy house was a royal session. The residing was a presiding. And such a rest of divine enthronement is the essence of the divine sabbath, the never ending seventh day of creation, which brought into a new, permanent phase the reality of the Glory-Spirit enthronement present from the beginning of creation. [Cf. *KP* 34-38.] That consummating of the original creation process in God's royal sabbatical session was redemptively recapitulated in the history of the production of the Solomonic temple. As we observed above, Solomon's temple was a representation of the cosmos and the constructing of it was a (re-)creation process. And in this recapitulation of creation on Zion, Yahweh's climactic enthronement-residence in the temple figures as the equivalent of the archetypal sabbath rest of the Creator.

Celebrating the event the Psalmist declares: "Yahweh has chosen Zion, he has desired it for his habitation. This is my resting place for ever more. Here I will sit enthroned" (Ps 132:13,14). Reflecting this same sabbatical concept earlier in the Psalm he prays: "Arise, Yahweh, from your royal resting place; arise from the ark of your sovereignty" (v. 8; cf. Num 10:35,36), the petition with which Solomon concluded his doxological prayer in the course of the festivities marking the completion of the temple project (2 Chr 6:41).

Being a recapitulation of the creational sabbath, God's enthronement in Solomon's temple was a typal anticipation of God's eternal sabbath-enthronement on the Har Magedon of the new heaven and earth, itself a continuation of the seventh day of creation.

From the beginning God held out to his people the eschatological prospect of participating in his sabbath rest. Agreeably, in the prototypal portrayal of the eschaton on Zion a sabbath rest for Israel is associated with Yahweh's sabbatical enthronement. Solomon extols the Lord for this when blessing the assembly gathered from the full extent of the promised kingdom to celebrate the completion of the temple (1 Kgs 8:65): "Blessed be Yahweh who has given rest to his people Israel according to all that he promised" (1 Kgs 8:56).

The sabbatical character of the divine enthronement episode is underscored by the double seven day duration (cf. 1 Kgs 8:65) of the observances that initiated the use of the temple house as the royal habitation of Yahweh, King of Israel. (For ḥānak, usually rendered "dedicate," to denote beginning the use of a house, cf. Deut 20:5.)

At Ararat, Noah consecrated the ark-kingdom to the Lord by erecting an altar and sacrificing token offerings emblematic of the kingdom – a priestly act well-pleasing to him (Gen 8:20,21). Similarly, king Solomon and all Israel with him confessed the temple-kingdom on Zion to be the Lord's domain. In token of this they consecrated to him altar offerings beyond the capacity of the regular bronze altar to handle. And God revealed his acceptance of this priestly tribute by a descent in fire to consume the sacrifices (1 Kgs 8:62-64; 2 Chr 7:1-7).

So was perfected the Mount Zion version of the Har Magedon schema, prototype of the days of the Son of Man, the antitypical history that issues in the consummation of the Har Magedon reign of the triune King of Glory.

Chapter Eleven

Har Magedon in the Messianic Finale

Danielic Preview

Introduction. Our transition from the old typal pattern to the New Covenant stage of the Har Magedon warfare will be by way of the prophetic visions of the Book of Daniel. They bridge the two in that they set forth clearly both the closing of the old order in the destruction of the theocratic kingdom of Israel and the establishment of the new messianic order. As we shall see, they reveal how the inauguration of the New Covenant antitype occurs before the termination of the Old Covenant type so that the new overlaps the old for a time.

Besides clarifying the nature of the linkage between the two eras, Daniel's prophecies provide an introduction to our survey of the Har Magedon paradigm in the messianic age by displaying that complete pattern within a relatively brief compass and in graphic fashion. Indeed, the seventy weeks prophecy of Daniel 9 by itself contains almost all the major elements of the pattern from the initiation of the New Covenant to the consummation of the kingdom, including a remarkably full revelation of the Messiah, the guarantor of the covenant. This passage will be treated at some length presently.

Daniel 2

Mountain of God imagery figures prominently in the vision of Daniel 2 (cf. Dan 11:45). There are two mountains. The first represents the Old Covenant kingdom of Israel, Zion, the provenance of Messiah, whose first advent is symbolized by the cutting of a rock from this mountain (Dan 2:34,45). Subsequently, the rock strikes and pulverizes the great image, symbol of the evil world power, and thereupon the rock assumes the form of a world-filling mountain (Dan 2:35,44). This portrays the second advent of Christ, the final judgment of the world, and the consummating of God's kingdom. The second mountain, the cosmic mountain that the rock becomes, is the antitypical Zion, the eternal Har Magedon.

The symbolism of the two mountains, one local, the other cosmic, brings out both the type-antitype continuity of the Mosaic and messianic kingdoms and at the same time the passing away of Zion, the earthly mountain of God, once the foundation was laid for the antitypical reality which it prefigured, the heavenly, everlasting Har Magedon.

This Daniel 2 vision of the eschatological enlargement of the mountain-kingdom echoes the Isaianic prophecy that at the end of the days the mountain of Yahweh's house would be exalted to the highest elevation, as the mount of gathering of all nations (Isa 2:2).

Daniel 9

The prophetic vision of the seventy weeks (Dan 9:24-27) was conveyed to Daniel by Gabriel in 539, the first year of Darius/Cyrus. [On this vision, see *CSW* 452-469.] According to Jer 25:11,12 the fall of Babylon would signal the end of an allotted seventy year captivity of Israel, and similarly in Jer 29:10 the Lord promises that upon the completion of the seventy years he would bring his people back from exile to their homeland. Daniel had witnessed the threatened judgment on Babylon in that first year of Cyrus, a round seventy years from the beginning of the exile, reckoned from the siege of Jerusalem by Nebuchadnezzar in 605 (recorded in Dan 1:1). It was a more precise seventy years if the captivity is reckoned from the death of Josiah in 609 (as is done in the genealogy of Jesus in Matthew

1). And now that Babylon had fallen Daniel's concern was that the seventy appointed years were completed according to his study of Jer 25:12 (cf. Dan 9:2), and yet the desolation of Jerusalem continued. If the Lord was to prove faithful to his promise, implicit in Jer 25:11,12 and explicit in Jer 29:10, he must not delay taking action to restore the mountain of his sanctuary (cf. Dan 9:16,20), and for such prompt restoration Daniel pleaded in his confessional prayer (Dan 9:3ff.; cf. Lev 26:40ff.).

In immediate response, Gabriel assured Daniel that God's decree (dābār) initiating the restoration had already been issued (yāṣāʾ) while he was praying (Dan 9:23). And, indeed, before Cyrus' first year was concluded, this heavenly decree was registered in earthly history in the decree of Cyrus legitimizing the return of the exiles and the rebuilding of the temple at Jerusalem – true to the prophecy of Jeremiah, as the biblical historians observe (2 Chr 36:22,23; Ezra 1:1-4).

After assuring Daniel that the restoration decree (dābār) had already been issued (yāṣāʾ), Gabriel proceeded to expound that decree in the vision (marʾeh) of the seventy weeks (v. 23b). The equivalence of the decree and the vision is evident from the parallelism of dābār and marʾeh in v. 23b. Moreover, in v. 25 the starting point of the seventy weeks is said to be the going forth of the decree to rebuild Jerusalem. That this is the decree which according to v. 23a had already gone forth is clear from the way v. 25 repeats the key terms of v. 23, namely, dābār, "decree," and yāṣāʾ (in the nominal form mōṣāʾ), "going forth." This evidence that the seventy weeks were already under way, together with the necessity for immediate action on the Lord's part in order to fulfill the promissory prophecy of Jer 29:10, puts it beyond question that the seventy weeks of Dan 9:24 began in that very year, 539 BC. Since the Messiah and the fall of Jerusalem in 70 AD are features of the seventy weeks, that period is longer than a literal 490 years. The seventy weeks of this vision must then be figurative.

The symbolism is that of ten Jubilee periods, which span all the history of God's kingdom from the typal restoration of Zion initiated in 539 BC to the final restoration and the eternal Jubilee. Confirming the presence of the Jubilee concept is the first subdivision of the seventy weeks, a Jubilee period of seven weeks (Dan 9:25). This one Jubilee period is set aside for the restoration of the old Jerusalem. That was the particular concern expressed in Daniel's prayer, but the divine response, while not neglecting the immediate concern, looks beyond it and reveals the prospect of the antitypical restoration of God's kingdom in the New Jerusalem, which would be the outcome of the ten Jubilees as a whole.

The vision opens with a declaration of the purposes the seventy weeks were designed to accomplish (v. 24). These are stated in six clauses (arranged in three pairs) suggestive of a creation motif, with six divine works culminating in the eternal Sabbath/Jubilee rest. The first pair, warning that a judicial end would be put to transgressing of the covenant, advises us that the restoration of Jerusalem in Daniel's time would not provide the permanent solution; it would not be the final, for ever manifestation of the kingdom. As the Jubilee symbol of the seven weeks intimates, that Old Covenant restoration event was indeed a triumphant redemptive deliverance and renewal, comparable to the exodus. But Israel was still under the Law, their possession of the typological kingdom still under the works principle, and like their forefathers they would inevitably fail. Once again Jerusalem would fall and the apostates would be dispersed. And this tragic termination of the Old Covenant order in 70 AD looms very large in the following verses of this vision.

If beyond the restoration from Babylon there was to be another national fall of Israel, there was also to be beyond that another, greater return from captivity, a new, antitypal exodus. This future hope is disclosed in the second and third pair of purposes presented in v. 24. These point us to Christ and the New Covenant consummation of the kingdom. The second pair, "to make atonement for iniquity and to bring in everlasting righteousness," is clearly a description of the saving mission of Christ Jesus. And the consummation of God's cosmic temple is in view in the prospect of the anointing of the holy of holies contained in the third pair of goals.

In Dan 9:25a the course of the seventy weeks is traced from the initiating decree to the Messiah-Ruler/Prince (Māšîaḥ Nāgîd), the coming One who ushers in the climactic seventieth week. The figure of the Māšîaḥ had been anticipated in the mention of the anointing (the verb māšaḥ) in the last of the purpose clauses in v. 24. Now our eyes are directed to him as the central, totally dominant figure of the vision, the One who will fulfill all the objectives of the seventy weeks – the judgment of the old order, the inauguration of the New Covenant, and the completing of the holy house of God on Har Magedon. As the prophecy unfolds he is designated by the two components of his compound title separately, thus Māšîaḥ in v. 26a and Nāgîd in v. 26b.

The sixty-nine weeks leading up to Messiah-Ruler are divided into seven weeks and sixty-two weeks (v. 25a). The time of restoration (the Jubilee period of seven weeks) is thus distinguished from the subsequent time of declension (the sixty-two weeks). Dan 9:25b focuses on this seven week period of the restoration of Jerusalem, Daniel's immediate concern, promising the successful rebuilding of the temple-city in spite of the opposition of adversaries (as later recorded in the historical accounts of 2 Chronicles, Ezra, and Nehemiah).

The seventieth week is the subject of the closing two verses of the vision. The opening event of this week is identified in v. 26a as following "after the sixty-two weeks" (i.e., after the sixty-ninth week). Reference is made to the week in its entirety in the phrase "in the course of the one week" (v. 27a). And the fall of Jerusalem is said to transpire "in the middle of the week" (v. 27b).

It is important for the proper interpretation of vv. 26 and 27 to recognize they have a parallel structure with correspondence between the successive three parts contained in each of the two verses. The A-sections deal with the covenant of the seventieth week, the New Covenant; both the B and C sections, with the terminating judgment on the Old Covenant order. The fact that the vision thus concludes with a heavy emphasis on the disaster of 70 AD reminds us that this vision belongs to the canon of the Old Covenant, where the divine lawsuit against the apostatizing nation is a major rubric of the prophets' message. Yet, while prosecuting the lawsuit of the Mosaic Covenant, the prophets also proclaimed the promises of the Abrahamic Covenant and thereby were heralds of the Messiah and the New Covenant. So too the prophecy of the seventy weeks makes known that before the collapse of the typal kingdom, the foundations of the enduring messianic kingdom would be laid.

A key term from the covenant vocabulary is found in each of the corresponding A-sections of Dan 9:26 and 27. In v. 27a it is bĕrît ("covenant") itself. In v. 26a it is kārat, the term commonly used for the cutting ritual in the ratification of covenants. This covenantal significance of the kārat act is then what is in view in the statement that "Messiah will be cut off and there will not be to him" (v. 26a). Resumed here are elements of Jacob's oracle concerning Judah (Gen 49:8-12) in which Judah's messianic descendant, Shiloh, is the coming one (as he is also designated in Dan 9:26b), the one to whom the Davidic sceptre and universal allegiance belong (cf. Ezek 21:27). Dan 9:26a prophesies that at his advent Messiah will not receive the honor rightfully his: "there will not be to him" the submission due to him as divine king. Instead he will be delivered over to death by the Old Covenant community, which will thereby fill up the measure of their iniquity. Yet in the unfathomable wisdom of God this cutting off of the Messiah is the legal basis for the New Covenant; his blood is "the blood of the covenant poured out for many for the forgiveness of sins" (Matt 26:28; Mark 14:24; Luke 22:20; 1 Cor 11:25).

It is with this messianic act of inaugurating the New Covenant that the seventieth week begins. Then in the course of that "one week" the Messiah will make the covenant to prevail (higbîr). He, the one, will succeed in bringing to realization all the blessings of the Covenant of Grace in behalf of "the many" (cf. Isa 53:11,12) – such is the assurance of Dan 9:27a, complementing the covenantal declaration of v. 26a. Higbîr does not refer to the initial making of a covenant but to the honoring and carrying out of the terms of an existing covenant. [On the verb gābar, see *CSW* 464-467.] The higbîr of v. 27a is not then synonymous with the kārat of v. 26a. The kārat-ratification of the covenant marks the commencement of the seventieth week; higbîr refers to the ensuing course of the covenant to the end of the seventieth week.

There should be no doubt that Messiah-Ruler is the subject of higbîr; he is the subject of all the acts in Dan 9:26,27. Significant in this regard is the relation of these verses to Isaiah 9 and 10, especially the dependence on Isa 10:21ff. attested by the unmistakable borrowings of the Isaianic thought and terminology. In Isa 9:6 [5] the Messiah is identified as ʾēl gibbôr, "the mighty God," and then in Isa 10:21 this messianic ʾēl gibbôr appears as the God of the covenant remnant in the midst of those acts of judgment that are prophesied in Dan 9:26b,c and 27b,c. Clearly, the messianic gibbôr figure of Isa 10:21 is the inspiration for the use of the related verbal form higbîr in Dan 9:27a, and Messiah-Ruler, whose name is ʾēl gibbôr, is the one who accomplishes the fulfilling of the covenant denoted by higbîr.

The cutting off of the Messiah (Dan 9:26a) is to be related to the second pair of purposes presented in v. 24. His undergoing the death of the Cross was the definitive act of his obedience, performed as the federal representative of "the many," his elect people. It was an atoning sacrifice for their sins (purpose three in v. 24). And it brought in everlasting righteousness (purpose four in v. 24); it was the one act of righteousness, the probationary victory over Satan that won for the redeemed entitlement to the everlasting blessedness of heaven.

Messiah's higbîr accomplishment (Dan 9:27a), his making the covenant to prevail for the elect, is to be related to the third pair of purposes in Dan 9:24. It moves beyond the securing of entitlement to heaven to the actual bestowal of the eternal inheritance. It involves the coming of the kingdom in fulfillment of all that God promised through his prophets (purpose five). As depicted in purpose six, this ultimate eschatological event is an anointing of the holy of holies. In view is the consummation of the Glory-Spirit temple. That Omega-event was typified in the anointing of the Mosaic tabernacle by oil and by Glory-cloud and in the similar filling of the Solomonic house of God by the Shekinah-Spirit. Like the final Har Magedon epiphany these episodes were occasions of divine temple entrance and enthronement. As observed above, the anointing (māšaḥ) of v. 24 must be related to the Māšîaḥ of v. 26a. We do not have to choose between identifying the anointed holy of holies as the anointed person or as the anointed Spirit-temple architecturally conceived. For Messiah, the Spirit-anointed person, is himself the temple of the Glory-Spirit (cf. John 2:19,20). [Cf. *GOM* 231-232.]

Daniel's intercession had been in behalf of the devastated temple mount of the old order (Dan 9:20) and he had been assured that the restoration he requested had already begun (vv. 23,25). Then in 9:26a Gabriel's prophecy had jumped ahead to the New Covenant order Messiah would institute. Now in 9:26b the subject is the relationship of this Messiah to the temple-city of the old order, which had been restored in Daniel's day but since then would have degenerated into such a perverse spiritual state that they had repudiated and cut off their promised Messiah (v. 26a). However, God had raised his Son from the dead and exalted him to his heavenly throne as a Nāgîd, royal ruler, over all nations. That is the title Isaiah gave Messiah when declaring that he would be the fulfillment of God's everlasting covenant with David (Isa 55:4), whose royal status had also been so designated (2 Sam 5:12; 6:21; 7:8; 2 Chr 6:5). Attached to the title Māšîaḥ in Dan 9:25, Nāgîd underscored Messiah's kingly office and now used separately in v. 26b it is the appropriate designation for Messiah as the ruler of Israel who brings judgment on the rebellious nation: "The army of the coming Ruler will destroy the temple city."

Jesus clearly refers to this passage in the parable of the wedding banquet, where he likens the Lord to a king who was enraged against his subjects for their violence against his messengers and "sent his army and destroyed those murderers and burned their city" (Matt 22:7; cf. 21:33-44). The destruction of Jerusalem by the Roman army in 70 AD is of course what is being predicted, the Roman army being called the Lord's army in that he sovereignly used it to accomplish his purposes of judgment. In Dan 9:26b the identification of the earthly army that would destroy the temple-city as the army of the messianic Nāgîd is comparable to the Lord's heavenly decree to restore Jerusalem (9:23) finding earthly expression in the decree of Cyrus, whose heart was moved by the Lord to act as a messianic shepherd of Israel (cf. Isa 44:26–45:13).

Paralleling Dan 9:26b, v. 27b foretells again the divine judgment on the temple-city. The correspondence of these two passages is highlighted by the sound and sense echoing of the verb yašḥît, "destroy" (v. 26b) in the verb yašbît, "make cease, bring to an end" (v. 27b), the latter a pun-reversal of the sabbath blessings of restoration in the Jubilee symbolism of this vision. Messiah-Ruler (subject of the action in v. 27b as in v. 26b) "will make sacrifice and oblation cease." As a priest who offers the true, once-for-all sacrifice, Christ made obsolete in principle the typal sacrifices of the Old Covenant. But the point of v. 27b, in correspondence to v. 26b, is rather that Christ as Ruler and Judge effected the outward cessation of the old sacrificial system by destroying the old temple. A significant new feature added in v. 27b is that Christ's judgment on apostate Jerusalem takes place "in the middle of the week" – the "one week" (the seventieth week) just mentioned in v. 27a. While the seventieth week as a whole is devoted to fulfilling for those in Christ the blessing sanctions of the New Covenant as the final administration of the Covenant of Grace, the terminating curse sanction of the Old Covenant is executed within this epoch. There is thus an overlapping of the Old and New Covenants, the old temple order retaining a qualified legitimacy for a while after the inaugurating of the New Covenant, even though the latter meant the obsolescence in principle of the old order (cf. Heb 8:13). The overlap is the period from the Cross to 70 AD and the practice of the apostles and early church, especially in Jerusalem, as recorded in the Book of Acts was in accord with this overlap situation.

The division of the seventieth week in the middle produces two symbolic periods of three and a half years each. The first is the overlap period extending to the fall of Jerusalem in 70 AD. The second covers the history of the church from its disengagement from the collapsed typal order in 70 AD to the consummation. The second symbolic three and a half year era reappears in the New Testament Apocalypse as a symbolic period which we will be identifying with the interim leading up to the antichrist crisis and the second advent of Christ.

The correspondence of Dan 9:26c and 27c is evidenced in their common emphasis on the finality of the judgment on Jerusalem expressed by the terms qēṣ, "end," and šeṭep, "overflooding" (cf. Isa 8:8) in v. 26c and kālāh, "complete destruction," in v. 27c. Even more clearly the parallelism appears in their both concluding with a reference to decreed desolations: neḥĕreṣet šômēmôt (v. 26c) and neḥĕrāṣāh . . . šōmēm (v. 27c).

Along with the overwhelming finality of the judgment, Dan 9:27 stresses the extremity of the offense that demanded such total desolation. It speaks of the messianic Judge as the Desolator (mĕšōmēm), the one who brings desolation upon the kānāp, "wing," of abominations. Citing this in his discourse on the coming fall of Jerusalem (Matt 24:15), Jesus foretells the existence (hestos) of "the abomination of desolation in the holy place." In this citation the "wing" of Dan 9:27c is absorbed into "the holy place."

In Dan 9:27c kānāp may be translated "extremity"(cf. Isa 24:16; Num 15:38) and the "extremity of abominations" understood as the turning of God's house, the holy place of prayer, into a den of satanic thieves (Matt 3:7; 12:34; 23:32,33; John 8:44) conspiring against the Most High and his Anointed (Acts 4:25-27). In effect, the temple itself as the embodiment of Israel's ultimate apostasy would be "the extremity of abominations" (Dan 9:27c) and the "abomination of desolation" (Matt 24:15).

Another possibility, suggested by the reference to "the wing of the temple" in Matt 4:15 and Luke 4:9, is that the kānāp of Dan 9:27c should be taken more concretely as the pinnacle of the temple. This could be a case of synecdoche, the pinnacle standing for the whole temple, which would again be "the abomination of desolation." Or the "abominations" might be an abstract designation for the defiled temple, with kānāp denoting the high point of the structure, an architectural figure for the heights of devilish defiance against the Lord of the Har Magedon temple-city on the part of the temple officialdom.

On any of these views of the kānāp, the seventy weeks prophecy foretells that Mount Zion, epitome of the old order, would become a pseudo-Har Magedon, provoking the wrath of Israel's rejected king and the sending of his army to reduce the abominable temple-city to desolation. With that word, "the desolate" (šōmēm), the vision ends. The different forms of the verb šāmēm found in Dan 9:27c are not to be confused. Měšōmēm denotes the actor, Messiah-Ruler, the Desolator. Šōmēm denotes the object of the action, Jerusalem, the desolate, the devastated.

Decretive terminology appears throughout the vision of the seventy weeks (including the opening and closing clauses – v. 24a and v. 27c) identifying the various events as the consequences of sovereign divine determination. The dominant picture is that of the Lord as "the great and fearful God who keeps covenant" (Dan 9:4). He executes the curse sanctions of the Torah covenant of works; hence unfaithful Jerusalem is devastated, once and again (cf. Dan 9:12,27). But he also unfailingly proves himself to be the covenant-keeping God in bringing to pass the promised blessing sanctions of the Covenant of Grace. And so before the old Jerusalem suffers its final devastation, the promised Messiah-Ruler inaugurates the New Covenant. Then in the course of the seventieth week, carrying out the divine decree, he brings his redeemed people into the fullness of their Jubilee inheritance. Both his terminating of the old order and his consummating of the new order proclaim the sovereignty of King Jesus, Māšîaḥ Nāgîd.

The prophecies of Daniel have provided us with an entrance into our survey of the Har Magedon paradigm in the messianic age. Next we shall examine the individual elements of that pattern in their historical sequence, using additional Old Testament and relevant New Testament data.

Christ, Covenant Grantee and Guarantor

Introduction: Covenant Theology. Via the prototypal Har Magedon kingdoms identified with Mount Ararat and Mount Zion we have now come to their antitype, the heavenly Har Magedon attained under the

New Covenant. This ultimate Glory realm is secured by the meritorious works of Christ Jesus. In accordance with the Father's commitments to the Son in their covenant of works, the Son became the grantee of the everlasting kingdom as the reward for his undertaking the role of second Adam and his triumphing in the probationary task of redemptive warfare against Satan, the archfoe of the holy mountain.

Exalted to the throne of Har Magedon on high, the Son in turn administers a covenant with his people in which by grace they become co-heirs of the kingdom with him. It is on the legal grounds of his one act of righteousness performed as their representative and credited to them that they become co-grantees with him. By his obedience as their Probationer, Christ the second Adam becomes the guarantor for his people of the covenanted kingdom of which he is the primary grantee.

Actually the Son's administering of the Covenant of Grace began at the initiation of redemption immediately after the Fall, the New Covenant being the culmination of the series of redemptive administrations. Because of this early origin of the Covenant of Grace we introduced a discussion of this covenant above in connection with our treatment of the primal prophecy of Messiah as the coming victor of Har Magedon (see Chapter Eight). It was there observed that Christ's covenantal administration of redemptive blessings from the Fall onwards was in anticipation of his later successful probation in the fullness of time. So certain was the Son's obedience in his probationary mission as second Adam, on which the elect's reception of eternal salvation and the Glory-kingdom depended, that he could engage in ministering the benefits of the gospel of grace to his people by the Spirit long before he came to earth. Our previous discussion in Chapter Eight should also be consulted for its comments on the relationship between the Father's eternal covenant of works with the Son and the Lord's covenant of grace with his people. It was there argued that although these two are interrelated they are to be carefully distinguished from one another, one notable distinguishing feature being the different roles of the Son in the two arrangements – Servant in the intratrinitarian covenant but Lord in the covenant of grace.

Har Magedon Setting

Christ's covenantal task was performed in a Har Magedon setting. For the typal kingdom of the Old Covenant with Mount Zion, the typal Mount of Assembly, at the center was the venue of his earthly life and messianic vocation.

It is not only where the temple mount itself is the location of Jesus' activities that the Har Magedon motif appears in the Gospels. It may also be seen in certain instances where we are told that some other mountain was the site of an outstanding event in the life of our Lord. Thus, early on in Jesus' ministry his foundational exposition of the nature and norms of his kingdom and associated covenant sanctions, beatitudes and curse threats, was delivered on a mountain (Matt 5:1). The strong resemblance of this to the giving of the foundational covenantal instructions at the typal Har Magedon of Sinai suggests that the mountain of "the sermon on the mount" too should be perceived as a Har Magedon.

Matt 28:16-20 records another Sinai-like covenantal proclamation on a mountain, this episode being near the close of Jesus' earthly ministry. Like the Matt 5:1 mountain, this mountain is in Galilee. (We shall comment further below on the nature of this so-called "Great Commission" as a promulgation of the New Covenant.)

The transfiguration of Jesus (Matt 17:1-13; Mark 9:2-13; Luke 9:28-36) and his ascension (Acts 1:6-12) also transpired on mountains and both of these had the chief identifying feature of Har Magedon – the Glory-cloud manifestation of God, with attendant heavenly beings. At the transfiguration the Glory overshadowed the mount as at Sinai. Peter calls this divine manifestation "the sublime glory" and refers to the site as "the holy mountain" (2 Pet 1:17,18). At the ascension, the Glory-cloud served at once as insignia of deity, heavenly veil, and divine chariot, functions associated with it elsewhere (cf., e.g., Ps 104:1-3; Dan 9:13,14).

The phenomenon of a customary central Har Magedon in a constellation of occasional holy mountains is analogous to the situation with respect to altars in the typal kingdom of Israel. In the old order there was a central altar associated with the Glory-Presence, which became stationary in the temple on Zion when God chose that site as the permanent place of habitation for his name. While the Mosaic law of the central altar prescribed that the ordinary sacrificial service, as performed particularly at the three principal festivals, should take place there, allowance was made for special altars in accordance with the fundamental principle that altars were authorized at (though only at) places of divine revelation, particularly theophany (cf. Exod 20:24; Deut 12:5a,11; 27:5ff.). [On the law of the altar see further *TGK* 80-82.] In view of the symbolic import of the altar as a mountain of God, this pattern of altar distribution affords more than an analogy; it actually exemplifies the weaving of the Har Magedon motif into the total symbolic fabric of Jesus' ministry.

Also contributing to this extended Har Magedon rubric in the covenant community of Jesus' day were the synagogues. The very designation of these structures as "gathering" places identifies them with Har Magedon, the Mount of Gathering (and with the ʾōhel môʿēd, the tent of gathering). Moreover, the functions of synagogue gatherings – the worship of God and covenant instruction – were functions of the temple on Zion. The association of the synagogue gatherings with the Sabbath further marks the synagogues as extensions of the Zion/Har Magedon symbolism.

Although the typological setting of Jesus' mission served by its symbolic arrangements to explain the meaning of that mission, the actual significance and impact of what Jesus did transcended the typal order. The latter was only an outward sign of the antitypical reality projected into its midst. While Jesus honored the prescribed arrangements of the old Torah covenant under which he was born, his ministry was in fact a priestly service in the true, heavenly Har Magedon sanctuary (Heb 9:11; 8:2), a once-for-all saving accomplishment that rendered obsolete the Mosaic kingdom and its typal Har Magedon order (Heb 7:18,19; 8:13).

Intimations of the passing of the old order and the transformation of the people of God under the New Covenant into a global community can be detected in the various extensions of Har Magedon symbols from Zion throughout the typal kingdom. Even more clearly anticipative of this imminent new universalism was the association of Jesus with the outlying areas. He was known as Jesus of Nazareth – Nazareth in Galilee of the Gentiles. And, due in part to his rift with the authorities in Jerusalem (which betokened the collapse of that central typal Har Magedon), his ministry gravitated away from Judea to the area beyond the Jordan and especially towards Galilee, with forays into Samaria and the region of Tyre and Sidon. Of special interest in this connection is the Galilee location of the two Har Magedon mountain episodes that bracket Jesus' ministry in the Gospel of Matthew. All such instances of the movement towards Gentile territory signalized the passing away of the old typal economy and Jesus' bringing in of the new order of the fullness of the Gentiles, the cosmic order of the heavenly Har Magedon.

Defence of Har Magedon

The kingdom in Canaan was a reinstituting of the Har Magedon centered kingdom in Eden (with adjustments to the postlapsarian, redemptive situation). Agreeably, Jesus' earthly ministry within this Har Magedon framework of the Old Covenant resumed the probationary kind of arrangement that obtained under the creational covenant of works. And for Jesus, as for Adam in Eden, the probationary task was one of defending the sanctity of the mountain of God against Satan, would-be usurper of the Har Magedon throne.

The similarity of Jesus' probationary conflict with Satan to that of the first Adam is most pronounced in the episode of his temptation by the devil as narrated in the Gospels. There is again a manifestation of the devil, and his objectives and strategies have not changed. Again he tempts the guardian of the holy mount to break the covenant with the Lord and render allegiance to himself. And again his seductive suggestion is "that the dominion and the glory belonging to image-of-God status (peculiarly so in the case of the messianic Son of God) might be attained at the hidden expense of defying the authority of God as expressed in specific covenantal stipulations." [On this see further *KP* 144-145.]

The Har Magedon dimension of this encounter is highlighted by the lofty mountain location of two of the temptations (such being the imagery even if a visionary element is allowed in these episodes). One is a very high mountain with an overview of the world. What transpires here recalls Mount Nebo, to which the Lord took Moses and from whose summit he showed his servant the typal kingdom land. That land of the Canaanite nations was of course at the Lord's disposal; he covenanted it to Abraham and his descendants and he was about to give it to them (Deut 34:1-4; Josh 1:1-5). When Satan, the tempter, in a strikingly similar situation presents himself to the One greater than Moses, the New Covenant mediator, as having authority to grant a vicegerency (under himself) over the nations, he is assuming divine prerogatives. But the mountain he commandeers is a pseudo-Har Magedon, a false throne-center of the cosmos. And the position to which he lures Jesus the Christ is that of antichrist, the beast (cf. Rev 13:2).

The second mountain of temptation is Zion itself, site of the holy city and the temple, typal reproduction of the heavenly Har Magedon temple. The Har Magedon character of this site is made the more conspicuous by the Scripture passage from which Satan would draw a rationale for Jesus casting himself down (Ps 91:11,12; Matt 4:6; Luke 4:10,11). For Psalm 91 extols the Lord as the overshadowing One, avian imagery elsewhere used for the epiphanic Spirit, the Glory-Temple atop Har Magedon, whence the Lord sends angels to minister to his people. More precisely this temptation takes place on the "wing" (pterugion) of the temple, apparently an elevated architectural feature (Matt 4:5; Luke 4:9). Use of the word "wing" here evokes Dan 9:27c, where, as we have seen, "wing" was a key term in the description of Zion turned by Satan into an abominable pseudo-Har Magedon.

Conquest of the Dragon

The Gospels reveal Jesus in the process of fulfilling the primal prophecy of Gen 3:15. He appears as a divine warrior locked in mortal combat with the devil. From the temptation onward he is successful in his defence of Har Magedon, stalwartly resisting Satan's challenge to the holy mountain. But more than that, his victory is a dispossessing of Satan, an expropriating of his kingdom, and ultimately a trampling of the serpent's head, a slaying of the dragon. For a sketch of this conflict we shall draw upon two passages in the New Testament Apocalypse.

Revelation 12. Revelation 12 portrays the dramatic confrontation of Jesus and the devil, the decisive battle in the Har Magedon warfare, as an unsuccessful attempt by the Satanic dragon to devour the messianic child born to the glory-arrayed woman (vv. 1-5). Her male child, a son of man figure, emerges from the ordeal triumphant, exalted to the Har Magedon throne of God, destined to rule with an iron sceptre over all nations – as prophesied in Ps 2:4-9. The dominion Jesus refused to accept from the tempter, he receives as the reward for his obedience to the Father.

The battle is pictured again in Rev 12:7ff., this time as a warring of Michael (the proper name of the messianic Angel of the Lord) and his angelic legions against the dragon and his demonic hosts. The devil's defeat is depicted as a being hurled down to earth from his position in the invisible realm of powers. This is Har Magedon imagery derived from the context of Isa 14:12, whose language Rev 12:9 echoes. The Isaiah passage describes the king of Babylon's antichrist aspirations to the heavenly throne on the Mount of Assembly and his ultimate doom, cast down to Sheol (cf. v. 15). The height from which Satan is said to be expelled in Rev 12:9 is the celestial mountain to whose lordship he was a pretender; it is Har Magedon turned into a pseudo-Har Magedon in the fantasy world of Satan's ambitions and lies. [On this, cf. Chapter Six above.]

The description of the devil in this connection as the one who has been the deceiver of the whole world (Rev 12:9) suggests that his casting down meant the loss of his hitherto universal dark sway; henceforth the light of the gospel of Christ would penetrate all the nations. This is confirmed in vv. 10ff., where the defeat and casting down of Satan are attributed to the church's martyr testimony to the blood of the Lamb.

The old deceiver is further identified in Rev 12:10 as the unrelenting accuser of those who hold the testimony of Jesus. To rebut his accusations Jesus must accomplish an atoning sacrifice. Only by the passive obedience of his submission to the Cross can Jesus silence Satan, the accuser of the brethren. The crushing of the serpent's head by the messianic seed of the woman is at the cost of the bruising of his heel. Hence the gospel that is heralded to the ends of the earth after Satan's expulsion from on high is a message of Christ crucified, the Lamb who was slain.

Scripture also identifies Satan as the one who has the power of death (Heb 2:14). To overcome him in this capacity, death must be conquered. And the glorified Jesus reassures John: "I am the living One; I was dead and behold I am alive for evermore. And I have the keys of death and Hades" (Rev 1:18). The gospel that advances across the earth as a result of the casting down of the devil is, accordingly, a preaching of Christ risen as well as Christ crucified.

By the Cross Jesus turns aside the sword thrust of Satan's accusations and by the resurrection he strips Satan of the weapon of death, freeing those who all their lifetime were held in bondage by their fear of death (Heb 2:15; cf. 1 Cor 15:56,57). It is by virtue of this double victory of

Jesus that Satan and his evil angels are cast down from the heights of Har Magedon. At the critical hour of his conflict with the devil, anticipating its outcome, Jesus declared: "Now is the judgment of this world; now shall the prince of this world be cast out. And I, if I be lifted up from the earth, will draw all men unto myself" (John 12:31,32). [Cf. *GOM* 102-104.]

Revelation 20. Another Apocalyptic representation of the encounter of Christ and the devil is found in Revelation 20. Once again the messianic victory is portrayed as a casting down of Satan. And again, here even more clearly, there is a curtailing of Satan's previous world-wide success as a deceiver of the nations. This restriction of his evil influence is symbolized as a binding and imprisoning of the dragon in the locked and sealed Abyss (vv. 1-3, cf. v. 7). [On the following cf. *GOM* 84, 85.]

The background of this imagery is discovered in Isa 49:24,25, particularly as that is adapted in the teaching of Jesus. The Isaiah passage speaks of the Servant of the Lord (vv. 1ff.). He will bring God's salvation to the ends of the earth (v. 6), calling the captives out of darkness (v. 9). Warrior imagery is used for the Lord's deliverance of his people: he will take them as plunder from the terrible adversary (vv. 24,25).

In a dispute arising from our Lord's casting out demons, he cites Isa 49:24,25, translating it into a statement about himself and Satan. The question in Isa 49:24, "Shall the prey be taken from the warrior?", is rephrased as "How can one enter the house of the strong man and spoil his goods?" (Matt 12:29; cf. Mark 3:27). The warrior imagery of the Isaiah passage is more explicit in the Lucan version: the strong man is one who is fully armed and, when overcome, has his armour taken away (Luke 11:21,22). In Isaiah 49 the Lord answers the question whether the prey can be taken from the warrior with the assertion that he would himself contend against the enemy and, yes, he would succeed in seizing the captive prey (v. 25). Applied to Jesus, he is the stronger warrior who spoils the prince of demons, by the Spirit-finger of God rescuing the demon-possessed from the devil's domination.

In Matthew and Mark the element of binding is inserted into the spoiling motif: to enter the house of a strong man and plunder it, one must first bind him (Matt 12:29; Mark 3:27). The figure of binding reappears and is indeed prominent in the resumption of the theme of Christ versus Satan in Revelation 20. This vision opens with a description of the angel from heaven as having a great chain (v. 1) and the primary action is the binding of the ancient serpent with that chain for a thousand years (v. 2).

It is clear from Jesus' saying about the stronger man that he is the one who binds and confines the dragon in Rev 20:1-3. Even if the angel in Rev 20:1 is not Jesus, he is the agent of Jesus; Jesus is the ultimate actor. It is, however, preferable to see this angel who casts down the dragon as the Michael (Christ) angel who casts him down in Rev 12:7,8 (cf. Rev 10:1,5,9; 18:1,21). Moreover, authority over the realm of death and Hades, symbolized by the angel's possession of the key to the Abyss in Rev 20:1, is claimed by Christ by virtue of his resurrection (Rev 1:18). [On this, cf. *IOS* 70-75, 82-84.]

The effects of Jesus' binding of Satan would be manifested throughout the "thousand years," the age of the church's carrying out of the Great Commission. But foretastes of that worldwide spoiling of Satan are already seen in the Gospel accounts of Jesus confronting the demonic agents of the devil and delivering their victims from Satanic tyranny (as on the very occasion of his saying about the binding of the strong man). [On this, cf. *GOM* 102-104.] It was indeed on the basis of our Lord's successful waging of this Har Magedon warfare during his earthly ministry that he became the grantee of the heavenly kingdom, in fulfillment of the Father's commitment to him in the intratrinitarian counsels of eternity.

Lord of the New Covenant

It was also on the meritorious ground of his probationary triumph over the evil one that the Son, the grantee of the kingdom, became the guarantor for his people's inheriting of the kingdom. This arrangement was administered through the New Covenant, of which Jesus is mediator-Lord. Ratification of this final administration of the Covenant of Grace took place on the Cross; Jesus' blood shed there was the blood of the new covenant. Then the declaration of the risen Lord on the Har Magedon mount in Galilee near the time of his ascension constituted the promulgation of the covenant (Matt 28:18-20). The Father's bestowal of the Holy Spirit at Pentecost was a confirmation that the ratificatory sacrifice of Jesus was accepted, that the covenant was operational, and that the Father had exalted his Servant-Son as Lord of the New Covenant. Like the Old Covenant the

New Covenant was sealed in a communion meal (Exod 24:9-11; Matt 26:20ff.; Mark 14:17ff.; Luke 2:14ff.; John 13). And as was the case with the Old Covenant, the status of the New Covenant as ratified and in force was attested in divinely inspired documentation – the four Gospels deposited in the canon of New Covenant Scripture.

The customary designation of the pronouncement of Matt 28:18-20 as "the great commission" does not adequately reflect its nature, which, as we have mentioned, was nothing less than the promulgation of the new constitutional order. In fact, its contents, a concise summary of the terms of the New Covenant, exhibit the essential three part structure of the treaty documentation of the Mosaic covenants. The three key components of these were the following: (1) The claims of the Lord of the covenant establishing his right to demand the allegiance of his people, particularly the claim of his very identity (cf. "I am," Exod 20:2). (2) The commandments, stipulating the duty of the covenant servants. (3) The sanctions of threat and promise, functioning as constraints on the servants' loyalty or as commitments on the Lord's part. [We are here following closely the treatment of this matter in *GOM* 166-173.]

In keeping with this treaty form, Jesus' declaration begins with his coronation claims, identifying himself as invested with cosmic authority (Matt 28:18b). In effect he announces to his disciples that all that Old Testament prophecy had foretold of the messianic Son – that he would destroy the beast power, that he would be enthroned on holy Har Magedon/Zion as judge of the nations, grantee of an imperishable kingdom – all was being fulfilled in him. The Father had given him all authority in heaven and on earth. By this self-identification as the Son of Man exalted to the pinnacle of heaven, conqueror of Satan, victor over sin and death, Jesus asserted his absolute claim on the disciples' covenantal confidence and commitment.

Proceeding to his sovereign charge, Jesus issued the New Covenant commission (Matt 28:19,20a), the central section of this covenantal formulation, after which the whole is usually named "the great commission." While this section corresponds formally to the commandments section of the Mosaic covenants, it differs functionally from the latter as the gospel of grace and truth that came by Jesus differs from the law given through Moses (John 1:17). Israel's obedience to the stipulations of the works arrangement mediated by Moses would be accepted as the legal ground of their continued possession of the typological kingdom. But Jesus does not summon the church to earn the eternal kingdom by obedience to the demands of the new covenant. Rather, it is as the one who, obedient unto the death of the Cross, has himself already merited salvation and the kingdom of glory for his church that Jesus commissions his disciples to go and disciple and baptize, gathering believers to the Lord of Har Magedon, to engage with him in the building of his eternal Glory-temple.

In Jesus' promulgation of the New Covenant the concluding third treaty section of constraints/commitments took the form of his promise to be with his people always (Matt 28:20b). The threats of curse and promises of blessing that Moses addressed to the Israelites were from the Lord's perspective his commitment to enforce the terms of the covenant. These covenant sanctions were divine guarantees that he would both punish rebellion and confer his promised blessings on covenant keepers. Jesus' climactic promise of his constant presence with his church was akin to that kind of guarantee of blessing. It did not, however, envisage the church as under probation like the nation of Israel under the law but as the persevering people for whose eternal kingdom blessings Jesus was the surety. And this commitment of his unfailing presence – in and through the Paraclete-Spirit whom he promised to send (John 15:26) – was an assurance to them of success in carrying out their otherwise impossible covenantal commission of world witness.

New Covenant Interim

Introduction. There is an interval in the messianic era between the inauguration of the covenant and the consummation of the kingdom. Contrary to the expectations of many in Jesus' day the advent of the Messiah did not mean the immediate realization of his visible reign over the earth. After his death and resurrection he went to the Father in heaven to prepare a place for his disciples, promising to come back and take them to be with him (John 14:3,28). There would thus be an interadvental period in which the church was in a waiting posture, looking for the second advent of Jesus, the reappearance of their high priest from behind the veil of the heavenly holy of holies, apart from sin, bringing salvation (Heb 9:28). This period of Jesus' absence emerges clearly in his parables. He likens it to the time when a master goes on a journey and after a lengthy absence returns to settle accounts with those he entrusted with talents to be used for him (Matt 25:14ff.; cf. Mark 13:34).

Evident again in this interadvental period are the same essential characteristics that were found in the interim periods of the typological histories leading up to the Har Magedon mounts, Ararat and Sinai/Zion. Of particular interest we find that true to the typological pattern, the community of the faithful in this final, climactic interim period does not yet take on the form of an outward kingdom on earth.

The 3½ Years Symbol

The 120 years duration of the interim before the Deluge was disclosed beforehand to Noah. And in the covenant with Abraham it was indicated that the interim before the promised deliverance and homecoming of his descendants would last for 400 years. Similarly we find that in the revelation concerning the course of the New Covenant there is a numerical index of the length of the interim, only now it is in the symbolic form of 3½ times or years. From our study of the seventy weeks prophecy in Daniel 9 we have found that this 3½ year period (i.e., the second half of the seventieth week) is the church age, more precisely the church age from the end of the time of the New Covenant's overlapping of the old order in 70 AD (the middle of the seventieth week) to the consummation (the end of the seventieth week). An examination of the contexts where this 3½ years symbol appears in the Books of Daniel and Revelation will bring out the major features of the interim phase of Har Magedon eschatology in the antitypical, messianic age.

Daniel 9. In the seventy weeks passage itself (Dan 9:24-27), the very fact that the 3½ year interim is part of the seventieth week provides a general indication of its nature. In the course of that week, initiated by the ratification of the New Covenant, Messiah-Ruler is engaged in making the covenant and its promises prevail for the many. Even though the coming of the kingdom in outward glory (symbolized in v. 24 as the anointing of the eternal, heavenly holy of holies) does not occur until the trumpeting of the final Jubilee at the end of the seventieth week, already during the seventieth week Christ is exercising his royal authority and his heavenly

Spirit-power unto the salvation of his people. In that respect the 3½ years interim is an age of realized eschatology, an age of the realization of the kingdom within.

Daniel 7. In Dan 7:25 the 3½ years symbol denotes a period in which the saints are dominated by the world power, symbolized by a little horn. The little horn arises as an eleventh horn on the fourth beast, which represents the Roman empire, and its oppressive rule continues until the divine advent in final judgment, when it is destroyed and the everlasting kingdom of the dragon-slaying Son of Man is established (vv. 22,26,27; cf. vv. 9-14). Thus, the 3½ times of the little horn, like the second half of the seventieth week in Daniel 9, covers the present church age, the interadvental interim. While the little horn's domination includes at its climax the antichrist crisis at the end of the interim, the little horn symbolizes the evil bent of the earthly nations throughout the interadvental period. As seen in Daniel 7 the interim is then characterized by an unrelenting persecution of the church. Not yet in the interim, the coming of the kingdom in glory for the saints of the Most High.

Daniel 12. Once again in Dan 12:7 the period denominated as 3½ times is one of persecution for the covenant community. The Daniel 12 context like that in Daniel 7 brings before us the climactic events at the end of earthly history – the appearing of antichrist (Dan 11:36ff.; cf. 2 Thess 2:3ff.), the advent of Christ as the Savior of his people, and the resurrection. Here it is Michael, the great prince, who arises as the protector of the saints from the rage of the antichrist (Dan 12:1ff., on which see further below), the role attributed in Daniel 7 to the Son of Man, destroyer of the little horn.

The reference to the 3½ times comes in answer to the poignant query, "How long?", prompted by concern for the suffering of God's people (Dan 12:6; cf. Pss 6:3 [4]; 80:4 [5]; 90:13; Isa 6:11; Dan 8:13; Zech 1:12). Solemnly declaring that the duration of the period in question will be 3½ times, the response warns that this time of persecution will culminate in the shattering of the power of the holy people (Dan 12:7).

In the account of the universal resurrection that follows the 3½ times (Dan 12:2) the saints, who awaken to everlasting life and glory, are described as the wise who have been instrumental in bringing many to righteousness (Dan 12:3). During the 3½ times they had been engaged as witnesses to the gospel, the wisdom and power of God unto salvation.

This martyr-testimony to Jesus by the church will again be found to be a prominent feature of the interadvental interim in other passages where the 3½ years symbol appears.

Daniel 2. One other passage in Daniel that should be mentioned here is the account of Nebuchadnezzar's dream in Daniel 2. It is comparable to Daniel 7 and 12 in theme and eschatological scope. Also, like them it occupies an A-section position in the over-all double-chiasm structure of the book beyond its introductory first chapter. Thus: A (Daniel 2) • B • A (Daniel 7) • B • A (Daniel 12). Though not denoted by the 3½ years symbol, the interadvental interim is present here. It is latent in the two stages in the career of the messianic rock: the cutting out of the rock is Christ's first advent and the rock's smashing of the great image is his judgment of the world at his second advent. What is to be noticed is that again here the entire in-between period is characterized by the presence of the world kingdom and its opposition to God's people. The colossus representing the evil imperial powers remains standing and fearfully dominant during the whole interadvental interim until sudden, total obliteration befalls it and the messianic rock-kingdom emerges from this final judgment as the eternal cosmic Har Magedon mountain (cf. vv. 35,44,45).

Revelation 11. Revelation 11–13 resumes and carries forward the eschatological perspective and symbolism of the Danielic prophecies just surveyed. We find again the horned beast power, blaspheming God and persecuting the saints, but also the ultimate victory of Michael, the messianic Son. And embedded in this framework of the messianic age are several references to the 3½ year interim, which exhibits here the same characteristics as it does in the Danielic passages.

There are two such references in Revelation 11. One is in verse 3, in the form of an equivalent, 1260 days. Here it denotes the term of the activity of the two witnesses, symbolic of the prosecution of the Great Commission by the church empowered by the Lord, the sovereign controller of all that transpires (cf. Dan 9:27a; Matt 28:18ff.). [On the menorah mission of the two prophet figures, cf. *GOM* 131-173.] It is evident that their mission, though successfully completed, has met with opposition from the unbelieving world devoted to the beast, which overpowers and kills the witnesses in the antichrist crisis at the end of the interim (vv. 7-10;

cf. Dan 7:21). Subsequently the martyrs are restored to life and raptured into heaven (vv. 11,12).

Besides the familiar features of the prophetic testimony and the persecution of the true church, the interim era in Revelation 11 is marked by the presence of an apostate church (an element which, though we did not reflect upon it above, was present in the broader context of the Danielic passages, especially in Daniel 8, 10, and 11). Symbolically, the apostate covenant community is portrayed as the outer court of the temple, not measured off as holy like the inner sanctuary, the true Israel (v. 2a). It is also portrayed as the erstwhile "holy city" of Jerusalem, "the great city" (cf. Jer 22:8; Ps 48:2) where the Lord was crucified, once a sacred divine residence but eventually turned into an abomination of desolations, a virtual Sodom or Egypt (v. 8; cf. Deut 32:32; Isa 1:9,10; Jer 23:14; Rom 9:29) or Babylon, as the great city is called elsewhere in the Book of Revelation. No longer sanctified by God's Presence the great city is abandoned to profanation by the heathen. Such is the significance of the trampling, the opposite of the measuring action of verse 1. And this Gentile trampling of the "holy city" is said to continue for forty-two months (v. 2b), another equivalent of the 3½ years, like the 1260 days in v. 3.

The interim is thus seen to be an era in which a false church co-exists with the true church (cf. v. 3). Just as the true Israel/Jerusalem of the Old Covenant is used to denominate its continuation, the church of the New Covenant, so (as in Revelation 11) the profaned, apostate Jerusalem of the Old Covenant is used as a figure for the false church in the New Covenant age. The false church is a modified development of the apostate covenant community of Israel. Hence there is ascribed to it the very fate that Jesus warned awaited the apostate Jerusalem for their repudiation of him: it was to "be trampled on by the Gentiles until the times of the Gentiles are fulfilled" (Luke 21:24; cf. Dan 8:13,14). "The times of the Gentiles" are the interim, the 3½ years, perhaps so called because it is the era when the gospel is presented to all the nations. This phrase in Luke 21:24 is possibly a Lucan reflection of the statement contained in the Marcan account of this discourse: "The gospel must first be preached to all the nations" (Mark 13:10; cf. Paul's declaration that the rejection of the hardened portion of Israel would continue "until the fullness of the Gentiles has come in" [Rom 11:25]). [See GOM 177-201 for an extended treatment of the interpretation of the harlot, the city Babylon, as an apostate ecclesiastical institution, the false church, the opposite and antagonist of the woman clothed with holy glory, the New Jerusalem, the true church.]

Revelation 12. The vision in Revelation 12 focuses on Christ's victory over the dragon at his first advent, but it also looks beyond that to the experience of the church in the interadvental period. And in that connection the 3½ years symbol of the interim appears twice (vv. 6 and 14). Both contexts are concerned with the situation of the community of faith (symbolized by the woman) after the departure of the victorious Christ to his throne in heaven and the hurling down of the great dragon to earth. Foiled in his attempt to do away with the messianic offspring of the woman, now exalted beyond his reach, the enraged Satan directs his attack against those who are accessible to him, the woman and the rest of her offspring, those who hold the testimony of Jesus. Though vulnerable and threatened, they are protected and preserved during the interim. This is the point in both v. 6 and v. 14. Rev 12:6 says the woman fled into the wilderness to a place prepared for her by God, where she can be sustained for 1260 days. Rev 12:14 says the woman was given the two wings of a great eagle so that she might fly to the place prepared for her in the wilderness, where she is sustained for a time, times, and half a time. Such is the interim condition of the church – a fugitive existence in the wilderness, not yet come to rest in the glory land. As faithful witnesses to the Lamb, God's people are overcomers (Rev 12:11, echoing the Revelation 11 identification of the interim as Great Commission time) and they are indeed sustained in the wilderness. Yet at the same time they are warred against by the dragon (12:17) and face martyr-death for their martyr-witness. It is as those who loved not their lives unto death that they overcome.

Revelation 13. Introduced in Rev 11:7, the figure of the horned beast (based on the imagery in Daniel 7) appears again in Revelation 13, now as the focus of the vision. The beast emerges from the chaotic deep at the behest of the dragon in a pseudo-creation event (13:1). In the sovereign purpose of God it is granted to the beast to continue as the blaspheming, persecuting agent of Satan for 42 months (13:5-7). This conflict of the evil imperial power with the saints goes on unabated throughout the interim, coming to a climax in an apparent, if ephemeral, triumph of the beast (13:7; cf. 11:7; Dan 7:21,25).

The Interim and Millennialism

The results of the foregoing survey of the 3½ years symbolism in the apocalyptic visions of Daniel and Revelation may be stated in terms of the different views entertained by the main millennial positions as to the state of the church in the interadvental age. Clearly the biblical evidence supports the view maintained by the advocates of amillennialism and (classical) premillennialism as over against that of the postmillennialists. We have found that the interim era is consistently represented as a time of struggle and tribulation for the church – which is the position of the amillennialists and the premillennialists. Nowhere countenanced is the notion that the covenant community is to assume visible, earthly theocratic form before the parousia-return of the theocratic King, as held by the postmillennialists (properly so-called – see further below). Although the premillennialists fail to recognize that the church age is the millennium, with respect to the crucial matters of the nature of the church's present mission and our pre-parousia hopes and expectations they are kindred spirits with the amillennialists in opposition to the alien mentality of theonomic postmillennialism.

In this connection the relevance of the covenant of the common grace order may be noted. Along with assurances of a relative stability of the realm of nature, that covenant guaranteed equal civil rights within the institution of the state for all the peoples of the earth as long as the earth endures. Ruled out, therefore, is the kind of theocratic enforcement of biblical religion in the common world that is advocated by the postmillennialists.

Stated in terms of our underlying thesis of the recurring Har Magedon pattern of eschatology, the conclusion we reach from the representations of the New Covenant interim in the 3½ years passages is that it is very much like the interims in the typological instances of that pattern. This conclusion could be supported by various other lines of exegetical and theological evidence. We might recall the statement of Jesus concerning the similarity of the days of Noah and of the Son of Man (Matt 24:37-41; Luke 17:26,27). Or we might show the likeness of the present church age to the patriarchal interim by pointing to the use of the patriarchs' mode of life as a model for the Christian life. A particularly pertinent example of this is Peter's identification of Christians as pilgrims and strangers in the world (1 Pet 1:1; 2:11; cf. Heb 11:9,13). At a deeper, spiritual level there is also the similarity of the Spirit's presence and working in the patriarchal and present ages – invisibly present but working mightily within for the transformation of individuals and the edification of the covenant community. And other features of the New Covenant might be adduced that show it to be like the typological interim eras, especially like the patriarchal interim in contrast to the era of the Israelite theocracy. What has been mentioned may, however, suffice for this purpose. But we shall round off this discussion of the New Covenant interim with a look at one more apocalyptic passage, one that will bring the millennial perspective to the fore again.

The Millennium Symbol (Rev 20:1-6)

Millennial Nomenclature. In Revelation 20 we come upon another numerical-temporal symbol for the interim – a thousand years. Amillennialists and postmillennialists are in agreement that the millennium is the present church age interim, while the premillennialists locate it in a future age. Postmillennialists fall in with the premillennialists in the (erroneous) view that the millennium is a time when God's people are organized as a visible kingdom exercising dominion over the earth. (There are self-styled postmillennialists whose millennial expectations stop short of the visible kingdom feature, but I am regarding that feature as definitive of the postmillennial position.)

With the qualification just mentioned, I am still using the customary labels here for the three main millennial positions. I suggest however that it would bring the heart of the eschatological issue into clearer focus if we labelled the options in terms of the relation of the coming of the Glory-kingdom to the final judgment/consummation, rather than in terms of the relation of the parousia to the millennium. We would then speak of the pre-consummation view, held by postmillennialists and premillennialists (the latter, however, regarding the kingdom as post-parousia, which, though mistaken, is less objectionable than the pre-parousia view of the postmillennialists) and the post-consummation view, held by the amillennialists alone.

Church Age Millennium. To demonstrate the identification of the thousand years of Rev 20:1-6 with the present church age (the 3½ years interim) we note the following: First, the millennium begins at the first advent. In our discussion of Revelation 20 above (under the heading "Conquest of the Dragon") we traced the binding of Satan (Rev 20:2) to our Lord's adaptation of Isa 49:24,25, identifying himself as the divine warrior, the stronger one who binds and plunders Satan, the great deceiver. And that process was already under way as evidenced in Jesus' deliverance of the demon-possessed. Also, as observed in that previous discussion, Revelation 20 and Revelation 12 are strikingly similar in their accounts of Christ's overpowering the dragon, "the ancient serpent, who is the devil and Satan" (Rev 12:9 and 20:2), the binding of him in Revelation 20 being equivalent to the hurling him down in Revelation 12. Since in Revelation 12 the casting of Satan out of heaven is an achievement of Christ's first advent, the same will be true of the binding of Satan that launches the thousand years in Revelation 20.

Second, the millennium ends at the antichrist crisis and the return of Jesus to execute final judgment on Satan's forces at the final battle, the battle of Har Magedon. Something of the exegetical case for identifying the millennium-ending battle of Rev 20:7-10 with the Rev 16:12-16 (and 19:17-21) battle of Har Magedon at the parousia was made earlier (i.e., in the chapter: "Har Magedon: The Mount of Assembly") and this will be developed further in our treatment of the antichrist crisis.

Corroborating the identification of the thousand years of Revelation 20 with the pre-parousia, church age is the repetition of the historical pattern of Revelation 11 in Revelation 20: the long period (the thousand years) culminating in a brief crisis (the "short time," v. 3) in Revelation 20 matches the 3½ years of prophetic witness followed by the 3½ days crisis in Revelation 11. The parallelism of the two passages is confirmed by the similar nature of the corresponding periods in each, both the longer periods being times of martyr-witness and both the shorter periods being a crisis resulting from the emergence of the evil power from the Abyss. And since the 3½ years in Revelation 11 symbolize the present church age from beginning to end, its Revelation 20 counterpart, the thousand years, must also be identified with the interadvental period.

Additional support for the millennium-interim equivalence is found in an especially intriguing passage in the eschatological teaching of the apostle Paul. That the restraint of Satan described in Revelation 20 belongs to the pre-parousia, interim era is shown by the Pauline version of this same time of restraint in 2 Thess 2:6,7. As pictured there the restraint is exerted against Satan's ultimate agent, the man of sin (or antichrist). The purpose of the restraint is to prevent the (pseudo-)parousia of antichrist from taking place prematurely. The restraint inhibits the escalation of the incipient antichrist spirit for a time. Then at the appointed time of the true parousia the restraint is withdrawn, permitting the open and full manifestation of antichrist, the prelude to Christ's advent in judgment on the lawless one (2 Thess 2:3-11). Likewise then the millennium era of the restraint of Satan spoken of in the parallel Revelation 20 passage is to be identified with the interadvental era concluded by the crisis and parousia.

This is perhaps the best place to address the question of the precise identity of the restraint/restrainer in 2 Thessalonians 2. Paul's teaching on the man of sin is rooted in the prophecy of this same development in Daniel 10–12 (note especially 2 Thess 2:4 and Dan 11:36). In Daniel's preview, the history of Antiochus Epiphanes, the second century BC analogue of the antichrist, merges into a prophecy of the latter (cf. Dan 11:21-45). And in connection with the events leading up to Antiochus it is revealed that the course of this earthly history interlocks with and is determined by the course of a warfare waged in heaven. The celestial conflict pits evil angels, who are identified with the Israel-dominating nations of Persia and Greece, against Gabriel and Michael, the guardian princes of God's people Israel. By resisting the demonic powers, Gabriel, with Michael's help as the decisive factor (Dan 10:13,21; cf. 12:1), restrains the escalation of evil in Persia and Greece in turn (Dan 10:13,20). Only at the divinely appointed time does the antichrist figure arise (cf. Dan 11:29; Rev 9:13,14). Like this prototypal pattern of restraint is the restraint of the development of iniquity referred to in 2 Thessalonians 2. It takes place in the realm of angels (with repercussions on earth) and the individual restrainer is Michael/Christ. The restraint on the satanic movement is initiated by Michael's casting the Devil down (Revelation 12) or, as stated in Revelation 20, by the messianic Angel's binding him and casting him into the Abyss. Though not eliminated altogether, the antichrist principle continues only in a mystery-restrained mode, not yet in outward pseudo-parousia form, not so until Christ relinquishes this restraining role (2 Thess 2:7). Removal of the restraint precipitates the final crisis, with the manifestation of antichrist and the counter manifestation of Christ, destroying the man of sin (2 Thess 2:8). Dan 12:1 describes this crisis of unsurpassed proportions (v. 1c) as the time when Michael, the one "who takes a stand (ʿāmad)" as the warrior-protector of God's people (v. 1b), will again take that stand (ʿāmad, v. 1a) and deliver his people (v. 1d; cf. Dan 11:1).

Pre-Kingdom Millennium. Demonstrating that the thousand years are the church age has involved mention of various facets of the millennium era. Now we want to concentrate on the key issue with respect to the nature of the millennium – its relation to the coming of the Glory-kingdom. We shall argue for what I proposed above to call the post-consummation view by showing that there is no basis in the contents of the Revelation 20 passage itself for the contention of the premillennialists and postmillennialists that the thousand years are a time of theocratic dominance for the people of God on earth. Specifically, such a terrestrial kingdom is not suggested by the binding of Satan (vv. 1-3) or by the granting of judicial authority to those on the thrones (v. 4) or by the first resurrection experience (vv. 5,6).

As for Jesus' binding of Satan we have seen that this had reference to deliverance from satanic deception and spiritual darkness and to release from enslavement by demons. Until Christ's first advent all the world outside Israel's limited orbit was snared in the delusion of the devil's deception. But with the binding of the strong warrior by the stronger One, the divine warrior, gospel light has penetrated the nations. The deceiver of souls no longer holds universal sway. During the millennium God is gathering from all the nations those who are coming to the knowledge of him through the enlightenment of the Spirit. The universal advance of the Word of God's saving truth, the consequence of the binding of Satan, continues through the thousand years era until the brief crisis at its close. But far from the thousand years being a time of political dominance for those who do not worship the beast or his image, their status is portrayed as that of souls who have been beheaded because of their testimony to Jesus (cf. Rev 20:4b).

Rev 20:4a describes the session of a tribunal given authority to judge. This recalls Dan 7:9ff. (and cf. Rev 4:2-4), where the heavenly Har Magedon court of the Ancient of Days is seated and proceeds to render a verdict in vindication of the saints of the Most High (cf. Dan 7:13,14,2,26,27). Similarly the judicial session in Rev 20:4a results in the vindication of the faithful (v. 4b), who would not therefore seem to be the occupants of the thrones. But even if the judges are understood as the saints delivering judgment in their own favor, that would not constitute evidence for the notion of an earthly millennial theocracy, for what is described is a celestial scene and martyr people in the intermediate state (as will be shown below).

The prospect of an earthly millennial kingdom infused with Glory elements would confront us in Rev 20:4-6 if the first resurrection spoken of there were a bodily resurrection of believers who then reigned with Christ for a thousand years. Such a co-existence on planet earth of glorified beings back from the grave with mortal humans would be a bizarre scenario, to say the least. But more important and decisive, the interpretation of the first resurrection as bodily is contradicted by the meaning of "first" (prōtos) in this context.

Premillennialists suppose that prōtos signifies first in a series of things of the same kind and therefore argue that the first resurrection must be bodily because (as we all agree) the second resurrection (Rev 20:12,13) is bodily. Actually, here in Revelation 20 and 21 prōtos denotes something of a different kind from what is called "second" or "new." Thus, in the vision of the re-creation in Rev 21:1ff., prōtos marks the present world order as different from the "new heaven and new earth." In contrast to the "new" enduring cosmos of the consummation, the present world – the prōtos world – is a world that is passing away. Further, among the prōtos things that are passing away is bodily death (Rev 21:4), and antithetically paired with this "first" death is "the second death," the lake of fire (Rev 21:8; cf. 20:6,14). Unlike the first death, the second death does not denote the loss of bodily life but something else, something which in fact is the sequel to bodily resurrection (cf. Rev 20:12-15) and is part of the eternal order (Rev 20:10). As the premillennialists themselves acknowledge, in the case of the first and second death pair, prōtos signifies a different kind of experience from "second." They are then being inconsistent when in the case of the first and second resurrection pair, which is intertwined with the first and second death pair in this same context (cf. especially Rev 20:6), they insist that both must be of the same (bodily) kind.

The question remains – what then is the first resurrection? As one of the "first things" it belongs to the present, passing age, not to the consummation order of new or second things. It cannot, therefore, be bodily resurrection to immortality and glory for that is a distinctive feature of the new, consummate cosmos. The answer lies in the striking paradoxical schema produced by the interlocking of the two antithetical pairs, first and second death and first and second resurrection.

In the case of the wicked the event of bodily resurrection is not called a resurrection "for the true significance of the event is to be found in the destiny in which it issues and in the case of the unjust the grave delivers them up (v. 13) only to deliver them over to the lake of fire (v. 15). Hence, the real meaning of the resurrection of the unjust to physical life is conveyed by the paradoxical metaphor of death, "the second death" (v. 14)." [This quotation is from *FR*, of which the present comments are a condensed version. Cf. also *FRR*.]

Similarly, paradoxical terminology is used in referring to the bodily death of the righteous. The real significance of their passage from earthly life is to be found in the nature of the intermediate state into which it translates them. And John sees the Christian dead, the souls of the martyrs beheaded for the testimony of Jesus, living and reigning with Christ for a thousand years (Rev 20:4b). As the event that introduces the Christian into the blessedness of this state of royal-priestly life in the presence of Christ in the heavenly church triumphant (vv. 4-6), bodily death is paradoxically called "the first resurrection." What for others is the first death is for believers a veritable resurrection. It is the first resurrection, to be followed by their second resurrection, a bodily resurrection, at the parousia after the thousand years when all the "first" things pass away and God makes all things new (Rev 21:4,5).

The interpretation of the first resurrection as the physical death of believers – in effect, the intermediate state of believers – is confirmed by the close correspondence of Rev 20:4-6 to other passages in Revelation containing visions of the intermediate state. One such passage is Rev 14:13. It is like the millennium passage in literary form, both of them belonging to the series of the seven beatitudes of the Apocalypse. Rev 20:6 affirms: "Blessed and holy is he that has part in the first resurrection" and Rev 14:13 declares: "Blessed are the dead who die in the Lord henceforth." Moreover, the nature of the blessedness of the martyrs is much the same in these two beatitudes. Rev 14:13 describes the intermediate state in sabbatical terms as a resting from labors. Now sabbath rest is a royal session, an enthronement after the completion of labors that secure the kingdom (cf., e.g., Isa 66:1). And such is the millennial living and reigning with Christ, a participation in Christ's royal sabbath rest. From this parallelism of the two passages we conclude that Rev 20:4-6, like Rev 14:13, describes the state of the Christian dead.

Particularly strong is the resemblance between Rev 20:4-6 and the vision of the intermediate state in the Rev 6:9-11 account of the opening of the fifth seal of the seven-sealed scroll. In both passages John sees "souls," souls described as slain or beheaded for their witness to the word of God. And like the souls in Rev 20:4-6 (and the blessed dead in Rev 14:13) the souls seen under the heavenly altar in Rev 6:9-11 are granted royal sabbatical repose. Other features common to both passages are the priestly identity of the martyr-souls and the favorable judgment already rendered for them, while they await God's punitive judgment against their wicked slayers. Clearly, Rev 20:4-6 has to do with the same situation as Rev 6:9-11 and again we are bound to conclude that the first resurrection must be the experience of death through which the Christian enters the blessed and holy intermediate state.

Another passage that closely parallels Rev 20:4-6 is the letter to the church in Smyrna (Rev 2:8-11). It speaks of martyrdom and it promises: "Be fruitful unto death and I will give you a crown of life . . . He that overcomes shall not be hurt by the second death" (vv. 10b,11b). This is the only occurrence of "the second death" in Revelation apart from the first resurrection context in Revelation 20. Also, the promise of "a crown of life" is the precise nominal equivalent of the verbal "they lived and reigned" in Rev 20:4. Note too the contextual references to the activity of Satan in both passages (cf. 2:9,10 and 20:2f.,7ff.). There might also be a relationship between the numerical symbols of the ten days of tribulation in Rev 2:10 and the thousand years in Revelation 20. If so, the intensifying of ten to a thousand and the lengthening of days to years would intimate that the present momentary suffering of the believers cannot be compared to the exceeding great glory that awaits them even in the intermediate state. To die and be with the Lord is far better. Once again then the interpretation of the first resurrection as the intermediate state is corroborated by the correspondence between Rev 20:4-6 and a passage descriptive of the blessedness of the martyr dead.

Conclusion. The two numerical symbols for the interim age represent two cosmographic perspectives. The 3½ years symbol views it from the perspective of the lower (earthly) register; the thousand years, the upper (heavenly) register.

As a truncated heptad the 3½ years signifies a stopping short of completeness. With respect to the devil's attempt to wipe out the church, the 3½ years duration of the beast's career indicates that Satan's effort is a failure; it falls short of ultimate success. With respect to the church militant's sufferings, the 3½ years suggests the Lord's shortening of the time for the elect's sake. And with reference to the church's eschatological journey, the 3½ years underscores the not-yet-sabbath status of the church militant, its present location in the wilderness, still on the way to the kingdom land of rest and glory.

The replacing of the 3½ years symbol by the thousand years in Rev 20:1-6 alerts us to the change in perspective here. The new perspective is identified by the context as that of the heavenly, intermediate state. Indeed, the use of the numerical symbol of a thousand itself suggests the heavenly perspective for elsewhere in apocalyptic symbolism a thousand characterizes celestial realities. There are the myriads of thousands of angels about the heavenly throne (Dan 7:10; Rev 5:11) and the millions of thousands of angelic troops loosed at the sounding of the sixth trumpet (Rev 9:16). The dimensions of the cuboid heavenly Jerusalem are twelve thousand stadia each (Rev 21:16) and the redeemed multitude before the throne, the fullness of the Jews and Gentiles, are in typological symbol a hundred forty-four thousand (Revelation 7).

As these examples show, a thousand connotes fullness, completeness. So also in Rev 20:1-6 a thousand signifies the completeness aspect of the intermediate state as over against the incompleteness of the earthly experience of the church. To be sure the intermediate state is a limited period, not yet the eternal sabbath, which does not dawn until the consummation, and accordingly the sabbatical seven is not used as a figure for its duration. But though not yet the eternal Sabbath/Jubilee, the intermediate state is for the saints a preliminary time of rest from their earthly labors (Rev 14:13). It is the end of the earthly pilgrimage stage. It is an arrival in the land of promise. And for such an eschatological state, the completeness connotation of a thousand made it an appropriate symbol.

Whether viewed from the earthly (3½ years) or heavenly (thousand years) perspective, the interim history of the church militant is a martyr age in the double sense of the church's witnessing to Christ and suffering for Christ. Indeed, that is what we find to be the nature of the church age no matter where we turn in the Scriptural canon of the New Covenant, in the historical narrative and ecclesiastical correspondence portions, as well as the apocalyptic visions.

Stated in terms of the principal antagonists, the church age interim is a time of continuous Har Magedon conflict between Christ and Satan. Satan opposes the advance of the gospel by persecution from without (through the institutional agency of the bestial imperial powers) and by perversion of the truth within (institutionalized in the apostate Babylon-church). Christ, enthroned above with all authority in heaven and earth, restrains Satan and the antichrist development. He not merely protects and preserves his remnant flock in their earthly wilderness but he empowers the church militant for its martyr-witness in fulfillment of the Great Commission. And he leads the martyr-slain through the valley of the shadow of death into their "far better" intermediate home and the peace of his Presence.

As for the millennial issue, the Scriptures are uniform in their depiction of the New Covenant interim as an age in which Christ, the King of kings, is already reigning invisibly by his Spirit within the hearts of his people in the world but does not yet terminate the arrangements promulgated in God's common grace covenant and hence (contrary to postmillennialism) does not yet establish his theocratic kingdom of glory on earth.

The Battle of Har Magedon

Introduction. At the climax of the ages-long Har Magedon conflict, the rebel aspirant to the throne of the celestial mount gathers his forces for a final assault against the holy city. The battle is joined when Christ the Lord of Har Magedon counterattacks with his heavenly army. The outcome of this battle of the great day, *the* battle of Har Magedon, is the triumph of Christ, the salvation of the saints, and the doom of Satan and all his evil followers. It will be recognized that this course of eschaton events

– a time of crisis for the saints with an ensuing divine judgment on the world – repeats the pattern found in the history that led to the typological episodes of kingdom consummation at Ararat and Zion.

The Antichrist Crisis

Global Challenge. In the interim passages we have been considering a concluding crisis appears repeatedly, a distinctive brief period whose fateful developments are the catalyst for the last great battle. Like the interim era it is identified by specific numerical symbols as well as more general terms indicative of its short duration.

It is a period of 3½ days (Rev 11:9), the time the two slain witnesses lie dead, following the 3½ years interim era of their testimony (Rev 11:3) and immediately preceding their resurrection-vindication (Rev 11:11f.).

It is the "short time" after the thousand years interim age (Rev 20:3), the time of the satanic siege of the beloved city, the precursor to the final judgment (Rev 20:7ff.).

It is the "little while" regime of the seventh head of the beast (Rev 17:10) at the end of the 3½ years interim period of the sixth head of the beast (cf. Rev 13:5), the "one hour" (Rev 17:12) in which the ten horns give their authority and power to the beast for the war against the Lamb.

Initiating this crisis is a divine removal of limitations imposed on the satanic rebellion during the interim era. Satan is released from the Abyss where he had been imprisoned during the thousand years (Rev 20:3,7). Expressed in terms of Satan's agent in Rev 11:7ff. – the beast ascends from the Abyss after the 3½ years church age career of the two witnesses and kills them, sparking a celebration in the great city for 3½ days, the crisis period. According to Revelation 17 this coming up of the beast out of the Abyss ends the present age, the time when he is under restraints so that it is said he "now is not" (v 8), and brings on the "little while" crisis in which the beast functions as a climactic eighth king via the seventh head and the ten horns (v. 11). That the beast's coming up from the Abyss is "a going to his destruction" (vv. 8,11) reminds us that this crisis unfolds in fulfillment of the purpose and decree of the Lord God, the Judge who reigns on Har Magedon.

Most explicitly, removal of previous restraint is cited in explanation of the antichrist crisis in 2 Thessalonians 2. And as we found in our discussion of that passage above, the Lord is the one who restrains the eruption of evil during the interim and accordingly he is the one who removes the restraint, so precipitating the time of crisis, the manifestation of the man of sin and the final battle.

In this Pauline apocalypse the man of sin event is identified as an apostasia (2 Thess 2:3). This apostasia is often understood as an apostate situation that forms the background context from which the man of sin emerges, but the particle kai connecting the apostasia and the manifestation of the antichrist is here explanatory, not supplementary: the antichrist eruption *is* the apostasia. In the LXX, apostasia renders Hebrew terms that signify treacherous covenant breaking (Mal 2:14,15) and, predominantly, rebellion against Yahweh, audacious repudiation of his lordship in favor of idol gods (cf. Josh 22:22; 2 Chr 29:19; 33:19; Jer 2:19). The antichrist episode is a resumption of Satan's challenge to the Lord of Har Magedon in Eden in the beginning, conspiring to overthrow him and to seize the cosmic throne on the heavenly mount (cf. 2 Thess 2:4).

Satan and Antichrist. In both the Genesis 3 and 2 Thessalonians 2 episodes Satan acts through an agent, the serpent and the man of sin respectively. A mysterious relationship obtains between Satan and the agents, a Satan-possession. Analogous to the tempter's appropriation of the serpent is the demons' occupying of the swine (Luke 8:32,33) and comparable to his fusion with the man of sin is the demons' possession of humans, subverting their sense of identity, renaming them as demons (e.g., Luke 8:30). A phenomenon even closer to Satan's entry into the man of sin is his entering into Judas, the betrayer (Luke 22:3). Both Judas and antichrist become extensions of Satan, organs of his attack on Christ, and both share in his doom, each being designated "son of perdition" (John 17:12 and 2 Thess 2:3).

Incarnation is not possible for Satan but satanic possession of or embodiment in the man of sin amounts to a pseudo-incarnation. Consequently, antichrist sustains a kind of messianic relation to Satan. In terms of the Revelation 13 symbolism – the dragon gives his power, throne, and great authority to the beast (vv. 2,4), preeminently to the antichrist culmination of the beast in its seventh/eighth head. The antichrist is Satan's vicegerent.

To be sure, the subordinate status inherent in messiahship is contradicted by the man of sin's claim to a name above all. Indeed this self-exaltation constitutes a rival claim in conflict with the claims of the one who has delegated his throne to him (cf. Rev 13:1,2). For in the satanic order of things there is no place for two claimants to the supreme height of the throne of Har Magedon. Satan cannot replicate the trinitarian Father-Son (Messiah) relationship, one in which the Messiah-Son together with the Father and the Spirit occupies the Glory-throne of all creation. Hence by his claim to deity above all deities the messiah figure that Satan spawns becomes in effect a rebel against his father. Such contradiction and division is to be expected in Satan's kingdom-house for he is the irrational spirit par excellence.

Counterproductive, self-destructive though it all is, Satan must plunge on with his counterfeit-messiah madness. The antichrist he authors and authorizes he also empowers; the coming of the man of sin is according to the energizing (energeia) of Satan (2 Thess 2:9). Thus empowered, antichrist performs supernatural signs by which those who reject the true Lord of Har Magedon are deceived into giving their allegiance to the false lord (2 Thess 2:9-12). The satanic counterfeiting of Christ and his mission goes beyond the performing of miraculous deeds intended to validate blasphemous claims. It involves the whole manner of the man of sin's appearing on the stage of history. His manifestation is called a parousia (2 Thess 2:9) and, like Christ's parousia, it results in a great gathering of humanity (a major feature of the crisis, as we shall be observing).

The element of deception brings out again the relation of the antichrist crisis at the end of history to the Genesis 3 episode at the beginning. In Eden too the supernatural sign, the speaking serpent, was a tactic in the devil's strategy of deception and there too the objective of the deception was nothing less than a realignment of the allegiance of the community of man, diverting it from the Creator Lord of Har Magedon to Satan, the rebel challenger.

As carried out in the antichrist crisis, the deception assumes global proportions. In both Old Testament and New Testament prophecy the (temporary) success of the satanic deception is depicted as a universal gathering of the forces of the nations against Har Magedon. Of the Old Testament instances we noted in our survey of this theme above (cf. Chapter Six) we shall consider further at this point only Ezekiel 38–39.

Gog of Magog and the Apocalypse. The Ezekiel prophecy is of special importance because it introduces the individual antichrist figure of Gog in connection with the theme of universal gathering against the Mount of Gathering. Gog's antichrist identity is established by the identification of Magog, his imperial base (Ezek 38:2,3), as the yarkĕtê ṣāpôn, "heights of (Mount) Zaphon" (38:6,15; 39:2), the equivalent of har môᶜēd/magedon in Isa 14:13. As we noted earlier, Gog's ideological claims to the mountain of deity are here given objective form as a separate, pseudo-Zaphon. It is from this false Har Magedon that he sets out against Zion, the true Har Magedon, with his universal gathering of troops, the hallmark of the antichrist crisis.

Confirming the identification of Gog as antichrist are "other features in Ezekiel 38–39, like the beast symbolism applied to Gog (38:4; 39:2) and numerous parallels to the judgment of the beast of Revelation in the description of God's destruction of Gog, most striking of these the feasting of the birds and beasts on the slain hordes (Ezek 39:4,17-20 and Rev 19:17,18). Likewise, parallels between Gog's career in Ezekiel 38–39 and that of the Pauline "man of sin" in 2 Thessalonians 2 corroborate Gog's antichrist identity. Thus, Gog's advance against Israel in a storm-cloud theophany (Ezek 38:9,16) matches the (pseudo-)parousia nature of the man of sin's appearance (2 Thess 2:9). Also, in both cases the Lord responds in the true parousia-advent with almighty vengeance (Ezek 38:18-23; 39:1-21 and 2 Thess 2:3-10)." [*GOM* 213 and *HMEM* 219ff.]

Ezekiel's mapping of the coalition of nations provides a graphic image of the universality of Gog's gathering of forces. Starting at Magog, the theocratic capital of Gog, and returning to that northern vicinity at the end (Ezek 38:2-6), the military nations are listed in clockwise order so as to form a great circle encompassing Zion at the center. This imagery is resumed in the Johannine vision of the satanic armies from the four corners of the earth encircling the beloved city (Rev 20:9). And Ezekiel's list of seven military nations and three mercantile peoples participating in the enterprise (Ezek 38:13) is itself based on the Genesis 10 table of nations, Magog and the nearby northern nations being placed there at the head of the list (vv. 2,3). It is thus suggested that after the expansion of the church in the Great Commission era, the Gog-antichrist crisis will witness a return to the days before the gospel age, when Satan was effectively the deceiver of the nations; indeed, a reversion to the ancient days of the world-wide prevalence of Babel-spirited nations bent on erecting pseudo-Har Magedons (Genesis 11).

Ezekiel's prophecy of the universal mustering of armies is taken up in a series of passages in the New Testament Apocalypse. These are chiastically arranged in the course of John's visions according to the subject(s) of the world-wide deception/gathering, thus: *(a)* Rev 12:9, the dragon, Satan. *(b)* Rev 13:14, the false prophet, agent of the (first) beast. *(c)* Rev 16:13-16 (cf. 17:12-14), the dragon, the beast, and the false prophet. *(b')* Rev 19:19,20, the beast and the false prophet. *(a')* Rev 20:7-10 (cf. v. 3), the dragon, Satan. The parallelism of the corresponding sections (with their immediate contexts) is reenforced by various details. For example, both *a* sections describe the dragon as "that ancient serpent called [or, who is] the devil and Satan." And both *b* sections refer to the miraculous signs performed by the false prophet and the receiving of the mark of the beast and the worshipping of his image by those who are deceived.

Since the identification of the episode at the close of the millennium (section *a'*) with the parousia event (referred to in section *c* and *b'*) is particularly important for the millennium debate, corroborative evidence will be in order. [What follows is an adaptation of the discussion in *HMEM* 218-221.]

That the satanic war of Rev 20:7-10 is the antichrist-Har Magedon battle of Revelation 16 and 19 is indicated by parallels between the careers of Satan and the beast. In Revelation 20 Satan emerges from his imprisonment in the Abyss, instigates the final challenge against the Lord and his city, and goes to his doom (vv. 7-10). The beast comes up out of the Abyss in the climactic stage of the eighth king, makes war against the witnesses of the Lamb in the true Jerusalem, and goes to his destruction (17:8-14; cf. 11:7,8; 19:20).

Our thesis is also confirmed by the fact that Ezekiel 38–39 proves to be the common source behind Rev 20:7-10 and the series of passages in Revelation referring to the antichrist-parousia event. The relationship of Rev 20:7-10 to Ezekiel 38–39, obvious enough from the adoption of the Gog-Magog terminology in Revelation 20, is also evidenced by a set of basic similarities: the marshaling of hordes from the four quarters of the earth (Ezek 38:2-7,15; 39:4; Rev 20:8); the march of the gathered armies to encompass the saints in the city of God, center of the world (Ezek 38:7-9,12,16; Rev 20:9); the orchestration of the event by God (Ezek

38:4,16; 39:2,19; Rev 20:3,7); the timing of the event after a lengthy period in which God's people were kept secure from such a universal assault (Ezek 38:8,11; Rev 20:3); the eschatological finality of the crisis (Ezek 39:22,26,29; Rev 20:10ff.); and the fiery destruction of the evil forces (Ezek 38:22; 39:6; Rev 20:9-10).

Just as clearly, the Gog-Magog prophecy of Ezekiel 38–39 is a primary source drawn on by Rev 16:14-16, 19:17-21, and the other Apocalyptic prophecies of the final conflict. Prominent in these passages is the major feature that marked the dependence of Rev 20:7-10 on the Ezekiel prophecy, namely, the universal gathering of the enemy armies (Rev 16:14-16; 17:12-14; 19:19; and compare 6:15 with Ezek 39:18-20), including too the historical setting of that event at the close of this world-age (Rev 6:12-17; 11:7-13; 16:16-17 [cf. 17:10-14]; 19:15-21), following an era in which it is given to the church to fulfill its mission of gospel witness (11:3-7; cf. 12:6,14). The features in Ezekiel 38–39 listed above in support of the identification of Ezekiel's Gog with the beast of Revelation are additional evidence to the same effect.

Millennial Implications. The conclusion is then amply warranted that Ezekiel 38–39 is the common source of Rev 20:7-10 and the passages earlier in Revelation that deal with the eschatological battle. This confirms the standard amillennial contention that the Gog-Magog episode of Rev 20:7-10 is a recapitulation of the accounts of the Har Magedon crisis in these other passages. And the capstone for that argument is what we have discovered about the relation of Har Magedon (môᶜēd) to the place of Gog's provenance, Mount Zaphon, the relationship established by the Zaphon connection in Isa 14:13, Psalm 48, and Ezekiel 38–39. It now appears that the very term har magedōn itself identifies the Rev 16:14-16 event as the Gog-Magog event of Rev 20:7-10.

Rev 20:7-10 is not, as premillennialists would have it, an isolated, novel episode not mentioned elsewhere in the Apocalypse. Rather it belongs to a series of passages, including Rev 19:11-21, which premillennialists rightly regard as referring to the antichrist-Har Magedon crisis and the parousia of Christ. It therefore follows that the thousand years that precede the Gog-Magog crisis of Rev 20:7-10 precede the Har Magedon-parousia event related in the other passages. Har Magedon is not a prelude to the millennium, but a postlude. Har Magedon marks the end of the millennium. And that conclusion spells the end of premillennialism.

The eschatological prospects presented in the series of Har Magedon passages also pose a considerable problem for the postmillennialists. Their supposition that there is to be in the present millennial age a fulfillment of the Old Testament prophecies of the coming of the kingdom in the form of worldwide political dominion clashes with the recurring Apocalyptic forecasts of a severe crisis for God's people. As we have seen, the renewal of Satan's status as the deceiver of the nations during this crisis at the end of the thousand years signifies a universal suppression of the gospel witness. This global curtailing of the church's hitherto mighty missionary outreach is vividly symbolized in Revelation 20 by Satan's amassed troops surrounding the camp/city of the saints, a hemming in of the light of salvation by Satanic darkness. And equally eloquent is the Revelation 11 symbolism of the silencing of the testimony to Jesus by the beast's slaying of the two prophetic witnesses on his ascent from the Abyss. Such is the scope and intensity of the antichrist's opposition to all worship except that offered to himself that even the false church is not tolerated. The alliance of the beast and the harlot (Rev 17:1-7) is terminated. Profaned ("trampled," Rev 11:2) by the nations during the interim era, the Babylon harlot is destroyed by the beast powers in the hour of the final crisis: "they will hate the harlot; they will make her desolate and naked and devour her flesh and burn her with fire" (Rev 7:16). Clearly, the enormity of the surge of evil world powers at the close of the church age contradicts the postmillennial expectation that all the nations will have been theocratized under the kingship of Christ during the millennium. As we shall be further observing below, the kingdom of glory comes only after the complete and final removal of all evil from the earth.

Latent in the Apocalyptic symbolism is an even more direct contradiction of dominion theology's postmillennial eschatology. The melding of church with the state and its coercive power, the arrangement which theonomic reconstructionism regards as the kingdom ideal to be attained during the millennium, is precisely what is anathematized in the Apocalypse as the harlot-Babylon church, the monstrous perversion of the true church.

The Parousia Day

Evocative of the Har Magedon judgment scene is the term "the day of the Lord" and variations thereof. These include: "the day of Yahweh of hosts," "the day of judgment," "the great day," "the great and terrible day of Yahweh," "the day of his coming," "the day when Yahweh takes action" (Ps 118:24; Mal 4:3 [3:21]), "that day," or simply "the day" (Mal 4:1 [3:19]). It is the particular occasions when the divine council assembles from time to time for judicial action that accounts for the use of this temporal terminology for the spatial reality of the heavenly court or the epiphanic Presence that is constitutive of that awesome place. A familiar instance of the latter is the designating of the second advent of the Lord Jesus as the "day" (1 Cor 3:13; Heb 10:25; cf. 1 Cor 4:3, where "day" signifies human judgment). Of incidental interest, the dual spatial (or theophanic) and temporal dimensions of "the day of the Lord" correspond to two meanings of the Magedon-term môʿēd: appointed place of assembly (especially the ʾōhel môʿēd, "tent of meeting") and appointed time of assembly (especially the sacred festivals).

Origins. The origin of the day of the Lord concept is found in the "days" of creation. As observed earlier, each of the six days contains a judgment pronouncement of the Creator, declaring the work of that day "good." But the seventh day is preeminently the day of the Lord. The sabbatical rest in which it consists is a royal-judicial session of the Judge of mankind and angelkind, an on-going work of judgment that occupies the Lord of Har Magedon until the consummation (cf. John 5:17). The temporal reality of the seventh day is thus identified with the spatial reality of the enthroned Glory-Presence, the central core and fullness of the supernal realm. The theophanic-cosmological and the eschatological dimensions of the day of the Lord thus intermesh from the very beginning in a heavenly register space-time continuum. [On the origin and other aspects of the day of the Lord, cf. *IOS* 106-115.]

Day of Covenant Judgment. As we trace the day-of-the-Lord judgments through the Scriptures we find that they are an enforcing of the dual curse-blessing sanctions of God's kingdom covenant, an implementing of the principal principle of covenant justice, whereby the Lord rewards with eternal life those who seek for glory, honor, and immortality and renders wrath to those who obey not the truth (Rom 2:5-8).

Gen 3:8 recounts the primeval day of the Lord following Adam's failure in the probation crisis of the creational covenant. By transgressing that covenant man had incurred its death curse and in response the Lord of the covenant came in judgment. His parousia, accompanied by cherubim and thunderous "voice" (the qôl yahweh), was a divine advent "as the (Glory-)Spirit of the (judgment) day." Again in this episode, as in the seventh day of creation, there is a blending of the theophanic-spatial reality (the Spirit) with the judicial-temporal function (the day).

Likewise in the administering of the Torah covenant the failure of the covenant people in their national probation led to a day of Yahweh, a day of reckoning. Pressing the Lord's lawsuit against the Israelites, his prophet-lawyers repeatedly warned that for those who did not honor their covenant obligations the coming day of the Lord would bring not light but darkness. Such a day of judicial darkness befell the nation in the calamity of the Babylonian exile and a second time in the 70 AD destruction of Jerusalem.

Beyond the typological day of the Lord that would terminate the Old Covenant order as threatened in the curses of the Mosaic covenants, the Old Testament prophets foresaw an eschatological day of the Lord, a final judgment event at the conclusion of the coming new covenant age. For God's redeemed people it would prove to be a day of vindication. But for those who spurn the invitation to come under the grace of the new covenant in Christ, the second Adam, making instead the wretched choice to remain under the works principle in the first Adam, this final day of the Lord would bring the unmitigated doom threatened against man in the primal covenant of works in Eden.

Sabbatical Symbol. Before proceeding to the New Testament developments, we shall take note of the sabbatical symbol of the day of the Lord. The revelation of the creation "week" culminating in the eternal seventh day of the Lord (a revelation presumably given to Adam in Eden) was at the same time an instituting of the Sabbath ordinance (Gen 2:3). Stamped on the course of man's earthly life, the Creator's seven day pattern with the seventh day a symbolic representation of the upper register seventh day was a continuing reminder of the heavenly day of the Lord. Keeping before man's eye his Maker's claim of cosmic sovereignty, the Sabbath ordinance called for an unconditional, unquestioning consecration to him. Agreeably, in the Sinaitic renewal of the Sabbath ordinance it is declared over and again that the Sabbath belongs to or is holy to Yahweh, the covenant Lord. The Sabbath also held out the promise that for the overcomers, the eschatological journey leads to union with their Lord in the Spirit and to sabbath rest beyond this world-time. It pointed to the consummated day of the Lord.

Like the history of the creation "week" in which it was embedded, the Sabbath ordinance was communicated to man only through special revelation. The specific sabbatical requirement of six days of kingdom work to be followed by a seventh day rest was a separately disclosed, sovereign provision of the creation covenant. It was not part of the general revelation of the moral will of God written on man's heart in creation and of universal obligation at all times. Certainly those who contend that it was cannot simultaneously hold that such an unchangeable moral imperative was later altered by changing the Sabbath day from the seventh day to the first day of the week.

Whatever the mode of its disclosure, the Sabbath was a creation ordinance and that is urged by advocates of the universality of the Sabbath in support of their view. What this argument overlooks is that the Adamic family in Eden, though it was indeed the whole world at that time, was a holy theocratic community in covenant relationship to their Creator-Lord. They were a universal-*covenant* community and the Sabbath ordinance was an article (and in fact a sign) of that covenant. To abstract the Sabbath from the framework of the Covenant of Creation (à la the fallacious nature-grace scheme) is to denature the biblical reality. The fact is that no evidence of the Sabbath's having been appointed to a non-covenantal group is to be found here in the Sabbath's origins as a creation ordinance.

Another customary argument for the universally binding nature of the Sabbath ordinance is that this view of it is required by its inclusion in the Decalogue revelation at Sinai (Exod 20:8-11). But false assumptions regarding the Decalogue inform this argument. To be sure these laws are for the most part universal moral norms. Taken as a whole, however, they are clearly presented in the Exodus narrative as part of a special covenant revelation of Yahweh given to his elect people Israel, not as a general revelation of law addressed to the world at large. Specifically, the ten commandments are the standard central stipulations section found in treaties of the Mosaic age and accordingly the documentary witnesses to this Sinaitic transaction are identified as "the two tables of the *covenant*" (Exod 31:18; 32:15; 34:29; Deut 4:13; 9:9,11,15).

Moreover, in this Sinaitic context the Sabbath ordinance itself is explicitly identified as an "everlasting covenant" and a "sign" of the covenant between God and his chosen people (Exod 31:16,17). It signifies that he, Yahweh, was sanctifying the recipients of the Sabbath sign (Exod 31:12), distinguishing them from the rest of the world, setting them apart as a holy kingdom people, peculiarly his own. The Sabbath symbol of the day of the Lord does not belong to the world, but, quite the contrary, was given to God's people Israel as a mark of distinction from the nations in general (cf. Deut 5:15).

Further, since the six days of divine work in the creation paradigm (cf. Exod 20:11) were holy kingdom-establishing activity, so too must be the six days of work in the Sabbath ordinance, which replicates that divine archetype. This means that Sabbath observance requires a theocratic as well as a covenantal setting, that is, a setting in which culture as well as cult is holy kingdom activity. Such was the case in the two historical situations where the Sabbath ordinance was clearly prescribed, i.e., in Eden and at the mount Sinai Har Magedon. If there was Sabbath observance in other covenantal contexts in redemptive history before the Law (e.g., the patriarchal community), it would be due to the presence there of an earthly altar perceived as a symbolic mountain of God, a stylized Har Magedon. Incidentally, this would be analogous to the way in which the presence of such altar-theocracies evidently provided the socio-political rationale for the practice of the required tributary tithe. In the New Covenant era beyond the demise of the Israelite theocracy, an era in which the common grace principle is uniformly operative, the theocratic context prerequisite to the six-work-days component of the Sabbath ordinance is missing. To contend that the Sabbath stipulation of the Old Covenant, designed for a theocratic community, has continuing normative status today, one must first fall in with the pernicious theonomic notions concerning the civil provisions of the Law.

Certain other considerations of a negative sort contradict the view that the Sabbath is a universal norm. In the post-Fall world the Sabbath is omitted from the provisions of the common grace order (cf. especially Genesis 3, 4 and 9). Also, insistence on Sabbath observance is absent from the decree of the Jerusalem council (Acts 15).

In short, there is no biblical evidence that the Sabbath ordinance was ever given to a universal (or restricted) non-covenantal group. Wherever it is found it is a mark of privileged, holy status and a sign of the covenant people's hope of the consummation of God's kingdom. Accordingly, even if Sabbath observance as prescribed in the fourth commandment were regarded as a continuing obligation under the New Covenant, it would still have to be recognized that this covenant sign appertained only to the covenant community of the church.

The question of the continuity of the Sabbath ordinance into the church age is the question of the relation of the Sabbath to the Christian first day of the week. This will be investigated below in connection with the resumption of our exploration of the day of the Lord theme.

Day of Christ. The eschatological day of the Lord foretold by the Old Testament prophets reappears in New Testament prophecies of the end of the world. It continues to be closely identified with the parousia-Presence of God and with divine judicial action, only now the day of Yahweh becomes the day of Jesus Christ and his parousia as Judge. A remarkable witness this to his deity! As Jesus testified, it is his identity as Son of man, that is deity (cf. Dan 7:13,14), that makes it appropriate for him to receive authority to execute judgment in the coming hour of the resurrection-judgment (John 5:26-29).

Christians awaiting that hour of the apocalypse of Jesus when they will be made manifest before "the judgment-seat of Christ" (2 Cor 5:10; cf. Rom 14:10, with textual variant "God" for "Christ") are assured that they will be found guiltless in that "day of our Lord Jesus Christ" (1 Cor 1:8). And as we observed above, Christ's disclosing of the judgment at his appearing is attributed in 1 Cor 3:13 to "the Day." Other variations of this terminology include: "the day of Christ" (Phil 1:10; 2:16); "the day of Jesus Christ" (Phil 1:6); "the day of the Lord Jesus" (1 Cor 5:5; 2 Cor 1:14; cf. 1 Thess 5:2). With reference to his parousia advent in judgment Jesus himself speaks of "his day" (Luke 17:24) and "the day when the Son of man is revealed" (Luke 17:30).

Rev 1:10 and the Sabbath. Rev 1:10 calls for special attention here. Describing his visionary experience, the apostle John writes: "I was in the Spirit on the Lord's day and I heard behind me a loud voice." In this statement the phrase "the Lord's day" (or "the dominical day," reflecting the replacement of the usual noun kurios by the adjective kuriakos) is often regarded as a designation of the day of corporate Christian worship, the first day of the week. It would then be another detail, along with the location of John on Patmos (v. 9), in the description of the circumstances of his receiving the apocalyptic visions. But we are alerted to a different interpretation by the striking similarity of this passage to the primeval judicial parousia narrated in Gen 3:8, both passages containing the same combination of features: the Spirit, the day, and the "voice." Indeed, Rev 1:11ff., elaborating on John's reception of the vision, locates the apostle in the heavenly judgment scene of the divine council, the scene which the Scriptures identify with the day of the Lord. The Glory-Presence of the divine Judge that dominates that scene is here a parousia of the Son of man, Christ the Lord, invested in the Glory-Spirit and surrounded by the angelic hosts, as we see in subsequent expanded descriptions of this scene (e.g., Revelation 4 and 5). Moreover, in the associated letters to the churches Christ functions as Lord of the covenant, engaged in the pronouncing of judgment on the work of his servants in the seven covenant communities (cf. Revelation 2 and 3), precisely as was the case in the Lord's thunderous advent in Eden as the Spirit of the (judgment) day. [Cf. *IOS* 123-124.]

This means that "on the Lord's day" in Rev 1:10 stands in appositional explanation to "in the Spirit," which regularly in the Apocalypse designates the upper register realm (cf. Rev 4:2; 17:3; 21:10). "The Lord's day" here does not refer narrowly to the final judgment day foretold by the prophets; it rather denotes the continuing judicial scene of the heavenly court in session (another instance of this temporal terminology being used for the permanent spatial reality of God's enthronement as Judge of the world). It might well be that the choice of the unusual kuriakos in Rev 1:10 instead of the customary kurios was to avoid the phrase's being misunderstood as a reference to the final judgment event.

A significant implication of our interpretation of this passage is that the messianic day of the Lord has an "already" as well as a "not-yet" aspect. It was inaugurated at the first advent of Christ through his resurrection and ascension. In the time of the apostle John the Son of Man had already assumed his place at the right hand of the Majesty on high, crowned with glory and honor (cf. Heb 2:9). There will be a climactic finale. The day of Christ the Lord will culminate in the parousia of Jesus in the glory of the Father with all the holy angels and in his consummating of the kingdom through a final, cosmic, redemptive judgment at Har Magedon. But "the Lord's day" of Rev 1:10 refers to the already realized heavenly enthronement of the Lord Jesus.

The arrival of the inaugurated messianic kingdom stage of the day of the Lord raises the question of the present status of the Sabbath, the symbolic day of the Lord prior to the New Covenant era. The dominant traditional approach maintains that the Sabbath ordinance continues to be in force, only the Sabbath day has been shifted from the end of the week to the first day, the day adopted by Christians for their assemblies and soon known as the Lord's day (appropriately so even if Rev 1:10 does not offer an inspired instance of this). Apart from this change in days it is held that the fourth commandment's regulations regarding the manner of Sabbath observance have been transmitted to the alleged New Covenant Sabbath.

But the difference between the old and the supposed new Sabbath is not as slight as it might seem. Actually in the hypothesized process of changing the Sabbath day from the seventh to the first day of the week the whole thrust of the symbolism of the sabbatical week gets radically altered. To understand the nature of the continuities and discontinuities in the history of the Sabbath ordinance we need to return again to its creational origins. With and through the instituting of the Sabbath in Eden the division of time into a recurring seven-day cycle was impressed on the life of the covenant people. This reckoning of time as a succession of weeks continues beyond the covenant in Eden throughout the history of the administration of the Covenant of Grace, including the New Covenant age. But the specific form of this covenant week is adjusted to the changing eschatological position of the covenant people. In particular, our present concern is to show that the New Covenant version of the generic covenant week differs radically from the covenant week as sabbatically structured in the beginning and again in the Law and, indeed, that the discontinuity is such as to preclude the identification of the New Covenant first day with the Sabbath prescribed in the fourth commandment.

To begin with the big, obvious difference – the relation of the one distinctive day in the week to the other six days is the polar opposite under the New Covenant order to what it was under the Old Covenant, now preceding rather than following the others. This is already a fatal objection to identifying the distinctive Christian day as the Sabbath, for the sequence of days with the Sabbath coming after the six days is an essential feature of the Sabbath ordinance. That is so for a couple of reasons. First, it is explicitly indicated in the fourth commandment that the Sabbath ordinance is designed to replicate the Creator's pattern of kingdom-producing work (i.e., the six days) which leads to the sabbath rest afterwards (i.e., the seventh day). This basic feature of the Mosaic Sabbath would be lost in a weekly pattern with a first day Sabbath. And second, the Sabbath ordinance is intended to convey symbolically the promise that the covenant people would attain to the eschatological sabbath rest (i.e., the seventh day) via a history of kingdom-cultural labor (i.e., the six days), in fact, as a reward for their carrying out the kingdom commission of the covenant. A first day Sabbath would fail to give expression to that eschatological-covenantal process.

Further, the difference between the covenant week in the Old and New Covenants is more than simply the different sequence of the six days and the one day. For, as we have seen, the cultural activities of God's people in the New Covenant age would not qualify as holy kingdom labors in the first place, inasmuch as they are common grace (i.e., non-holy, non-kingdom) activities. As such there is no place for them to function symbolically at all within the schema of the holy covenant week. Like the sixty-two weeks in the seventy weeks pattern of Dan 9:25, the six days following the first day serve only to fill out formally the imagery of the generic covenant week. Only one day then has special significance in the covenant week under the New Covenant – a major difference from the sabbatical week appointed in the Law, in which the six days also have their own sign value.

Moreover, the special character of that one distinctive weekly day in the Christian calendar is of a different kind than that exhibited by the sabbatical seventh day. Unlike the latter, whose observance took the form of a symbolic imitation of a divine paradigmatic event (viz. the Creator's seventh day cessation of work), the Christian practice of the first day does not involve such re-enactment. Its special significance does not lie in the realm of symbolic dramatization by the observant community at all. It is simply the set time for believers to come together to meet with the Lord.

Otherwise stated, the Decalogue's Sabbath ordinance differs from the Christian first day in that it involves both time and place (more specifically, a holy theocratic kingdom place) whereas the latter involves only time.

This tends to be obscured once special buildings are erected to facilitate the assembly of Christians for worship (in itself an innocent and inevitable development) and these structures come to be entitled "sanctuaries" and begin to incorporate temple features, like the altar, into their architecture and furnishings (a lamentable development).

A further problem for the traditional view of the Sabbath ordinance is that under the Old Covenant the weekly Sabbath was integral to a typological network of sabbatical festivals which, along with the whole system of types, became obsolete once the antitypical New Covenant order was established. The obsolescence of these sabbatical days is confirmed by the apostle Paul's observations in Rom 14:5; Gal 4:10; and Col 2:16,17. The interpretation of these passages is much debated but the most that might be extracted in support of Sabbath day observance under the New Covenant is that though not mandated for Christians it is to be tolerated, or rather was tolerated for a while. The rationale for this Pauline policy of leaving it to the individual conscience would be found in the overlap of the old and new orders until 70 AD and the temporary continuance of the validity of the old temple system. However, not only did that situation come to an end at the destruction of Jerusalem but the Sabbath observance temporarily tolerated was the old seventh day Sabbath. Continuing the typological Sabbath permanently into the New Covenant age contravenes the teaching of the Book of Hebrews that Jesus has secured the antitypical sabbath estate (sabbatismos, Heb 4:9) that still remained to be attained after Joshua brought Israel into the typical sabbath rest in Canaan (Heb 4:8). It denies in effect that the entry of man into the divine sabbatical rest that was promised in the typological Sabbath of the creational and Sinaitic covenants has been realized through the resurrection of the God-man, Jesus Christ, and his ascension to the heavenly heights of Har Magedon. It fails to recognize that the premessianic Sabbath symbolism was a temporary, passing shadow and that Christ is the abiding substance (Col 2:17), the antitypal sabbath rest.

Another serious theological problem besets the identification of the Christian first day as the Sabbath. The Sabbath ordinance of six days of kingdom labor leading to the reward of sabbath rest was not only a component of the premessianic typological system but, as a sign of the Torah covenant, it was an exponent of the works principle that governed Israel's possession of the typological kingdom under the Law. The alleged continuance of the Sabbath in the church would carry that principle of works with it into the New Covenant administration of Gospel grace. The advocacy of such a continuance of the Decalogue ordinance of the Sabbath is therefore, in effect, a Judaizing contention.

The risen Christ by his precedent setting first-day-of-the-week appearances to his disciples (cf. Luke 24:13ff.,36ff.; John 20:19-23,26ff.) appointed the time for believers to come together to meet with him henceforth. In ordering a weekly cycle he was authorizing the continuation of the covenant week into the New Covenant era, only now it appertained solely to the cultic sphere of the life of God's people; it was no longer a cultural-cultic sabbatical week. With this instituting of the Christian first day of the week, the sabbatical ordinance of the Decalogue was abrogated, replaced by the dominical week. And this means that contrary to traditional Sabbatarianism the distinctive first day of the new, dominical week is not a modified residue of the Sabbath day of the fourth commandment, governed by the rules for Sabbath observance, such as the prohibition of various non-cultic activities.

Octave Day Assemblies. Some further, more positive explication of the first day of the week is in order. A good name for it would be Assembly Day (yôm môᶜēd), Magedon Day. It is the day for the people of God to gather as the ekklesia. This earthly gathering is not a mere symbol of the Mount Zion above and the assembly there of the Lord and his angels and the spirits of just men made perfect (Heb 12:22-24). It is an actual earthly extension of that heavenly reality. Hence, the angels are present (1 Cor 11:10; cf. Rev 1:20). And like the assembly on high this holy cultic gathering has a judicial character. There is here an exercising of the keys of the kingdom; the sanctions of the covenant are declared, benedictions and anathemas (cf. Revelation 2 and 3). This is not yet the full assembly, the final eternal day of the Lord, but it is already a participation in that day through the Spirit.

The first day gatherings are in celebrative commemoration of the exaltation of Jesus as Lord through the first-day-of-the-week events of his resurrection and his bestowal of the Spirit on the church at Pentecost, which was the confirmation of his lordship. A brief supportive comment on this dating of the Acts 2 Pentecost is injected here in view of disagreement on the matter. The identity of the Sabbath in the phrase "the day after the Sabbath" in Lev 23:15 is disputed but on either interpretation (i.e., whether the first day of the Feast of Unleavened Bread or the Saturday in the week of the feast) it will have been Saturday in the year in question, when the fourteenth of Abib, Passover (cf. Exodus 12; Leviticus 23; Deuteronomy 16), fell on Thursday evening/Friday. Hence "the day after the Sabbath" from which the fifty days to Pentecost were counted was Sunday and accordingly the Pentecost advent of the Spirit came on a first day of the week.

Reflective of the nature of the "coming together" of the ekklesia (1 Cor 11:17,18,33,34) on the first day as an acknowledgment and celebration of Jesus' lordship over the household of God, the meal of which they partook on that occasion, the showing forth of his death until he comes, is called the Lord's (kuriakos) supper (1 Cor 11:20). And as we have noted, the day of assembly itself came to be known as the Lord's (kuriakos) day (or dominical day), a showing forth of Christ's lordship until he comes. The ekklesia gathering on the first day is an interim form of his parousia until the parousia of the final day of the Lord in redemptive judgment.

Both forms of the covenant week, the one with the seventh day Sabbath and the first day arrangement, give expression to the dominion of the covenant Lord. However, though they have this feature in common, the first day, as we have demonstrated, is not to be identified as a continuation of the Sabbath. Analogous is the relation between the Paschal Feast and the Lord's Supper. Both are meals of covenant communion and both are said to belong to the Lord (cf. Lev 23:6) but nevertheless the Lord's Supper of the New Covenant is not to be identified with the Paschal meal and is not subject to the various regulations governing the latter. Similarly, baptism and circumcision both symbolize covenant judgment ordeals and function as signs of covenant membership appointed for those who profess the faith and their children, but baptism is not circumcision. Likewise, though both are Lord's days, the Christian first day is not the Sabbath.

The Christian first day is an octave day, a heptad plus one, the climactic eighth day of an ogdoad. This ogdoad pattern of a unit of seven (or multiple sevens) plus one is exhibited in the ceremonial calendar of the Old Covenant. In the Feast of Booths, for example, the seven days of offerings are crowned by an eighth day of holy convocation (Lev 23:33-36), a day of solemn rest like the first day of that feast (Lev 23:39), but an octave higher. Pentecost involves a heightened form of this numerical scheme, a fiftieth day after a period of seven times seven or forty-nine days (Lev 23:15,16). Likewise, the Jubilee year is a fiftieth year, the plus one year after seven sabbath years (Lev 25:8-10). Among its counterfeits of Christ and his kingdom, the satanic enterprise has its pseudo-version of the octave pattern. The beast is an eighth head, the climax of the seven heads. But it fails to bring its heptad series to a successful conclusion. It does not gain the heights of Har Magedon; quite the opposite, it descends to perdition (Rev 17:11). Christ, however, is the true octave figure and his resurrection day (celebrated in the first day assemblies of the ekklesia) betokens the consummate perfecting of Har Magedon. Allusive as they are to the timing of the resurrection of Christ ("as it began to dawn towards the first day of the week") the first day gatherings of the church proclaim that he is the victor over the Enemy and the tomb, the true One, the antitype of the old theocratic kings in the typological era of sabbath cycles, the legitimate vindicated Lord of Har Magedon whose reign has already been inaugurated.

Easter Sunday, the precedent setting first day, is bound to the immediately preceding seventh day in the triad of days (Friday-Saturday-Sunday) that constitutes the climactic, triumphant encounter of Jesus with Satan and his victory over death, the "three days and three nights in the heart of the earth" (Matt 12:40). That original dominical day was therefore a first day after the Sabbath, a seventh day plus one, an eighth day, an octave first day. And such then are the subsequent dominical days of ekklesia assembly.

Both Israel's Sabbath and the church's octavized first day lift up the eyes of God's people to the consummation of Har Magedon. The Sabbath points to the consummation as completion, as arrival at the eschatological goal of the original creation. The octave dominical day points to the consummation as a commencement, as the launching into the realm of the new creation. Or better, it presages the unending continuance, the everlastingness, of the consummated cosmos. In the numerological code of the Scriptures this octave one is a cipher for infinity; it signifies the eternity of Har Magedon consummated. Speaking of things touching Christ, the true, octave King of kings, the doxology that ascends from the octave first day assembly confesses to him: "Thy throne, O God, is for ever and ever" (Ps 45:6 [7]).

Har Magedon Gatherings

Pre-Parousia Gatherings. Acts of divine gathering with Mount Magedon as their ultimate destination are a prominent feature in the prototypal judgment days. The Noahic household was gathered into the ark, a sanctuary in the midst of the world-destroying divine judgment and a refuge from the tyrannical Cainite dynasts. And in that vehicular symbol of the cosmic kingdom the covenant community, gathered out of the perishing world, was bound for the Har Magedon mount of Ararat. A gathering of a different sort was going on outside the ark, a clambering to higher ground as the waters of judgment rose relentlessly, eventually prevailing over the mountains and thereby over the swarm of doomed mankind herded on those heights. In the exodus judgment that redeemed God's people from the house of bondage, the Mosaic nation was gathered out of the land of Egypt to the Har Magedon assembly at Sinai. Also entailed in that act of redemption was the Lord's sovereign gathering of the pharaoh's hosts to their doom in the sea. The dual gatherings involved in these redemptive judgments manifested contrasting judicial verdicts of vindication and condemnation and were themselves a part of the process of executing the corresponding dual sanctions of salvation and destruction.

This Har Magedon phenomenon of gathering is found again in the antitypal day of the Lord. That two-sided final judgment is also depicted in Scripture as a double gathering at the Mount of Assembly. We shall return to this ultimate, second advent gathering but first want to indicate how pervasive this feature of gathering is by observing how it figures in the other main periods of the messianic administration of the kingdom, namely the interim and the crisis. As we shall see, a variety of specific images are used to portray the Har Magedon gatherings: agricultural harvesting, military mustering, and the homecoming of dispersed people.

The interim gathering is a harvesting of the mission field of the world. Jesus commissioned his disciples to this harvest-gathering, a task already urgent at that time (John 4:35-37; cf. Luke 10:2; Matt 9:37,38). In that context he declared the hour was come to move on from the old holy mountains to the true (i.e., heavenly) center of worship in the Spirit (John 4:23,24), the celestial Zion/Har Magedon. During the interim those rescued by the power of the gospel from the deception of Satan are being gathered from all nations into the ekklesia assembly, the church on earth and the church already in the heavenly assembly on mount Zion above. This gathering is a harvest of firstfruits unto God and the Lamb (Rev 14:1,4; on the use of firstfruits imagery for believers cf. Rom 16:5; 1 Cor 16:15; Jas 1:18).

The church militant laboring in the mission field is God's agent but ultimately God is the Harvester. It is by his Spirit that the menorah mission will be accomplished (Zech 4:6; cf. *GOM* 136-141). It is Jesus who will gather together into one those from among scattered humanity who are predestined to be the children of God (John 11:52). The particular kind of gathering referred to in this prophecy is one familiar from the Old Testament, the bringing back home of a scattered people. More specifically the image is drawn from the typology of the Israelites exiled in Babylon and then restored to Jerusalem, a history which reproduces the situation of mankind, scattered from Paradise but regathered in Christ to the holy mountain of God (cf. Deut 30:4,5; Isa 43:5,6; 66:19-21; Jer 23:3; 29:14; 31:8,10; 32:37; Ezek 11:17; 20:34,41; 28:25; 34:13; 36:24; 37:21,22; 39:21; Ps 107:2,3). The prophesied arrival at the goal of the antitypical paradise takes us beyond the interim to the consummation, but the restoration of the elect from the diaspora of humanity is already a work in progress during the interim age of the church, busy at its gathering task in the fields ripe for harvesting.

The gathering at the antichrist crisis is of a military sort. It is the mustering of the hordes of Gog and Magog for the final battle of Har Magedon. This global campaign of deception by the dragon, the beast, and the false prophet (Rev 16:14,16; 19:19; 20:8; Ezekiel 38 and 39; Ps 48:4; Zech 12:3) is a satanic counterfeit of Christ's imminent gathering of the redeemed. At the same time, as Ezekiel's prophecy of the event emphasizes (Ezek 38:4,16,17; 39:2,17), this amassing of armies is God's doing. He releases Satan from his millennial imprisonment (Rev 20:7) and uses him as his instrument (like heart-hardened pharaoh of old) to gather the wicked forces to the mountain of God, the place of their execution (cf. Isa 66:18; Joel 3:2; Mic 4:12,13; Zech 14:2). The antichrist crisis, the terminal episode in earth history, merges into the judgment event that introduces the eternal state. For the wicked the gathering at Har Magedon for the great battle turns into a gathering into the winepress of eternal perdition.

Dual Parousia Gathering. At the parousia there is a dual gathering to Har Magedon for final judgment, with consignment of all men to either the supernal garner or the infernal pit. The motif of this double harvesting is sculptured in high relief in Rev 14:14-20.

The two divisions of mankind contrasted in this passage are referred to in the immediately preceding context. Those who are gathered in the grain harvest (vv. 14-16) are the hundred forty-four thousand described in vv. 1-5, followers of the Lamb, redeemed from mankind as firstfruits for God. They represent the attainment of the full complement of the servants of God promised to the martyr suppliants in Rev 6:9-11 (cf. Rev 14:13). They are the company portrayed in the double vision of the hundred forty-four thousand and the great multitude from all nations in Revelation 7 (i.e., the church depicted first in typological, then more literal fashion). They stand with the Lamb on Mount Zion and sing the new song before the Har Magedon throne.

Those who are gathered in the grape harvest (Rev 14:17-20) are the worshippers of the beast described in vv. 9-11. They drink the wine of God's unmitigated wrath and the smoke of their fiery torment goes up for ever and ever.

It is the apocalyptic advent of Christ on the world stage at the crisis that sets in motion the whole resurrection-judgment complex of events. The Son of Man is the great gatherer who orders and oversees the dual harvest of the final redemptive judgment. John the Forerunner foretold this dual gathering role of Jesus: he would baptize with the Spirit and fire, clearing his threshing floor, gathering the wheat into the granary and burning the chaff with unquenchable fire (Matt 3:11,12; Luke 3:16,17). And Jesus himself declared in the kingdom parable of Matt 13:24-43 that at the end of the age it is he who shall send his angels on their double harvest mission. Agreeably the dual gathering of Rev 14:14-20 is conducted by Jesus and his angels. The passage opens with the epiphany of the Son of Man, with golden crown and seated on a white cloud, insignia of deity (cf. Dan 7:13,14; Rev 1:13). He proceeds to harvest the grain while an associate angel gathers the vintage of the earth destined to be crushed in the winepress of divine wrath.

The Gathering of the Elect. Christ, raised from the dead, was the "firstfruits." Those who are his at his coming are the rest of the harvest (1 Cor 15:20-23), the grain harvest of Rev 14:16. Summoned from the grave (or, if bodily alive at the parousia, transported from the midst of the crisis-conflict with Satan), transfigured in the twinkling of an eye, they are gathered up in the clouds to meet the Lord in the air (1 Thess 4:14-17; 2 Thess 2:1; 1 Cor 15:51-54). That this word of comfort is immediately addressed to those concerned about believers who had fallen asleep in Jesus (1 Thess 4:13) tells us that reunion with our loved ones in the Lord is one aspect of the joy of this harvest gathering, a joy perfected by our being caught up together into the presence of our Savior to be with him always (1 Thess 4:17).

The resurrection-gathering of the saints effects a separation of the sons of the kingdom from the seed of the evil one. This separation is brought out graphically in our Lord's teaching concerning the day of the Son of Man, the day like the Noahic day of judgment. Coming on the clouds of heaven with power and great glory (cf. Matt 16:27; 2 Thess 1:7) he will send out his angels with a loud trumpet call to gather his elect from one end of heaven to the other (Matt 24:30,31), but also to gather all evildoers out of his kingdom (Matt 13:41). One of two men in the field will be taken to safety and one left for desolation. One of two women grinding at the mill will be taken and the other left (Matt 24:39-41). The angel reapers will perform their twofold task: the weeds (the Satan-sown wicked) will be gathered and bound in bundles to be burned in the furnace of fire and the wheat (the righteous) will be gathered into the barn, destined to glow like the sun in the kingdom of their Father (Matt 13:30,39-43).

In thus separating the elect from the reprobate the resurrection-gathering is a phase of the final judicial process, an identifying of individuals as belonging to one or the other category. It is a public disclosure of verdicts reached in the divine court, with all in heaven and earth as witnesses. Moreover the resurrection-glorification of those in Christ confirms their justification and vindicates them in their controversy with Satan's offspring, validating their claim to be the true heirs of the Har Magedon kingdom. This judicial aspect of the event comes to expression in Jesus' eschatological teaching in his portraying the finale of history as a courtroom proceeding, a holding of judgment in the court of heaven: when the Son of Man comes in his glory with all the angels he will sit on the Glory-throne and all peoples will be gathered before him. He will separate the sheep from the goats. Pronouncing the benediction of the Father on the sheep, he will invite them to inherit the kingdom of eternal life, prepared for them from the foundation of the world. And pronouncing the goats accursed, he will dismiss them to the eternal fire prepared for the devil and his angels (Matt 25:31-46).

The combination of this courtroom metaphor with the familiar battlefield metaphor for the climactic confrontation event matches the dual role of Har Magedon, the focus of the resurrection gatherings, as both the site of the battle and the site of God's judgment throne and court. Actually, the battle *is* the judgment process. It is a variety of the judicial technique of trial by ordeal in which the outcome of the combat signifies the verdicts of approbation or condemnation.

The saints are not simply passive spectators in the final judgment. In both martial and juridical portrayals an active role is attributed to them. In the military scenario Christ is the divine warrior, the champion who triumphs in the trial by ordeal combat against Satan, but the gathered redeemed participate with him in crushing the serpent's head (Rom 16:20; cf. Rev 2:16,17). It is by the blood of the Lamb that Satan is overcome but the triumph is also affirmed of the company of martyr witnesses (Rev 12:21). Christ's gathering of his people is therefore a mustering of troops for the final battle of Har Magedon. The count of their assembled hosts, twelve thousand from each of the twelve tribes (Rev 7:1-8; 14:1) is reminiscent of the military census records of Israel (cf., e.g., Num 1:2ff.). And when the Faithful and True rides forth to judge and make war (Rev 19:11) those who are arrayed in the white linen of his righteousness follow in his train as "the armies of heaven" (Rev 19:14). To these overcomers it is given to share in Messiah's prerogative of shattering the evil powers like a potter's vessel (Rev 2:16,17; cf. Ps 2:9). In a prophecy of the gathering of the nations against Zion, Micah, incorporating agricultural imagery into the military picture, declares that God will gather those nations as sheaves to the threshing floor and will commission the daughter of Zion to rise and thresh them and, ox-like, beat them in pieces with bronze hoofs and iron horns. The prophet Zechariah employs even fiercer figures for the role of the Lord's people in the day of judgment: God will turn them into weapons of war, bow and arrow and warrior's sword, and like wild beasts they will roar and devour and be satiated with the blood of the foe (Zech 9:13-15; cf. Isa 41:15,16).

In the courtroom imagery of the final judgment the saints' role vis-à-vis their satanic adversaries is that of judges. This is in keeping with man's original assignment as guardian of Har Magedon to judge Satan, banishing him from God's holy presence. Paul assumes that this judicial role of the saints is a matter of common knowledge: "Do you not know that the saints will judge the world . . . that we will judge angels?" (1 Cor 6:2,3; cf. Heb 2:6-8). Beyond the final judgment this royal-judicial dignity is perpetuated in Christ's granting to the overcomers to sit with him on his throne (Rev 3:21; cf. Dan 7:27; Matt 19:28; Luke 22:30).

The resurrection-metamorphosis of the saints is not only a rendering of judgment that declares them to be the legitimate claimants to the eternal kingdom; it is an actual passage into the Glory-world. Indeed this assimilation or incorporation of redeemed mankind into it is a constitutive element in the instituting of the eternal order. Resurrection and final judgment may then be subsumed under the palingenesis (Matt 18:29), the regeneration of the cosmos.

The in-a-moment, in-the-twinkling-of-an-eye nature of the particular episode of the glorifying of the saints at the parousia (1 Cor 15:51,52) is not explicitly affirmed of the complex of parousia, resurrection, judgment, and palingenesis as a whole. In fact, surveying the significance of the various facets of this stupendous cosmic event as revealed in battle and courtroom imagery leaves us with the impression that a (perhaps considerable) period of time must be involved. Yet when we analyze the eschaton experience of the elect, each aspect of it seems to entail the simultaneous presence of the others. The same is true in the case of those whose dreadful portion is among those who people Hell. That would suggest that the re-creation resulting in the eternal Glory-order of the new heaven and earth transpires in a moment, a singular instant of divine apocalypse, an Omega-radiation answering to the Alpha-radiation that produced the Glory-realm with its angelic hosts at the origin of the cosmos in the beginning.

Whether the transition occurs in a moment or over a more extended time, a daunting ultimate culture shock would seem to await us frail mortals in crossing the boundary into the Glory-dimensioned world of God and the angels. But we will not fear for "Thou art with me." Though the mountains topple into the heart of the sea and the earth melts, God is our refuge and strength (Psalm 46; cf. Joel 3:16). Our Maker-Lord, who has gone before us to prepare a place for us, has surely arranged for us in his love and wisdom a transfer into that new world that is not merely psychologically manageable but an occasion of ecstatic wonder and the joyous peace of arrival at home at last. Indeed through all the generations he has already been providing such a blessed passage for his people, shepherding them through the valley of death's shadow into the light of his Glory-Presence beyond the veil (Luke 16:22; Ps 17:15).

In connection with their glorification believers alive at the parousia receive a blessing gained by the departed saints at their death/"first resurrection," the perfecting of their sanctification. Glorified and sanctified beyond the possibility of sinning the redeemed are completely equipped for their eternal state of existence in the realm of consummated Har Magedon. That cosmic holy of holies, tabernacle of the God of Glory, is the heavenly garner into which Christ, the Harvester of the grain, gathers his people.

The Gathering of the Reprobate. Given authority to execute judgment (John 5:27; Acts 17:31), the Son solemnly announces that the hour is coming when all who are in the tombs will hear his voice and come forth, those who have done good to the resurrection of life and those who have done evil to the resurrection of judgment (John 5:28,29), shame and everlasting contempt (Dan 12:2). Here again the eschaton event of universal resurrection issues in a clear demarcation between the elect and the reprobate and activates the eternal decrees with respect to their opposite destinies.

Like the rendering of the favorable judgment on the elect, the adverse judgment against the reprobate registered in the resurrection-separation is imaged in Scripture by intertwined military and juridical metaphors. Put in terms of the martial metaphor, the resurrection of the ungodly gathers them into the ranks of the devil's massive forces marshalled against the Lamb and the ekklesia, and the final judgment assumes the form of a last great battle between the two gathered hosts, gathered from heaven and earth and hell. The satanic gathering against Har Magedon provokes a counter gathering of the holy legions of heaven led by the Lord, intent on redemptive vengeance, bent on treading the evil hosts in his anger and trampling them in his wrath (Isa 63:1-6; cf. 13:2ff.). By way of further attestation to these antithetical gatherings, a short medley of passages from biblical seers, prophets and apostles:

On that day when the Lord gathers all the nations against Zion for battle he will seek to destroy them all (Zech 12:1-9). He will come with all his holy ones and fight against those nations, smiting them with panic and punishing them with consuming plague (Zechariah 14).

Brought out by God (Ezek 38:4,16,17; 39:2) at the end of the days from the pseudo-Zaphon against the true Har Magedon and the covenant people gathered from the nations, antichrist Gog of Magog with all his assembled troops will be utterly destroyed. The measure of their multitudes will become the measure of their debacle. Aspiring to the peak of Zion (ṣîyyôn) they end up in a grave in the valley, their carcasses flagged by burial markers (ṣîyyûn). They will be devoured by the wild creatures of field and sky invited by the Lord God to the sacrificial feast he prepares for them. For his anger will be aroused and he will rain destruction upon them, earthquake, pestilence, sword, hailstone, fire and brimstone, so bringing glory to his name as all nations witness the judgment which he executes (Ezekiel 38,39).

At the time of the end, the antichrist king of the north will exalt himself above the God of gods (Dan 11:36). Storming through the nations with his marshalled forces, military and maritime, in his mad fury he invades the Glory-land and positions himself against the holy mount of Glory (Dan 11:41,44,45a). But there he meets with divine judgment from which none can help as Messiah-Michael arises for the salvation of God's people, and there at Har Magedon he comes to his end (Dan 11:45b–12:1; cf. Dan 7:9-11,21,22,26).

When the man of sin appears at the climax of Satan's campaign of world deception (2 Thess 2:3,4,9-11) the Lord Jesus will be revealed from heaven with his mighty angels in flaming fire, taking vengeance (2 Thess 1:7,8). In that day when he comes to be glorified in his saints he will slay the lawless one with the breath of his mouth and destroy him by his parousia epiphany (2 Thess 2:8).

After the thousand years, when Satan, the beast, the false prophet and the kings of the earth with their armies are gathered to attack Har Magedon and besiege the city/camp of the saints (Rev 16:13-16; 19:19; 20:7-9), the Word of God, the Faithful and True, the Lord of lords, will ride forth with his priestly armies to encounter them. From his mouth issues a sharp sword to smite the nations. Those slain by the divine warrior will be devoured by the birds of prey, gathered for the great supper of God. The One who judges and makes war in righteousness will tread the winepress of the fury of the wrath of God the Almighty. The fate of all his foes marshalled against Har Magedon is to be cast into the lake of fire, the second death, to be tormented day and night for ever and ever (Rev 19:11-21; 20:9,10).

Portrayed according to the martial metaphor, such is the nature of the gathering of the reprobate for final judgment.

Pictured according to the juridical metaphor, the battlefield of the final conflict becomes the courtroom and the battle a legal trial by ordeal, an ordeal by dual combat between Christ and Satan, the champions of the opposing armies of the redeemed and their evil adversaries. In terms of this imagery the reprobate, raised from the dead and drafted into the devil's legions assaulting Har Magedon, find that they have been summoned there from the grave to present themselves at the tribunal of the Lord God on that holy mount. As described by the prophet Joel, God's gathering of the wicked deposits them in the Valley of Jehoshaphat, the place of the last great assize. Multitudes, multitudes of the warriors of the nations gathered in the valley of decision; for the day of the Lord is near in the valley of decision. There he sits to judge all the nations, commanding his warriors to put in the sickle for the harvest is ripe and to tread the overflowing winepress. From Zion, his holy mount of gathering, the Lord roars and the lights of heaven are darkened and heaven and earth are shaken (Joel 3:9-17).

The great white throne judgment episodes of Daniel 7 and Revelation 20 are other notable instances of the portrayal of the satanic beast's overthrow and destruction as a courtroom transaction. As pictured in Daniel's vision, the little horn's blasphemies and suppression of the saints of the Most High are the occasion for the heavenly court to sit in judgment in the presence of the Ancient of Days on his throne of fire (Dan 7:9,26). The books are opened and the torrent of consuming fire, the ordeal instrument, streams from the judgment throne, overwhelming the devil's agent. The trial by ordeal thus declares that the beast's dominion was taken away and given over to the Son of Man, fellow of the Ancient of Days and representative-champion of the saints in the judicial combat (Dan 7:8-27).

In the Revelation 20 depiction of the resurrection-judgment a courtroom vision is juxtaposed to a battle vision. In vv. 7-10 (a recapitulation of the Har Magedon battle scene of Rev 16:12-16 and 19:11-21) the forces of antichrist Gog besieging the city of the saints are consumed by fire falling from heaven. Then in the vision of vv. 11-15 John sees the great white throne and on it the Judge from whose presence the earth and heaven flee away. Standing before the throne are the dead, great and small. They are judged according to what was written in the books and all whose names are not found in the book of life are sentenced to the lake of fire along with the devil, beast and false prophet (cf. Rev 19:20; 20:10).

Consummation of the Har Magedon Kingdom

Catharsis

The territory occupied by the covenant people must be free of defilement because the Holy One dwells in the midst of them (cf. Num 35:34). Catharsis of the earth therefore necessarily precedes the inauguration of God's glory kingdom. This cosmic depuration, accomplished through the eschatological resurrection and final judgment, includes the elements of ethnic cleansing, deconstruction of human culture, and decontamination of nature.

Ethnic Cleansing. Here we will be covering some of the same ground as in our discussion of Har Magedon gatherings, especially the gathering of reprobate individuals into the winepress of wrath, which itself echoed material in our treatment of the antichrist crisis. But the angle of vision will be different. Our interest here is in the cathartic effect the excising of the collective company of the reprobate has on the earth as the realm that becomes kingdom domain in the consummation event.

The final judgment is redemptive; it secures various soteric benefits for God's people. Over against the charges of the adversary-prosecutor it affirms with finality the acceptance of the elect with their holy Creator through the merits of Jesus, guarantor of the Covenant of Grace. Besides sealing their salvation from the wrath of God, the final judgment delivers them from the hostility of evil men. This follows the pattern of the typological judgments. It was when the prediluvian dynasts threatened the continuation of Seth's diminishing line that God's saving intervention came in the form of the Deluge judgment that overwhelmed the world of the self-deifying oppressors. It was when the chariotry attack of Yahweh-challenging pharaoh was about to overrun and crush the fleeing Israelites that the Lord rose up in judgment, overthrowing the Egyptian forces in the sea. Similarly in the eschaton event, it is when the little horn has hemmed in the saints that the Ancient of Days comes in judgment and they are rescued from the beast power (Dan 7:21,2). It is when antichrist Gog and Magog have surrounded the ekklesia-camp that the judgment fire falls on them, ending their siege of the saints (Rev 20:9). Both type and antitype final judgments are thus redemptive acts in that they save God's people from the power of their hellish foes.

More than overthrowing the dominion of the enemy powers, the final judgment terminates their very presence. "Behold, the day of the Lord comes cruel and with wrath and fierce anger to make the earth a desolation, and he will destroy the sinners out of it" (Isa 13:9). In the coming day of his advent the Lord Jesus will take vengeance on all those who do not know God and do not obey the gospel. All those who did not believe the truth but had pleasure in unrighteousness will undergo the punishment of eternal destruction, separated from the presence of the Lord and from the glory of his majesty (2 Thess 1:8,9; 2:10-12). The Lord executes a thorough ethnic cleansing of the satanic genotype. The genocide is total; all fallen men and angels are eliminated from the world of the saints. This complete removal of Satan and his seed is a prerequisite for establishing the Glory-kingdom among men (logically so, even if chronologically they are simultaneous, complementary aspects of the final judgment event).

The typological judgment episodes exemplify this principle too. The ungodly of the world that then was were erased en masse by the Deluge as a prelude to the settling of the ark, symbol of the consummate kingdom of the new heaven and earth, on the Ararat Har Magedon. The Canaanites must be obliterated by the Israelites in a holy war of annihilation to make way for setting up Yahweh's kingdom. The promised land must be hallowed, a holy territory free of the devotees of demonic Baals must be secured before a sanctuary might be erected for the divine Glory or a royal house be built for the throne of the messianic king (cf. Ps 106:34-39). In keeping with this typological paradigm the coming of the antitypal kingdom of glory does not precede the elimination of the Satan-allied population of planet earth. It is only at the final judgment, when deceived men, small and great, all who receive the mark of the beast and worship his image, have been cast into the lake of fire, the second death, that the eternal holy city descends from heaven (Rev 20:15; 21:5-8; cf. 19:18).

Stated in terms of the millennial issue, it is after "the thousand years," which lead up to the final judgment, that the kingdom comes in power and glory. We shall pursue this matter further below.

Extermination of the reprobate cancels the covenant of common grace. As long as the present earth endures the wicked are guaranteed co-existence with the righteous in a commonwealth order of earthly life that affords a measure of temporal benefits to all (cf. Gen 8:20–9:17). But at the appointed time this age of divine forbearance, during which God's people emulate their heavenly Father by treating their enemies with forgiving love, will come to an end. The time will arrive for the new ethics of final judgment that summons the saints to holy hatred of the ungodly and to the execution of the ban of utter destruction against them (Lev 27:29; Josh 6:17). That ethic of imprecation and execration, of dispossession and obliteration, was introduced in the history of Israel's conquest of Canaan as a prototypal anticipation of the final judgment. It was there an exceptional, intrusive feature within the broader, underlying common grace order, a temporary, limited abrogation of the principle of commonness, forewarning the world of God's intention to apply this holy war ethic on a global scale in the coming hour of final judgment. The genotype of the wicked is an endangered species, inexorably destined to become an extinct species in the lake of fire.

Deconstruction of Human Culture. When the apostle Peter warns of the dissolving of the earth in the final day of the Lord he includes with the earth "the works that are on it" (2 Pet 3:10). Above (in Part One, Chapter Three) we have interpreted these works as the works of man, his cultural formations, infected by evil since the Fall. That culture is embodied in political structures, in the city of man, which metastasizes into the cult of man with human rulers demanding for themselves the adoration that belongs to the Creator alone. Possessed of the antichrist spirit they seek to suppress and eradicate the covenant people. We see this malformation of the city in the typological histories: in the reign of terror of the self-styled "sons of the gods" in Noah's day, in the Babel enterprise, in the Egyptian enslavement of Abraham's descendants. And we see it in the present antitypal age in the opposition of imperial powers to the church. Common grace provision though it is, the state is so warped by sinful humanity that the Scriptures portray it as a draconic beast with proud head and lethal horns raised up against God and his people. The city of man becomes an idol, the quintessential work of man's hands (cf. Isa 2:8).

This idolatrous imperial superstructure that fallen man has imposed on the infrastructure of the earth is to be dissolved along with the earth, Peter warned. And other biblical voices sound similar warnings. In setting forth some of the relevant data in key apocalyptic passages we shall at the same time be calling attention to what is revealed concerning the temporal relation of the termination of the city of man to the advent of God's glory kingdom, a sequence that has a decisive bearing on the millennial issue.

In Haggai's prophecy of the shaking of heaven and earth the focus is on the collapse of the throne of the kingdoms of the nations. That is ground zero, the seismic center of this cosmos-quake. And the flowing of the treasures of the nations into God's kingdom house, filling it with splendor, is the sequel to the cosmic catastrophe (Hag 2:6,7,21,22; cf. Heb 12:26). This sequence is present again in Daniel's prophecies of the final judgment of the world kingdom. In Daniel 2 the world-image is first struck and pulverized and carried away leaving not a trace, and then the messianic stone that delivers the annihilating blow becomes an earth-filling mountain, the kingdom of the God of heaven that shall never be destroyed (Dan 2:44). Similarly in the vision of the end of the world in Daniel 7, the people of the Most High do not receive the kingdom of glory and universal dominion until the parousia of the Son of Man and the final, total elimination of the beast with ten horns and its eleventh horn in the consuming fire which issues forth from before the Ancient of Days (Dan 7:21,22,26,27). And in the apocalyptic prospects of John, the Glory-adorned bride-city New Jerusalem, epiphanic epicenter of the new heavens and earth, is at its appearing a wholly holy realm. There is no vestige of the city of man. The dragon empire in its totality – beast, false prophet, and all their followers small and great, who receive the mark of the beast and worship its image – has been previously banished to the lake of fire (Rev 21:8,27; 22:15). That does not transpire until the last judgment (Rev 20:7-15; cf. 19:20,21). Hence, only after that consummating judgment – and therefore after the "thousand years" that lead up to that judgment – does the Glory-kingdom of the Lamb-Lord descend from heaven.

In addition to this consummate, eternal Glory-kingdom, the premillennial and postmillennial views would posit an earthly theocratic kingdom during the millennium – a kingdom of long duration (if not literally a thousand years) yet transitional, not permanent, a premature Glory-kingdom, less than ideal. Truth be told, what they propose is a bizarre mongrel hybrid. But the basic difficulty for those pre-consummation views is that the Scriptures disallow the notion of such a sea to sea global theocracy before the final judgment, whether with the visible personal presence of Christ as world sovereign (premillennialism) or without it (postmillennialism). According to the Scriptures the bestial imperial power retains its place on the world stage in unbroken continuity throughout the church age right up to the final judgment. Thus in Daniel 7 the little horn of the fourth beast, symbol of the world power in the present interim era, continues in its God-defying and saints-persecuting character until the (Danielic) great white throne judgment. It not only continues but prevails over God's people, necessitating his parousia intervention in that final judgment to rescue the godly remnant on earth. Likewise in the Book of Revelation, world domination by the draconic beast continues through the church age in a succession of representatives symbolized by a series of horns culminating in the seventh/eighth horn(s), the antichrist climax of the city of man (Rev 13:5; 17:9-14). It continues until the (Apocalyptic) great white throne judgment with no hiatus in which to insert a prolonged, universal, external sway of a messianic theocracy as hypothesized in premillennialism and postmillennialism.

There is no transitional millennial semi-glory kingdom. There is only the full-fledged kingdom of Glory and that does not make its appearance before the final and complete evacuation of the archenemy of Har Magedon and his individual and institutional minions. Advocated by the amillennialists alone, the post-consummation view of the coming of the kingdom in glory is demanded by the biblical sequence of ethnic cleansing and deconstruction of the city of man before kingdom consummation.

Decontamination of the World of Nature. While for the wicked the final judgment terminates the benefits of common grace, for the saints it brings to an end the time of their enduring the afflictions due to the common curse on the natural order. In Revelation 21 the common curse phenomena are called "the first things," things that pass away, making way for the eternal order of new things (vv. 1-4; cf. 22:3; Isa 65:17-25). Specified are (the first) death and the associated culture of pain and tears and the grave (Rev 20:13,14; 21:4; cf. Isa 65:19). The whole complex of the common curse is summed up in death, the extremity of that curse that warps man's experience of procreation and labor through all his transient generations after the Fall (cf. Gen 3:16-19)

The replacement of the first things by the new things, especially the removal of death and Hades, amounts to a clearing away of pollution from man's natural environment, a sanctifying of the earth itself. For the human dead, buried in the ground, pollute the earth. Isaiah, tracing the death curse on the earth to Adam's breaking of the creational covenant (Isa 24:5,6), depicts the earth as mourning along with its human occupants, bemoaning the netherworld fate that has befallen it (Isa 24:4,7ff.). In this context (i.e., Isa 24:1–27:1) the prophet foretells the eschatological cleansing of the corpse-corruption from the earth by means of the resurrection. He pictures the resurrection as the emptying out of a vessel filled with the dead (Isa 24:1-3), as the removal of a death shroud (Isa 25:6-8), and as the taking away of a veil-like covering that conceals the dead (Isa 26:19–27:1). [See further *DLM*.]

Reference was made earlier to Paul's restating of Isaiah's message in Rom 8:18-25. The apostle declares that the creation itself is groaning along with believers because it has been subjected to a state of corruption and decay. However, the earth will be delivered from its polluted condition as global cemetery by the resurrection, particularly the redemption of the bodies of the saints. This focus on the experience of believers is to be expected in treating of the resurrection as a redemptive accomplishment, but a special reason for it is that the plea of the earth to be rid of the corruption of human corpses is accompanied by another cry from the ground, the cry of the innocent blood of the martyrs that stains the soil (cf. Ps 106:38; Job 16:18). This is a cry for an atoning covering, for vindication and vengeance. Such was the cry from the ground that opened its mouth to receive Abel's martyr blood (Gen 4:10,11; cf. Heb 2:24). To this cry too the resurrection and final judgment are the desired response. The Song of Moses concludes with the assurance that the stain of the blood of the Lord's martyr people will be covered by the blood of their slayers (Deut 32:43; Num 35:33). [Cf. *GOM* 89-91.] And Isaiah's celebration of the Lord's resurrection triumph over death concludes with the promise to the saints that in the coming day the earth will no longer suppress their cry. Their appeal for vindication will be heard. Their Lord will come forth from his place to punish the inhabitants of the earth. His people will be made alive and the earth will be delivered from the bondage of corruption and purified from the stain of innocent blood (Isa 26:20–27:1; cf. Rev 6:9-11).

Here again in the depurating of nature the biblical sequence of events rules out theories of a millennial establishment of a kingdom of glory. For the "first things" of the common order that obtains throughout the present interim age, things that would be incompatible with a millennial reign of Christ in glory, do not give way to the new things of the new creation until the final judgment and the universal resurrection (Rev 20:7–21:4) and thus not until after the thousand years are ended. The (first) death is indeed the last enemy to be subdued (1 Cor 15:26). Until Christ subdues death at the last trump the earth remains the arena of the incessant Har Magedon conflict of satanic subversion and messianic subjugation.

The problem of corruption posed by Hades is actually one of cosmic proportions. It is not just a matter of freeing the earth of its cemetery status, but of eliminating Hades as the intermediate realm of the damned, fallen angels as well as fallen men. To deal with this God has prepared a separated place in the consummated order for the devil and his angels, a place to which reprobate men are also banished (Matt 25:41; Rev 20:15; 21:8). This realm, sealed off from the domain of the new heaven and earth, is symbolized by a lake of fire, the realm we call Hell. God has created Hell as a decontaminating, hermetically sealed black hole against the time when he will consummate his holy kingdom. Into this lake of fire unclean Hades is cast (Rev 20:14). Hell thus serves as a cosmic catharsis.

At the same time, Hell as the punitive (second) death of the reprobate satisfies the requirement for a forensic covering of martyr blood (cf. Num 35:33). The redemptive counterpart to this is the atoning sacrifice of the Cross, the shedding of Christ's blood as a covering for the bloodguiltiness of the elect.

Pleroma

With our arrival at the finale of the ages-long Har Magedon warfare (Part Three) we are brought back to the issues covered in Part One of this investigation. We attempted there to integrate the biblical intimations concerning the nature of heaven and its eschatological history with the current surmisings of cosmologists, especially on the question of the cosmic endgame. (A re-reading of Part One might be found useful as we return to this subject of the consummation.)

It was remarked in Part One that the metamorphosis or glorification of redeemed humanity was the principal operative mechanism in the consummating event. We shall reflect a bit further on this metamorphosis and then comment on its outcome, the consummate kingdom of heaven. In our analysis of the eternal order the concept of pleroma (fullness) will come to the fore. The catharsis, the negative, cosmos-emptying aspect of the final judgment, paves the way for its positive counterpart, the filling of the cosmos that brings Har Magedon to a final state of pleroma.

Glorification-Metamorphosis. Glorification of the saints at Christ's second advent is a vanquishing of death whether the objects of this divine action are those who are still alive at the parousia or those who had previously experienced "the first resurrection" (i.e., those who had died). For the former, glorification is a conquest of death in that it involves a transition from a mortal condition to a state of immortality (which is not merely unending life but glorious, eternal life). For the latter, glorification involves resurrection, victory over the grave, restoration of bodily life, and that of the immortal kind.

Until the parousia-consummation, glorification is a soteric benefit that belongs strictly to the "not yet" aspect of eschatology. It is "already" only in the case of Christ, the firstfruits, whose exaltation included his permanent transfiguration.

By this metamorphosis the *imago dei* in man is perfected. It imparts the third glory component of the image, physical luminosity, bodily splendor, the eschatological blessing promised in the creational covenant as the reward of successful covenant probation. The other two glory elements of the *imago dei* were bestowed on man in preliminary form at the beginning. After the Fall they are restored in measure to God's people by redemptive grace and will be perfected in them when they are glorified. These are the glory of ethical excellence and the glory of dominion over the cosmos.

Ekklesia Pleroma. Turning now to the relation of the glorification of the saints to change in the cosmos at the consummation we begin by restating a point made in our discussion of this subject above (i.e., in Chapter Three). Those who are glorified are thereby equipped for the perception of and participation in the Glory-dimensioned realm. Newly opened to them, heaven is for them a new place, whatever objective alterations of the cosmos do or do not follow upon the final judgment. Actually, an objective change in heaven is involved in the glorification event itself. For it incorporates the elect of all ages bodily into the Glory-temple. This gathering of redeemed, glorified mankind into heaven changes heaven; it introduces the pleroma of Christ's body, the church, into the heavenly scene. Our exploration of this pleroma aspect of the consummate Har Magedon will be by way of a review of some of the more salient prophetic-apocalyptic imaging of the eternal realm.

Taken up into the Glory-Spirit realm, John found himself atop the "great high mountain," on which he saw the temple-city Jerusalem descending (Rev 21:10). This was an apostolic reprise of Ezekiel's visionary experience when "the hand of Yahweh" (i.e., the Glory-Spirit) brought him to "the very high mountain" in the land of Israel on which the temple-city was situated (Ezek 40:2; cf. 20:40; 43:12). And in another Johannine vision of this holy height it is explicitly called "Mount Zion" (Rev 14:1). The "great high mountain" in the climactic vision of the new heaven and earth in Rev 21:10 (cf. vv. 1ff.) is then clearly Har Magedon, mount of God's enthronement.

The new creation setting of this mountain-city-temple in Revelation 21 directs us back to the original creation for its rootage and there we find that pleroma prospects are in view from the very beginning. Mandated in the creational covenant is the pleroma program of increasing and filling the earth. Mankind was commissioned to subdue the earth and develop the holy city, extending it to the global dimensions of Megapolis fullness. Proffered in this pleroma commission (accompanied by the Sabbath ordinance) was a divine promise that in the narrow way of covenant faithfulness man would attain to the eschatological fullness.

In his preparing of the garden in Eden (Gen 2:8,9) the Creator provided man with a paradigm for performing the cultural assignment of developing the city. For the garden arrangement represented a cultural ordering of the natural world. It was a bounded area (cf. Gen 3:23,24), shaped and stocked to accommodate its human occupants. While the boundaries served to consecrate the garden as sacred space, they also marked off man's domain from nature not-yet-culturally-structured. The garden was incipient city of God. Confirming the garden's nature as polis and indeed as prototypal Metapolis, Revelation 22 incorporates elements of the garden of Eden like the tree and river of life in its portrayal of the eternal city, New Jerusalem (vv. 1,2).

As the resumption of such paradise features in the new heaven and earth shows, the eschatology of the creational covenant is, with redemptive adaptations, continued in the program of salvation. Accordingly, in our survey of the earlier, typological eras of the Covenant of Grace we found again prototypes of the holy city on the mountain – the ark-kingdom on Ararat and the temple city Jerusalem on Mount Zion. The pleroma theme of subduing and peopling the earth also emerges again, particularly in Israel's occupation of the promised land to its full extent, presaging the messianic fullness.

Similarly in the prophetic visions of God's Old Testament spokesmen the eternal kingdom-city is characterized by pleroma; to these visionaries it was revealed that the local, typological Zion would make way for the cosmic Har Magedon. Thus (as previously noted) in Daniel 2 the mountain that represents the Old Covenant kingdom does not cover the whole canvass and is indeed overshadowed by the colossus symbolizing the world power, but the mountain emblematic of the kingdom of the Messiah (the stone cut from the old mountain) is described as a "great mountain" that "(fills) the whole earth" (v. 35). This antitypical mountain is the pleroma that follows the catharsis effected by the messianic stone's annihilation of the gigantic world image.

Prophesying of this eschatological fullness, Isaiah declared that Zion, the temple mountain, would be established at the end of the days as the highest of the mountains, a heavenly mount to which many people will come. It will become the pleroma peak of Har Magedon, the gathering place of all the nations (Isa 2:2ff.; cf. Mic 4:1ff.).

The pleroma aspect of the consummated Har Magedon city appears again in John's apocalyptic visions. We have had occasion above to mention that in Revelation 7 the redeemed, depicted in the typological imagery of the twelve tribes of twelve thousand each (Rev 7:4-8; cf. 14:1), are also more literally described as a great multitude beyond numbering from all nations, tribes, peoples and tongues, worshipping with all the angels of heaven at the throne of God and the Lamb (Rev 7:9-12). The city descended from heaven on the great high mountain has pleroma proportions; its length, breadth and height are each 12,000 stadia (i.e., well over a thousand miles), mirroring the typological number of completion used in the description of the city's population (Rev 21:16; cf. 7:4-8). The eschatological remnant in this Christ-ark is not a Noahic handful but a messianic myriad. The New Jerusalem is filled with the innumerable hosts of heaven and earth.

This city of cosmic plenitude is Christ's bride, the church (cf. Rev 21:9,10), and in Pauline terms the church consists of the fullness of Israel and the fullness of the Gentiles (Rom 11:12,25), together totalling the predestined pleroma of the new humanity in Christ. Using the figure of the head and body for Christ and the church the apostle declares Christ's body to be the pleroma, the fullness of him who fills all in all (Eph 1:23; 4:10). As second Adam, Christ takes up the creational commission given to the first Adam to fill the earth with descendants. He fulfills this kingdom mandate by fathering a cosmos-filling family through Spirit-effected regeneration (cf. Isa 53:11; John 1:13; 3:3ff.; Heb 2:13). The cosmic scope of this church-body pleroma is underscored in the Ephesians 1 context by what is affirmed of Christ as the head. It was the Father's good pleasure that in the fullness of the times he should unite under Christ's headship all things in the heavens and on earth (v. 10). In fulfillment of this sovereign purpose he exalted Christ to his right hand in the heavens far above every name in this world and that which is to come, giving him this headship over all things for the church, the cosmic pleroma he generates by the Spirit (vv. 20-23; cf. Eph 4:13).

Parousia Pleroma. Along with the pleroma of Christ's mystical body, the fullness of the elect of mankind, there is another pleroma, a pleroma of the divine Presence. And as we examine the biblical data relevant to this parousia pleroma it will emerge that there is a remarkable union between it and the pleroma of the church in the theanthropic Christ.

Viewed as a temple or holy of holies (cf. Rev 21:16) the celestial city, New Jerusalem, is the place where the Shekinah appears, where God tabernacles among his people (Rev 21:3; cf. Ezek 37:26,27). John describes this holy city on the high mountain as "having the glory of God" (Rev 21:11; cf. Ezek 43:2-4); it is the site of his personal epiphanic Presence. In Isaiah's vision of the consummation the association of the Glory-Spirit theophany with Zion-Jerusalem is climactic: the Lord will create the theophanic cloud (cf. Gen 1:1,2) over the whole site of Mount Zion and her assemblies; over all the holy mount the Glory will be a sheltering pavilion (Isa 4:5,6; cf. Rev 15:8). And this Glory-Presence is a pleroma Presence. The fullness aspect of the Glory Spirit suggested in Isa 4:5,6 is clearly indicated in Isaiah 6: the Glory robes and smoke-cloud of the divine Presence enthroned among the seraphim fill the temple (vv. 1-4; cf. Exod 40:34,35; 1 Kgs 8:10,11). Likewise in Ezekiel's vision of the eschatological temple the Glory of the Lord fills the temple (43:4,5; cf. 10:3,4; 44:4) and in Rev 21:22 God is identified with the temple structure of the holy cosmic city in its totality.

Earlier we observed that there are two phases in the epiphanic manifestation of the God of Glory. At the Alpha-radiation of Gen 1:1 the endoxate Spirit (Gen 1:2) was the Glory pleroma that filled the cosmic temple. Then in the course of redemptive history divine epiphany entered a new phase through the Incarnation of the Son.

The theanthropic Christ, in whom the pleroma of deity dwells bodily (Col 1:19; 2:9) and who fills the cosmos through his church, is also bonded with the Glory-Presence pleroma that fills the heavenly temple. Thus, the Apocalypse conjoins the Lord-Lamb with the enthroned King of Glory when identifying the latter as the temple, the fullness of the cosmos city (Rev 21:22; cf. 22:1; John 2:19-21). And in the portrayal of that temple-city as "having the glory of God" the Lamb-Lamp parallels the Glory-Light of God (Rev 21:11,23).

Such bondings are not just between the second and third persons of the Trinity; the full trinitarian oneness of deity is reflected in apocalyptic visions of the divine Glory-Presence pleroma. In Revelation 1 this trinitarian unity is signalized by the benedictory salutation (vv. 4,5) from the three persons of the Godhead – from the One who is, was, and is to come (itself a formula shared by the first and second persons, cf. v. 8); from the seven-fold Spirit pleroma; and from Jesus Christ. Then the vision of the incarnate Son (vv. 12ff.), drawing upon previous prophetic visions (particularly those in Daniel 7 and Ezekiel 1), portrays him as one with the Spirit and with the Father. Like the Danielic Son of Man he is transported on the Glory-cloud and invested with the transfiguring Spirit. And he also possesses attributes of the Ancient of Days: white of raiment and hair, enthroned as heavenly Judge. He who has seen the Son has seen the Father (John 14:9).

Christ: Mediator of Pleroma Union. The church pleroma, the bride-wife of the Lamb (Rev 21:9) is one with him who, himself incarnational epiphany, is one with the endoxate Spirit epiphany. By virtue of her mystery marital union with the God-man in the Spirit (Eph 5:31,32), the church participates (without blurring the Creator-creature distinction) in these Son and Spirit epiphanies. Agreeably, the wife of the Lamb shares with God in his identity as the cosmic temple city (Rev 21:9-12,22; cf. 1 Cor 3:16; 2 Cor 6:16; Eph 2:20-22), the two simultaneously filling the cosmos. Also, to the overcomer Jesus promises: "I will grant him to sit with me on my throne even as I overcame and sat down with my Father on his throne" (Rev 3:21).

Jesus Christ, the God-man, is then mediator of a union of the human pleroma with the divine pleroma. This wondrous oneness is the fulfilling of the petition-claim of Jesus as our successful covenant Probationer: "Holy Father, keep them in thy name which thou hast given me, that they may be one, even as we are one" (John 17:11) . . . "that they may all be one, even as thou, Father, art in me and I in thee, that they also may be in us" (John 17:21) . . . "The glory which thou hast given me I have given to them, that they may be one even as we are one, I in them and thou in me, that they my be perfected into one" (John 17:22,23).

Final Epiphany: The Theanthropic Principle. In the purposing and accomplishing of this oneness of God and man, this communion of the Holy One with erstwhile sons of wrath, we have the ultimate in the revelation of God's name. In keeping with the preredemptive situation, the creational epiphanation of the Spirit was fashioned to reveal God's wisdom and power, his holiness and justice, goodness and love. But the full revelation of the nature of God (the prime objective of creation) was to include the manifestation of a supreme love, the love of God that we see in the compassion, mercy, and grace of our Redeemer, "the lamb that was slain" (Rev 5:6-13; 13:8). It was to redound "to the praise of the glory of his grace" (Eph 1:6; cf. vv. 11,12). Bringing about as it does this fullness in the revelation of God, the incarnational epiphany of the theanthropic Christ is the final epiphany.

Pointing to the remarkably precise physical adjustments that had to obtain in the evolving universe for human existence on planet earth to be possible, cosmologists call this cosmic dynamic "the anthropic principle." For our part, operating within a theistic-presuppositional framework we would see the data enlisted in support of the anthropic principle as bearing witness to God as the Architect-Designer who ordered the whole cosmic process with a view to his creation of mankind. In terms of this proximate divine purpose the visible universe is, after all, geocentric and anthropocentric.

But this is only part of a larger, theocentric programme. We will want to affirm that not the emergence of man but the pleroma revelation of God is the endgame of creation. God's name is God's endgame. Agreeably, the prime petition is "hallowed be thy name" (Matt 6:9; Luke 11:2). And, as we have observed, the glorified God-man, Savior-Head of the pleroma of God's elect and participant in the divine Glory pleroma, is the Omega revelation of God's name. The anthropic principle must be held in subordination to the theanthropic principle.

From the perspective of historico-causative sequence we have asserted the priority of the creation order and its eschatology as the foundational paradigm, of which the redemptive-Christological order is a secondary adaptation. However, while the theanthropic-redemptive order is historically subsequent and secondary, it has priority status when viewed within the framework of God's eternal decrees. For within the eternal simultaneity of the divine decrees priority is a matter of telic ultimacy. And the theanthropic pleroma is the sovereignly ordained cosmic telos (Col 1:16).

Entailed in this teleological priority is a formative relation to the precursive course of the cosmos; the decreed eschatological epiphanation of the God-man Redeemer dictates the shape of the whole anterior historical process, both creational and lapsarian. Stated in architectural metaphor, the consummate Glory-temple projected in the divine Builder's achitectonic conception, though not erected until after the laying of the preconsummation foundations, predetermines the form and dimensions of those foundations. More specifically, two consequences of the predestinating of the theanthropic pleroma as the ultimate telos are that creation includes the making of an image-of-God earthling, the first Adam, and secondly that the creational covenant issues in the Fall of man. The resultant predicament of a world lost in sin in turn occasions the divine response of incarnational epiphany and the soteric mission of the second Adam, the theanthropic Savior – the response with the priority of telic ultimacy, the response which is formative of the situation to which it responds.

Detemporalizing the priority that obtains in God's decrees does not dissolve the paradox of divine sovereignty and human responsibility. That remains (cf., e.g., Acts 2:23; Rom 3:7,8; 9:14ff.), a reminder of the basic theological-religious distinction between us creatures and our Creator, the Lord of Har Magedon, our Father in heaven, whose thoughts and ways are beyond our fathoming.

The Gospel of Har Magedon

The cosmic endgame prospect of the double (divine and human) pleroma bound together in the theanthropic Christ is presented to us in gospel mode. It comes as an invitation to an eschatological banquet on Har Magedon. In Isaiah's words, on that day when Yahweh of hosts reigns on Mount Zion in his Glory-parousia (Isa 24:21-23), he "will make on this mountain a feast for all peoples" (Isa 25:6). And the herald of this messianic good news is exhorted to get up to a high mountain and shout, "Behold your God. Behold the Lord Yahweh comes with might . . . He will feed his flock like a shepherd" (Isa 40:9-11; cf. 52:7). The Har Magedon banquet is the marriage supper of the Lamb and those who are invited to come and enjoy without price (Rev 22:17) are pronounced blessed (Rev 19:9).

Referring to this banquet in a kingdom parable (Luke 14:16ff.) Jesus tells us that in the face of the rejection of his invitation by many, the householder persists in gathering guests, determined that his house be filled (v. 23). The harvest-gathering to which Jesus commissioned the church will be completed. The eternal good pleasure of him who accomplishes all things according to the counsel of his will (Eph 1:11) will be fulfilled: Christ will be the firstborn among many brethren (Rom 8:29). The Son will receive his request that all whom the Father had given him be with him where he is to behold his glory, the glory the Father gave him in love before the foundation of the world (John 17:24). The predestined pleroma in Christ will be assembled in fullness of joy before his parousia-Presence on consummated Har Magedon, Mount of Gathering.

Appendix A

Space and Time in the Genesis Cosmogony*

To rebut the literalist interpretation of the Genesis creation "week" propounded by the young-earth theorists is a central concern of this article. At the same time, the exegetical evidence adduced also refutes the harmonistic day-age view. The conclusion is that as far as the time frame is concerned, with respect to both the duration and sequence of events, the scientist is left free of biblical constraints in hypothesizing about cosmic origins.

The opening section gives a biblico-theological sketch of the two-register nature of cosmology as presented in Scripture. The second major section shows how two-register cosmology informs and shapes the treatment of both the space and time dimensions in the Genesis prologue. It is found that a metaphorical relationship obtains between the two levels, the heavenly level (upper register) being described in figures drawn from the earthly level (lower register). As for the seven-day scheme, it belongs to the upper register and is, therefore, to be understood figuratively, not literally. The point of the concluding section is that Genesis 1, on any view that identifies the narrative order with the temporal sequence, would contradict the teaching of Gen 2:5 concerning the natural mode of providence during the creation process.

---

* Originally published in *Perspectives on Science and the Christian Faith* 48:1 (1996): 2-15.

An *apologia* is needed for addressing again the question of the chronological data in the Genesis creation account. Simply put – the editor made me do it. Over thirty years ago, I made an exegetical case for a non-literal interpretation of the chronological framework.[1] In the interval, that approach has found increasing acceptance. Its most distinctive argument, derived from Gen 2:5, has occasionally been incorporated in studies with similar views of the chronological issue.[2] Advocacy of the literalist tradition, however, is as clamant as ever, and it was thought that a more accessible statement of my exegetical arguments could prove useful at this date.

In preparing the restatement another line of exegetical evidence has come to the fore in my thinking. It concerns a two-register cosmological concept that structures the whole biblical cosmogony. This matter developed into the main point and has become in this essay the umbrella under which the other, restated arguments are accorded an ancillary place here and there. My *apologia* concludes then with a claim of adding something somewhat fresh to the old debate.

Two-Register Cosmology

Central in biblical revelation is the relationship of God, whose dwelling place is heaven's glory (Ps 115:16), to man on earth. A two-register cosmos is thus the scene of the biblical drama, which features constant interaction between the upper and lower registers.[3]

From the perspective of man (more precisely, of man in his pre-Consummation state), the heavenly register is an invisible realm. However, heaven is not to be thought of as occupying a separate place off at a distance from the earth or even outside the cosmos. Heaven and earth relate to each other spatially more after the manner of (speculated) dark matter and

---

[1] "Because It Had Not Rained," *The Westminster Theological Journal* 20 (1958): 146-157.

[2] Cf. H. Blocher, *In the Beginning* (Downers Grove: InterVarsity, 1984); C. E. Hummel, *The Galileo Connection* (Downers Grove: InterVarsity, 1986); R. Maatman, *The Impact of Evolutionary Theory: A Christian View* (Sioux Center: Dordt College Press, 1993).

[3] Theological differences aside, the cosmology of mythology is analogous. Indeed, mythology may be defined formally precisely as a portrayal of human affairs in terms of a dynamic interrelating of divine and human realms.

visible matter. When earthlings experience a proleptic opening of their eyes, they see that the very spot where they are is the gate of heaven (Gen 28:16,17), filled with heavenly chariots of fire (2 Kgs 6:17).

Reference to the invisible realm as "above" is simply a spatial figure based on a natural analogy between what is physically higher and what is more exalted in dignity and honor. This same analogy accounts for the designating of the invisible sphere by the name of the upper level within the visible world. Visible space is itself divided into heaven and earth (and, in tripartite formulations, the waters under the earth). The visible heaven consists of the star-studded canopy of the sky overhead, with the clouds, the waters that are above the earth. Taking its name from this above-section of visible space, supernal space (the above-section of the two-register cosmos) is then called "heaven."[4] Further, when the heavenly Glory is revealed in visible theophany, it is a manifestation in clouds and related phenomena. So close is the association of God's dwelling and actions with the visible heaven (cf., e.g., Ps 104:2-4) that it may be difficult to determine in given cases whether "heaven" refers to the visible or invisible heaven, or both at once.[5]

The two-register character of biblical cosmology, relative as it is to man's preglorification status, is not permanent. It belongs only to the first stage of an eschatological movement that was integral to creation from the beginning and leads to a final stage of Consummation. As we trace this eschatological development, an important feature that emerges is the archetype-replica (original-likeness) relationship between the upper and lower registers.

From the beginning, God's presence was peculiarly and preeminently associated with the invisible heaven. That was where he dwelt, the site of his enthronement (cf., e.g., Deut 26:15; 1 Kgs 8:39,43,49; Pss 11:4; 102:20 [19]; 103:19; Isa 66:1; Matt 5:45; 7:21). It was there that he manifested his Glory to the angels, the Glory that fills invisible space and makes it a temple, the Glory-epiphany that is itself God's temple. But though the invisible, upper register heaven was God's true sanctuary, the earth also

[4] Similarly, the depths of the sea or subsurface earth metaphorically signify the infernal realm.

[5] "Heaven of heavens" (cf. Deut 10:14; 1 Kgs 8:27; Neh 9:6; Pss 115:16; 148:4) apparently distinguishes a "higher" heaven, possibly the clouds of heaven (the water "above the heavens," cf. Ps 148:4) or the invisible heavens.

was at the first the scene of a special visible divine presence.[6] Invisible space was the holy of holies; and visible space (visible heaven and earth) was a holy place. Creation was sanctified in all its spatial dimensions, with lower register space a replica of the upper register archetypal temple.

Eden was the sacred center of the earthly reproduction of the heavenly reality. Here in the garden of the Lord, the Spirit-Glory that fills the heavenly temple was visibly manifested on the mountain of God (cf. Isa 51:3; Ezek 28:13ff.; 31:8f.), the vertical cosmic axis linking heaven and earth. The revealed presence of the King of Glory crowning this sacred mountain marked the earth as a holy theocratic domain. Reflecting the identity of Eden as a sanctuary was the priestly responsibility assigned to man to guard the garden from profanation (Gen 2:15). The sequel underscores this. When man forfeited his priestly role, guardianship of the holy site was transferred to the cherubim (Gen 3:24). They were guardians of the heavenly temple throne and the extension of that function to Eden accents the identity of this earthly spot as a visible reproduction of the temple above.[7]

Man's fall radically altered the way the replication of holy heaven on earth was to unfold. As a consequence of the breaking of the creation covenant, the Glory-theophany was presently withdrawn and the earth, though still under the sovereign control of the King of heaven, was left an unsanctified place. Only by way of redemptive intrusion does theophany-centered holy place reappear in the otherwise non-holy, post-Fall world – most prominently in the cultus of Israel's typological theocratic kingdom.

Where sanctuary does emerge again on earth, its nature as a copy of the heavenly archetype is emphasized. The tabernacle and temple, restorations of Eden's sanctuary with cherubim-guarded throne of God, are made after the pattern of the upper register temple revealed to Moses and Solomon.[8]

---

[6] For elaboration of this theme see my *Kingdom Prologue* (privately published, 1993), pp. 31, 32.

[7] Ibid.

[8] The tabernacle and temple were so designed that both in their horizontal and vertical sectioning they also portrayed the visible register of the cosmic temple with its corresponding partitioning. Cf. my *Images of the Spirit* (Grand Rapids: Eerdmans, 1980), pp. 39-42 (hereafter, *Images*).

They point ahead typologically to the apocalypse of the heavenly temple at the end of the ages. At that consummation of redemptive history, presaged by the Sabbath ordinance, the visible-invisible differentiation of space comes to an end as the heavenly Glory is unveiled to the eyes of redeemed earthlings, their perceptive capabilities transformed now by glorification. The boundary of heaven and earth disappears. All becomes one cosmic holy of holies. God himself is the Glory-temple, the true temple, archetype and antitype of prototypical temples and provisional theophanies.

Redemption is a way of achieving the original telos of creation despite the Fall. A successful probation by the first Adam would have led through a cosmologically two-register history to an eschatological climax at which Eden's Glory would have been absorbed into the surpassing heavenly Glory. At the dawning of the eternal Sabbath for humanity, all space, without distinction any longer of upper and lower cosmological levels, would have become a consummate revelation of the Glory of heaven's King. Because of the Fall, that eschatological omega-point had to be won by the second Adam.

Two-register cosmologies left their imprint on the form of ancient graphic and literary materials in a variety of ways. A quite literal case of the two-register format is seen in graphic representations like the Assyrian reliefs that picture the king in a lower register, whether driving forward in battle or returning triumphantly, and in a higher register the god in a matching stance.[9] The Book of Job offers a clear instance of the shaping of a piece of literature by the two-layer cosmology. In the prologue, heavenly scenes (Job 1:6-12; 2:1-6) alternate with closely related earthly scenes (Job 1:1-5,13-22; 2:7-10). A similar movement from the upper to the lower register is found throughout the Book of Revelation. Each series of visions of happenings on earth is introduced by a disclosure of the heavenly control center of the universe, where the earthly judgments are decreed and whence their executive agents descend. With its characteristic opening of the heavens, the apocalyptic genre is a place we naturally expect to find

---

[9] This example thus contains the additional feature of the likeness of the lower to the upper phenomenon. Comparison of these reliefs with literary accounts of warfare as a two-level affair involving earthly conflict of nations below and divine or angelic contention in the heavens (cf. Dan 10:12,13,20,21; Zech 9:13,14) illustrates how these cultural media can be mutually illuminating.

the formative impact of two-register cosmology on literature. Another such place is a cosmogony like the Genesis prologue.

Cosmology of the Genesis Prologue

The creation prologue (Gen 1:1–2:3) presents a theological mapping of the cosmos with space and time coordinates. Both these dimensions exhibit the biblical two-register cosmology, a construct that functions as an infrastructure of the entire account. And this, we discover, has a decisive bearing on the interpretation of the chronological data.

The Space Coordinate

Two-Register Space

Genesis 1:1. What this opening verse states is that God, in the beginning,[10] created both the upper and lower spatial spheres. "The heavens and the earth" is not just a merismus, a pair of antonyms which as a set signifies totality. The phrase rather denotes concretely the actual two components that together comprehend all of creation. That does indeed amount to everything, but in translating, the separate, specific identity of each of these two components must be preserved. One thing demanding this is that verse 2, resuming "the earth" of verse 1, treats it by itself as a distinct, individual sphere.[11]

More precisely, what Gen 1:1 affirms is that God created not just the spatial dimensions immediately accessible to man, but the heavens too, that is, the invisible realm of the divine Glory and angelic beings. This interpretation is reflected in the apostle Paul's Christological exposition of Gen 1:1, declaring that the Son created "all things that are in heaven and that are in earth, visible and invisible, whether they be thrones, or dominions, or principalities, or powers" (Col 1:16; cf. John 1:1-3).

---

[10] For a discussion of bĕrēšît, see below.

[11] See further W. P. Brown, *Structure, Role, and Ideology in the Hebrew and Greek Texts of Genesis 1:1–2:3* (Atlanta: Scholars Press, 1993), p. 102, n. 12.

Similarly Nehemiah, reflecting on the Genesis creation account, finds a reference there to the invisible heaven of the angels (Neh 9:6), and the only possible referent is "the heavens" of Gen 1:1 (and the reference to that in Gen 2:1, if the latter summation does in fact include Gen 1:1, not just 1:2-31).[12]

Moreover, in the context of Genesis 1 itself, the visible "heaven" or "firmament" (v. 8) is derived from what is called "earth" in verses 1 and 2. Hence, the "heavens" that are distinguished from that "earth" in verse 1 must be the invisible heavens. This would not necessarily be the case if verse 1 were a summary heading for the entire account. But what Gen 1:1 says about "the beginning" cannot be summing up the entire process of creation, for the allusions to the bĕrēšît of Gen 1:1 in Prov 8:22,23 identify that "beginning" as prior to (not coextensive with) the developments traced in Gen 1:2ff. Though it is an independent statement, Gen 1:1 is, therefore, not a heading but a declaration concerning the initial phase of creation history.

Some oppose construing Gen 1:1-2 as I have because, they insist, the phrase "the heavens and the earth" always signifies the finished product, the well-ordered, occupied universe, and hence "the earth" that appears in that phrase in verse 1 cannot be the unfinished, uninhabitable place called "earth" in verse 2.[13] But contrary to this often repeated claim, in other appearances of the phrase "(the) heavens and (the) earth" in Scripture, the idea that these realms were finished and inhabited is not what is signified by this phrase itself but would have to be supplied by the context. And even if all references after Gen 1:1 happened to be to a heaven and earth in such a finished state, that would not be determinative for the Gen 1:1 context, which deals with the very process of developing the product from an empty to a furnished condition.[14] In fact, it may well be that in all the appearances of "(the) heavens and (the) earth" (over half of which are

---

[12] The same question arises in Exod 20:11. On this, see the discussion of the phrase "the heavens and the earth" below.

[13] If one does so insist, then recognition of what Proverbs 8 reveals about bĕrēšît in Gen 1:1 would compel adoption of some variety of the discredited gap theory to account for the earth in Gen 1:2.

[14] Cf. the observations of A. Heidel, *The Babylonian Genesis* (Chicago: U. of Chicago Press, 1963), p. 91.

allusions to the creation account, acknowledging the Lord as the maker of heaven and earth), the phrase signifies precisely the invisible and the visible realms, and thus the whole two-register world.

There is, therefore, no reason to resist the clear direction of Prov 8:22-23 for the interpretation of Gen 1:1 as referring to an earlier juncture, not to a later stage when the earth had become habitable for man. In point of fact, though the visible realm, the "earth," was not completed until the end of the creation "week," completion of the invisible heavenly realm (with its angelic hosts) had evidently been accomplished "in the beginning." Job 38:7 indicates that the celestial sons of God existed at the point in earth's development described in Gen 1:2ff. Thus, in view of the close allusive relationship of Job 38 to Genesis 1, Job 38:7 also furnishes independent support for the interpretation of "the heavens" in Gen 1:1 as the invisible sphere of the angels of God.

Gen 1:1, therefore, states – and how eminently fitting is this affirmation for the opening of the canonical Scriptures – that God in the beginning made the whole world, both its upper and lower spatial registers, both its invisible and visible dimensions, heaven and earth, all.

Genesis 1:2. Both invisible and visible space, introduced in Gen 1:1 as "the heavens" and "the earth" respectively, appear again in verse 2. Focusing on the lower register, this verse describes the earth at an early inchoate stage (v. 2a and b). But it also prepares for the following account of how this uninhabitable world was transformed into a paradisiacal home for man by pointing to the God of the invisible heaven, present above the darkness-enshrouded waters of the earth below (v. 2c). This creative Spirit-Presence is depicted in avian metaphor[15] as hovering in fostering fashion above the world. As shown (for one thing) by the striking echo of Gen 1:2 in Deut 32:10,11, the "Spirit" here refers to that heavenly epiphany which is known in its manifestation within the visible world as the Shekinah, the theophanic cloud of glory.[16] Including as it does then the Spirit-Glory of the temple in heaven along with the earth below, Gen 1:2 carries forward the two-register cosmology contained in verse 1.

---

[15] On the common use of avian imagery for deity in the ancient Near East see my "The Feast of Cover-over," *Journal of the Evangelical Theological Society* 37 (1994): 497, 498 (hereafter, "Cover-over"). Cf., e.g., in pharaonic nomenclature the Horus (or serekh) name.

[16] For an extensive treatment of this see my *Images*.

Genesis 1:3–2:3. The several creative fiats by which visible space gets fashioned into a habitable world in the course of the six days (Gen 1:3ff.) are sovereign decrees. They clearly evoke the throne of the King of Glory, the King invisible, the only God, dwelling in light unapproachable (1 Tim 1:17; 6:16). Each such fiat, therefore, signals the continuing presence of the upper register sphere in the panoramic scenario of the creation narrative. That these fiats emanate from the invisible heavens is indicated with particular clarity in the account of man's creation in God's image. For there (Gen 1:26) the divine fiat takes the consultative "let us" form that reveals the setting to be the angelic council,[17] the judicial assembly which is a regular feature in disclosures of the heavenly reality denoted "Spirit" in Gen 1:2.

Another index of the continued inclusion of the heavenly register in the scene is the motif of the divine surveillance and judgment found in the refrain: "and God saw that it was good" (Gen 1:4,10,12,18,21,25,31). For repeatedly conjoined with statements that the invisible heaven is the site of God's temple-throne is the declaration that from there he engages in a judicial scrutiny of the world. From that throne "his eyes behold, his pupils try the sons of men" (Ps 11:4c). It was from his throne in heaven that the divine Masterbuilder looked down, saw the unfolding work of his hands, and pronounced it "good," that is, in perfect accord with his architectonic plan (cf. Prov 8:30,31).

Further, the full two-register cosmology comes to expression in the fiat-fulfillment format, which is the basic structure of each of the six day-stanzas. While the "let there be" is uttered at the upper register, the "and it was so" transpires at the lower register. The fiat of the Logos-Word above is executed by the Spirit in the earth below.[18]

Once again and quite directly God's throne in the upper section of the two-register cosmos is alluded to in statements about the Creator's seventh day rest, which is his heavenly enthronement (Gen 2:2b,3b). The earthly register is also included in the day seven section, for along with the Creator's

---

[17] Cf. *Images*, pp. 22, 23.

[18] This alternating sequence of heavenly and earthly scenes is similar to the pattern of the prologue to Job. The similarity is not just formal, for in each case what takes place in the lower register is determined by the sovereign word of God revealed in the heavenly council.

Sabbath of royal resting above, it also contains the appointment of the Sabbath ordinance for human observance of earth below (Gen 2:3).[19]

Table 1. Two-Register Space in Genesis Prologue

	Verse 1	Verse 2	Days 1-6	Day 7
Upper Register	heaven	Spirit	fiats	God's Sabbath
Lower Register	earth	deep	fulfillments	Sabbath Ordinance

The summary chart of the space dimension theme in the Genesis prologue (Table 1) shows that two-register cosmology is present not only as a concept but as a pervasive factor in the organization of the composition. Additional evidence of its influence on the literary structure of the passage will be noted below.

Replication Relationship of the Two Registers

The lower register relates to the upper as replica to archetype. Before seeing how that comes to expression in the creation account, we must call attention to how the six days fall naturally into two triads, one dealing with creation kingdoms and the other with the creature kings given dominion over them. As frequently noticed, the two triads run in parallel with obvious correlation of their successive members.[20]

---

[19] Space and time are conceptually correlative in the Sabbath. In our analysis of the time coordinate of this cosmological charting the Sabbath will be given closer consideration.

[20] This will be spelled out in our discussion of the replication relationship of the two registers. Evidence will appear there for preferring the kingdom-king analysis of the themes of the two triads over something more general, like regions and their occupants or habitations and inhabitants.

The earthly products of the first three days mirror one or another characteristic of the invisible heaven, the above realm, the realm of light and overarching Glory (Gen 1:2). The day-light called forth on day one was a replica of that Glory-light. The bright firmament-vault of day two was so much the likeness of its archetype that they shared the same name, "heaven" (Gen 1:8). The lofty trees, the climactic fruit of day three, are used in Scripture as an apt figure for the cosmos (cf. Dan 4:10-12). With their high spreading branches a realm for the birds of the heaven, they are comparable to the firmament-heaven in which the birds fly (Gen 1:20), a towering image pointing to the overarching Spirit-heaven above.

Moving on from copies of the heavenly kingdom to images of the heavenly King, the second triad of days presents creature kings whose roles in the hierarchy of creation are earthly reflections of the royal rule of the Creator enthroned above. Royal terminology is explicitly used for the luminaries of day four. In that they regulate the cycle of light and darkness, they are said to "rule over" the kingdom of day and night produced on day one (Gen 1:16; cf. Ps 136:8,9). God's blessing-mandate to the creatures of day five closely resembles the dominion mandate afterwards given to man. In each case royal occupation of the assigned domain is to be accomplished by being fruitful, multiplying, and filling (Gen 1:22,28). So the birds and fish would exercise their rule over the sky and sea, the kingdom realms of day two. Incidentally, the birds of day five and the luminaries of day four – both associated with the "firmament of heaven" (Gen 1:14,15,17,20) – are like the King of heaven in other ways besides their ruling function. The birds' overshadowing of their nests (Deut 32:11) and the luminosity of the sun and moon become biblical figures for the Glory-Spirit as a protective covering, the heavenly Sun and Shield (cf. Ps 84:12 [11]).[21] Culminating the series of earthly replicas of the Creator-King is the final creature of day six, man, the image of God and his holy angels (Gen 1:26). In this earthling, made like unto the Glory-Spirit with respect to the threefold glory of royal dominion, moral excellence, and (in eschatological prospect) visual luminosity,[22] creaturely reproduction of the heavenly King of kings is perfected.

---

[21] Cf. my "Cover-over."

[22] Cf. my *Images*.

The replication motif emerges distinctly on day seven in the Sabbath ordinance, designed to call man to the imitation of the divine sabbatical pattern. Discussion of this will be deferred, however, until we are dealing with the time coordinate of the Genesis cosmology.

As a final illustration of replication in the spatial dimension, we turn to the way the two-register pattern of the total cosmos, visible and invisible, is repeated within the visible, lower register by itself in its subdivision into an upper realm (heaven) and a lower realm (earth). This secondary, replicated two-register structure is highlighted by the arrangement of the contents of the two parallel triads of days according to their upper or lower location.

The first members of each triad are related to the upper level, the heaven: the light of the sky on day one and the heavenly luminaries on day four. The third members belong to the lower level, the earth: the land and its vegetation on day three and the land animals and man on day six. And the second members are strikingly designed to serve as links between the first and third members. For these middle units of the two triads each combines both upper and lower levels: the sky and the sea in day two and the birds of the air and fish of the sea in day five.

Table 2. Location of Triads' Productions

First Triad		Level		Second Triad
day one	—	upper	—	day four
day two		{ upper / lower }		day five
day three	—	lower	—	day six

Here again we see that the two-register cosmology construct was a decisive factor in determining the literary shape of the Genesis prologue.[23]

The Time Coordinate

Space and time, the cosmological coordinates, are correlative. Interlocking of the two is pronounced in God's seventh day rest, a temporal concept that connotes the spatial reality of the holy site of God's enthronement. Also indicative of their correlation is the giving of the temporal names "day" and "night" to the spatial phenomena of light and darkness (Gen 1:5). It is inevitable then that the two-register structuring of the spatial dimension will also be found in the temporal dimension, and with it the archetype-replica relationship between the two registers. We have seen that by reason of this replication relationship earthly things are a rich source of metaphor for the realities of the invisible heaven. God is portrayed as hovering like an eagle over its nest and as resting like a man after his work is done (cf. Exod 31:17); upper register space is designated "heaven" after the upper level of visible space; etc. We naturally expect then that in the case of time, as of space, the upper register will draw upon the lower register for its figurative depiction. Hence, when we find that God's upper level activity of issuing creative fiats from his heavenly throne is pictured as transpiring in a week of earthly days, we readily recognize that, in keeping with the pervasive contextual pattern, this is a literary figure, an earthly, lower register time metaphor for an upper register, heavenly reality.[24]

---

[23] These data also attest further to the parallelism between the successive members of the two triads of days.

[24] Following nineteenth century theologian W. G. T. Shedd, C. J. Collins identifies the creation days as an anthropomorphism, part of an extended anthropomorphic portrayal of the Creator as the worker-craftsman; cf. "How Old Is The Earth? Anthropomorphic Days in Genesis 1:1–2:3," *Presbyterion* 20 (1994): esp. 117, 118 (hereafter, "How Old"). As over against the literalists, this is moving in the right direction. But the explanation needs adjustment, for not all the metaphors used of God are anthropomorphic (cf., e.g., the avian image in Gen 1:2) and some of them refer to heavenly realities other than God. It is rather a matter of two-register cosmology and an archetype-ectype relationship between the entire two registers in both their spatial and temporal dimensions.

Lower Register Time

Twin Record. Earthly time is articulated in the astronomical phenomena that measure off and structure its flow. It is the astral-solar-lunar relationships of the earth that define the units, the years and the days, in which man experiences (lower register) time. They produce the sequence of light and darkness that marks the days. They arrange the signs in the sky that announce the seasonal round of the years. Time is named, its meaning is expressed, in this system of calibration. The establishing of this regulatory order by which lower register time is defined and in which it has its being is recorded in the creation account. Twice in fact: once at the beginning of the first triad of days (Gen 1:3-5) and a second time at the beginning of the second triad (Gen 1:14-19).

Temporal Recapitulation. The non-sequential nature of the creation narrative, and thus the non-literal nature of the creation "week," is evident from the recording of the institution of lower register time in both the first and fourth day-sections. This point must be developed here because of its importance as an independent argument against the solar-day and day-age views and because the exegesis involved is preparatory to other arguments below.

The forming and stationing of the sun, moon, and stars are attributed to day four. Their functions with respect to the earth are also stated here, first in the fiat section (Gen 1:14,15) and again (in reverse order) in the fulfillment section (Gen 1:16-18). They are to give light on the earth and to rule by bounding light/day and darkness/night, as well as by demarcating the passage of years and succession of seasons. These effects which are said to result from the production and positioning of the luminaries on day four are the same effects that are already attributed to the creative activity of day one (Gen 1:3-5). There too daylight is produced on the earth and the cycle of light/day and darkness/night is established. In terms of chronology, day four thus brings us back to where we were in day one, and in fact takes us behind the effects described there to the astral apparatus that accounts for them. The literary sequence is then not the same as the temporal sequence of events.

To avoid this consequence, alternative interpretations of day four have been sought. According to one proposal, the luminaries (though unmentioned previously) were in existence before the point in time dealt with in day four and were indeed present at day one as the source of light spoken of there.[25] Day four describes simply their coming into sight, not their creation. Any such view is falsified by the language of the text, which is plainly that of actual production: "Let there be . . . and God made . . . and God set (lit., gave)." The attempt[26] to override this language cannot be passed off as just another instance of phenomenological description. The proposed evasive tactic involves a very different notion – not just the general denominating of objects according to their everyday observed appearance at any and all times, but the relating of a specific event at a particular juncture in the creation process as though witnessed by an observer of the course of events, someone who at the moment reached on day four is supposed to catch sight of the luminaries, hitherto somehow hidden, perhaps by clouds. Disclaimers notwithstanding, this proposal is guilty of foisting an unwarranted meaning on the language affirming God's making and positioning of the luminaries. In the accounts of the other days, everybody rightly recognizes that the same language of divine fiat and creative fulfillment signifies the bringing into existence of something new, not just a visual detecting of something that was there all the while. And there is no more excuse for reducing divine acts of production into human acts of perception in day four than there would be elsewhere.

Some advocates of the controverted approach to day four acknowledge more forthrightly its distinctiveness and develop more fully its peculiar feature of the seer figure.[27] An attempt is made to explain the precise sequence of the entire creation narrative by the exigencies of the visual experience of the hypothesized human spectator, as he is conducted through all the successive scenes. Besides the basic objection that it is belied by the language of origination used for the day four event, this form of the observer hypothesis is beset with a special problem of its own. Its suggested guided-tour perspective is a feature of apocalyptic visions and there the presence of the seer figure is plainly mentioned. He is in fact the one who narrates the visions unfolding before him. No such figure is introduced in the creation account; the alleged human spectator is a fiction imposed on the text contrary to its non-visionary genre.

[25] I would agree that this is in fact a correct view of the day one situation, but not that that situation was before day four.

[26] For a recent example, cf. Collins, "How Old," p. 123, n. 55.

[27] A recent case is D. L. Roth, "Genesis and the Real World," *Kerux* 9 (1994): 30-54.

Recognizing that the actual making of the luminaries is related in day four, but still trying to avoid the conclusion that the narrative order is thematic rather than sequential, some would subordinate the statement about the making of the luminaries (vv. 16,17a) to the statement about their purpose or functions (vv. 17b,18a), alleging that the only distinctive new development of day four is that these functions then become operational. But the primary declaration that the luminaries were made cannot be eliminated as a day four event in that way – no more so than the statement in the day two account that God made the firmament may be reduced to the idea that a previously existing firmament began to perform its stated purpose of dividing between the waters above and below (Gen 1:6,7). Moreover, this minimalist view of day four would share the fatal flaw of all views that eliminate the forming of the luminaries from the happenings of day four: it would leave day four with no new contribution, for all the functions mentioned there are already said to be operative in day one.[28]

Also entailed in the minimalist interpretation of day four is the pluperfect rendering of the verbs expressing the making of the luminaries in the fulfillment section (vv. 16,17), introduced by "and it was so" (v. 15b). If adopted, the pluperfect could not be restricted to these verbs. For consistently in Genesis 1, what immediately follows the fiat and the "and it was so" formula that answers to the fiat is a detailing of what God proceeded to bring into being in execution of the fiat. In day four then the verbs of fulfillment in verses 16,17 cannot be pluperfect with respect to the fiat of verses 14,15a. Temporally they follow the fiat, which means the fiat would have to be put in the same pluperfect tense as its subsequent fulfillment, yielding the translated "And God had said." That is, day four as a whole would have to be cast in the pluperfect, and that with reference to the time of the events in the preceding days. Ironically, such a translation would make explicit the non-chronological sequence of the narrative, the very thing the pluperfect proposal was trying to avoid.[29]

---

[28] The role of ruling cannot be isolated as a new function distinct from those mentioned in day one. In Gen 1:18 ruling the day and night is explicated as dividing the light from the darkness (equivalent to dividing the day from the night, v. 14).

[29] A pluperfect rendering of the *wayyiqtol*-form introducing this section is grammatically defensible, precisely because it begins a paragraph, and that would bring out the true temporal relationship of Gen 1:14ff. to what immediately precedes. But though this

Understandably dissatisfied with the contrived nature of these attempts to avoid acknowledging that the act of making the luminaries was a day four event, other opponents of the non-sequential view of the creation narrative have been driven to seek a solution in a reinterpretation of day one. They would account for the presence of light and the cycle of day and night in day one by positing for this point in time some light source other than the one whose origin they admit is assigned to day four and which (according to their commitment to the temporally sequential order of the narrative) did not, therefore, exist until three days (or ages) after day one.

Some speculate about a supernatural light source, a manifestation of divine glory in space. But that distorts the eschatological design of creation's history, according to which the advent of God's Glory as the source of illumination that does away with the need for the sun awaits the Consummation.[30] Indeed, the assumption of such a supernatural mode of ongoing providence during the creation week is contradicted by the assumptions that inform Gen 2:5ff.[31]

No more satisfactory is the suggestion that the hypothetical lighting system was some natural arrangement. That would raise questions about the wisdom of the divine procedure. Why would God create such a vast cosmic order only to discard it three days (or ages) later? Why create a replacement cosmos to perform the very same functions already being performed perfectly well by the original system?[32] Like the gap theory of Gen 1:2, this scenario, with its mid-course cosmic upheaval and starting over, would introduce a jarring, discordant note into the simple, stately symphony of the cosmic house-building – planned, performed, and perfected by the all wise master builder.

---

would establish my thesis without more ado, I would retain the translation, "And God said (v. 14) . . . and God made" (v. 16) in order to preserve the picture of seven successive days, leaving it to the other available evidence to demonstrate the figurative nature of this picture and the dischronologized sequence of the contents of the days.

[30] Note also that the presence of this divine Luminary puts an end to the cycle of day and night instituted on day one (Rev 22:5).

[31] On this, see below.

[32] Indeed, in line with the anthropic principle, the original system would necessarily have been virtually the same as its replacement. Cf. R. Maatman, *The Bible, Natural Science, and Evolution* (Sioux Center: Dordt College Press, 1970), p. 111; A. Lightman, *Ancient Light* (Cambridge, Mass.: Harvard U. Press, 1991), pp. 117-121.

Any such approach that disconnects the luminaries of day four from the light of day one, denying the cause-effect relationship of the two, violates the overall thematic scheme of the creation narrative. As we have seen, the successive members of the first triad of days correspond to the successive days of the second triad, the relationship of each matching pair being that of creation kingdom (theme of the first triad) to creature king (theme of the second triad). The correspondence is especially close in the day one-day four pair. It is clearly the light phenomena (kingdom) of day one over the which the luminaries (kings) of day four rule, producing and regulating it. Temporal recapitulation most certainly occurs at day four and hence there is no escaping the conclusion that the narrative sequence is not intended to be the chronological sequence.

Upper Register Time

The Beginning. As observed above, the allusions in Prov 8:22,23 to the bĕrēšît of Gen 1:1 show that this "beginning" precedes the situation surveyed in Gen 1:2ff. It stands at the head of the creation days. While belonging to the creation week,[33] it marks the interface of precreation and the space-time continuum, pointing back to what is signified by "was" in the identification of God as the one "who is, and who was, and who is to come" (Rev 1:8). In Gen 1:1 the "beginning" is peculiarly associated with God himself. Similarly, echoes of bĕrēšît in the Scriptures focus on divine acts and intratrinitarian relationships back of creation. Equating the beginning with a stage "before the earth was," Prov 8:23 asserts that the personified divine Wisdom was present with God at the beginning (cf. Col 1:17). The prologue of John's Gospel identifies "the beginning" in terms of the relationship between God and the Logos, who was God and made all things (John 1:1-3), the one who identifies himself as "the beginning of the creation of God" (Rev 3:14; cf. Rev 21:6; 22:13; Col 1:15-18) and speaks of the glory he had with the Father "before the world was" (John 17:5).

---

[33] This conclusion is required by Exod 20:11, particularly if the "heaven" it refers to as being made during the "six days" includes the invisible heavens, whose formation, unlike that of the earth, was exclusively within "the beginning."

All indicators tell us that "in the beginning" belongs to the upper register, where Father, Son, and Spirit act together in sovereign purpose, word, and power to create the world. "In the beginning" is a time coordinate of invisible space. Entry into the six days that it is, "the beginning" serves to identify them as also belonging to the invisible cosmological register.

The Seventh Day. God is present at the beginning of creation; he *is* "the beginning." He is also "the end," for he appears at the completion of creation as the Sabbath Lord. The seventh day has to do altogether with God, with the upper register. The divine rest which characterizes the seventh day is the reign of the finisher of creation, enthroned in the invisible heavens in the midst of the angels.[34] It is precisely the (temporary) exclusion of man from this heavenly Sabbath of God that gives rise to the two-register cosmological order. At the Consummation, God's people will enter his royal rest, the seventh day of creation (Heb 4:4,9,10), but until then that seventh creation day does not belong to the lower register world of human solar-day experience. It is heaven time, not earth time, not time measured by astronomical signs.

Not only the identification of the Sabbath rest with God's royal session on high, but the unending nature of that seventh day of creation differentiates it from earthly, solar-days. Consisting as it does in God's status as the one who has occupied the completed cosmic temple as the King of Glory – a status without the possibility of any interruption or limitation – the seventh day is in the nature of the case unending. This is confirmed by the treatment of the theme of God's "rest" in Hebrews 4. That rest is identified in verses 3 and 4 as God's seventh day of Gen 2:2 (which is quoted). The passage then expounds God's rest as an ongoing reality, entrance into which is the eschatological hope of God's people (see esp. vv. 10,11; cf. John 5:17). If the seventh day were not an unending Sabbath-rest for God but a literal day, would the next day be another work day, introducing another week of work and rest for him, to be followed by an indefinite repetition of this pattern? Are we to replace the Sabbath-Consummation doctrine of biblical eschatology with a mythological concept of cyclic time?[35] In the Genesis prologue the unending nature of

---

[34] Cf. my *Kingdom Prologue*, pp. 22-25.

[35] The issue of creation-consummation eschatology is theologically crucial, for bound up with it is the Bible's doctrine of the covenant with its decisive probationary crisis and the principle of federal representation.

God's Sabbath is signalized by the absence of the evening-morning formula from the account of the seventh day.

The Six Days. Under consideration here is the series of six numbered days plus the accompanying evening-morning refrain. This refrain is not to be connected with the solar time phenomena of days one and four, for it is not confined to those two contexts but is included in all six day-sections and in every case is immediately conjoined to the numbered day. The imagery of the evening and morning is simply a detail in the creation-week picture. This refrain thus functions as part of the formulaic framework of the account.

The question whether the references to the six days (with their evenings and mornings) describe lower register time phenomena or whether they belong to the upper register is answered in favor of the latter by the interlocking of the six days on both sides with upper register temporal features. Certainly the six days are part of the same strand as the seventh day, and the "beginning," as suggested above, is to be taken as the threshold of the creation week. Psalm 104 reflects this by similarly bracketing its treatment of the works of the six creation days (vv. 5-26 or 30) with upper register scenes of God in heaven, before (vv. 1-4) and after (vv. 27 or 31-35).

The six evening-morning days do not then mark the passage of time in the lower register sphere. They are not identifiable in terms of solar days, but rather relate to the history of creation at the upper register of the cosmos. The creation "week" is to be understood figuratively, not literally – that is the conclusion demanded by the biblical evidence.

Replication: The Sabbath Ordinance

Rounding out the series of acts of spatial and temporal replication in the Genesis prologue is the reproduction of the pattern of the Creator's time in the instituting of the Sabbath ordinance.[36] This ordinance superimposed a special temporal grid on the calendar of days and seasons marked by astronomical sequences. The Sabbath was designed for symbolic purposes

[36] For a discussion of the Sabbath as a creation ordinance, see my *Kingdom Prologue*, p. 50.

within the covenant community, as a sign calling to consecration and the imitation of God and as a seal promising consummation of the kingdom to the covenant keepers.[37] By this promise the Sabbath reminds us that lower register history as a whole is patterned after upper register time in that it is a Consummation-directed eschatological movement. The weekly scheme of the Sabbath ordinance portrays this overall seventh-day-bound design of lower register time, while it also symbolically mirrors the archetypal heavenly creation week itself.

Exod 20:11 brings out explicitly that the continuing earthly pattern of sabbatical weeks is a human copy of a divine original. Within the two-register cosmology of the creation account with all its replications of upper register realities in the lower register world, all of them reproductions with a difference, there can be no doubt about the figurative nature of the relationship of the Sabbath ordinance to God's upper register creation week. The gratuitous insistence of literalists that the terms of the Sabbath ordinance in Exod 20:11 demand that the creation week be one of literal solar days is contradicted by the metaphorical character of the whole series of creation replications to which the original Sabbath ordinance (Gen 2:3) belongs. Like man's nature as image of God, man's walk in imitation of God's sabbatical way is not a matter of one-to-one equivalence but of analogy, of similarity with a difference. Like all the other lower register replicas, the sabbatical week of the ordinance is a likeness of its original, not exactly the same; it is an earthly metaphor for the heavenly archetype.

The Genesis prologue thus concludes with the record of the instituting of the lower register phenomena that provides the figurative chronological framework on which this literary composition has itself been constructed, the seven-day metaphor employed for the time dimension of God's creating the heavens and the earth.

Cosmogony and Providence

Our argument for the metaphorical nature of the creation week has included evidence that the narrative sequence of Genesis 1 is determined by thematic factors and is not intended to correspond to the actual temporal

[37] Ibid., pp. 51, 52.

sequence, as maintained by both the solar-age and day-age views. For further light on this issue we now turn to Gen 2:5-7.

The Genesis 2 Context

After the prologue, Genesis divides into ten sections with a refrain formula ("these are the generation of N." [lit.]) serving as the heading for each.[38] In keeping with the uniform meaning of this formula, Gen 2:4 signifies that what follows recounts not the origins but the subsequent history of the heavens and the earth. Gen 2:5ff. is thus identified as a record of the sequel to the world's creation, not as a second account of creation. This section does, however, pick up the story within the creation period (as does the next section at Gen 5:1ff.). In doing so it incidentally reveals something about the nature of divine providence during the creation week, something that cannot be accommodated by strictly sequential interpretations of Genesis 1.

Genesis 2 fixes attention on the lower register and, more precisely, on Eden as it sets the stage for the covenant crisis of Genesis 3. Here again the arrangement of the narrative is thematic rather than strictly chronological. At the beginning (vv. 5-7) and end (vv. 18-25) the man and woman, the human principals in the probationary crisis, are reintroduced (cf. Gen 1:27). The middle of the chapter describes the site of the dramatic event (vv. 8-14), calling attention to the two critical trees in the midst of the garden (v. 9), and it reports the covenant stipulations on which the decisive testing was based (vv. 15-17), here too emphasizing the probation tree (vv. 16,17). Genesis 2 having thus set the scene with its major features (the man, the woman, and the judgment tree), Genesis 3 proceeds to relate the fateful action.

From this overview of Genesis 2 it is evident why, in the narrative of man's creation (vv. 5-7), the origin of vegetation (and thus of trees) is intertwined with his. Also, looking back at Genesis 1, we can now appreciate the artful designing that brought the first triad of days to a climax in trees and the second triad in man, so anticipating the crucial connection of the two unfolded in Genesis 2 and 3.

---

[38] Cf. ibid., pp. 6, 7.

Exegesis of Genesis 2:5-7

To bring out the sovereign lordship of Yahweh-Elohim in establishing the covenantal order of man in the garden, under probation with its demands and promises, both represented by trees, the account takes us back to a time before there was a man or a garden and trees in order then to tell us how the Lord proceeded to form the man, plant the garden, and make its trees grow.

Gen 2:5a says that at a certain time and place within the creation process vegetation did not yet exist. The language allows that the earth as a whole is referred to but the area particularly in view might be the Eden region, on which the following narrative focuses. Absent at this point in time were all plants, whether belonging to the unpeopled wilderness or to cultivated areas.

Gen 2:5b explains why Yahweh-Elohim had not yet produced the vegetation. Rain is needed for the preservation and growth of plants, and God had not yet initiated the rain cycle. Of course, man can compensate for the local lack of rainfall by constructing an irrigation system, but man was not on the scene either. It is the assumption underlying this explanation for the timing of the creation of vegetation that confirms the conclusion that the Genesis 1 narrative is not chronologically sequential. To this we shall presently return.

Gen 2:6 tells of the provision of a supply of water, the absence of which had previously delayed the appearance of vegetation. Whatever the meaning of the Hebrew ʾēd (traditionally "mist"), this verse cannot be describing another circumstance adverse to plant life (like chaotic flood waters), for the effect of the ʾēd was a beneficial watering, such being the consistent meaning of the verb šāqâ.[39] Verse 6 must then be relating a new development, not something concurrent with the situation described in verse 5. For otherwise verse 6 would be affirming the presence of the supply of water necessary for the survival of vegetation at the very time

---

[39] Ancient Near Eastern cosmogonies contain the motif of an absence of water that is subsequently remedied, with fruitful fields resulting. Examples are the Sumerian myth of *Enki and the World Order* and the Akkadian *Myth of Anzu*. For discussion see R. J. Clifford, *Creation Accounts in the Ancient Near East and in the Bible* (Washington, DC: The Catholic Biblical Association of America, 1994), pp. 34f., 84.

when verse 5b says the absence of vegetation was due to the lack of such a water supply. The context thus demands the translation: "but an ʾēd began to rise," an inceptive meaning that is agreeable to the usage of the imperfect form of the verb employed here.[40]

The ʾēd in verse 6 answered to the previous lack of rain in verse 5b. If the ʾēd does not refer to rain but to some satisfactory alternative, the previous absence of that alternative should have been included in verse 5b in the listing of the missing sources of water. Indeed, if the ʾēd solution is not equatable with the rain whose absence was the problem, the citing of the absence of rain in verse 5b would itself be stranded as an irrelevance. These considerations argue in support of the identification of the Hebrew ʾēd with the Eblaite ì-du, "rain-cloud."[41] Also, the one other context where ʾēd is found is all about rain-clouds. That passage, Job 36, extols the greatness of God, who spreads the clouds abroad and sends down showers on man, so giving food in abundance (vv. 26-33). Verse 27a speaks of God's drawing forth the drops of water and then, repeating the image, the parallel clause in verse 27b adds the source from which the rain is distilled, namely the ʾēd, apparently the rain-clouds. Similarly in Genesis 2 the originating of the ʾēd as a watering system (v. 6) is implicitly attributed to Yahweh-Elohim by virtue of the previous tracing of the absence of that provision to his determination (v. 5b). Another Joban echo of this is heard in Job 38:25-30. Challenging Job's knowledge of storm phenomena, the Lord illustrates his own creation-wide sovereignty by the example of his provision of rain and vegetation, not just in agricultural areas but in the wilderness where no man is.

---

[40] See the discussions of preterital *yiqtol* in P. Joüon and T. Muraoka, *A Grammar of Biblical Hebrew* (Rome: Pontifical Biblical Institute, 1993), pp. 368-9 and of incipient past non-perfective in B. K. Waltke and M. O'Connor, *An Introduction to Biblical Hebrew Syntax* (Winona Lake: Eisenbrauns, 1990), pp. 503-4. Cf. S. R. Driver, *A Treatise on the Use of the Tenses in Hebrew*^{2} (Oxford: Clarendon, 1881), pp. 27, 36ff. Suggested examples, besides cases involving stative verbs, include Gen 37:7; Exod 15:5,12,14; 2 Sam 15:37 (cf. 16:15); 1 Kgs 7:7,8; Jer 6:14.

[41] Cf. M. Dahood, "Eblaite ì-du and Hebrew ʾēḏ, 'Rain Cloud,'" *Catholic Biblical Quarterly* 43 (1981): 534-38. Other suggested etymologies for ʾēd produce meanings like flood or subterranean rivers, which break through and water the surface. On such interpretations (and on the rain-cloud view too) the ʾereṣ from which the ʾēd ascends could be the deeps beneath the earth (cf. Exod 15:12).

The springing forth of plants (at least the wild plants that need only the rain, not man the cultivator) is taken for granted in Gen 2:6 as a consequence of the provision of the prerequisite water, a consequence occurring before the creation of man (v. 7). Even the Lord's planting of the garden with its trees (v. 8) is not to be located after the creation of man, since the form of the verb for planting can express the pluperfect.[42] In the absence of rainfall, man can dig irrigation ditches to bring the necessary water to his cultivated land,[43] and therefore, to round out the explanation of the absence of vegetation in Gen 2:5b, the absence of man was added to the absence of rain. But once God had caused it to rain, the Eden-garden could be planted without man being yet present.

When, therefore, the creation of man is narrated in Gen 2:7, this act is not subordinated to the theme of the production of vegetation. However symbiotic the relationship of man and the cultivated plants, man was not made for the plants but the plants for man. The report of man's creation (v. 7) stands apart as an independent statement announcing the presence of the main party in the upcoming probationary crisis to take place in connection with the trees of the garden – the theme of the following narrative.

Genesis 2:5 and the Creation "Week"

What was the nature of divine providence during the creation "week"? More specifically, by what means did God preserve such things as he had brought into existence? Embedded in Gen 2:5 is an answer to that question that has decisive implications for the interpretation of the chronological framework of the creation account.

Whatever uncertainty may perplex the exegesis of various details in Gen 2:5-7, the point I am now making does not depend on the adoption of a particular interpretation of any of these details. It rests on – indeed, consists in – the simple, incontestable fact that Gen 2:5 gives an explanation, a

---

[42] Compare the similar grammatical-compositional situation in Gen 2:19, which surely does not intend to suggest that the animals were made after the creation of Adam and his experience in the garden described in verses 7-18.

[43] This is a function of mankind featured in the ancient cosmogonies.

perfectly natural explanation, for the absence of vegetation somewhere within the creation "week."[44] Gen 2:5 tells us that God did not produce the plants of the field before he had established an environment with a watering system, the natural, normal precondition for plant life. The assumption underlying Gen 2:5 is clearly that a natural mode of divine providence was in operation during the creation "days."

Acts of supernatural origination did initiate and punctuate the creation process. And had God so pleased, his providential oversight of what he had created might also have been by supernatural means during that process. Gen 2:5, however, takes it for granted that providential operations were not of a supernatural kind, but that God ordered the sequence of creation acts so that the continuance and development of the earth and its creatures could proceed by natural means. This unargued assumption of Gen 2:5 contradicts the reconstructions of the creation days proposed by the more traditional views.

The scenario conjured by the literalists' solar-day interpretation is, in fact, utterly alien to the climate and tenor of Gen 2:5. Within the flurry of stupendous events which their view entails, each new cosmic happening coming hard on the heels of the last and all transpiring within a few hours or days, the absence of vegetation or anything else at any given point would not last long enough to occasion special consideration of the reasons for it. Within that time-frame such a question would be practically irrelevant. Gen 2:5 reflects an environmental situation that has obviously lasted for a while; it assumes a far more leisurely pace on the part of the Creator, for whom a thousand years are as one day. The tempo of the literalists' reconstructed cosmogony leaves no room for the era-perspective of Gen 2:5.[45]

And in specific contradiction of the disclosure of Gen 2:5, both the solar-day and day-age theories must assume that God used other than

---

[44] One thing showing that the situation described is within the six-day era is that man was not yet present. My essential contention is not affected whether the lack of vegetation mentioned be earth-wide or local (the Eden area) and no matter to which "day" the vegetationless situation pertains.

[45] Endorsing my argument as originally published, H. Blocher examines the criticism of it by E. J. Young (*Studies in Genesis One* [Philadelphia: Presbyterian and Reformed, 1964], pp. 58-65) and concludes that Young "misses the main point" (*In the Beginning*, p. 56, n. 56).

the ordinary secondary means in the providential sustaining and further shaping of what his creative word had called into being.

We have already seen that any view that insists day four presents events chronologically later than those in day one must posit some means other than the sun, moon, and stars of day four, something extraordinary or even supernatural, to account for the effects of light and the day-night cycle mentioned in day one. It would also have to be by some such means that the vegetation whose production is described in day three was sustained apart from the presence of the normally prerequisite sun of day four. Likewise, on any strictly sequential interpretation of the narrative, the existence of all flora (day three) before any fauna (days five and six) would include extraordinary means of preservation in those symbiotic situations where the survival of a particular kind of vegetation is dependent on the activity of animal life. And of course the existence of the earth itself on day one confronts the traditional approaches with a gigantic exception to normal providential procedure. For according to them the earth would have come into existence by itself as a solitary sphere, not as part of the cosmological process by which stars and their satellites originate, and it would have continued alone, suspended in the spatial void (if we may so speak) for the first three "days" of creation. All the vast universe whose origin is narrated on day four would then be younger (even billions of years younger) than the speck in space called earth. So much for the claimed harmony of the narrative sequence of Genesis 1 with scientific cosmology.[46]

In short, if the narrative sequence were intended to represent the chronological sequence, Genesis 1 would bristle with contradictions of what is revealed in Gen 2:5. Our conclusion is then that the more traditional interpretations of the creation account are guilty not only of creating a conflict between the Bible and science but, in effect, of pitting Scripture against Scripture. The true harmony of Genesis 1 and Gen 2:5

---

[46] Some of these problems of sequence (but not the major one involving days one and four) would be resolved by a variation on the day-age view which allows that the days may overlap. The idea is that while what is described as happening on a given day must have begun to happen before the next day's developments began, the completing of the earlier day's creative work would have overlapped the activity of subsequent days. This contrived interpretation not only fails to salvage the chronological sequence, but it actually amounts to a virtual acknowledgment that chronological sequence yields to thematic interests in the ordering of the days.

appears, however, and the false conflict between the Bible and science disappears, when we recognize that the creation "week" is a lower register metaphor for God's upper register creation-time and that the sequence of the "days" is ordered not chronologically but thematically.[47]

[47] In this article I have advocated an interpretation of biblical cosmogony according to which Scripture is open to the current scientific view of a very old universe and, in that respect, does not discountenance the theory of the evolutionary origin of man. But while I regard the widespread insistence on a young earth to be a deplorable disservice to the cause of biblical truth, I at the same time deem commitment to the authority of scriptural teaching to involve the acceptance of Adam as an historical individual, the covenantal head and ancestral fount of the rest of mankind, and the recognition that it was the one and same divine act that constituted him the first man, Adam the son of God (Luke 3:38), that also imparted to him life (Gen 2:7).

Appendix B

Har Magedon: The End of the Millennium*

Some sixty years ago C. C. Torrey published a study of Har Magedon that has not received the attention it deserves.[1] His explanation of the Hebrew terms transliterated into Greek as har magedōn (Rev 16:16) is accepted in the present article and additional evidence for it adduced. Further, it will be shown how this interpretation leads to the recognition that Har Magedon is Mount Zaphon/Zion and that the Har Magedon battle is the Gog-Magog crisis of Ezekiel 38–39. This in turn proves to be of critical significance in the millennium debate. For it adds a final, decisive point to the traditional amillennial argument for the identification of the conflict marking the end of the millennium (Rev 20:7-10) with the climactic battle of the great day of the Lord to which the Apocalypse repeatedly returns, as in the Rev 16:12-16 account of the Har Magedon encounter itself and the Rev 19:11-21 prophecy of the war waged by the messianic judge.[2]

---

* Originally published in *Journal of the Evangelical Theological Society* 39 (1996): 207-222.

[1] C. C. Torrey, "Armageddon," *HTR* 31 (1938) 237-248.

[2] See also Rev 6:12-17; 11:7-13,18; 13:7; 14:17-20; 17:11-14. Cf. M. G. Kline, "A Study in the Structure of the Revelation of John" (unpublished). A full exposition of the recapitulatory structure of Revelation will be found in the forthcoming commentary on this book by G. Beale in NIGTC.

I. Har Magedon, The Mount of Assembly

1. *Derivation from* har môᶜēd. Har is the Hebrew word for mountain. The meaning of magedōn is disputed. The most common view, following the variant reading mageddōn in Rev 16:16, identifies it as Megiddo, site of notable battles in Israel's history (Judges 5; 2 Chr 35:22-25) and thus an apt designation for the place where "the battle of the great day" occurs. In addition to the frequent objection that there is no mountain of Megiddo, the area being rather a vast plain, Torrey stressed the fact that the vicinity of Jerusalem is where biblical prophecies uniformly locate the eschatological crisis in which the armies of the nations assemble against God and his people.[3] He cited passages like Zechariah 12 and 14, Joel 3 [4], Isa 29:1-7, and, of particular relevance, Rev 14:14ff. (esp. v. 20) and 20:7ff. (esp. v. 9), which parallel 16:14-16 in the structure of the Apocalypse.[4]

Torrey's own solution, developing an earlier conjecture by F. Hommel, was to trace har magedōn to the Hebrew har môᶜēd (cf. Isa 14:13), "Mount of Assembly." He noted the appropriate association of har môᶜēd with Jerusalem and dealt with the question of transcriptional equivalence. The apparent differences between the Hebrew har môᶜēd and the har magedōn rendering can be readily accounted for. Representation of the consonant ᶜayin by Greek gamma is well attested. Also, in Hebrew -ôn is an afformative to nouns, including place names.[5]

2. *Antipodal to the Abyss.* Supportive of the derivation of har magedōn from har môᶜēd is the fact that each of these expressions in its single biblical appearance is paired with Hades as its polar opposite on the cosmic axis. In the Isa 14:13 context the contrast is drawn between the heights to which the king of Babylon aspires as the site of his throne and the depths to which he is actually to descend. He will not ascend to the har môᶜēd, above the stars of God, to the yarkĕtê ṣāpôn, "heights of heaven," as he boasts (vv. 13-14), but will be brought down to the yarkĕtê bôr, "depths of the Pit" (v. 15).[6] Correspondingly, in the Book of Revelation har magedōn

---

[3] The prophetic idiom is typo-symbolical, not literal, but that is a separate issue.

[4] Cf. Ps 48:1-8 [2-9]; Isa 24:21-23; Mic 4:11-13; Zeph 3:8.

[5] Examples especially pertinent in the present context are ṣāpôn, ʾăbaddôn, and the spelling of Megiddo as mĕgiddôn in Zech 12:11.

[6] For further discussion of the terms yarkĕtê and ṣāpôn see below.

(16:16) is contrastively paired with Abaddōn (9:11), another Hebrew term, here the name of the angel of the Abyss, and in its OT appearances a synonym of Sheol (Job 26:6; 28:22; 31:12; Ps 88:12; Prov 15:11; 27:20). The Abaddon of Rev 9:11 is then the equivalent of the Sheol and Pit of Isa 14:15. And the har (mountain) element in har magedōn (Rev 16:16) of course contrasts with the Pit of Abaddon, as does the har in har môᶜēd (Isa 14:13).

That har magedōn is to be perceived as paired with Abaddōn even though they do not appear in the same immediate context is indicated by certain factors besides their antipodal semantic relationship. One is that in the Book of Revelation these two terms, and these alone, are described as Hebraisti, "in Hebrew."[7] Another factor is their parallel placement in the literary structure of the Apocalypse: Within an overall chiastic arrangement they appear in the corresponding series of the trumpets and the bowls of wrath, in each case at the climax.

In short, then, we find that in Isaiah 14 and the Book of Revelation there are matching antonymic pairings of har môᶜēd and har magedōn with the pit of Hades. Within the framework of this parallelism the har môᶜēd of Isa 14:13 is the equivalent of the har magedōn of Rev 16:16 and as such is to be understood as its proper derivation and explanation. Accordingly, har magedōn signifies "Mount of Assembly/Gathering" and is a designation for the supernal realm.

As an appendix to this point we would note that the term môᶜēd, if seen as the Hebrew behind magedōn, provides a further point of linkage for the pairing of har magedōn and Abaddōn. For in Job 30:23 the Death/Sheol realm denoted by Abaddōn is called the bêt môᶜēd, "house of gathering." Though Job longs to come to God's place of judgment, the heavenly council gathered on the har môᶜēd, he is sure only of being brought down with all who live to their common appointed gathering, their house of gathering (bêt môᶜēd) in Sheol. The association with môᶜēd, "gathering," thus shared by Abaddon and Har Magedon intensifies the irony of those biblical passages where someone finds himself in Abaddon/Sheol who had laid claim to Har Magedon or gathered forces against it.[8]

---

[7] Perhaps a desire to flag the correspondence with Abaddōn prompted the addition of -ōn to magedōn.

[8] For a similar situation involving the ʾōhel môᶜēd, the tent of gathering, compare the experience of Korah in Numbers 16.

3. *Hebraisti.* There is another overlooked clue to the meaning of har magedōn in Rev 16:16 itself. As noted in the discussion of the relationship between har magedōn and Abaddōn, each term is identified as Hebraisti (which can refer to Aramaic as well as Hebrew). Our clue has to do with a stylistic feature characterizing the appearance of such transliterated words in the Greek text of the NT: These words are regularly accompanied by an explanation of some sort, even by a translation sometimes. The Abaddōn counterpart to har magedōn in Rev 9:11 is a good example: "They had a king over them, the angel of the Abyss, whose name in Hebrew is Abaddon, and who has in Greek the name Apollyon (Destroyer)."

By way of further illustration it will suffice to mention those instances where the transliterated word is specifically identified as Hebraisti. These turn out to be all the more apropos in that this use of Hebraisti is an exclusively Johannine trait within the NT, with four instances in John's gospel besides the two in Revelation.[9] In three of the cases in the gospel the word in question is the name of a place. In each case the context furnishes at least an identification of the place thus denoted, even if not a translation. In John 5:2 Bethesda (with variants Bethsaida, Bethzatha, Belzetha) is identified as a particular pool in Jerusalem having five porches or colonnades. Similarly, in John 19:13 the Aramaic Gabbatha (of uncertain meaning) is identified by the Greek term Lithostrōton ("stone pavement or mosaic"), the designation of Pilate's judgment seat to which Gabbatha is appended. In the case of the reference to the site of the crucifixion in John 19:17 the Greek name Kraniou ("of the skull") affords the translation of the Aramaic name Golgotha, which is added to it.[10] In John's resurrection narrative the Aramaic rabbouni is at once explained by the Greek didaskale, "teacher" (John 20:16).

This consistent pattern creates a strong presumption that an accompanying explanation will be found in Rev 16:16 for har magedōn, the place name there with the Hebraisti label. Such an explanation can be shown to be present once it is recognized that har magedōn is based on har môᶜēd. The semantic connection is between Magedōn and the main verb in the statement: "And he gathered (synēgagen) them into the place

[9] Cf. nai, amēn (Rev 1:7).

[10] The explanatory role of the Greek is clear in the Aramaic-Greek sequence found in Matt 27:33; Mark 15:22.

called in Hebrew Har Magedon." The verb synagō interpretively echoes the noun magedōn – he gathered them to the Mount of Gathering. In effect it translates magedōn, establishing its derivation from môʿēd, "gathering." Synagō is indeed the verb used in the LXX to render yāʿad ("appoint"; niphal "assemble by appointment"), the root of môʿēd (an appointed time or place of assembly).

An instructive parallel is found in Numbers 10, where an interpretive wordplay affords an explanation of ʾōhel môʿēd, "tent of meeting/gathering," which symbolically points to the same heavenly reality that the har môʿēd represents.[11] Directions are given to Moses that at the sounding of a certain trumpet signal "the whole assembly (ʿēdâ, from the root yāʿad) shall gather (yāʿad) unto you at the entrance to the Tent of Meeting (ʾōhel môʿēd)" (v. 3). The verb of gathering that brings out the significance of ʾōhel môʿēd is rendered in the LXX of Num 10:3 by the same synagō that explains har magedōn in Rev 16:16.[12] Num 10:3 thus corroborates our view of how synagō functions in Rev 16:16.

We conclude that the evidence of the Hebraisti clue in Rev 16:16 clinches the case for the har môʿēd derivation of har magedōn.

II. Har Magedon, Mount Zaphon/Zion

Appositional to har môʿēd in Isa 14:13 is the phrase yarkĕtê ṣāpôn (Zaphon). Accordingly, what is disclosed about ṣāpôn, and particularly yarkĕtê ṣāpôn, in this and other contexts will contribute to our picture of the har môʿēd and thus of Har Magedon. The data that emerge through the Zaphon connection will also be found to confirm further the derivation of har magedōn from har môʿēd.

1. *Zaphon, realm of deity.* In texts from Ugarit on the north Syrian coast, Zaphon is the name of a mountain about thirty miles north of Ugarit that was regarded as the residence of Baal.[13] As a localized representation of the cosmic

[11] On this see further below.

[12] For other examples of yāʿad translated by synagō in the LXX cf. Neh 6:2,10; Ps 48:4 [5].

[13] "Zaphon" has been traced to ṣpw/y, "to look out" (used e.g. in Ps 66:7 for God's surveillance of the nations from the heights of heaven), or to ṣpn, "to hide." Opinions differ on whether its application to Mount Zaphon was direct or secondary, with a (storm)wind as the primary designee.

abode of the gods, Mount Zaphon shared its designation with the celestial realm. In the OT, ṣāpôn means "north."[14] But it may also denote Zaphon, the terrestrial mountain;[15] or Zaphon, the mythological realm of the gods; or, as a demythologized figure, the heaven of the Lord God; or the holy mountain of God, Zion, as the visible earthly projection of God's heaven.

The phrase yarkĕtê ṣāpôn appears in Ps 48:2 [3]; Isa 14:13; Ezek 38:6,15; 39:2. Its meaning is clearly seen in Isaiah 14, where it stands in apposition with phrases (including har môᶜēd) that refer to the heavens to which the king of Babylon aspires and in opposition to the yarkĕtê bôr into which the king will actually be cast. Some commentators, especially those who see a reference not to Zaphon the mountain of Baal but to a mountain of El farther north, would translate "the distant north." It is evident, however, from the contrastive pairing with yarkĕtê bôr, the Pit of Sheol, that yarkĕtê ṣāpôn concerns a vertical, not horizontal, dimension. It refers not to a quarter of the earth but to a level of the cosmos, denoting the supernal realm, the celestial zenith, while its antipodal opposite, yarkĕtê bôr, denotes the infernal region, the netherworld nadir. In these phrases yarkĕtê, which in the singular means "side" and in the dual "recesses, extreme parts," signifies the remotest reaches, the utmost height or depth.[16]

There are other passages where ṣāpôn has been understood as referring to the celestial realm. One is Ps 89:12 [13]. Above, it was cited as a possible instance of ṣāpôn as Mount Zaphon. Favoring that is the conjoined mention of mounts Tabor, Hermon, and Amanus (taking ymn as an alternative for ᵓmn), the mountain of El. Another view is that ṣāpôn here signifies "clouds," an appropriate pairing being produced by emending yāmîn to yammîm, "seas." Problematic for the rendering "the north and south" is the absence of a concept parallel to this in the context. What does parallel God's creating of ṣāpôn and the south (v. 12 [13]) is God's founding of the heaven and earth (v. 11 [12]). This favors understanding ṣāpôn as

---

[14] Most now explain this as another instance of naming quarters of the globe after prominent topographical features, in this case after Mount Zaphon to the north of Israel.

[15] Ezek 32:20; Ps 89:12 [13] are possible instances of this usage.

[16] The semantic equivalent of yarkĕtê ṣāpôn is found in the Ugaritic ṣrrt ṣpn, apparently meaning "insides/heart of Zaphon." Interestingly, one text in which this expression appears deals with a pretender to the divine throne – namely, with Ashtar the Rebel's futile attempt to ascend to Zaphon and occupy the throne of Baal.

the heavens, with its lower cosmic counterpart designated "south" as a play on the meaning of ṣāpôn as "north." Note also this psalm's emphasis on God's heavenly throne site (vv. 5-8,13-14 [6-9,14-15]).

Job 26:7 is one of two passages in Job that contain a similar use of ṣāpôn.[17] Here again the perspective is cosmic with references to the upper and lower extremes of creation in illustration of the universal scope of God's providential control. Sheol and Abaddon appear in v. 6 representing the lower region, and v. 7 then adds: "He spreads out ṣāpôn over emptiness; he suspends the earth on nothing." Clearly, a vertical rather than horizontal dimension is in view. The ṣāpôn is the sky above the earth.[18] But beyond that, as the preceding mention of Sheol/Abaddon suggests, the visible heavens point to the invisible heaven of God's abode.

The Zaphon with which har môᶜēd (and thus har magedōn) is equated in Isaiah 14 is the celestial realm of deity. It should also be noted that through the tying in of the heaven-defying king with the yarkĕtê ṣāpôn in this passage, the antichrist associations of Har Magedon in the Rev 16:16 episode begin to come into focus here.

2. *Zaphon/Zion.* In Psalm 48 the yarkĕtê ṣāpôn connection yields the identification of Har Magedon with Zion, the earthly counterpart of the heavenly dwelling of Israel's God-King. The opening verses of this psalm introduce its celebration of the supremacy of Yahweh, the Suzerain, and his mountain-city: "Great is Yahweh, and greatly to be praised, in the city of our God (v. 1 [2]a,b,c); the mountain of his sanctuary, paragon of peaks, joy of all the earth (vv. 1 [2]d,2 [3]a,b); Mount Zion, the heights of Zaphon,[19] city of the Great King (v. 2 [3]c,d,e)."[20] Linking the city and

---

[17] The other is Job 37:22; on this see below under the discussion of Ezek 1:4, another such passage.

[18] The astronomical reference in v. 7a is to the pole of the ecliptic, devoid of stars (so M. M. Kline in unpublished address). Another view is that ṣāpôn refers to the clouds suspended in the sky. Cf. J. De Savignac, "Le sens du terme *Ṣâphôn*," *UF* 16 (1984) 273-278.

[19] There is no comparative preposition before yarkĕtê ṣāpôn and no need to take this as *comparatio decurtata* (cf. GKC 118r).

[20] This arrangement (contrary to the numbered verses) into three triplets (A.B.C.) brings out some artful poetic features: the correspondence of the three cola (a.b.c.) of B and C (on the equivalence of Bc and Cc, cf. Isa 24:10-11); the summary inclusio provided by Cc with Aa-c. In biblical and mythological texts reference to the exalted throne-city of deity tends to prompt clusters of descriptive phrases in apposition.

mountain of God, this passage declares Zion-Jerusalem to be the yarkĕtê ṣāpôn. This establishes that har môᶜēd (appositional to yarkĕtê ṣāpôn in Isa 14:13) is Mount Zion, and thereby that har magedōn is related to the city of Jerusalem (and not to be explained by Megiddo).

This identification of har môᶜēd is also attested by passages (like Ps 74:4; Lam 2:6) that speak of Zion as the place of God's môᶜēd and the assembled congregation (ᶜēdâ) of his people, and most graphically by the locating of the ʾōhel môᶜēd, "tent of meeting," and its temple continuation on Zion.[21] In the ʾōhel môᶜēd God met (yāᶜad) and spoke with his people (Exod 25:22; 29:42-43; Num 17:4 [19]), his presence being mediated through the Glory theophany enthroned amid the cherubim. The tent was thus an earthly replica of the divine council in heaven, where the Most High sits as King surrounded by his assembled hosts.[22]

The relevance of Psalm 48 for Har Magedon extends beyond its identification of yarkĕtê ṣāpôn, the har môᶜēd equivalent, with Zion/Jerusalem. This psalm also relates how the rebellious kings gather (yāᶜad) there against Yahweh (v. 4 [5]), who shatters their advancing forces and secures the eschatological peace of his city (vv. 5ff. [6ff.]). All the key elements of the Har Magedon event of Rev 16:16 are united here in connection with the har môᶜēd (Zaphon) site, a signal corroboration of the explanation of har magedōn as har môᶜēd.[23]

Har môᶜēd/magedōn is then the place of God's royal presence, whether heavenly archetype or earthly ectype, where he engages in judicial surveillance of the world (Lookout Mountain); where he gathers the gods (cf. Ps 82:1) for deliberation (Council Mountain); where he musters his armies for battle (Marshal Mountain); where he assembles the company of his holy ones, spirits of just men made perfect with myriads of angels (Ecclesia Mountain).[24] Echoing Psalm 48, Heb 12:18-29 displays these

---

[21] Cf. Ps 15:1. Similarly in Canaanite mythology the tent of the deity and his mountain are conjoined.

[22] Cf. Ps 78:69. On the replication of the heavenly archetype in the tabernacle see M. G. Kline, *Images of the Spirit* (Grand Rapids: Baker, 1980) 39-42.

[23] The same situation obtains in Ezekiel 38–39, to be examined presently.

[24] In secular texts both the Greek ekklēsia and equivalents of môᶜēd are used for a civil assembly. An example of the latter is the designation of the Byblos assembly in the Wen-Amun text.

varied facets of Har Magedon, Mount of Gathering, and identifies it as Zion, heavenly Jerusalem, city of the living God, the Great King.

The story of the earthly Har Magedon goes back to the beginnings of human history when this mountain of God rose up as a cosmic axis in Eden. There the battle of Har Magedon was joined as Satan challenged the God of the mountain and overcame the first Adam, the appointed guardian of the garden-sanctuary.[25] In redemptive history Zion was a typological renewal of Har Magedon, the setting at the dawning of the new covenant age for another momentous encounter in the continuing warfare, this time resulting in a decisive victory of Jesus, the second Adam, over the evil one. The typological Zion/Jerusalem provides the symbolic scenery for prophecies of the climactic conflict in the war of the ages. Through his antichrist beast and his allied kings gathered to Gathering Mountain, Satan will make his last attempt to usurp Har Magedon. But the Lamb, the Lord of the mountain, and his assembled armies will triumph in this final battle of Har Magedon, the battle of the great day of God Almighty (Rev 16:14-16; 19:11-21; 20:7-10).

III. Har Magedon and Magog

Following the trail of har magedōn back to har môᶜēd has led us to examine a set of OT passages containing the phrase yarkĕtê ṣāpôn. From the first two (Isaiah 14; Psalm 48) it has appeared that har môᶜēd/magedōn is identifiable with Mount Zaphon/Zion. Ezekiel 38–39 is a third such passage, and here we discover a fundamental correspondence between the Zaphon/Magedon and Gog-Magog concepts. That means that the Har Magedon crisis of Rev 16:14-16 (and the series of parallel passages in Revelation) is to be identified with the millennium-ending Gog-Magog event of 20:7-10. For the Revelation 20 passage is replete with allusions to Ezekiel 38–39, including, along with the explicit mention of Gog and Magog, the distinctive central theme of Ezekiel 38–39, the universal gathering of the world forces to destroy God's people and their catastrophic overthrow by the descent of fiery judgment from heaven.[26] Accordingly

[25] See M. G. Kline, *Kingdom Prologue* (privately published, 1993) 76.

[26] For further details see below.

it is generally acknowledged that Ezekiel's prophecy and the vision of the loosing of Satan after the thousand years in Revelation 20 describe the same eschatological event.

A main consideration in establishing the identity of the Revelation 16 Har Magedon crisis and the Ezekiel 38–39 Gog crisis (and thus the Revelation 20 Gog crisis) is the antichrist element common to both.[27] The antichrist identity of the dragon-like beast in the Har Magedon episode would be acknowledged by most, irrespective of their millennial preferences. For the continuity of this beast of Revelation 16 with the fourth beast of Daniel 7 (in the final phase of its little-horn expression) is obvious, and in Daniel an alternative representation of this bestial eschatological foe is the self-deifying king of Dan 11:36, the figure interpreted by Paul as the antichrist (2 Thess 2:4). It remains now to show that the antichrist element is also conspicuously present in Ezekiel 38–39 among the other major features of this Gog-Magog prophecy that appear again in the Apocalyptic accounts of Har Magedon.[28] Gog's antichrist characteristics may best be elicited through an examination of his provenance and his destination.

1. *Provenance of Gog.* A description of Gog's place of origin is included in the opening account of his hostile advance with his military forces against the community of God's people (Ezek 38:1-13). A condensed recapitulation of this portrayal of Gog appears as an introduction (38:14-16) to the next section, which presents God's judgment on Gog (38:17-23), and once again by way of introduction (39:1-2) to the final section, which contains a double elaboration of the divine judgment (39:3-8; 39:9-29).[29]

---

[27] "Antichrist" is used here in the popular sense, as a designation for the man of sin figure referred to in 2 Thess 2:3-10.

[28] It may be recalled that such Har Magedon features were observed in the other yarkĕtê ṣāpôn passages. Psalm 48 relates the marshaling of enemy forces against Zaphon/Zion, and in Isaiah 14 the antichrist aspect of Rev 16:16 episode is articulated in the aspirations of the king of Babylon, a prototypal antichrist who claims for himself supremacy on har môᶜēd.

[29] The two elaborations on the destruction of Gog are arranged in thematic parallel, each treating in turn (1) the destruction of Gog's weaponry (vv. 3,9-10), (2) death-burial (vv. 4a,11-16), (3) banquet (vv. 4b-5,17-20), and (4) devastation of the nations (vv. 6a,21).

Whatever details are omitted from the two abbreviated recapitulations of the opening section, one feature included each time is Gog's provenance, the yarkĕtê ṣāpôn (Ezek 38:6,15; 39:2). It is from the heights of Zaphon that God brings Gog with all his armies to overthrow them on the mountains of Israel. Gog is characterized by the antichrist syndrome: He is a pretender to the throne of heaven. The correspondence of his experience to the king of Babylon typology in Isaiah 14 is seen in the ironic motif of the polar contrast between his pretensions and his actual fate. Challenging Yahweh's sovereignty on Zion, Gog would take possession of the mountain heights of Israel. But he ends up with his vast military array in the depths of a valley. He lunged for a heavenly throne but plunged into a netherworld grave. Not the lofty polis (city) of the divine Suzerain but a necropolis was his destiny.

The ironic reversal is underscored by puns. Instead of the glory of ṣiyyôn (Zion), Gog's hallmark will be ṣiyyûn (Ezek 39:15), the marker that flagged for burial the corpses of his forces. The valley where his armies were buried is called the valley of the ʿôbĕrîm (Ezek 39:11), "those passing through or across," a term used for the dead, those who cross over from this world to the next.[30] In that sense will they turn out to be ʿôbĕrîm who set out to be ʿôbĕrîm in the sense of invaders traversing the land of Israel as conquerors.[31] Another name given to the burial valley is gêʾ hămôn gôg (Ezek 39:11),[32] "valley of the multitude of Gog." It recall's God's wordplay interpretation of the new name, Abraham, he gave to Abram as a gift of grace: ʾab hămôn gôyîm (Gen 17:4-5), "father of a multitude of nations." In quest of such name-fame Gog mustered his multitudes, but his hămôn-name proclaimed his shame. Whereas ʾab hămôn gôyîm prophesied of Abraham's innumerable descendants out of all nations, elect in Jesus Christ and co-heirs with him of the kingdom of eternal life, the similar sounding gêʾ hămôn gôg signified the mountains of skeletons of Gog's hordes, cleared from God's kingdom land and cast into gêʾ hinnōm, the Gehenna valley of the dead, where the fire is never quenched.

---

[30] Cf. Job 34:20; Ps 144:4. See M. S. Odell, "The City of Hamonah in Ezekiel 39:11-16: The Tumultuous City of Jerusalem," *CBQ* 56 (1994) 479-489.

[31] Cf. Ezek 14:17; Zech 9:8.

[32] Cf. hămônâ (Ezek 39:16).

The antichrist character of both the king of Babylon in Isaiah 14 and Gog in Ezekiel 38–39 is brought out by their connection with the yarkětê ṣāpôn. Gog, however, is not just an OT prefiguration but the antichrist of the final crisis. In Rev 20:7-10 the Gog-Magog assault on Zion marks the end of the millennium. Within Ezekiel 38–39 indications also abound of the eschatological finality of the Gog crisis. As in Revelation 20, it comes after a long age of secure preservation for God's people (Ezek 38:8) – in NT terms, after the age in which the church, though sorely persecuted, is preserved by the Lord to complete the great commission task (cf., e.g., Rev 11:7). And as the judgment on Gog in Revelation 20 merges with the resurrection of the dead for final judgment (20:11-15), so God's judicial deliverance of his people from Gog in Ezekiel 38–39 institutes for them the eternal state of unending, never-again-disturbed felicity (39:21-29).

"Your [Gog's] place" (mĕqômĕkā) stands in Ezek 38:15 (within the first recapitulation section) as a substitute for the previous "land of Magog" (Ezek 38:2; cf. 39:6). Indeed, the term may reflect an etymological play on Magog. Māqôm would interpret the mā- in Magog (explained either by the Akkadian māt, "land of," or as the Hebrew noun prefix signifying "place").[33] The second syllable of Magog would then be taken as the name Gog, a name borne by an earlier Anatolian king (Gugu or Gyges) and here created out of Magog to serve as a symbolic pseudonym for the future antichrist foe. In any case "your [Gog's] place" certainly functions in this context as an equivalent of land of Magog. And since "your place" is identified as yarkětê ṣāpôn in Ezek 38:15,[34] its equivalent, Magog, is likewise identified as yarkětê ṣāpôn – and thus as har môᶜēd/magedōn.

In fact māqôm could by itself, like yarkětê ṣāpôn, carry the idea of divine dwelling site. In Deuteronomy māqôm is used repeatedly for the place God would choose for his throne and residence – namely, Jerusalem (e.g. Deut 12:5,14; 14:22-23; 15:20). In 2 Chr 36:15 it is used by itself as the designation of God's temple. It is equated with the mountain of Yahweh (Ps 24:3) and refers to God's royal abode in heaven (Isa 26:21; Mic 1:3). In the light of this usage, "your [Gog's] place" in Ezek 38:15 would by itself seem to signify the position of supreme divine authority

---

[33] As in māqôm itself.

[34] Cf. Ezek 38:2-6, where Magog (v. 2) and yarkětê ṣāpôn (v. 6) form an inclusio for the survey of nations gathered by Gog.

that Gog claimed. Along with yarkĕtê ṣāpôn it would be an expression of Gog's antichrist pretensions. The theme that thus emerges in Ezekiel 38–39 is that of Gog's coming from his place to challenge God at his place.

The Ezekiel 38–39 account of Gog's Zaphon provenance harks back to the Noahic chapter in the story of the mountain of God. The list of nations gathered by Gog begins and ends with northern nations near Gog's land of Magog (Ezek 38:2-6). Also, in the basic passage identifying Gog (38:2-3) and in the second recapitulation of it (39:1) Gog is titled Prince-Head of (Anatolian) Meshech and Tubal. Included in the mountainous territory of these northern nations was the Ararat region where Noah's ark came to rest.

Noah's ark was designed as a replica of the three-story universe, the cosmic city-temple of God (cf. Isa 66:1).[35] Established in sabbatical rest on the Ararat mountaintop, the ark was a redemptive restoration of the mountain of God in Eden, itself a replica of the heavenly Zaphon.

Supportive of the allusive relation of Ezekiel 38–39 to the flood event is the fact that the list of the seven military nations gathered by Gog, along with the three mercantile peoples introduced in 38:13, is patently based on the Genesis 10 list of nations that developed in the postdiluvian movement of the Noahic families out from Ararat. Indeed, the northern nations more closely associated with Gog, and Magog itself, appear at the head of the Genesis 10 list (vv. 2-3).

Understood against this Ararat background, Gog's pretensions are again exposed as nothing less than claiming for himself the headship over the traditional mount of deity in his ancestral land in the north. Genesis 11 reports that the Babel-builders attempted a rebellious restitution of the lost Eden/Ararat mountain of God. Gog takes the challenge against the God of Zaphon to the ultimate, antichrist stage.

2. *Destination of Gog.* As related in Ezekiel 38–39, Gog's antichrist challenge takes place according to God's preannounced purpose and his sovereign orchestration of the event. Lured by the Lord to this final confrontation, Gog advances against "the mountains of Israel" (39:2,17). It is God's chosen Mount Zion in the heart of these mountains that is his central point of attack. As in the case of the mustering of the bestial armies in Revelation 16, the destination and intended target for Gog and

---

[35] See Kline, *Kingdom Prologue* 139-140.

his hosts is Har Magedon, where the Lord's Anointed is enthroned at his right hand.

The indications for this are clear, even though Zion is not mentioned by name in Ezekiel 38–39. God does speak of the mountains of Israel as "my mountains" (38:21) and of the land of Israel as "my land" (38:16). Implicit in that is the royal mountain-city where Yahweh dwells and rules over the mountainous domain he claims as his own. Also, such a capital city on the cosmic mountain was regarded as the center of the earth, and in 38:12 Gog is described as scheming to assault the people of God dwelling at "the center (lit. navel) of the earth."[36] In that concept Gog's real objective is exposed – Yahweh's Mount of Assembly, rival to Gog's pseudo-Zaphon. In the Revelation 20 version of Ezekiel 38–39, Gog's armies are explicitly said to compass "the beloved city" (v. 9), which is Jerusalem/Zion.

Though the term ṣāpôn is not applied to the mountain of God's Presence in Ezekiel 38–39, it is so used at the beginning of the book to denote the divine source of the prophet's visions. In Ezek 1:4 the storm-wind (rûaḥ sĕᶜārâ),[37] the fiery cloud (ᶜānān) that is the theophanic chariot, is said to come from Zaphon.[38] The same term for storm, sĕᶜārâ, is used for God's golden whirlwind confrontation of Job (Job 38:1; 40:6), for the theophanic chariot in Elijah's translation into heaven (2 Kgs 2:1,11), and for the storm chariot of the divine warrior advancing above his people as their defender (Zech 9:14). Ezekiel saw the theophany "coming" not as a storm moving across the earth from the geographical north[39] but as a parousia advent out of heaven. Ezek 1:4 is an expansion of the introductory statement (v. 1) that heaven was opened and Ezekiel saw visions of God. The storm-cloud theophany of v. 4 corresponds to the visions of God in v. 1, and the ṣāpôn of v. 4 is the heavens of v. 1. Divine appearances are comings, advents. Anticipatively setting the scene for Yahweh's revelation to Job out of the theophanic storm (sĕᶜārâ, Job 38:1), Elihu announced

---

[36] Cf. Ezek 5:5.

[37] The combination of rûaḥ with sĕᶜārâ involves a play on rûaḥ as both wind/breath and Spirit, frequent in references to the Glory-Spirit theophany.

[38] Haṣṣāpôn exhibits the use of the definite article for unique objects, like the sun; cf. GKC 126, 2(c).

[39] This is the common interpretation of haṣṣāpôn. Confusingly it identifies sĕᶜārâ as the stormy approach of enemies from the north (a recurring theme in Ezekiel, to be sure) after first recognizing that it is the Glory theophany of Yahweh.

that God's awesome golden majesty was "coming." Indeed, it was "coming from ṣāpôn" (Job 37:22).[40] The ṣāpôn of Ezek 1:4 is then the heavenly site of God's Glory, the celestial place of God's enthronement,[41] here opened up to be accessed by Ezekiel, as was characteristic of the call experience of OT prophets. It is therefore in keeping with an attested concept and terminology of Ezekiel if we interpret the Ezekiel 38–39 scenario as a coming of antichrist Gog from his pseudo-Zaphon to challenge Yahweh on his true Zaphon. Agreeably, Gog's coming is portrayed in 38:9,16 as a coming like a storm-cloud over the land and thus as a counterfeiting of the storm-cloud parousia of God's Glory by a pseudo-parousia.

The antichrist identity of the Gog figure of Ezekiel 38–39 is evidenced by the identification of this archenemy with the pseudo-Zaphon in the north and by his gathering of his universal hordes against Mount Zion, the authentic Zaphon/Har Magedon.

Some detect in this motif the influence of the myth of the conflict between the gods of order and the chaos powers. In Ugaritic texts, for example, it is in connection with Baal's sovereign station at Zaphon that he must do battle against such rival divine beings. And with respect to Ezekiel 38–39 in particular, M. C. Astour suggests a more specific inspiration in the Cuthean Legend of Naram-Sin, which relates the ordeal of that king against northern hordes that are the embodiment of chaos demons.[42] But whatever imagery of the chaos myth has been taken up into the Scriptures, it appears there as demythologized figures of speech. In the Bible the conflict is not cosmological-existential but redemptive-eschatological.

3. *Millennial applications.* According to the premillennial position, the thousand-year era of Rev 20:1-6 with the Gog-Magog episode at its close (vv. 7-10) follows chronologically the judgment of the antichrist beast portrayed in Rev 19:11ff. A common and telling criticism of this view calls attention to various points of identity between the Rev 20:7-10 crisis

[40] See the comments above on the use of ṣāpôn in Job 26:7 for the cosmic north, heaven, the polar antithesis of Sheol/Abaddon.

[41] In Ezek 3:12 this locus of God's Glory is called "his place," another term for the seat of divine sovereignty. The vision of the Glory-Spirit in Ezekiel 43 (explicitly linked, v. 3, to the prophet's opening vision) describes it as "the place of my throne" (v. 7).

[42] M. C. Astour, "Ezekiel's Prophecy of Gog and the Cuthean Legend of Naram-Sin," *JBL* 95 (1976) 567-579.

and the one referred to in 19:11ff. (and the series of parallel Apocalyptic passages, including 16:14-16).

The war (polemos) of Rev 20:8 is certainly "the war of the great day of God, the Almighty," the battle of Har Magedon described in 16:14-16. In each case it is the war to which Satan, the dragon, gathers the nations of the whole world. This universal gathering against the Lamb and the city beloved of the Lord is also referred to as Satan's deception of the whole world through the signs wrought by his agents, the beast from the sea and, particularly, the false prophet. Indeed, this theme of the deception-gathering appears in a series of five passages in the Apocalypse, concentrically arranged according to the subject(s) of the action, with 16:13-16 the centerpiece and 20:7-9 the concluding member. Satan as the ultimate deceiver is the subject in the first member of the chiasm (12:9) and in the last (20:7-9), where the deception is specified as the gathering. The false prophet, acting in association with the dragon-like beast, is the subject in the second member (13:14), which speaks of his world-deceiving signs, and in the fourth (19:17-20), where his deceptive signs are identified with the gathering of the kings of the earth against the messianic horseman and his armies. At the center of the chiasm (16:13-16) all three subjects appear together as the source of the demonic signs by which the kings of the whole earth are gathered to Har Magedon for the great war. This identification of Satan with his two agents in the disastrous enterprise is also brought out in the fifth member of the chiasm (20:10).[43]

The identity of the war of 20:7-10 with the antichrist-Har Magedon battle is further indicated by other parallels between Satan and the beast. In Revelation 20 Satan emerges from his imprisonment in the Abyss, instigates his final challenge against the Lord and his city, and goes to his doom (vv. 7-10). The beast comes up out of the Abyss in the climactic stage of the eighth king, makes war against the witnesses of the Lamb in the true Jerusalem, and goes to his destruction (17:8-14; cf. 11:7-8; 19:20).

Our thesis at this point is that Ezekiel 38–39 proves to be the common source behind Rev 20:7-10 and the series of passages in Revelation referring to the antichrist-parousia event. Cataloguing the details that substantiate this will at the same time underscore and supplement the evidence cited

---

[43] The NIV foists a pluperfect sense on the verbless clause that refers to the fate of the beast and false prophet.

above for the correspondence of Rev 20:7-10 and the other Apocalyptic passages with one another.

The relationship of Rev 20:7-10 to Ezekiel 38–39, obvious enough from the adoption of the Gog-Magog terminology in Revelation 20, is also evidenced by a set of basic similarities: the marshaling of hordes from the four quarters of the earth (Ezek 38:2-7,15; 39:4; Rev 20:8); the march of the gathered armies to encompass the saints in the city of God, center of the world (Ezek 38:7-9,12,16; Rev 20:9); the orchestration of the event by God (Ezek 38:4,16; 39:2,19; Rev 20:3,7); the timing of the event after a lengthy period in which God's people were kept secure from such a universal assault (Ezek 38:8,11; Rev 20:3); the eschatological finality of the crisis (Ezek 39:22,26,29; Rev 20:10ff.); and the fiery destruction of the evil forces (Ezek 38:22; 39:6; Rev 20:9-10).[44]

Just as clearly, the Gog-Magog prophecy of Ezekiel 38–39 is a primary source drawn on by Rev 16:14-16; 19:17-21 and the other Apocalyptic prophecies of the final conflict. Prominent in these passages is the major feature that marked the dependence of Rev 20:7-10 on the Ezekiel prophecy – namely, the universal gathering of the enemy armies (Rev 16:14-16; 17:12-14; 19:19; and compare 6:15 with Ezek 39:18-20), including too the historical setting of that event at the close of this world-age (Rev 6:12-17; 11:7-13; 16:16-17 [cf. 17:10-14]; 19:15-21), following an era in which it is given to the church to fulfill its mission of gospel witness (11:3-7; cf. 12:6,14).

Further (and of central interest in this essay), the Har Magedon of Rev 16:16 is identifiable with Mount Zaphon, the provenance of Gog in Ezekiel 38–39. Particularly important is the significance of this location for the identity of Gog. His claimed lordship over the Zaphon site of the divine council, a challenge to the true Lord of Har Magedon, reveals the Gog of Ezekiel 38–39 to be the bestial antichrist agent of Satan in the Apocalyptic prophecies of the war of the great day. Such self-exaltation over all that is called God is the affront of this man of sin that provokes the parousia of the Lord Jesus to overthrow and destroy him (2 Thess 2:3-10). The pseudo-parousia attributed to this antichrist, a spectacle of satanic deception (2 Thess 2:9), is another feature found in Ezekiel's

[44] Some of these points were mentioned earlier by way of demonstrating that the Gog of Ezekiel 38–39 is the final antichrist.

prophecy where, as we have noted, Gog's coming is portrayed as an advent in storm-cloud theophany (Ezek 38:9,16). Also, beast symbolism is used for the antichrist phenomenon in Revelation, and beast imagery is applied to Gog in Ezek 38:4; 39:2. Extensive evidence of the Ezekiel source is afforded by the Apocalyptic accounts of God's judgment on the beast. Instruments of judgment mentioned by both Ezekiel and John include earthquake (Ezek 38:19-20; Rev 6:12; 11:13; 16:18-20), sword (Ezek 38:21; Rev 19:15,21), and destructive hail and fiery brimstone (Ezek 38:22; 39:6; Rev 16:21; 19:20). Most striking is the distinctive motif of God's summoning the birds and beasts to feed on the carcasses of the defeated armies Gog had gathered, the banquet theme elaborated in Ezek 39:4,17-20 and incorporated into the account of Christ's victory over the beast and his assembled armies in Rev 19:17-18.

The conclusion is amply warranted that Ezekiel 38–39 is the common source of Rev 20:7-10 and the passages earlier in Revelation that deal with the eschatological battle. This confirms the standard amillennial contention that the Gog-Magog episode of Rev 20:7-10 is a recapitulation of the accounts of the Har Magedon crisis in these other passages. And the capstone for that argument is what we have discovered about the equation of Har Magedon (môᶜēd) with Gog's place, Magog, the equation established by the Zaphon connection in Isa 14:13; Psalm 48; Ezekiel 38–39. It now appears that the very term har magedōn itself identifies the Rev 16:14-16 event as the Gog-Magog event of 20:7-10.

Rev 20:7-10 is not, as premillennialists would have it, an isolated, novel episode, not mentioned elsewhere in the Book of Revelation. Rather, it belongs to a series of passages, including Rev 19:11-21, which premillennialists rightly regard as referring to the antichrist-Har Magedon crisis and the parousia of Christ. It therefore follows that the thousand years that precede the Gog-Magog crisis of Rev 20:7-10 precede the Har Magedon-parousia event related in the other passages. Har Magedon is not a prelude to the millennium, but a postlude. Har Magedon marks the end of the millennium. And that conclusion spells the end of premillennialism.

The conclusion that Har Magedon is the end of the millennium also contradicts the preterist approach to the Apocalypse. Preterists interpret the series of passages (except for Rev 20:7-10) that we have taken as prophecies of the final conflict as referring instead to past events, like the fall of

Jerusalem or the collapse of the Roman empire. This approach with its drastic reductions of the Apocalyptic emphasis on the final global Gog crisis is understandably popular with postmillennialists, whose distinguishing notion is that the present age, the millennium, is – at least in its latter phase – a time not only of surpassing evangelistic success for the church but one of outward prosperity and peace.[45] Indeed, postmillennialism of the theonomic reconstructionism variety, in keeping with the theonomic insistence that Torah legislation enforcing the theocratic order is definitive of the church's duty today, anticipates that the millennial success of the church's mission will involve its worldwide political dominance and the forcible elimination of public practice of non-Christian religions. They expect a fulfillment in this church age of the OT prophecies of the restoration of the kingdom in the dimension of external dominion to the ends of the earth.[46]

For such postmillennial expectations, the biblical forecast of a global surge of anti-Christian forces as the immediate precursor of the parousia is obviously a problem. The postmillennialists' strategy is to confine the problem to Rev 20:7-10 by adopting the preterist approach and then to try to minimize the enormity of the crisis described in that passage. But once the preterist option is removed, their exegesis loses all plausibility as they attempt to deal with the whole series of Har Magedon-Gog passages and the recurring, progressively elaborated theme of the worldwide suppression of the gospel witness in which the millennium issues. Actually, Rev 20:7-10 by itself refutes the postmillennial projections, for it is evident there that the nations of the world have not become officially "Christianized" institutions during the millennium.[47] That is in accord with the consistent eschatological pattern of Scripture. In the visions of Daniel 2 and 7, for example, the imperial power clearly retains its beast-character throughout

---

[45] The postmillennial label is often given to those whose optimism is limited to the evangelistic sphere. See below for a suggested revision of millennial terminology.

[46] Cf. D. Chilton: "All nations are absolutely required to be Christian, in their official capacity . . . Any nation that does not submit to the all-embracing rule of King Jesus will perish; all nations *shall* be Christianized . . . in this world as well as in the next," *The Days of Vengeance* (Forth Worth: Dominion, 1987) 489, commenting on Rev 19:16.

[47] This problem drives some to the so-called consistent preterist position, which extends the preterist hermeneutics to Rev 20:7ff. and so regards as past history what all others recognize as events that will usher in the world to come.

history, ultimately prevailing against the saints. Not until the parousia of the Son of Man and the final, total elimination of the bestial empire do the people of the Most High receive the kingdom of glory and universal dominion.

Recognition of the identity of the Har Magedon and Gog-Magog events thus proves to be decisive for the rejection of any view, premillennialist or postmillennialist, that understands the millennium as an age that witnesses the fulfillment (at least in a provisional form) of the OT prophecies of the coming of God's kingdom in external earthly grandeur. The kingdom of glory does not come until final judgment is executed against antichrist/Gog, and therefore not before the end of the millennium. There is no transitional stage in its appearing between the first and second advents of Christ. The glory kingdom comes only as a consummation reality and as such it abides uninterrupted, unchallenged for ever and ever.

Here is the fundamental difference in the eschatology of the several millennial views, the difference that our names for them should reflect. Two of the views are pre-consummation. They hold that a (transitional) realization of the OT prophecies of the kingdom as an external imperial power occurs during the millennium and thus before the consummation. These two can be distinguished from each other in terms of how they relate the millennium to the parousia as pre-parousia (the postmillennialists) and post-parousia (the premillennialists).[48] The amillennial position alone represents the post-consummation view of the coming of the kingdom of glory.[49]

---

[48] Their shared pre-consummation status signalizes a hermeneutical kinship between theonomic postmillennialists and (dispensational) premillennialists: Both fail to understand the typological nature of the Israelite theocracy.

[49] Within the post-consummation view there is room for differing expectations as to the extent of the church's missionary success and of Christian influence on culture, as long as the latter is perceived within the limits imposed by the terms and guarantees of God's covenant for the common order (cf. esp. Gen 8:20–9:17). It is a basic theological flaw in all pre-consummation views that their millennial scenarios entail violations of those divine covenantal commitments.

Appendix C

Death, Leviathan, and the Martyrs: Isaiah 24:1–27:1*

A series of Isaianic oracles concerning the nations (chaps. 13–23) culminates in a section popularly known as the Isaiah apocalypse[1] (chaps. 24–27). From 27:2 on, the focus of this section is on Israel, its fall and fullness.[2] (More than is generally recognized, Paul tapped this vein for his discussion of Israel in Romans 9–11.) In Isa 24:1–27:1 there is a broader, universal perspective.[3] The present essay will concentrate on this first part of the "apocalypse," treating it as a distinct composition and attempting to show how the subject of death, or better, the Lord's conquest of death, permeates and structures its contents. Some contribution may thereby be made to the higher critical debate, at least as to the unity of the material. But my primary interest is in opening up exegetically Isaiah's pastoral

* Originally published in *A Tribute to Gleason Archer*, ed. by Walter C. Kaiser, Jr. and Ronald R. Youngblood (Chicago: Moody Press, 1986) 229-249.

[1] The form-critical assessment expressed by this label is disputed, other genres (including cantata) being proposed.

[2] At the close, however, the focus seems to widen (cf. 27:13).

[3] Isa 24:1–27:1 and 27:2-13 are alike in their eschatological extension to the final divine advent.

theology of death and resurrection and judgment. And in the process, I also want to explore the extraordinary influence exercised by 24:1–27:1 on subsequent biblical revelation, particularly on certain major eschatological passages in the New Testament.

Victory Over Death

Three passages celebrating Yahweh's victory over death occupy the key positions in the structure of Isa 24:1–27:1.[4] They frame the composition with introduction (24:1-3) and conclusion (26:19–27:1) and form its central apex (25:6-8). Each, by means of its own distinctive image, graphically depicts a dramatic reversal that overtakes the realm of death.

The Devourer Devoured

I shall start with Isa 25:6-8, the centerpiece of the composition,[5] and its picture of the eschatological banquet. To appreciate the point of this imagery it is necessary to recall the reputation of the grave as the great devourer. Sheol opens wide its spacious maw and swallows down victims insatiably.[6] But at the banquet for all peoples "in that day" (cf. v. 9) a remarkable reversal will take place. The Lord will become the devourer[7] and death, the famed and fearful swallower, will itself be swallowed up (v. 8).[8]

---

[4] The customary chapter partitioning (except for the separation of 27:1 from chap. 26) appropriately marks the main divisions.

[5] Within chap. 25 itself this passage stands in the center between two confession sections (vv. 1-5; 9-12).

[6] Isa 5:14 speaks of Sheol making wide its throat (or enlarging its appetite) and opening its mouth without limit to engulf the multitudes descending therein. In the Ugaritic texts Mot, the god of death, is similarly described (*UT* 67, i 6-7). Cf. also Exod 15:12; Num 16:30,32,34; 26:10; Deut 11:6; Ps 106:17; Prov 1:12; Hab 2:5.

[7] It is particularly as the consuming theophanic fire that God is the devourer (cf., e.g., Exod 24:17; Deut 4:24; 9:3; Ps 21:9 [MT 10]; Isa 29:6; 30:27,30).

[8] Announcements of God's judgments on His enemies frequently involve such radical reversals. The evil that they have purposed or perpetrated boomerangs against them.

Perhaps the banquet scenario in 25:6-8 was prompted by the desire to exploit the identity of death as the swallower.[9] However, the divinely hosted banquet is a standard feature in visions of the life to come in biblical and extrabiblical literature. Moreover, the victory banquet is a regular element in the epic pattern of the conflict of the hero-deity and the monstrous power of disorder and death, which is in evidence elsewhere in the passage. In any case it was the communion meal of the elders of Israel on the mountain of God after the Exodus-triumph over the dragon (Exod 24:9-11)[10] that provided the specific typological model for Isa 25:6-8. For "on this mountain," the location assigned to the banquet in 25:6-7, refers back to the 24:23 scene of the Glory epiphany before the elders on Mount Zion, and that in turn clearly recalls the banquet scene at Sinai (cf. Exod 24:10-11).

The image of death as the swallower, alluded to in Isa 25:6-8, leads naturally to the further image of death as a cover. Thus in the Numbers 16 narrative the earth opens its mouth and swallows the rebels (v. 32) and then closes over them and covers them (v. 33; cf. Ps 106:17). The covering, concealing aspect of the grave is prominent in the concluding treatment of the victory over death in Isaiah 26:21, but it is probable that here in 25:7 there is also reference to the grave, the swallower, as a cover over all peoples. In parallel with God's swallowing of death (v. 8) we read of His swallowing "the face of the wrapping that enfolds[11] all peoples, the woven thing woven over all the nations" (v. 7). This woven covering is most likely a shroud.[12] But this is apparently a figure for the grave, the universal shroud that covers all humanity in their common lot of death.[13] It could then be that the explanation of the "face"[14] of the shroud is to be found in the common expression "the face of the earth," inasmuch as it

---

[9] Variations on this image recur as a kind of leitmotiv of the haunting presence of death throughout this composition.

[10] Use of the dragon-conflict pattern for the Exodus history in poetic portions of the Bible is well known.

[11] Cf. the use of lwṭ in 1 Sam 21:9 (MT 10); 1 Kgs 19:13.

[12] Some take it as a mourning veil, others as the net by which death ensnares its victims, a widely attested image.

[13] Cf. Hab 2:5; Josh 23:14.

[14] The "face" of the shroud in Isa 25:7 might also allude to the face-portraits on mummy cases and on coffins with anthropoid lids.

is this face, or surface, of the earth that constitutes the covering shroud over Sheol's occupants.[15] The two instances of Yahweh's swallowing (blᶜ) would then together encompass as their twin objects death (v. 8) and Hades (v. 7).

Quoting Isaiah's forecast of the swallowing of death (25:8), Paul identifies this banquet of everlasting victory with the believers' ultimate putting on of the glory of incorruption and immortality (1 Cor 15:54).[16] And the apostle John portrays this death of death in his account of the resurrection (the "second resurrection" in the first/second death/resurrection scheme of Revelation 20–21)[17] as a casting of death and Hades (or the "first death" in that same scheme) into "the second death," the lake of fire (Rev 20:14; cf. 21:4).

The Vessel Emptied

Anticipating the master theme of Isaiah 24–26, the opening verses (24:1-3) foretell the Lord's mighty overthrow of death. The theme is expressed in terms that suggest that here at the beginning death is already being thought of as the greedy, gluttonous devourer, filled with generations on generations of mankind. In 25:8 the great reversal is a matter of the swallowing of the swallower. Here it takes the form of the upending and emptying out of what had been a filled container.[18]

"See, Yahweh pours out the netherworld and empties it out; He turns it upside down and scatters out its occupants" (v. 1). The verb bqq, "empty out," onomatopoetically imitates the gurgling sound of water plopping out of a bottle. It is here reinforced by the similar sounding blq: bôqēq . . . ûbôlĕqâ.[19]

---

[15] To be judged to eat dust forever was for the serpent to be cursed with death. But Yahweh's swallowing of the earth-cover of death and the grave is a banquet of resurrection life forever, a devouring-death of death. Anticipating this eschatological banquet is the sacramental supper of the Lord, in which a feasting on Christ's death celebrates His victory of life.

[16] Cf. also 2 Tim 1:10.

[17] Cf. Meredith G. Kline, "The First Resurrection," *WTJ* 37 (1975): 366-75.

[18] Jer 51:34 combines the imagery of Isa 24:1-3; 25:6-8 in one picture of destruction in terms of devouring, monster-like swallowing, filling the maw, and emptying a vessel.

[19] Nominal derivatives of these two verbs appear as synonyms in Nah 2:10 (MT 11), a passage descriptive of the judgment of Nineveh, which has just been likened to a pool

The use of ʾereṣ for the netherworld is now well recognized.[20] In the present general context note, for example, "the realm (ʾereṣ) of the shades" (26:19).[21] The "face," pānêhâ, combined here with the verb ʿwh, "bend low,"[22] to express "turn upside down" apparently refers to the ground as surface of the grave,[23] which is compared to the top of a vessel bent over or upturned to pour out its contents.

According to the customary view of 24:1-3, it introduces the theme of the desolating of the earth, which is then traced further in the rest of chapter 24. But as interpreted above, this opening passage depicts the ultimate repair of the situation lamented in the immediately following verses and hence serves as an introduction not to chapter 24 alone but to the entirety of Isaiah 24–26. The interpretation of this passage as an opening statement of the main overall theme of the resurrection victory is corroborated by its closing formula: "For Yahweh has spoken this word" (v. 3). Such an assurance of the certainty of fulfillment is better accounted for if what has just been foretold is not merely the desolation of the earth but the astounding prospect of the termination of the sway of death. Moreover, the one other place within Isaiah 24–26 where essentially this same formula of divine utterance appears is at the close of the climactic assertion of the resurrection in 25:6-8.

The resurrection-judgment, according to 24:1-3, is universal. This is suggested by the paired listing of the representatives of opposite ends of the socioeconomic spectrum of mankind (v. 2).[24] Subsequently the

---

draining away (v. 8 [MT 9]). Also the emptying process in both passages is equated with a plundering (bzz) of the plunderer (Isa 24:3; Nah 2:9 [MT 10]). Cf. Jer 48:11-12.

[20] The word ʾereṣ does not thereby denote two entirely distinct entities. It is rather that the earth as the receptacle and covering of the dead becomes functionally the grave or netherworld as one aspect of its total historical identity.

[21] A parallel phrase in 26:19 is "the dwellers (šōkĕnê) of the dust," an equivalent of "its [the netherworld's] inhabitants (yōšĕbêhā)" in 24:1.

[22] Cf. Ps 38:6 (MT 7).

[23] On the possible resumption of this concept of the face of the earth in 25:7 see above. The Sumerian myth *Inanna's Descent to the Netherworld* (117, 123) refers to an entrance gate Ganzir, called the "face" of the netherworld. The familiar imagery of the gates of death is found in Isa 38:10. Cf. Ps 9:13-14 (MT 14-15); Matt 16:18; Rev 1:18.

[24] Similarly in Rev 20:12 "the great and the small" indicates the totality of the dead who are delivered up by death and Hades and the sea to stand before the judgment throne (cf. also 19:18). The appearance of the sea with death and Hades in 20:13 is

theme of the termination of death becomes more specifically occupied with the resurrection of the people of God. Thus in 25:6-8 and 26:19 and following, this theme finds expression within the genre of hymnic praise, the saints celebrating the resurrection as God's saving triumph that delivers them from the Satanic hosts. Not merely excluded from that salvation, the wicked are viewed along with death as the enemy from whom God rescues His own. But before the focus is narrowed down to the meaning of the resurrection for the redeemed, 24:1-3 presents the broader picture of a general resurrection, an emptying out of all the contents of the death-vessel without distinction.[25] All that death has swallowed down will be cast out at the resurrection. So death's historical role comes to an end: The first death undergoes the second death.

The Veil Removed

The covering aspect of Sheol, the natural concomitant of its identity as the devourer, is once again present in the final picture of the resurrection-victory over death in 26:19 and following. Previously the face of the earth (or netherworld) was viewed as the cover of a vessel (24:1) or as an enveloping shroud-cover (25:7), but here it is a veil-like covering that conceals the dead (26:21b). The blood of the slain sinks into the earth. The dead disappear into Sheol, concealed behind earth's covering of soil and stone. Death is the "hidden" place (Job 40:13). Resurrection is then an uncovering, an unveiling, a revealing of the concealed. "The earth shall disclose her blood and no more cover her slain" (Isa 26:21b).

---

one of numerous instances of the conceptualization of death as the waters of the deep. This identification of the netherworld with the waters of the sea perhaps contributed to Isaiah's imaging of death as a bottle or skin whose liquid contents are to be poured out. Conceivably Rev 20:12-13 reflects such an understanding of Isa 24:1-3. Cf. B. F. Batto, "The Reed Sea: Requiescat in Pace," *JBL* 102 (1983): 27-35; "Red Sea or Reed Sea?" *BAR* 10/4 (1984): 57-63.

[25] Nevertheless the resurrection experience means different things for the godly and the wicked, as appears in the perspective of 25:6-8; 26:19ff. In the language of Revelation 20, what is the second resurrection for those written in the book of life is the second death for those who are not.

It is clear from the context that the slain in view are the martyrs, as typical of all the faithful. For the passage opens with the declaration that the dead who belong to the Lord shall arise in joy (v. 19), and it continues with a special encouragement to God's people in contemplation of their experience of death (v. 20).[26] Moreover, immediately connected with this revealing of the blood of the slain is the assurance of the divine advent to punish their wicked oppressors (v. 21a).

In this connection I want to point out the Isaianic roots of a misunderstood Pauline concept in Romans 8. To do so it will first be necessary to discuss the relationship of the context of Isa 26:19 to the context of 24:4. With its announcement of the uncovering of the earth and the resurrection-manifestation of the saints, the former passage answers redemptively to what the latter says about the earth in mourning over the curse of death and especially over the polluting stain of innocent blood. One indication that this mourning does have to do with death is the contrastive correspondence between the situation mourned in the context of 24:4 and the celebration of the conquest of death in chapter 25, especially verses 6-8. A comparison shows sorrow replaced by joy, sighs by songs of praise, the languishing of earth's fruit by a lavish feast of fat things full of marrow and flavorful wine, well refined. In Isaiah 24 the curse that is grieved over is one that "devours the earth," decimating its population (v. 6). This is the motif of death as the never-sated devourer, which 25:6-8 takes up in its answering prophecy of the devouring of the devourer.

In the context of 24:4, what makes the earth groan is that it is obliged to become the grave, to cover over the human dead. But the relationship of that passage to 25:6-8, which has a redemptive focus on God's people, argues for a special (even if not exclusive) concern with the death of the righteous in the former. Pointing in the same direction is the explanation given in 24:5 for the entrance of death and the resultant mourning of the earth: "The earth is profaned (ḥānĕpâ) under its inhabitants." In view of the use of ḥnp elsewhere for polluting the ground by spilling innocent blood on it,[27] it appears that the sin against God's covenant by reason of which the earth suffers defilement and mourns is hostility vented on the covenant faithful, resulting in their martyrdom.

[26] On this see further below.

[27] See Num 35:33; Ps 106:38.

When the profaned, mourning earth of the 24:4 section is understood in this way, it becomes apparent that 26:19 and the verses that follow, like 25:6-8, answers directly to the earlier passage, proclaiming the resurrection-conquest of death as the resolution of earth's grievance.[28] Earth's accursed role as concealing the grave of the not-yet-vindicated people of God comes to an end when the martyrs are revealed and arise and the cry of their blood is heard and honored in heaven.

Until that deliverance from death's curse, the earth bemoans its role as netherworld. Isa 24:4 pictures the realm of nature as joining together with man in sighs over death. This brings to mind at once the similar thought in Romans 8. Paul says that creation groans together with those who have the firstfruits of the Spirit (vv. 19-23). Even the more precise image of the groaning of birth-travail (Rom 8:22) reflects the Isaiah 24–26 context. For in 26:16-18 God's people, struggling in the warfare against the enemy until God grants them the resurrection deliverance (v. 19), are likened to a woman crying out in birth pangs.[28] Moreover, just as the groaning of travail in 26:17-18 is followed by the resurrection-revealing of God's people (vv. 19-21), so in Romans 8 creation's groaning in birth pangs (v. 22) is in expectation of the resurrection of the children of God mentioned in the next verse (v. 23). Indeed, quite an extensive correspondence can be traced between these Pauline and Isaianic passages. Other features of 26:19–27:1 to be dealt with below are reflected in the latter part of Romans 8, such as the justification of believers in the face of Satanic accusation and the persuasion of God's presence and love in the experience of death. It is also remarkable that just as Isaiah moves from these themes into the question of Israel, its fall and fullness, in chapter 27, so does Paul in Romans 9–11 and (as we have observed) in such a way that his line of thought and imagery show dependence on Isaiah 27.

From this mutually illuminative relationship of Isaiah 24–26 and Romans 8 one perceives that the "bondage of corruption" over which,

---

[28] The use of nĕbēlâ, "corpse," in 26:19 echoes nābĕlâ, "it [the earth] withers (or dies)," in 24:4. The verb nābēl contributes to the alliterative quality of 24:4, but its choice there was probably also prompted by the preceding imagery of the emptied pitcher (cf. nēbel, "skin bottle") and the following motif of the silenced music (cf. nēbel, a musical instrument).

[29] A similar combination of ideas and imagery is found in Hos 13:13-14.

says Paul, the creation groans (Rom 8:21) is the earth's being subjected to the fate of covering the blood of the innocent and concealing the corpses of the saints.[30] The term for corruption, phthora, is the one that describes physical death in the resurrection context of 1 Corinthians 15,[31] another passage with clear connections with Isaiah 24–26.[32] And in Romans 8, as we have seen, what the earth looks forward to in hope as its deliverance from this corruption is precisely the resurrection of the righteous. As the repeated references to their resurrection in verses 19, 21, and 30 indicate, that event is not merely the occasion of the earth's deliverance but is itself the liberation from the corruption over which the earth groans.[33] By reason of the swallowing up of death in resurrection-victory, "the reproach of God's people" – the vanity of corruption from which until now the earth groans to be released – "is removed from all the earth" (Isa 25:8).

This discussion should not be closed without attention being drawn to another connection between Isaiah and Paul. Specifically, it again concerns Isaiah 24–26 and Romans. There is a general persuasion abroad

---

[30] Whatever wider reality might be suggested by "the whole creation" (Rom 8:22), the critical element in the idea is the earth's character as grave of the saints. If one is not persuaded that the earth's groaning in Rom 8:21 is specifically due to its entombment of the martyr-righteous, preferring still to see this verse as a reflection on Gen 3:17 (i.e., as a general curse affecting all mankind), then it must at least be recognized that that curse consists particularly in the reversal of the earth's original subservient relationship to mankind whereby man now is overpowered by the earth and ultimately reduced to the condition of "dust unto dust" (Gen 3:19).

[31] See vv. 42,50.

[32] Note particularly the quotation of Isa 25:8 in 1 Cor 15:54. Verse 55 continues with a quotation from Hos 13:14, which falls within a section of Hosea's prophecy where extensive interdependence with Isaiah 26–27 has been noted. See n. 29 above and J. Day, "A Case of Inner Scriptural Interpretation: The Dependence of Isaiah 26:13–27:11 on Hosea 13:4–14:10 (Eng. 9) and Its Relevance to Some Theories of the Redaction of the 'Isaiah Apocalypse,'" *JTS* 31 (1980): 309-19.

[33] In Rom 8:19 the "revealing (apokalypsis) of the sons of God" for which creation waits is customarily identified as the manifestation of the saints with Christ in glory; cf., e.g., Col 3:4. But discovery of the relation of Romans 8 to Isaiah 24–26 and of its concern with the earth's deliverance from profanation through the corruption of death suggests that the apokalypsis is the emergence of the righteous from their concealment in the earth (as in Isa 26:21), the uncovering that is the prelude to the manifestation in glory. Cf. J. Plevnik, "The Taking Up of the Faithful and the Resurrection of the Dead in 1 Thessalonians 4:13-18," *CBQ* 46 (1984): 274-83.

that Genesis 3 is without influence on theological developments in the rest of the Old Testament.[34] And when Genesis 3 is thus regarded as an isolated, unfruitful phenomenon, Paul's federal-covenantal reconstruction in Romans 5 is left without a supportive canonical linkage. But Isaiah at least (not to assess other suggested connections) can be adduced as a bridge between Moses and Paul in this matter. What the prophet says in the context of 24:4 must be recognized as a significant source for the covenantal theology of death in Rom 5:12 and the verses that follow. Isaiah deals there with death as a curse. Like Paul, Isaiah teaches that death entered the world through the entrance of sin – indeed, through the sin of breaking "the ancient covenant" in Eden – and that death so passed unto all men, devouring the earth's population, generation after generation (24:5-6; cf. v. 20).

Vindication of the Martyrs

Associated with death in Isaiah 24–26 as allied enemies of the saints are Satan and, more conspicuously, his human accomplices. And the final proclamation of the resurrection in 26:21 depicts it not only as a redemption of believers from the prison of death (v. 21d) but as a vindication of the martyrs against these Satanic persecutors: "The earth shall disclose her blood" (v. 21c). The cry of the martyrs' blood will be heard. At the resurrection they will have their day in court.[35] For the Lord will come forth "to punish the inhabitants of the earth for their iniquity" (v. 21ab). Vindication of the Lord's people will not stop short of taking vengeance on their primeval adversary, the serpent-devil (27:1). What is said in 26:21–27:1 about the coming vindication of the saints is a concluding summation; the theme of the enemies and their subjugation is under development throughout chapter 24–26. This material will be examined, dealing in turn with Satan and his demonic hosts and then with the evil world-power.

---

[34] For a recent representative statement see L. R. Bailey, Sr., *Biblical Perspectives on Death* (Philadelphia: Fortress, 1979), p. 53. He insists that, apart from the possible exception of Genesis 2–3, mortality is not associated in the OT with guilt and punishment.

[35] Cf. Gen 4:10-11; Job 16:18; Rev 6:9-11; 8:3ff.; 11:18; 19:2.

Judgment on Leviathan

Included in the final portrayal of the resurrection triumph over death is the judgment of Leviathan (Isa 27:1).[36] This serpentine symbol in the Bible often signalizes the demonic dimension of a situation. Sometimes the dragon is a figure for Satan himself, as in Rev 12:9; 20:2, and here in Isa 27:1.[37] Inasmuch as the devil is the one who has the power of death (Heb 2:14),[38] it is understandable that he and death should be found together here in common undertaking and common judgment. The same combination is found in Rev 20:10-14.

There is indeed a curious overlap in the attributes and activities of death and the devil in biblical representations of them. They even share the same name, or epithet: Belial.[39] Like death, the devil is depicted as the swallower, if not through the Belial designation then at least in Rev 12:4, where the dragon is seen ready to devour the messianic child, and in 1 Pet 5:8, where the Adversary is compared to a lion on the prowl,[40] seeking to devour believers. Similarly, Satan's human agents are portrayed as Sheol-like swallowers of the godly. The description of these enemies in Ps 73:9

---

[36] Isa 27:1 continues the judgment theme of 26:21 (note pqd, "punish," in both verses). Together the two verses deal with the final judgment of the evil occupants of both earth and heaven. Cf. 24:21-22. "In that day" in 27:1 forms an *inclusio* with 26:1. (It is a question whether the same phrase at the beginning of 27:2 introduces the following vineyard song, as is likely, or possibly belongs with 27:1.)

[37] Isa 27:1 closely resembles a passage in a mythological text from Ugarit (*UT* 67, i 1-3). Such mythological use of the dragon figure is a corruption of the tradition of the serpent-agent of Satan in the fall episode. In biblical texts like Isa 27:1 the dragon imagery is a demythologized, poetic adaptation.

[38] This characterization of the devil is explained by his critical role in the entrance of sin into the world, through which death also found entrance. Moreover a continuing agency of Satan in the infliction of death is suggested in Job 2:6 (and, on one interpretation, in 1 Cor 5:5).

[39] Note the parallelism of death and Belial in Ps 18:4 (MT 5) and 2 Sam 22:5. Belial (or Beliar) is used for Satan in 2 Cor 6:15. This is of special interest for this Isaiah context. If blyyᶜl is derived from blᶜ, "swallow," cf. Isa 25:7-8. If it is explained as bly plus ᶜlh, "none comes up," cf. 26:14. In Job 7:9 lōʾ yaᶜăleh describes the one who descends into Sheol. Isa 26:14 uses qwm, not ᶜlh, but in Ps 41:8 (MT 9) qwm with negative stands parallel to blyyᶜl.

[40] Behind this usage is probably the judicial surveillance conducted by Satan with a view to his accusing function, as in Job 1:7 and 2:2.

with gaping mouth reaching from heaven to earth reflects strikingly the description of Mot in the Ugaritic mythology.[41] And like the devil they are more specifically compared to lions eager to devour the righteous.[42] Death, on its side, shares with the Satan-Adversary in his identity as the enemy. Paul in his discussion of the resurrection in 1 Corinthians 15 characterizes death as "the last enemy" (v. 26), and possibly there is some (or even considerable) precedent in the Psalms for designating death as the foe.[43] Quite natural then is the conjunction of death and the devil in Isa 24:1–27:1. In particular, the aptness of Isaiah's concluding word on the judgment of Leviathan (27:1), appended to his final account of the resurrection-victory over death, can be appreciated.

The disclosure concerning Leviathan in 27:1 is adumbrated in 24:21-22. It is indicated there that the saints' warfare is on two levels. For behind the hostility displayed by earthly oppressors is a hidden, demonic enemy on high: "In that day Yahweh will punish the host of the height on high and the kings on the ground below" (v. 21). On high an army of evil beings is associated with the devil in his cause (cf. Rev 12:7-9). God's judicial intervention[44] against them will come "after many days" (v. 22b), at the final cosmic catastrophe (v. 20) and the revelation of the Parousia-Glory (v. 23).[45] This judgment

---

[41] Cf. *UT* 67, ii 1-3.

[42] See e.g. Pss 10:9; 17:12; 35:17,25; cf. 5:9 (MT 19); 124:3-6.

[43] Cf., e.g., Pss 31:8 (MT 9); 61:3 (MT 4). For a survey of the evidence in the Psalms adduced by M. Dahood for death as the foe see N. J. Tromp, *Primitive Conceptions of Death and the Nether World in the Old Testament* (Rome: Pontifical Biblical Institute, 1969), pp. 110-19.

[44] The verb pqd, "punish," used in the first colon of v. 21 is repeated at the close of v. 22 as an *inclusio*. Hence the same judgment is in view in each case. "After many days" (v. 22b) is equivalent to "in that day" (v. 21a).

[45] "Before his elders will be the Glory" (v. 23). After the introduction (24:1-3) two sections on earth's desolation (vv. 4-13; 16b-22) alternate with two brief sections describing the final epiphany and the response thereto (vv. 14-16a; 23). Verses 14-16a form an intricate chiasm produced by lexical and morphological pairings. In the terminal parts of the chiasm the eschatological theophany is denoted as the Majesty (gʾwn) and the Beauty (ṣby), in the middle parts as the Name (Yahweh). The Glory (kbwd) of v. 23 is the corresponding reference to the Parousia in the second epiphany section. Further on in 24:15 the ʿl-kn is perhaps to be taken as a divine title, "the Most High, the Upright." Following a suggestion of L. Viganò, W. H. Irwin argues for this in "The Punctuation of Isaiah 24:14-16*a* and 25:4*c*-5," *CBQ* 46 (1984): 215-19. A chiastic structuring is, however, still preferable to Irwin's overall stichometric analysis.

of the demonic host on high is the same as the judgment of Leviathan announced in 27:1.[46]

Something of the nature of the judgment on Leviathan referred to in 27:1 may be discerned from the equivalent disclosure in Rev 20:10a. There the devil's doom takes the form of the lake of fire, the second death. That realm is one of forever-continuing torment (v. 10b), and accordingly, the fate of Satan and others relegated to it is not absolute erasure from existence. The second death is existence on the other side of an impassable gulf from the cosmos proper. To be cast into the lake of fire is to cease to figure or function in heaven and earth as the consummated kingdom of God. Satan slain, or banished to the second death, no longer participates in the creation proper. He no longer functions as the power of death or otherwise affects the glorified saints.[47] Such existence, cut off from rapport with God's realm of life, is a death-existence.

Implicit in the nature of the resurrection of God's people as a judgment-victory over the devil (27:1), the one who has the power of death, is the justification aspect of the vindication of the godly. For inseparable from Satan's identity as possessor of the power of death is his role as "the accuser of our brethren . . . who accuses them before God day and night."[48] It is through his tempting to sin and then prosecuting for sin (the ultimate duplicity) that he has come to wield the power of death. Therefore God's

---

[46] A question arises as to the relation of the imprisonment in 24:22a and the binding of Satan in Rev 20:2-3. If that imprisonment is equated with the judicial intervention announced in v. 21 and again in v. 22b, then it will not correspond to the thousand-year confinement of the devil in Rev 20:2-3 but to his subsequent eternal doom (20:10). If, however, the imprisonment of v. 22a is understood as pluperfect with respect to the judgment of v. 21 (and thus too as preliminary to the same judgment as mentioned again in v. 22b), it would then be equivalent to Rev 20:2-3, and the "many days" could correspond to the "thousand years." In this case the subject of the imprisonment might better be viewed as only the demonic host, not the earthly kings. The word bôr, "pit," often used as a synonym of Sheol, also denotes a place of confinement and torment for demons. See Luke 8:31 (cf. Matt 8:29); Rev 9:1,2,11; 11:7; 17:8; 20:1,3.

[47] The Son of God came so that through death He might "render inoperative" him that had the power of death (Heb 2:14) and death itself (1 Cor 15:26; 2 Tim 1:10).

[48] It is just after a reference to Satan in terms distinctly reminiscent of 27:1 that this identification of him as the Accuser is given in Rev 12:10. The echo of 27:1 is all the clearer if the disputed adjective bārîaḥ means "primeval" and thus corresponds to the "ancient" serpent of Rev 12:9.

resurrection-conquest of Satan as possessor of the power of death is at the same time a triumph over him as the accuser of the brethren. And in the judicial ordeal before God's throne, to defeat the accuser in his quest for a verdict of condemnation is to seal the verdict of justification in behalf of the accused.[49]

The conclusion that the resurrection-victory of God's people involves their justification is also arrived at if the resurrection as a victory over death is considered. For death entered the world through sin, in condemnation for the breaking of the primeval covenant. Hence deliverance from death through resurrection in Christ is a reversal of condemnation. It publicly registers the verdict of justification secured by the merits of Christ. This verdict answers to the prayer of the blood of the martyrs that is disclosed at the resurrection (26:21), inasmuch as that blood has been pleading not only to be avenged through the judgment of the enemy but to be recognized as righteous blood, righteous through the advocacy of the blood of the Lamb (cf. Heb 12:24; Rev 12:11a). Agreeably, in the vision of the intermediate state in Rev 6:9-11, the martyrs awaiting the final avenging of their blood on the earth-dwellers already receive a foretaste of that judgment by being acknowledged as justified through the bestowal of white robes, emblematic of their righteousness (cf. Rev 19:8).

It follows that what 26:14,19 say about not participating or participating in this resurrection may be construed as legal pronouncements of condemnation and justification respectively. These two verdicts are formulated as a clearly matching contrastive pair. The wicked dead, true to their name "sons of Belial/Perdition," will not rise again (v. 14).[50] But God's dead, something of a contradiction in terms according to the argument of Jesus for bodily resurrection,[51] shall come to life (v. 19).[52] The promise of resurrection,[53] "your dead shall live" (v. 19a), is a verdict of justification. It

---

[145] Cf. Zechariah 3.

[146] Context must be ignored to take this as a denial of a universal resurrection. See the discussion of 24:1-3 above and n. 78 below.

[147] See Matt 22:32; Mark 12:27; Luke 20:38; cf. John 5:21.

[148] For this meaning of ḥyh see 1 Kgs 17:22; 2 Kgs 13:21; Job 14:14; Ezek 37:3,5,6,9,10,14.

[149] For a recent survey of the evidence for interpreting 26:19 and context in terms of physical resurrection see F. C. Hasel, "Resurrection in the Theology of the Old Testament Apocalyptic," *ZAW* 92 (1980): 271-76.

is comparable to "the just shall live," the justifying verdict pronounced on the righteous believer in Hab 2:4. There too we find a contrasting verdict against the wicked.[54] The lōʾ-yāšĕrâ in v. 4a (however the grammar as a whole is construed) must refer to God's verdict of condemnation[55] on the proud sinner, a verdict to which "shall live" in v. 4b corresponds. And Paul, citing this passage in Gal 3:11, confirms not only that "shall live" is a verdict but that it is indeed a verdict of justification. For he parallels this life obtained by the righteous through faith in Jesus Christ with the verdict of justification, which, he asserts, was not obtainable through the principle of works operative in the law.[56]

Subjugation of the World-City

The ancient dragon directs his assault on the faithful through the earthly agency of the dragonlike beast (cf. Rev 12:17–13:7). Inevitably, at the judgment, the beast shares the dragon's doom in the lake of fire (cf. 20:10). The place prepared for the devil and his angels is the fitting fate of the seed of the serpent, for throughout history they have exhibited their father's spirit of self-assertion in blasphemous defiance of God and murderous hatred of His people.[57] An antichrist propensity infects the apostate city of man from the days of Cain onwards, erupting virulently in the reign

[54] Heb 10:37-38 connects Isaiah 26 and Habakkuk 2 by (apparently) introducing its citation of Hab 2:4 with the "yet a very little while" of Isa 26:20 (LXX). Cf. the echo of Isa 26:11 in Heb 10:27. Also note in Hab 2:5 the reference to the insatiable appetite of death, devourer of all peoples, the central concern and pervasive image of Isaiah 24–26. Further, the patient waiting in faith for the eschatological divine intervention encouraged in Hab 2:3 is a major emphasis in the Isaiah passage (e.g. 25:9; 26:3,4,8,9,20).

[55] Preponderantly the verb yšr is used in the registering of assessments. Such is also the tradition of interpretation reflected in the LXX as quoted in Heb 10:37.

[56] The function of resurrection to life as the rendering of a verdict of justification should be borne in mind in dealing with Paul's expression "justification of life" (Rom 5:18) and his statement that Jesus "was raised for our justification" (4:25). On the principle of works in the Mosaic economy see Meredith G. Kline, "Of Works and Grace," *Presbyterion* 9 (1983): 85-92.

[57] See n. 42 above for the attribution to these human enemies of the same lionlike rapacity that distinguishes the devil and death.

of the sons of the gods at the climax of prediluvian history (Gen 6:1-4) and in the final manifestation of the beast in the man of sin.

This two-tiered structure of the Satanic enterprise has already been encountered within Isaiah 24–26. In 24:21 the kings of the ground below and the demonic hosts above are listed together as the joint objects of divine vengeance.[58] Elsewhere Isaiah suggests the bond of identity between these companies by applying to the earthly forces of evil the term mārôm, which in 24:21 distinguishes "the host of the height on high" (hammārôm bammārôm). Thus 24:4 notes that even the "height (mĕrôm) of the people of the earth" are among the death mourners.[59] And 26:5 prophesies judgment against "the ones who dwell in the height (mārôm)," further identified as "the lofty city."

Under the present major heading of the vindication of the martyrs it is the enmity of Satan's earthly agents against God's people that calls for particular attention. Isa 25:10-12 contains a distinctive treatment of this enmity. Moab, inveterate foe of Israel, serves as representative of the hostile world. Disdainful of the presence of the Glory-hand of God on "this mountain" (v. 10), that is, Zion (cf. 24:23; 25:6), Moab extends[60] its grasping hands "in the midst of it" (v. 11a), to seize all it can from Israel.[61] The full extension of its clutching embrace is compared to a swimmer's stretching forth his hands in a sweeping stroke (v. 11b). In this greedy grabbing by Moab a replication of the insatiable appetite of Sheol-death[62]

---

[58] What is depicted as a single judgment episode here in 24:21-22 is related twice in the Book of Revelation because of the thematic arrangement of its visions: once in Revelation 19 from the perspective of the beast and kings of the earth, and a second time in Revelation 20 from the perspective of the career of Satan.

[59] Pretensions to deity by mortals are repeatedly mocked by reminders of mortality. See Gen 6:3; Isa 14:9ff.; Ezek 28:9; cf. Ps 82:7.

[60] This same idea is again expressed by the verb prs in a similar context in Lamentations 1: "The adversary has spread out his hands over all her [Jerusalem's] desirable things" (v. 10a). Interestingly, the adversary who thus profanes the sanctuary is further defined in v. 10c in terms of the law of Deut 23:3 (MT 4) forbidding the Moabites and Ammonites to enter the assembly of the Lord. Also note Moab's involvement in the destruction of Judah (2 Kgs 24:2).

[61] For this same imagery elsewhere in Isaiah see 10:10,14; 11:14.

[62] In the motif of Mot's prodigious appetite, his hands figure as scoops (cf. *UT* 67, i 19-20). By them he also grasps his victims (cf. *UT* 2059, 21-22). For similar biblical references to the hands of Sheol see Ps 89:48 (MT 49); Hos 13:14.

is again met with. Moab's rapacious lust is totally frustrated, however, as God brings down into the dust "his pride with the catch[63] of his hands" (v. 11c).

The enmity of the world-power is also mirrored in the prayers of the saints. Out of the midst of their struggle against the overwhelming might of the oppressor they raise their cry, seconding the call of the martyrs' blood for divine retribution. Isa 26:8-9ab describes the constancy of the saints in such expectant prayer for God's decisive acts of judgment,[64] indignant as they are at the obdurate obtuseness of the unrepentant, unrelenting wicked in the absence of such judgments (vv. 9cd,10).[65] Verses 7 and 11 articulate their actual petitions.[66]

---

[63] Like pēras earlier in v. 11, ʾorbôt is followed by "his hands" and should be understood in a way that brings out this connection. That is achieved if one regards the noun as related to ʾrb, "lie in ambush," and as denoting plunder or prey – here the treasure that had been seized by Moab's outstretched hands. This results in a further point of likeness of this agent of the devil to death, for the latter is pictured as ensnaring its prey (cf., e.g., Ps 18:5 [MT 6]). So too is the devil (2 Tim 2:26).

[64] "Yes, for the way of your judgments we call upon you, Yahweh; our soul's longing is for (the revelation of) your memorial Name. In my soul I long for you in the night; yes, in my inmost spirit I yearn for you in the morning." In vv. 8,9b God's "judgments" are His judicial acts of deliverance. The "Name" (v. 8) is the theophanic Presence or Parousia. Note the chiastic structure with the repetitive taʾăwat-nāpeš (v. 8b) and napšî ʾiwwîtîkā (v. 9a) in the center and the corresponding ʾap clauses with their semantically matched verbs in the first and fourth cola (vv. 8a,9b).

[65] "Only when your judgments are on the earth do the inhabitants of the world learn righteousness. If the wicked is shown compassion, he does not learn righteousness; in a land of fair dealings the one who is evil does not see the majesty of Yahweh." In vv. 9d,10a ṣedeq refers to God's acts of judgment. In v. 10b the waw of ûbal is emphatic with postposition of the verb. Thus understood, an excellent parallelism obtains between the two cola of v. 10. In v. 9c, W. H. Irwin reads kĕʾaššēr "correct, set right," instead of kî kaʾăšer; cf. his "Syntax and Style in Isaiah 26," *CBQ* 41 (1979): 246.

[66] "Let there be a way of justice for the righteous, O Upright One, may you make level the path of the righteous" (v. 7). "Yahweh, let your hand be lifted high; let those who do not see see. Let them be dismayed at the fury of your forces; by the fire of your enmity consume them" (v. 11). Verse 7 is an example of the form in which the b-element is a single word (here, as often, a vocative) serving both a-sections. The first colon contains an interrupted construct chain. Possibly mêšārîm refers to the concrete mēšarum-act. Verse 11 is a further petition for the Parousia (cf. the "hand" of God and the angelic armies). Note again the theme of Yahweh as the true devourer who consumes the hostile would-be devourers.

Again in 26:17-18 the antagonism of the world-power is reflected in the confession by the godly of their helplessness to prevail in the battle against the foe. In childbirth, as it were, they manage to bring forth only wind (vv. 17-18ab). They acknowledge: "Victory we cannot achieve (naᶜăseh) on the earth; the inhabitants of the earth do not fall" (v. 18cd).[67]

But what God's people cannot achieve for themselves He accomplishes for them: "Every achievement in our behalf (maᶜăśênû) you have accomplished for us" (26:12). The section on their powerlessness to overcome the enemy (26:16-18) leads at once into the closing prophecy of the resurrection as the Lord's redemptive triumph, vindicating His people over against the world-power (26:19ff.).

One subtle device tying the resurrection announced in 26:19 to the preceding description of the saints' battle with the world-power (v. 18) is the double use of the verb npl, "fall,"[68] to highlight the contrast being drawn. In verse 18d the godly lament their inability to make their enemies "fall" dead in battle. Then in verse 19 God is said to make His dew "fall" on the dead, bringing them to life.

Renderings of verse 19 as though it continued the figure of childbirth (v. 18ab) are unacceptable. The figure has meanwhile shifted in verse 18c to that of military salvation or victory. Moreover, npl is not attested elsewhere in biblical Hebrew for childbirth, whereas it is used for battle casualties (cf. Num 14:29; Jer 9:21). Also, consistently in this context "the inhabitants of the world" are the wicked foe (cf. esp. vv. 9,21).

Again, to interpret tpyl in verse 19b as "give birth," with "earth" as subject, is to undo the parallelism between verses 19c and 19d and particularly to lose the obvious relationship, both sonant and semantic, between tappîl and ṭal, "dew." For the use of npl for the falling of dew on the ground see 2 Sam 17:12. Therefore verse 19cd should read: "For the dew of dawn[69] is your

---

[67] On this see further below.

[68] Enhancing the npl wordplay in 26:18 is the use of nĕbēlâ, "corpse" (v. 19). As observed above (n. 28) this also recalls the verb npl in 24:4, another context that is concerned with death and mourning and also contains a case of paronomasia using npl and nbl. Note the use of npl in 24:20 (itself a parallel to 26:14).

[69] On ᵓôrôt as "lights, dawn" cf. ᵓūrîm, "East" (24:15). Dawn fits well with waking from sleep (hāqîṣû). For the association of dew and dawn cf. Exod 16:13; Judg 6:38; Ps 110:3. On resurrection and dawn cf. Hos 6:2-3. On light and life cf. Job 3:16; 33:28; Ps 49:19

[God's] dew, and on the land[70] of the shades you make it fall."[71] The "land of the shades" continues the focus of verse 19ab on "the dwellers in the dust," the martyred saints called "your [God's] dead." Restored by God's revivifying dew, they sing in the exultation of their vindication.

Most directly and emphatically the retribution-vindication aspect of the resurrection of the martyrs is expressed in 26:21. God's decisive intervention will take the form of a descent from His heavenly Temple (v. 21a; cf. Mic 1:3) for the purpose of exacting recompense (v. 21b), and that with immediate reference to the appeal of martyrs' blood revealed (v. 21c) and the witness of God's slain released from the grave (v. 21d).

Once and again in Isaiah 24–26 the city is used as a figure for the hostile world-power. Judgment is in store for this city (24:10-12; 25:2,12; 26:5-6) and its kings (24:22; 26:5,14). In the case of both the city (25:12; 26:5-6) and its proud citizenry (26:5), these prophecies of final retribution are couched in the imagery of the primeval curse on the serpent (Gen 3:14-15), the humbling in the dust and the trampling under foot. Isaiah thus anticipates the apostle John's theme of the dragonlike beast sharing the dragon's doom. He makes the same point more explicitly in his prophecy of the powers in the heavens and the kings on earth imprisoned together in the pit (24:21-22).

Perhaps the delineation of the judgment of the world-city is intended to conjure up the netherworld scene. The realm of the dead was conceptualized as a city with its entrance gates (cf. 24:12),[72] and various characteristic features of the netherworld appear in the picture of the devastated world-city in chapters 24–26. It is a joyless desolation (24:7-12),[73] an eternal[74]

(MT 20); 56:13 (MT 14). Whether ᵓôrôt is understood as dawn, or herbs, or (Elysian) fields (so Mitchell Dahood, *Psalms*, AB, 3 vols. [Garden City, N.Y.: Doubleday, 1966-1970], 1:222-23), the idea is that of the enlivening effect of dew.

[70] Cf. above (n. 21).

[71] Dahood, *Psalms*, 1:223, takes tpyl from the verb nbl: "But the land of the shades will be parched." On this basis Irwin ("Syntax," p. 258) suggests a wordplay with tappîl calling to mind tabbîl, i.e., the earth gives birth to the shades it had parched. Earlier he took tappîl from pll, "moisten": "It will moisten the land of the shades" (*Isaiah 28–33: Translation with Philological Notes*, BibOr 30 [Rome: Pontifical Biblical Institute, 1977], p. 20).

[72] Cf., e.g., Ps 9:13 (MT 14), which contrasts the gates of death with the gates of Zion (v. 14 [MT 15]), and Isa 38:10. On Mot's city cf. *UT* 51, viii 11.

[73] Cf. Ps 73:18-19; Ezek 26:20.

[74] On the use of "eternity" for the netherworld (including its gates) in the OT and literature of the biblical world see A. Cooper, "Ps. 24:7-10: Mythology and Exegesis," *JBL* 102 (1983): 37-60.

ruin (25:2),[75] laid low in the dust (25:12; 26:5-6).[76] On this interpretation the world-city is mocked with the irony of its downfall. It conspired with the prince of death to usurp the status of Zion, heavenly city of life, but it ends up as a necropolis, the netherworld city of the dead.[77]

From this land of no return the persecutors of the saints do not arise (26:14; cf. 24:20).[78] The contrast between their fate and the resurrection affirmed for the martyrs (26:19) underscores the vindicatory nature of the latter.

In sum, then, according to Isaiah 24–26 an army of enemies is associated with death in warfare against the saints, but divine vengeance will befall them all on the day of resurrection. A similar perspective informs Paul's teaching on the resurrection: Death is "the last enemy" to be abolished by Christ in a process that involves His putting "all His enemies under His feet" (1 Cor 15:25-26).

---

[75] If MT is followed, the third colon in 25:2 should be translated: "(You have turned) the city into a palace of strangers." The mēᶜîr of the first and third cola are thus treated identically. The full pattern, "from . . . to," established in the first colon continues with ellipsis of "from" in the second colon and "to" in the third. For the role of "strangers" as desolators see v. 5 (cf. Isa 1:7). In the Sumerian composition *Lamentation over the Destruction of Ur* the goddess Ningal bewails the fact that a "strange city" and "strange house" have replaced her demolished dwelling. The fall of Jerusalem is bemoaned in almost identical fashion in Lam 5:2. J. A. Emerton emends the mēᶜîr in Isa 25:2c to muᶜar, hophal participle of ᶜrr, translating "the palace of foreigners is destroyed" ("A Textual Problem in Isaiah 25:2," *ZAW* 89 [1977]: 72). Cf. Isa 23:13 for ᶜrr with ʾarmôn, "palace," paralleled moreover by sym and lĕmappēlâ, as in 25:2ab.

[76] Cf., e.g., Gen 3:19; Job 10:9; 17:16; 21:26; 34:15; Pss 22:15 (MT 16); 90:3. In the Akkadian myth *Descent of Ishtar to the Netherworld*, dust and clay are said to be the fare of the netherworld (obv. 8). A fate decreed there is the curse of having the "food of plows" as food (rev. 23-24). Cf. Gen 3:14.

[77] This same ironic reversal becomes a major motif in Ezekiel's prophecy of Gog (Ezek 39:11-16). Gog aspires to the mount of God but must settle for the immortality of the cemetery city of Hamonah.

[78] Their resurrection experience is a passage from Sheol to the second death. They do not return to their historical freedom vis-à-vis the godly. They are not present in God's eternal cosmic kingdom of life to threaten again the peace of the righteous. Cf. above the discussion of the judgment on Leviathan; cf. also nn. 25, 50.

Invitation to the Martyrs

Even before death is ultimately abolished, it undergoes for the martyr-people an intermediate transformation. In the light of their coming resurrection-vindication, death assumes for them a different face. It becomes something that can be welcomed. The language of invitation becomes appropriate for it: "Come, my people, enter into your inner rooms and close your doors about you. Hide yourselves for a brief moment, until the wrath has passed by" (Isa 26:20). The term ḥeder, "inner room," used for private rooms like the bedchamber, is combined with death in Prov 7:27: "the chambers of death."[79] The house or room, particularly a sleeping chamber, is a natural image, elsewhere attested, for Sheol.[80] Certainly then the invitation of Isa 26:20, embedded as it is in a context of death and resurrection, is to be understood as welcoming God's people into the inner room of death, as into a sanctuary.

Quite clearly Isaiah is alluding to the enclosure of the Noahic family within the ark-house[81] for their passage through the waters of death. In the flood narrative Noah receives an invitation from God to enter[82] the virtual burial chamber (Gen 7:1). There is a fastening of the door behind the occupants (Gen 7:26).[83] The ark as burial room functions as a refuge until the time of wrath on the hostile world-power has passed.[84] Meanwhile the occupants of the ark anticipate their eventual resurrection-exit and the perfecting of their vindication.

According to Isa 26:20 death for the redeemed has been radically altered, from confining covering to covert.[85] This same view of the death of the righteous is expressed in 57:1-2. There it is seen as a gathering away

---

[79] Cf. ḥdry šʾwl in 1QH x 34. In Phoenician and Punic ḥdr means "grave, netherworld."

[80] Cf. Tromp, *Primitive*, pp. 156-59.

[81] Cf. *KP* 225-27.

[82] As in Isa 26:20, the verb is bwʾ.

[83] As in Isa 26:20, the verbal phrase is sgr bʿd.

[84] Isa 26:20 also recalls the securing of the Israelites behind their bloodsmeared doors in Egypt while the Lord's judgment passed through (ʿbr, Exod 12:23, as in Isa 26:20).

[85] Cf. Job 14:13-15. Job longs for Sheol as a temporary hiding place from wrath until the resurrection.

from evil and an entering into peace and rest.[86] Sheol's repute as an "eternal house" is refuted by the interim character and indeed relative brevity attributed to its continuance in 26:20. Implicit in the temporal limit of "a brief moment" is the hope of the resurrection, when all the enemies have been abolished and there is no longer need for the refuge provided by death.[87] Meanwhile death has lost its terror. The great enemy is obliged to serve the saints as a friend. Yahweh's triumph over Mot has begun.

Subsequent biblical revelation concerning death reflects quite specifically the Isaianic disclosures, with the perception of death as a veritable blessing and the invitation to experience it as a temporary sanctuary until the resurrection-vindication.

In Dan 12:13 the invitation, "Come my people," of Isa 26:20 is made individually personal. Daniel is invited: "As for you, come!"[88] Under discussion in the context are the persecution of the covenant people and the ultimate resurrection of glory for "the wise." The invitation is immediately preceded by a beatitude pronounced on those who wait in faith for the time of deliverance. That Daniel's invitation does indeed contemplate his death becomes evident once the verse is properly punctuated: "Until the end you shall rest.[89] And then at the end of the days you will stand [or arise] in your allotted inheritance."[90] In the first instance, as in the second, "the end" refers to a historical climax of collective eschatology, not to the individual end of Daniel.[91] It is rather the verb "rest" that refers to his death, in agreement with the earlier Isaianic assessment of the death of the godly.[92]

A series of passages in the Book of Revelation presents again this distinctly Isaianic perspective on the death of the righteous: 2:10; 6:9-11; 14:13; 20:4-6.[93] In all these passages the godly are viewed as under

---

86 Cf. Pss 36:7-12 (MT 8-13); 57:1 (MT 2).

87 Heb 10:37, apparently citing Isa 26:20, identifies the brief time as that still remaining until the second coming of Christ. Cf. n. 54 above.

88 As in Isa 26:20 the imperative is lēk.

89 The key to the verse division is this emphatic waw with postposition of the verb.

90 For gôrāl in this sense see Judg 1:3; Ps 125:3; cf. Col 1:12.

91 On qēṣ see also Dan 12:4,6,9, noting especially the correspondence of vv. 4 and 13.

92 As in Isa 57:2 the verb is nwḥ. Cf. Job 3:17.

93 Rev 14:13; 20:6 are in the form of beatitudes. Cf. Dan 12:12.

persecution. The beast power, or even the devil himself, appears in the nearby contexts. But the saints are faithful unto death, and their martyr blood cries out for avenging.[94] Also, the intermediate state of death is perceived as a royal sabbatical resting until the historical strife is over.[95] This interval of waiting will be short.[96] And finally, the continuity of John, the New Testament seer, with Isaiah, the Old Testament prophet, is exhibited in their common portrayal of death as having been fundamentally changed for the redeemed of the Lord. In Rev 20:4-6 this transformation is expressed by identifying the Christian's death as "the first resurrection."[97]

---

[94] See Rev 6:10.

[95] Esp. Rev 6:11; 14:13.

[96] Esp. Rev 6:11; cf. 2:10.

[97] See Kline, "The First Resurrection." Cf. Rev 12:11. There the martyr victims are proclaimed victors. It is in and through their faithfulness unto death that they are overcomers, secured from the second death, assured of the second resurrection (cf. Rev 2:11).

CPSIA information can be obtained
at www.ICGtesting.com
Printed in the USA
BVHW042031140321
602307BV00019B/274

9 781498 248044